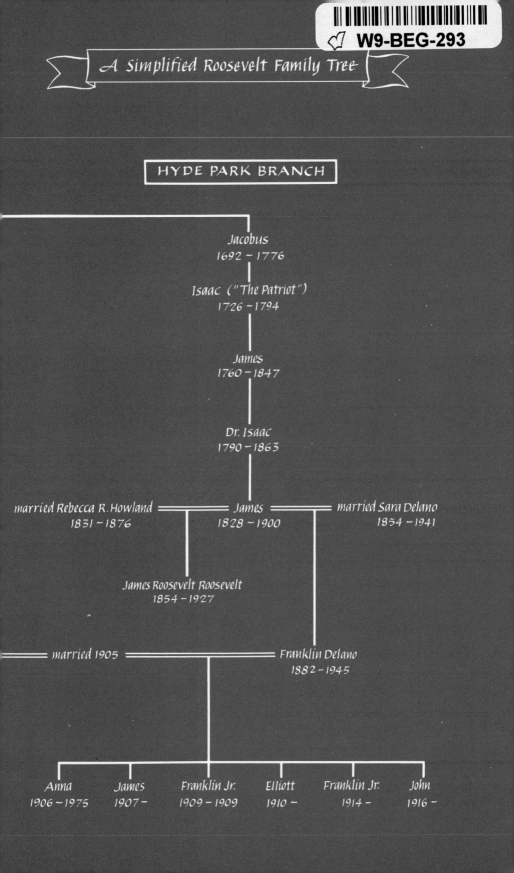

The
Roosevelt
Chronicles

The
Roosevelt
Chronicles

Nathan Miller

DOUBLEDAY & COMPANY, INC., GARDEN CITY, NEW YORK   1979

For
Jeanette

ISBN: 0-385-12754-5
Library of Congress Catalog Card Number 78–1212
Copyright © 1979 by Nathan Miller

INTRODUCTION

The story of America is the story of its families. Some are more distinguished than others, but all have made a contribution to the making of the nation. The Roosevelts, whose story is told in this book, played an important role in the development of the United States, and, in fact, the first sixty years of this century could well be called the Age of the Roosevelts. Emerging unexpectedly from a localized prominence in New York, they produced two of the greatest American presidents and a woman who well deserves the accolade of First Lady of the World bestowed upon her.

Patriots and parasites, saints and sinners, reformers and machine politicians, inventors and country squires, parade through the pages of this book. But it is not intended as a series of individual biographies or a genealogical study. Nor is it a sociological tract or a study of the effect of environment or genes. It is essentially the panorama of a family—a panorama reflected against the kaleidoscopic background of more than three centuries of American life.

A few words of explanation are in order as to why I have referred to the Roosevelts by their given names. It is not out of any sense of familiarity, but because of necessity. This seemed to be the best way to handle a situation in which all the participants have the same last name. No disrespect is intended for persons living or dead.

I am indebted to numerous librarians and archivists for help in gathering material for this book, particularly Dr. William R. Emerson and the staff of the Franklin D. Roosevelt Library at

Hyde Park; Wallace F. Dailey, curator of the Theodore Roosevelt Collection at the Harvard College Library; Dr. John A. Gable, executive director of the Theodore Roosevelt Association, and the staffs of the Reading Room at the New-York Historical Society and the Local History Reading Room of the New York Public Library; the Manuscript, Stack, and Loan divisions of the Library of Congress and the Montgomery County (Md.) Public Library.

Special recognition is due P. James Roosevelt, past president of the Theodore Roosevelt Association, and Dr. Gable, its executive director who read the manuscript and offered advice and counsel as well as suggestions for changes and improvements, and to Theo Lippman, Jr., Stanley Weiss, and Joseph D. Lichtenberg, M.D., who read selected portions of it. I also wish to express my appreciation to Franklin D. Roosevelt, Jr., for permission to quote from documents on file in the Roosevelt Library. And a debt of gratitude is owed to my able and sympathetic editor at Doubleday, Lisa Drew, and to her assistants, Lisa Healy and Mary Trone.

Nathan Miller

Chevy Chase, Maryland

PROLOGUE

Franklin D. Roosevelt was in high spirits. Barely suppressing a mischievous grin, he gazed out over the sternly disapproving faces of the Daughters of the American Revolution gathered in full panoply before him on April 21, 1938. It was a sight to chill the blood of the most hardened politician. Sensing a confrontation in the making, a sizable corps of newsmen and photographers had accompanied the President on the short trip from the White House to Constitution Hall, where he was to make the traditional welcoming speech to the DAR. Flashbulbs rippled across the vast chamber like heat lightning, and one exploded unexpectedly in Roosevelt's face. Momentarily startled, he recovered quickly and archly told his audience: "I see you are still in favor of national defense."

The wave of laughter that rolled over the some three thousand delegates belied the tension that existed between them and the President. For four years, Roosevelt had avoided the group's annual Continental Congresses, claiming the press of business prevented his attendance. In reality, although the President was as tradition-loving as any member of the DAR, he regarded the rigidly conservative society as hopelessly out of step with the times. The DAR was one of the most militant of the New Deal's critics, and the delegates had that very morning given overwhelming approval to a series of resolutions roundly condemning most of Roosevelt's policies. Now he savored a surprise guaranteed to wilt the orchid corsages pinned to their ample bosoms.

A band blared "Hail to the Chief" as Roosevelt appeared at the

flower-banked rostrum—Washington florists said their sales had
increased 300 percent during the convention—but his reception
was only coolly polite. "I couldn't let a fifth year go by without
coming to see you," the President began, brushing off the perfunctory welcome with a toss of his leonine head. Pointing out
that he had lacked the time to prepare a formal speech, he said
that at first he had thought of preaching on a text, but had decided instead to present the text without the sermon. "I think I
can afford to give you the text because it so happens, through no
fault of my own, that I am descended from a number of people
who came over in the *Mayflower*. More than that, every one of
my ancestors on both sides . . . every single one of them, without
exception, was in this land before 1776. And there was only one
Tory among them."

For the first time, the President was greeted with enthusiastic
applause. This was the kind of language the delegates expected
and understood. Having successfully lulled them into a false
sense of security, Roosevelt unveiled his text. "Remember," he
said, "remember always that all of us, and you and I especially,
are descended from immigrants and revolutionists."

There was a sound like air being sucked out of the hall. The
rest of the brief presidential remarks, extolling the DAR's educational programs, was all but ignored as the delegates sat in
shocked silence. By the time they had recovered their sense of indignation, Roosevelt had departed with a jaunty wave and a
high-octane smile. But his words seemed to reverberate about
Constitution Hall, repeating themselves over and over again. "All
of us . . . are descended from immigrants and revolutionists . . .
immigrants and revolutionists."

It is a distinction of which the Roosevelts have always been
proud.

Chapter I
ROOSEVELT ROOTS

Beyond the wooden palisade that marked the outer limits of New Amsterdam, a horse whinnied and shook in its harness. The first touch of spring had come early to Manhattan, enfolding the clearings scattered haphazardly about the island in warm friendliness. Planting time was at hand and Claes Martenszen van Rosenvelt had been laboring since daybreak with a crude hoe in his fields which lay just below the slopes of Murray Hill. Behind him plodded his wife, Jannetje, patiently sowing the freshly turned earth with Indian corn. Working together from sunup to sundown, they wrested a bare living from the reluctant land for themselves and their growing brood of children—and planted the roots of the Roosevelts deep in the soil of the New World.

Unlike many prominent American families, the Roosevelts have never exhibited an overwhelming pride of ancestry. Franklin Roosevelt often regaled visitors to his home on the Hudson at Hyde Park with hints of the skeletons supposedly lurking in the family closet. Waving toward one or another of the family portraits on the wall, he would gleefully call this ancestor "an old drunk" or that one "a reprobate." Other Roosevelts have been equally irreverent about their forebears. Theodore Roosevelt described the family's founding father as "our very common ancestor" and observed that he had come to America in the seventeenth-century version of steerage. And Alice Roosevelt Longworth, his outspoken daughter, hazards the opinion that Claes may have been a rogue "two leaps before the bailiff."

"Hell's bells!" Princess Alice once told Cleveland Amory, the society historian, "the Roosevelts aren't aristocrats at all in the sense of the word as I use it. As a matter of fact, I like the word 'patrician' better but the Roosevelt family aren't that either. It's nonsense. The Roosevelts were Dutch peasants who achieved burgherhood by making respectable marriages—which few of them, I might add, have done since."

In contrast to the family's later prominence, the arrival of the first Roosevelts in America was completely unheralded. No records have been found that show when Claes and Jannetje set foot in the bustling Dutch village at the tip of Manhattan. "All I know about the origin of the Roosevelt family in this country," Franklin Roosevelt, one of the clan's most assiduous genealogical students once said, "is that all branches bearing the name are apparently descended from Claes Martenszen van Rosenvelt, who came from Holland sometime before 1648—even the year is uncertain. Where he came from in Holland I do not know, nor do I know who his parents were. . . ."

Like many immigrants to America before and since, Claes shed all his yesterdays on the Atlantic passage. No one knows how old he was, what he looked like, whether he was tall or short, light or dark. One of the few clues to his past is his name. Rendered into English, it is Nicholas, son of Martin, of the Rose Field. In those days, Dutchmen took in addition to their baptismal names that of their father and the locality from which their family came. The family name, spelled in a dozen different ways in the old records —Roosinffelt, Rosewelt, Rosvelt, and Rasswelt, among others—indicates that the ancestral home of the Roosevelts was the village of Oud-Vossemeer on the island of Tholen at the mouth of the Rhine, where there was once a tract of land known as *het rosen velt*, or the field of roses.

Today, we can only guess at the reasons that had prompted Claes and Jannetje to emigrate to America. One thing is certain— the decision required either considerable courage or desperation, for Holland was enjoying the greatest prosperity in its history. The Dutch had, after eighty years of struggle, finally thrown off the yoke of Catholic Spain, and were entering a Golden Age. Energies and skills that had been devoted to war were released for peaceful purposes, and Holland had become the commercial center of Europe. Never before had the living standards of her people been so high, and it was not a time when most Dutchmen wished to abandon their country.

Ships flying the red, white, and blue tricolor of the Dutch Republic returned home with the riches of the Indies, and her prosperity was the envy of her neighbors. With this wealth came the desire to have all the luxuries that money could buy. Great houses were built and filled with the finest furnishings and linens, and their walls were hung with the paintings of Rembrandt, Vermeer, and Hals. Amazed visitors noted that the Dutch not only washed their hands after meals as was the common custom in an age when table utensils were few but also did so even *before* eating.

Claes and Jannetje may have decided to emigrate to America because they had not shared in the general prosperity. Perhaps the family had been ruined in the "tulipmania" that had swept Holland in the 1630s—a wild speculation in bulbs. Perhaps the family holdings on Tholen had been innundated by a storm that had ruptured the dikes that kept the sea at bay. Or perhaps the family had suffered such reverses in the long struggle with Spain that Claes, impelled by the restlessness that affected many people in those years, decided to strike out for new worlds to conquer.

Traces of the family still preserved at Oud-Vossemeer indicate that Claes was not nearly so "common" as his descendants sometimes claim, however. Bordered by dikes, or polders, and crisscrossed by drainage ditches, the flat, green fields about the village stretch to the horizon. Random windmills, a few clumps of trees, and the steeple of the Dutch Reformed Church stand stark against the sky. Three of the clan, Marinus van Rosevelt and his sons, Hendricus and Pieter, served the community as treasurer, and the father rests in the churchyard under a stone which reads: "Marinus van Rosevelt, in his life Burgomaster and inspector of dikes, died Jan. 29, 1710." The church's silver baptismal font is engraved with the name of its donor, "the lady Catharina van Rosevelt," and the twelve-bracketed chandelier was the gift of Johannes van Rosevelt, "one-time schoolmaster and verger of Oud-Vossemeer," who died in 1787.

Hanging prominently in the nearby Town Hall is a picture of the goddess of justice, painted by Jacob Xavery in 1753. It is framed by the coats of arms of fifteen prominent local families in-

cluding that of the Van Rosevelts—a silver shield emblazoned
with a lion and surmounted by three roses. Their motto was *Qui
plantavit curabit*, or "He who has planted will preserve," which
has been adopted by the American Roosevelts. The Van Rosevelt
family of Tholen persisted down through the nineteenth century
when its most distinguished representative was Johannes F. A. C.
van Rosevelt, a civil engineer who mapped the colony of Surinam,
or Dutch Guiana, so ably that all later surveys have been based
upon his work. Claes's wife, Jannetje, was the daughter of
Thomas Samuels, an Englishman living in the Netherlands. Like
the little band of Pilgrims who had temporarily settled in Leyden
prior to making their way to the New World in 1620, he may have
been a dissenter who fled to Holland so he could freely practice
his religion.

Curiously, the scattered references to Claes in the records of
New Netherland usually refer to him by a series of nicknames:
Kleytjen, Klein Klassje, and Cleyn Claesjen, which mean Little
Claes, Claes the Little One, or just plain "Shorty," giving rise to
the idea that Claes may have been a small man. Or perhaps he
may have been something of a giant, and his neighbors, with a
touch of heavy-handed Dutch humor, may have joked about his
size. Looking at his descendants, many of whom were—and are—
rather big men, the latter could well be the case. The fact that
Claes was known as the Little One has inspired a family tradition
that he had been to the New World before arriving with Jannetje
—that he was a mysterious adventurer also called Kleytjen, who
figured prominently in the exploration of what became New
Netherland.

In 1613, some thirty-five years before Claes is believed to have
first set foot on American soil, this Kleytjen was a member of the
crew of a Dutch ship which sailed up the Hudson, where her
captain planned to trade for pelts with the Indians. Unfortunately, she caught fire and burned to the water's edge. While a
new vessel was being built, the Little One and two other young
sailors either joined a roving band of Indians or were taken into
"protective custody" by them. Over the next two years, they wandered through the back country of eastern North America. The
French explorer Samuel de Champlain evidently heard of the
trio, and according to his diary, thought they were prisoners.
Eventually, Captain Cornelius Hendricks ransomed Kleytjen and

his shipmates from the Indians in exchange for a few baubles. Using information provided by the former captives, he prepared a detailed map of the mid-Atlantic region which he sent back to Holland along with notes based on "what Kleytjen and his Companions have told me of the situation of the Rivers and the places occupied by the tribes. . . ."

This is indeed a swashbuckling tale—the stuff of which legends are made—but it is highly improbable that the resourceful Kleytjen and Claes van Rosenvelt were one and the same. If this were true, Claes would have been more than fifty years old when he returned to New Amsterdam, which seems unlikely because he sired six children after settling in America.

In the 1930s, when anti-Semitism flared throughout the world in the wake of Adolf Hitler's rise to power and hatred of Franklin Roosevelt was at its peak, there were unsubstantiated claims that the forebears of the Roosevelts were Jews. Usually advanced to support them was the fact that no record of the marriage of Claes and Jannetje has been found in the records of the Dutch Reformed Church at New Amsterdam—conveniently ignoring the fact that they were probably married in Holland. One virulently anti-semitic tract preserved in the files of the Roosevelt Library at Hyde Park, "The 'Roosevelt' Family as Jews," claims that the family is descended from one "Rossacampo," a Spanish Jew who fled to the more tolerant Netherlands to escape the horrors of the Inquisition. These rumors became so prevalent that the President took the opportunity offered in 1935 by an inquiry from the editor of the Detroit *Jewish Chronicle* to state that despite all his efforts, he knew little about his ancestors. "In the dim, distant past, they may have been Jews or Catholics or Protestants," he wrote. "What I am more interested in is whether they were good citizens and believers in God. I hope they were both."

The town in which Claes and Jannetje found themselves after a hazardous voyage to the New World was not the quaint and tidy village of Washington Irving's fictional Father Knickerbocker, where red-faced burghers and their broad-beamed *Fraus* made merry. The reality was far grimmer. Founded neither as an outpost of empire like Virginia to the south nor as a haven from religious persecution like Massachusetts Bay to the north, the origins of New Netherland were narrowly commercial. The Dutch

West India Company, which ruled the colony from Amsterdam, regarded it merely as a springboard for winning control of the rich fur trade of the Hudson Valley. Everything was subordinated to the scramble for pelts and profits.

In 1626, two years after the original Dutch settlement up the Hudson at Fort Orange (now Albany), Peter Minuit had bought title to Manhattan Island from a band of roving Indians for twenty-four dollars' worth of beads and trinkets, and New Amsterdam quickly became the colony's most important port.* With about half of New Netherland's entire population of some fifteen hundred persons, it was already a cosmopolitan town. Exploring their new home, Claes and Jannetje would have been surprised by what one visitor called "the arrogance of Babel." Eighteen different languages were spoken there, it was said. Because of the reluctance of Dutchmen to leave the civilized comforts of Holland, the West India Company had been forced to resort for the bulk of its colonists to a melange of nationalities: French-speaking Walloons from the southern Netherlands, Huguenots from France, and a scattering of Scandinavians, Germans, Spaniards, Danes, Italians, Bohemians, and Jews. English freethinkers who had fled the rigid puritanism of New England were also welcomed, and there was a sizable contingent of black slaves, who were usually well treated by the Dutch. Swaggering privateersmen, teetering on the thin edge between legalized hijacking and piracy, also frequented the lusty and brawling town.

New Amsterdam was a compact village, so Claes and Jannetje would have had a clear panorama from river to river if they looked up the island from its tip. Lower Manhattan was considerably narrower in those days, before the shoreline was filled in. The East River lapped up to what is now Pearl Street, and Greenwich Street marked the shore of the Hudson River. Nostalgic Dutchmen were reminded of home by a canal crisscrossed by narrow little bridges which ran along the present length of Broad Street, and by the slowly turning sails of scattered windmills. The southernmost point was at State Street, and the town's northern

* This may not have been the slick deal that it is often portrayed. The Indians from whom the Dutch bought Manhattan did not live there and thus had no valid title. And if they had been able to invest the twenty-four dollars at 6 percent interest compounded annually, one writer estimates that this sum was worth in excess of $17 *billion* in 1973—considerably more than the assessed value of all the island's real estate at the time. Robert Sobel, *The Money Manias* (New York: Weybright and Talley, 1973), p. 10.

boundary was marked by the wooden palisade that gave Wall
Street its name. Outside this wall were a few orchards and farms,
or *bouweries.*

Fort Amsterdam, which occupied the area now bounded by
Bowling Green, Whitehall, Bridge, and State streets, appeared
from the water to be an imposing work. In reality, it was something of a public joke. The structure consisted of star-shaped
earthen walls upon which stone facing was placed from time to
time. Usually, the stones quickly disappeared, for the colonists,
no respecters of authority, appropriated them for building materials. Rooting pigs had undermined the walls, which appeared to
be in danger of tumbling down on the heads of the garrison if
any of its four brass cannon were fired. Within the fort were such
civic buildings as the barracks, the twin-peaked Dutch Reformed
Church, the jail, the council chamber, and the governor's residence, occupied since 1647 by crusty, peg-legged Peter Stuyvesant. Leading north from it was a wide street known as the
Breede Wegh, or Broad Way.

Perhaps as many as a hundred houses fronted on the handful
of streets, most of them a story and a half high, and usually built
of wood, including the chimneys. Soon after taking up the reins
of power, Stuyvesant had ordered a switch to brick and also established a night watch to guard against the danger of fire. All
had the customary Dutch front door cut horizontally in half, and
small-paned windows protected by heavy wooden shutters. As
in Holland, buildings were set gable end to the street, and had
neat and pleasant gardens behind them where householders
grew flowers, fruits, and vegetables. Traditional Dutch tidiness
did not extend beyond the front doors of the burghers, however.
Only the area around the waterfront had been paved with stones;
the rest of the streets were usually churned into seas of mud
when they were not covered with clouds of dust. Refuse and garbage were thrown into the roadways where roving pigs feasted
on it. Outhouses were sometimes placed haphazardly in the
streets with the same disregard for elementary sanitation.

One of the first things that Claes and Jannetje must have noticed about New Amsterdam was the abundance of drinking
places. According to census made about the time of their arrival,
the town had seventeen licensed taverns and perhaps half again
as many speakeasys. Thus, about a quarter of all its houses were

used for sale of alcoholic beverages. Copious quantities of beer, rum, and schnapps poured down the gullets of the colonists, and when times were flush, their tastes turned toward French brandy. Taverns existed for all economic and social groups. The gentry favored the two-story-high City Tavern at what is now the northwest corner of Pearl Street and Coenties Slip. One of the most prominent structures in town, it was eventually taken over as the City Hall, or Stadt Huys. Most watering places were far less grand, however. They usually consisted of a single, low-ceilinged room that reeked of stale beer, sweat, and tobacco. Passersby could hear raucous singing or drunken arguments emanating from inside, and deadly knife fights were not unknown. Claes and Jannetje van Rosenvelt may well have looked at each other and wondered uneasily whether they had done a wise thing in coming to America.

In the beginning, the Dutch West India Company, concerned only with the profits to be made in the fur trade, had regarded farmers as little more than a necessary evil, and was in no hurry to attract them. When it finally realized that its vast and empty holdings were a tempting target to the neighboring English, the company resorted to a semifeudal system of patroonships to populate the land. Anyone who brought over fifty families at his own expense was offered an extensive tract with full baronial privileges—such as establishing their own magistrate courts, the control of hunting and fishing on their property, and monopoly of trade with the Indians. The best land along the Hudson was gobbled up in this manner, with Killiaen van Renssalaer, a wealthy Amsterdam diamond merchant and a company director, securing a tract estimated at 700,000 acres. But New Netherland was a high-risk, low-profit proposition, and wealthy stay-at-homes expressed little interest in the patroonships. With the conspicuous exception of Rennsalaerswyck, most did not prosper, and were soon returned to the company. Eventually forced to face reality, the directors at last made it easier for less opulent settlers to own land. Claes van Rosenvelt availed himself of the opportunity soon after his arrival.

Claes and Jannetje took up residence on a forty-eight-acre farm a few miles beyond the outer limits of New Amsterdam. Adjoining a *bouwery* owned by Governor Stuyvesant, it was located in one of the best agricultural areas of Manhattan, nestled between Murray Hill and a swampy region to the south. Claes's land was well watered and contained a duck pond, near which he built a simple cottage. In terms of the modern city, the farm was approximately bounded on the north by Thirty-fourth Street, on the south by Thirty-first Street, on the west by Fifth Avenue and on the east by Lexington Avenue, while Madison Avenue cut right through it. Two centuries later, Theodore Roosevelt was born at 28 East Twentieth Street, only a half mile from where his ancestor had first established himself. The area was known as Rose Hill, and Claes may have given it this name in memory of the family acres back in Holland.

Farming on the frontier was not a task for the easily discouraged. Fields had to be cleared and there was the endless job of cutting or burning down trees and grubbing out rocks and stumps. The encroaching wilderness had to be held at bay; fences erected to prevent livestock from wandering away in the tangle of underbrush and to keep the deer that still roamed Manhattan from nibbling at the crops of corn, wheat, and beans. A watch had to be maintained for marauding wolves, and there was always the danger of Indian attack on isolated, outlying farms. Only a few years before, Stuyvesant's predecessor, William Kieft, had stirred up the Indians by scheming to gain control of their lands without bothering about the usual palaver and gifts. In little more than two years, countless Dutchmen fell victim to the scalping knife and tomahawk as the Indians sought revenge. With their fields lying fallow and their homes burned, the colonists finally managed to persuade the West India Company that Kieft had outlived his usefulness.

Life was hard and work never-ending, but Claes and Jannetje, apparently industrious and thrifty, prospered in their new home. Soon, the first of their children was born, a son who was named Christaen. His baptism was recorded at the Dutch Reformed Church in New Amsterdam on October 23, 1650, but he died in infancy. Over the next six years, Jannetje gave birth to three daughters: Elsje, born in 1652; Anna Margaret, in 1654, and Christina, in 1656. Two years later, the couple had another long-awaited son, a healthy baby whom they named Nicholas, after the proud father. As soon as they were able to perform them, the children were given simple chores about the farm—running errands, bringing in wood and water, weeding the garden, picking berries on the adjoining hillside, and dropping seeds at planting time.

Like other farm families, Claes and Jannetje sold the produce not required for their own needs in New Amsterdam. On market day, they loaded the children and whatever they had to sell on a springless little cart and jolted down the rutted road to town. Under Kieft's inept rule, the farmers had no stalls and merely dumped their produce on a tarpaulin spread on the ground near the waterfront and waited for customers. Often, they waited in vain as there were no fixed market days. Fruits and vegetables quickly spoiled in the hot sun or rain. One of Stuyvesant's first acts was to establish market days and to erect covered stalls in an area off Maiden Lane which became known as the Marckveldt, or market field.

Leaving their wives and children to tend their stalls, Claes and his fellow farmers from Haarlem at the northern end of Manhattan, Breukelyn across the East River, and Staaten Eylandt made their way to the nearest tavern, where over foaming pots of beer and long clay pipes, they discussed the events of the day—and denounced the incompetence of the West India Company and the iron-fisted rule of "Hardheaded Pete" Stuyvesant.

Stuyvesant was the best governor New Netherland ever had, even though he was hot-tempered and dictatorial. Faced with demands from some of the colonists for a probe of Kieft's corrupt regime, he flatly refused. He realized full well that if he permitted an investigation of his predecessor's affairs—no matter how warranted it might be—a precedent would be established that could haunt him if his successor chose to investigate his conduct. Noting that Kieft had been brought down by appeals directly to Holland, Stuyvesant warned: "If anyone during my administration, shall appeal, I will make him one foot shorter, and send the pieces to Holland, and let him appeal that way."

Rumblings of discontent about Stuyvesant's dictatorship multiplied. "Our great Muscovy Duke goes on as usual," complained one Dutchman. "He proceeds no longer by words or writings, but by arrests and stripes [the lash]." The old statement that a corporation has no soul was never truer than in New Amsterdam. Convinced they were being treated little better than indentured servants by the company, the frustrated settlers took to smuggling and other forms of illicit enterprise to make their fortunes. They believed that greed was the underlying policy of the government; that taxes were levied without consideration of the ability to pay; that the company siphoned off money that never returned; and trade restrictions encouraged monopolies, which made it difficult for honest men to earn a living. So when a small British fleet appeared off the town in 1664 and demanded that the Dutch surrender, Stuyvesant stomped his wooden leg in vain. New Amsterdam became New York without a shot and almost without a tear.

By then, Claes van Rosenvelt had been gathered to his fathers. He died in 1659, leaving Jannetje with four small children to raise and pregnant with a fifth. She did not long survive the birth of another daughter, Anna, born in 1660. Under Dutch law, the welfare of orphans was placed in the hands of orphanmasters who appointed guardians to make arrangements for their care and education. The order establishing such a guardianship for the children of Claes and Jannetje, dated December 10, 1660, is the first substantial reference to the Roosevelts in the records of New Amsterdam:

> Whereas *Jannetje Tomas*, widow of *Cleyn Classie*, commonly called so, has lately died, leaving besides some property five minor children, so that it has become necessary, to appoint administrators of the estate, therefore the Orphanmasters herewith qualify as such administrators *Tomas Hall* and *Pieter Stoutenbergh*, who are ordered to make an inventory of the estate, real and personal property, values and debts due by others, to settle all and make a report to this Board for future disposal.

Claes and Jannetje must have accumulated property of some value because the guardians were in and out of court over the next several years trying to collect debts owed the estate and fighting off claims against it. The Rose Hill Farm was apparently sold and the proceeds invested in a trust fund for the support of the children, who had been parceled out among various families. Young Nicholas was entrusted to the care of Metje Grevenraet, a respectable woman living in New Amsterdam. A kinswoman of Metje's, Christina Grevenraet, had been a witness at the baptism of Christina van Rosenvelt on July 30, 1656, so it is possible that the families were related. Metje was paid 200 guilders annually for the boy's care, but when he grew older, this sum was increased to 250 guilders. A farmer named Casper Samler purchased the Rose Hill Farm, and his cottage, located a little to the northeast corner of Madison Avenue and Twenty-seventh Street, was the last farmhouse on Madison Avenue.

Chapter II
OTHER BRANCHES, OTHER TREES

With the first glint of dawn, a huddle of men and women had come on deck, anxiously straining their eyes to the west for a glimpse of the New World. For more than two months, the *Mayflower* had been buffeted by Atlantic storms, and only the hardiest had survived the passage. Now excitement crackled among her passengers as signs of a landfall appeared imminent. In the pale light of November 10, 1620, a lookout high above the pitching deck made out a faint line to the starboard and gave a long-drawn-out cry: "Land, ahoy! Land ahoy!" Some of the excited passengers shed tears of joy; others dropped to the knees in grateful prayers of deliverance. Among them was Isaac Allerton—first of the Roosevelt's English ancestors in America.

In contrast to the shadowy Claes Martenszen van Rosenvelt, Allerton's movements—and somewhat shady dealings—have been amply documented. Tight-fisted and with the ethics of a gypsy horse trader, he was eventually banished from Plymouth by his Pilgrim brethren when these "pure and Unspotted Lambs of the Lord" discovered that he had fleeced them. This cost him his place in history, but the very survival of the colony owes much to the hardheaded business sense of the man who has been called "the first Yankee trader."

Born in London about 1586, Allerton was apprenticed to a tailor and then set himself in this trade. Unlike most Englishmen of his class, he managed to learn to read and write and became deeply concerned by the religious conflicts that raged at the turn of the seventeenth century. The Protestant Reformation had come to England as a result of Henry VIII's lust for Anne Boleyn, but there were those who claimed that the reforms had not gone far enough. Known as Puritans, they demanded an end to frivolity, extravagance, and moral corruption in the Church of England and wished to establish a New Jerusalem in which men could conduct their lives according to the precepts of the Bible. They called for an end to the existing religious hierarchy of archbishops, bishops, and deans and all clergy above the rank of parish priest, and proposed a federation of independent parishes in its place.

Although the basic underpinning of Puritanism was religious, it had economic, social, and political overtones as well. Emphasizing hard work rather than mysticism, the movement had special appeal to artisans, tradesmen, and other members of the aspiring middle class, such as Isaac Allerton. Over the years, Puritanism became the cutting edge of their demands for greater participation in the process of government. In the boisterous and lusty Merrie England of the Elizabethans, the Puritans were denounced as dour, bloodless, and bigoted, and their attitude aroused popular hostility. Queen Elizabeth had no stomach for disputation over religious dogma, but her successor, James I, assailed by a Puritan divine as "God's silly vassal," would not permit his authority as head of the Church of England to be questioned. "I will *make* them conform," he thundered, "or I will harry them out of the land!"

One of the bands of Puritans harried out of the country was led by William Brewster, and had made their homes in Scrooby, a village in the north of England. To avoid the scoffs and jeers of their neighbors, they fled to Holland in 1609, first making their home in Amsterdam and later at the university town of Leyden. Allerton, whose Puritan convictions had led him to Holland before the Scrooby group, was already residing at Leyden and joined their congregation. Energetic and enterprising, he had prospered, and like several other members of the congregation, became a Dutch citizen. The simple lives led by the Puritans and the impassioned preachings of their leaders attracted some Dutchmen and French Huguenots to join the group—among them a young man named Philippe de la Noye, whose family had aided the Englishman. Allerton married Mary Norris, another member of the sect, and they had three children in the next few years—a period in which his influence grew within the congregation.

Although Leyden was a secure and pleasant refuge, the Puritans were restless. Some believed greater opportunities could be found in the New World while others feared that their offspring would lose their English heritage and language if they remained much longer in Holland. As early as 1617, they opened negotiations with the Virginia Company which held a charter from James I for a great sweep of the Atlantic coast from what is now Maine to North Carolina and had established a colony at Jamestown a decade before. After considerable discussion, a group of "merchant adventurers" formed a new joint stock-company to finance a colony to be established at the northern reach of the English claim in America.

A measure of Isaac Allerton's importance can be gauged by the fact that he was chosen to secure one of the two ships to be used by the colonists. He purchased and refitted a small vessel called the *Speedwell*, which turned out to be one of the few business mistakes he ever made. The craft proved to be unseaworthy, and twice the expedition had to return to port so that she could be repaired. Finally, most of her passengers, including the chagrined Allerton and his family, transferred to the *Mayflower*, and on September 6, 1620, she sailed out into the uncertainties of the broad Atlantic in the worst season of the year. "All great and honourable actions are accompanied with great difficulties and must be both enterprised and overcome with answerable courages," wrote William Bradford, one of the Puritan leaders, in his chronicle of their adventures.

Two months later, as the *Mayflower* rocked in the swells off the barren dunes of Cape Cod after a tempestuous voyage, her company signed a compact in which they agreed to be ruled by the will of the majority until a permanent government had been organized. And so this group of weavers, smiths, tailors, carpenters, printers, bakers, and other such ordinary folk thus established the tradition of self-government in America. Isaac Allerton's bold signature is the largest on the page, just below that of Governor John Carver, William Bradford, Edward Winslow, and William Brewster.

Few colonists have been so poorly prepared for life in the wilderness than the small band that settled at Plymouth. They knew

little about farming, but luckily they found some fields that had
been cleared by the Indians that were ready for planting. Before
the first grim winter was over, half the company had died, including Allerton's wife. But they were undaunted. "They knew
they were pilgrims and looked not much on those things, but lift
up their eyes to the heavens, their dearest country, and quieted
their spirits," wrote Bradford in a passage that eventually caused
the *Mayflower's* company to become known as the Pilgrim Fathers. With the death of Governor Carver, Bradford was chosen
to succeed him and Allerton was named his assistant. Together,
they preserved the colony through its worst trials.

Four years later, in 1625, the colony faced a financial crisis.
The merchant adventurers in London, wearying of the settlement's failure to show a profit, announced that they would no
longer provide financial support. The settlers looked about for
someone qualified to deal with the stockholders, and chose Allerton. Having been selected by the colony's financial backers to
oversee the distribution of the supplies and tools sent out from
England and recently married to the twenty-four-year-old Fear
Brewster, daughter of the church elder, William Brewster, he
had the confidence of both sides.* He returned to London for the
first time in more than five years and convinced forty-two of the
original investors to sell their interest to the colonists for eighteen
hundred pounds, payable over nine years. Allerton, who had developed an insight in the way business operated, also managed to
borrow an additional two hundred pounds for the purchase of
fresh supplies and a stock of cattle at a rate of interest considerably below that which the settlers had heretofore been able to
arrange.

Upon his return to Plymouth, the assistant governor was hailed
as the colony's savior. The arrangement to buy out the stockholders staved off immediate dissolution and provided the settlers
with autonomy for the first time—subject to a mortgage, of
course. Allerton's plan was "very well liked and approved by all
the Plantation, and consented unto," wrote Governor Bradford.
Still unresolved, however, was how the payments agreed to by
their emissary would be met, inasmuch as they couldn't even pay

* Fear Brewster was not the only one of Elder Brewster's children to bear a
memorable name. His son was called Wrestle, no doubt for "wrestling with the
devil."

their current debts. The solution was found when "seven or eight of the chiefs of the place," including Allerton, agreed to jointly underwrite the amount promised the stockholders. In return, the "undertakers" received a monopoly on the colony's fur trade and were to be given annual tribute of corn or tobacco from each of the settlers.

In the general satisfaction with Allerton's arrangements, few noticed that the ship on which he had returned from London carried "some small quantity of goods under his own particular," which he sold at a profit. This was "more than any man had yet hitherto attempted," noted Bradford with some dismay because it was against the settlers' basic tenets for one of them to profit from another. But the governor was willing to overlook this transgression because Allerton "had otherwise done . . . good service." Undaunted by criticism, Allerton was convinced by the profits that he had earned from this enterprise that vast riches lay within his grasp ready for the taking.

Over the next several years, he made repeated trips across the Atlantic in which he accomplished much for the colony—and for himself. He arranged for the emigration of the remainder of the Leyden congregation, secured fresh loans at advantageous rates of interest that freed the colony from the constant specter of bankruptcy, and obtained an agreement that gave the Pilgrims exclusive rights to the fur trade on the Kennebec River in Maine. In the meantime, Allerton, in league with some of the less scrupulous London stockholders, grew rich at the expense of his fellow "undertakers." The amount of bedding, clothing, shoes, hats, pins, and cloth being brought into the colony for private sale increased until some ships seemed to be carrying more of his goods than that of the "undertakers."

Muttering mounted when Allerton's partners noted his goods "were so intermixed with the goods of the General as they knew not which was theirs, and which was his, being packed up together." If a ship were lost at sea, the loss could be charged completely to the "undertakers." And when a shipment was unpacked, it was usually discovered that the most readily salable items belonged to Allerton. Many suspected that the assistant governor was playing "his own game" but he was stoutly defended by his "beloved and honoured" father-in-law, William

Brewster, whom no one wished to offend, so "they bore with much in that respect."

Nevertheless, Allerton overreached himself. Without consulting anyone, he brought over a new preacher for the congregation in 1628, the incumbent having been ousted from his pulpit for allegedly plotting against the colony's leadership. The man selected, a Reverend Mr. Rogers, turned out to be a poor choice. Bradford described him as "crazed in his brain," and the colonists were put to the cost of not only bringing him over from England but sending him back. Allerton was severely criticized for having chosen him and for the expense entailed. But this was nothing compared to his next move. The following year, he returned from London with a new secretary whose appearance in the colony created tumult and consternation. He was Thomas Morton, who had been banished from Massachusetts a few years before as an "unworthy man and instrument of mischief."

The story of Morton of Merrymount, as he was known, provides one of the few touches of humor in the bleak saga of the Pilgrim Fathers. A lawyer, of whom it was said he "left his country for his country's good," Morton established a colony that became known as Merrymount, near the present site of Quincy, which attracted a group of rollicking bachelors, who scoffed at the Puritan way of life. Writing of Morton and his followers, Bradford thundered:

> They fell to great licentiousness and led a dissolute life, pouring out themselves into all profaneness. And Morton became Lord of Misrule, and maintained (as it were) a School of Atheism. And after they had got some goods into their hands . . . by trading with the Indians, they spent it as vainly in quaffing and drinking, both wine and strong waters in great excess. . . . They also set up a maypole, drinking and dancing about it many days together, inviting the Indian women for their consorts, dancing and frisking together like so many fairies, or furies rather; and worse practices. . . .

Although Bradford does not mention it, the Pilgrims were worried by more than the neighbor's morals. Despite their frolics, the settlers of Merrymount were serious rivals in the fur trade, venturing as far as the Kennebec in search of pelts. To facilitate this business, Morton sold guns and "strong waters" to the Indians. Pilgrim trappers and fur traders began to see Indians armed with muskets, and fearing an eventual attack, they resolved to put their competitor out of business. Captain Myles Standish took a small detachment and captured Morton while most of his supporters were away. Standish and some of the others demanded that Morton be summarily hanged, but he was shipped back to England on the next available vessel.

Now the smirking fellow was back again—and handpicked by no less than the assistant governor to serve as his secretary. This was too much; Morton was immediately arrested and banished from the colony. Allerton's judgment was questioned for having made such an insulting appointment, and after further suspicions were roused by his business dealings, he was dismissed as the colony's agent. An investigation of his accounts revealed that they were "fouled up in obscurity, and kept in the clouds, to the great loss and vexation of the plantation." More than two years were required to unravel them, and it was found that under Allerton's vaunted business management, large sums of money had vanished into thin air. Bills and receipts did not exist for substantial sums allegedly paid out, the colony's debt had increased tenfold in only four years, and one thousand pounds was still owed on the mortgage given the original stockholders. No one was safe from Allerton's machinations. "Yea, he screwed up his poor father-in-law's account," Bradford reported, with Brewster being saddled for charges "blown up by interest and high prices." In all, Allerton was said to have gouged his partners for at least two thousand pounds—a substantial sum in those days. Some of it had gone into purchasing a profitable brewery in England, as well as other enterprises.

Banished from the colony in 1631, Allerton went to live in Marblehead, where he added insult to injury by going into direct competition with the Pilgrims for the beaver and otter of the Kennebec and in the Maine fisheries. When he made a flying visit to Plymouth, he was called "to account for these and other gross miscarriages," says Bradford. "He confessed his fault and promised better walking, and that he would wind himself out of these courses so soon as he could, etc." Despite these promises, however, Allerton went his way, flouting his former brethren and adding to his profits. Soon, he had eight fishing vessels in his employ and had established a trading post at Machias in Maine. These investments proved profitable, but in a few years Allerton suffered severe reverses. The French swept down from Canada and destroyed his trading post, several of his fishing boats were lost at sea, and his warehouse at Marblehead caught fire and burned. And the local authorities, persuaded by the Pilgrims that "he loves neither you nor us," finally ordered him to leave the colony.

Allerton went to New Amsterdam, where he was welcomed by the Dutch and established himself as a merchant. For the next two decades, he divided his time between a home and warehouse on Pearl Street and the new and growing town of New Haven to the north—which gave him the right to trade in both the English and Dutch holdings in North America and the Caribbean. One wonders if he ever had any dealings with Claes Martenszen van Rosenvelt, and if so, what these two Roosevelt ancestors thought of each other. When Governor William Kieft touched off his bloody war with the Indians, Allerton and Thomas Hall, who later became one of young Nicholas Roosevelt's guardians, were among a council elected by the citizenry to deal with the emergency. Allerton had his own share of legal difficulties, however. According to the records of the town clerk, an Irish bond servant named Dorothy Lock

appeared in Court, complaining that Mr. Isaac Allerton, had beaten her, as appears by the marks, because Jonathan Kammentie, Allerton's servant, had carnal conversation with her, saying she was now about six weeks with child from him; requesting that she be permitted to marry said Jonathan and that Allerton may allow it. She is promised her freedom from her master, Jan Coort. The Court decides, that Dorothy may summon Mr. Allerton and meanwhile the Officer may investigate the matter.

The case had a happy ending, for Jonathan and his colleen were allowed to marry. Over the years, Allerton spent more of his time in New Haven, continuing his speculations with seeming profit, and built himself "a grand house on the creek with four porches" from which he could see across Long Island Sound. There he died in 1659, supposedly a wealthy man. But it was soon discovered that despite all his maneuverings and ventures, he was insolvent, and his estate consisted primarily of uncollectable debts. Perhaps the final word had been pronounced a quarter century before by William Bradford, who had written: "With pity and compassion touching Mr. Allerton, I may say with the Apostle to Timothy (1 Timothy vi.9) 'They that will be rich fall into many temptations and snares,' etc., 'and pierce themselves through with many sorrows,' etc; 'for the love of money is the root of all evil.'"

Shortly after the Pilgrims had celebrated the first Thanksgiving in October 1621, a ship was sighted making for Plymouth. Without contact with the outside world for a year and suspecting that she was a Frenchman come to raid the colony, the settlers were mustered by Myles Standish, and "every man, yea, every boy, that could handle a gun was ready" to beat off the invaders. Much to the relief of the anxious settlers, she broke out the red cross of St. George. The vessel was the *Fortune*, carrying thirty-five passengers, most of them members of the Leyden congregation who had been unable to sail in the *Mayflower*. Among them was nineteen-year-old Philippe de la Noye, one of the French Huguenots who had thrown in their lot with the English Puritans.

There is a family tradition that Philippe had fallen in love with Priscilla Mullins, who had sailed in the *Mayflower*, and he had followed her across the ocean. If so, she turned down both him and the redoubtable Captain Standish for John Alden, who was persuaded to speak for himself. For the next dozen years, the young Frenchman lived the life of a solitary farmer and surveyor before marrying Hester Dewsbury of Duxbury in 1634. When the Pequot Indians resisted white expansion into the Connecticut River Valley three years later, Philippe was among the ninety volunteers who shouldered muskets and joined a punitive expedition led by Captain John Mason.

Learning that the Indians were concentrated in a fortified village to the east of the Thames River, Mason's men sailed into Narragansett Bay in small boats, scrambled ashore, and marched some thirty miles overland. Undetected by the Indians, they surrounded the palisade, and at dawn on May 26, 1637 the screaming whites attacked the sleeping village. They easily broke through the feeble defenses and put the huddle of huts to the torch. To prevent any of the Pequots, many of them women and children, from escaping, the militiamen and their Indian allies established a ring about the flaming settlement. "We had sufficient light from the word of God for our proceedings," said one of the soldiers.

Those that escaped the Fire were slain with the Sword . . . and very few escaped. The Number they thus destroyed, was conceived to be above Four hundred. . . . [It] was a fearful sight to see them thus frying in the Fire, and the streams of Blood quenching the same; and horrible was the stink and scent thereof; but the Victory seemed a sweet Sacrifice, and [the English] gave praise thereof to God. . . .

Following his participation in this ruthless act of vengeance, Philippe returned to his farm, and fathered a large number of children, including two sons, Jonathan and Thomas. Over the years, the family name, written as Delaneaux, Delannoy, and Delanow, was finally anglicized to Delano, although another branch preferred Delannoy. In 1676 Jonathan Delano, following in the footsteps of his father, took part in an expedition that captured King Philip, an Indian chieftain whose warriors were terrorizing the frontier settlements of New England. As his reward for gallantry, young Delano was given a sizable grant of land near what is now New Bedford. He took his new bride, Mercy Warren, granddaughter of Richard Warren, another of the *Mayflower*'s passengers, to live there. When the whaling industry began to flourish, the Delanos prospered with it, and ships owned by Jonathan's descendants carried the American flag around the world.

Thomas Delano, his brother, had already achieved a distinction of another sort. He may have been a participant in one of America's first "shotgun" marriages. Although Priscilla Mullins had turned down his father in favor of John Alden, their daughter, Mary, found Thomas irresistible. The records of the Plymouth colony show that on October 30, 1667, Thomas Delano was fined ten pounds for "having carnall copulation with his *now* wife before marriage," by a court presided over by John Alden. The exact date of the young couple's wedding is carefully omitted from the record, although the year is given as 1667. Their child, a boy who was named Benoni Delano, was born on the day his father was fined—providing every indication that Thomas and Mary had gotten to the preacher just in time.

While Roosevelt ancestors were thriving and founding what were to become various branches of the clan in New Amsterdam and New England, another contribution to the family melting pot was being made in the South. As the seventeenth century drew to a close, the Parliament of Scotland, in one of its last official acts before the nation was unified with England, established a trading company similar to those organized by the English and Dutch. But instead of launching a colony on the forbidding coast of North America, the Company of Scotland chose Panama, or Darien, for a settlement designed to restore the fortunes of the nation. The project was the brainchild of William Paterson, a brilliant but erratic Scot who had helped found the Bank of England. Having heard Darien described as a lush and beautiful country where the soil yielded fruit without labor and rich deposits of gold abounded, Paterson conjured up a vision of a mercantile colony astride the Isthmus—the "door of the seas, and the key of the universe"—which would control the trade of the world.

Although there is no record that Paterson had ever seen Darien, normally hardheaded Scotsmen rushed to invest in his scheme or to enroll as settlers. The fact that Darien was under the control of Spain had little effect on their ambitions. It was as if the gray clouds that hung low over Scotland had suddenly parted, flooding the countryside with Caribbean sunlight. Within a short time, eager subscribers had poured as much as a million pounds into the company's coffers. Finally, all was ready, and on July 26, 1698, almost the entire population of Edinburgh poured down upon Leith to watch five ships crammed with some twelve hundred men, women, and children drop down the Firth of Forth and head for the open sea. A hard-bitten lot—unemployed soldiers, dissolute younger sons, poverty-stricken farmers, and a few ambitious artisans—the emigrants shared only one thing in common: the dream of a pot of gold at the end of the rainbow. Most of them would never see home again.

Hundreds of other prospective settlers had been turned down because of the lack of space, and were eager to sail in later ships. Among them was Alexander Stobo, a newly ordained minister of

the Church of Scotland. It was just as well, for if he had known
the fate of those who had gone before, he would probably have
abandoned any plans to join them. At first all went well under
the direction of Paterson, who with his wife had gone to Cale-
donia, as the colony was called. But the arrival of the Scots
caused a general alarm. The Spaniards besieged the settlement,
and the English colonists in the Caribbean, jealous of the new
settlers, refused to send supplies or other assistance. Fever, intense heat, disease, and hunger thinned their ranks and Paterson's wife was among those who died. Most of the settlers were
drunk all the time and the settlement collapsed into paralyzed in-
ertia. It was decided to abandon the colony. Sick with fever, Paterson was unable to resist, and he was carried aboard one of the
ships, his golden dream gone aglimmering. Two shiploads of sur-
vivors reached New York and a third came to anchor at Jamaica.

While these misfortunes were taking place, another expedition
sailed from Scotland, this one carrying Stobo, his wife, Elizabeth,
and three other clergymen who were to serve as missionaries.
They were horrified by what they found at Darien. "Expecting to
meet with our friends and countrymen," wrote one of the min-
isters, "we found nothing but a vast howling wilderness . . . we
looked for Peace but no good came." Soon, the preachers were
spending most of their time burying victims of the fevers emanating from the fetid jungle, so they had little time to minister to the
needs of the living. The horror was multiplied by the raucous
shouts of drunken Highlanders and Elizabeth Stobo feared for
her safety. "Our land hath spewed out its scum," Stobo wrote his
superiors in Scotland. "We could not prevail to get their wick-
edness restrained, nor the growth of it stopped."

Once again, the Spaniards lay siege to the settlement. With
fever raging among them and realizing resistance was useless, the
Scots accepted an offer from the enemy which allowed them to
depart in three ships with flags flying and drums beating. And so,
on April 12, 1700, ended the "noble undertaking" that was to re-
trieve Scotland's fortunes. The vessels drifted aimlessly about the
Caribbean with one of them sinking on the reefs near Cuba, and
the others, battered and dismasted by storms, arrived off Charleston, South Carolina, in pitiful condition.

According to a family tradition, a message was received on the
Rising Sun, one of the ships, requesting a Scots minister to come

ashore to officiate at a wedding. Stobo answered the call and his wife went with him. Following the service, the Stobos were invited to spend the night in the town. In another less complimentary version, the minister and a handful of others were said to have deserted the stricken vessel in a longboat. Be that as it may, their decision to go ashore was a stroke of luck. The next night, a hurricane shattered the ships to matchwood and they sank with all hands. Stobo had little compassion for those who perished. "It was the Lord's remarkable mercy that we were not consumed in the stroke, with the rest," he declared. "They were such a rude company, that I believe Sodom never declared such impudence in sinning as they."

Convinced that he had seen the miraculous hand of God at work, Stobo settled in Charleston. His daughter, Jean, later married James Bulloch, another Scots parson newly arrived in America. The young couple went to live in Savannah, where they began a family that was to become prominent in the affairs of Georgia. Nearly a century and a half later, their great-granddaughter, Martha Bulloch, married a visiting New Yorker named Theodore Roosevelt. A son of this union was destined to build the canal that eventually made William Paterson's dream a reality.

Chapter III
THE FIRST NICHOLAS

Rattling drums and the crash of salutes marked the ceremonies in which the flag of Britain replaced the Dutch tricolor over Fort Amsterdam on September 8, 1664. Perhaps Nicholas van Rosenvelt, a tow-headed lad of six "who wore knickerbockers and wooden shoes," was taken by Metje Grevenraet, with whom he lived, to witness the act that formally transformed New Amsterdam into New York. Like any small boy, he must have jumped up and down in excitement. English became the official language of the colony, Fort Amsterdam became Fort James, and the burgomaster, schepens, and schout became the mayor, aldermen, and sheriff. Some Dutchmen changed their names, with Carel van Brugge, for example, becoming Charles Bridge. Yet, like many momentous events, the transition from Dutch to English rule did not greatly alter the daily lives of ordinary citizens. New York remained a Dutch town in appearance, spirit, and culture for at least another generation.

For little Nicholas, life followed the usual pattern of the typical Dutch schoolboy—with one major exception. He was an orphan and undoubtedly grieved for the parents whom he had hardly known. But he had much to fill his days, and the memories of small children are fickle. Recollections of his parents probably dimmed with time. In winter he trudged—perhaps not too willingly—from Metje's house to either the public school held in the City Hall or to one of the private institutions that taught a smattering of Latin as well as basic reading, writing, and ciphering. Both schools emphasized the religious education of their charges, and students were expected to know their Scriptures or face a hiding. There, Nicholas learned to write a spidery hand. After school and when the day's chores were done, he went ice skating on the frozen ponds scattered about Manhattan or on the canal where Broad Street now runs. In summer he knew the friendly warmth of the sun, the touch of the cool, soft earth against bare feet. With his friends, he swam in the East River, went fishing or hunting for waterfowl along its banks, and learned to bowl on one of the greens about town.

And there were the traditional Dutch festivals, to be awaited with anticipation. The good burghers of New York continued to follow the customs of their homeland, and five major festivals were celebrated—Kerstydt (Christmas), Nieuw Jaar (New Year), Pass (Easter), Pinxter (Whitsuntide), and San Claes (St. Nicholas Day), which occurred on December 5. Gifts were given the children on St. Nicholas Eve and dances and feasts were held. Such occasions were so marked with hilarity that the magistrates were often forced to restrain the most boisterous of the merrymakers. Thus, Nicholas grew into young manhood in circumstances little different from when Manhattan had been a Dutch colony.

Nevertheless, the English had a fine eye for property, and under their rule, much real estate changed hands and the boundaries of New York began to expand. Isaac Bedloe obtained a patent to an island in the harbor then known as Great Oyster Island which he named after himself. Today, it is known as Liberty Island because two centuries later it became the site of the Statue of Liberty. An island in the East River off mid-Manhattan was purchased by Captain John Manning, the colony's ranking military officer. Later, it was to become known as Blackwell's Island, then Welfare Island, and finally Roosevelt Island. Ferries began operating across the Harlem River, and a Barbados merchant named Morris purchased part of the Bronck estate transforming that part of the Bronx into Morrisania. The British also confirmed most of the remaining patroonships and, calling these holdings manors, allowed them to expand.

In 1673, when Nicholas was fifteen, war again erupted between England and Holland, bringing unexpected excitement. In the absence of Governor Francis Lovelace, a powerful Dutch armada of twenty-three vessels suddenly appeared off the town, and in a startling reversal of fortunes, demanded its surrender. Captain Manning could offer little resistance. He had but a handful of troops under his command and the walls of Fort James were in no better repair than when it had been Fort Amsterdam. While the English anguished over the obvious necessity of surrender, Dutchmen rejoiced. Some rowed out to the Dutch ships riding majestically offshore and reported the sorry state of the fortifications. Others formed a "fifth column" that spiked the guns hastily set up on the waterfront.

Manning dispatched a message to the Dutch admiral asking why the Dutch had come "in such a hostile manner." The answer was to the point. The Dutch said they had returned to take back "what was theyr own, and theyr own they would have." Stalling for time, Manning then asked to see the admiral's commission. That officer replied that it lay in the mouth of the stubby black cannon protruding from the sides of his ships, and if the English persisted in refusing to surrender, he would show it. Growing weary of the game at last, the Dutch opened fire on the fort. Some six hundred men were landed, and with the support of several hundred Dutchmen of all ages, of whom Nicholas might have been one, they advanced on the town. Manning promptly surrendered, and New York, now renamed New Orange, passed once again under the Dutch flag. But Dutch control lasted only fifteen months, for they relinquished all claims to New Netherland at the end of the war. Surrounded by English colonies and unattractive to Dutch settlers, the colony had little value to Holland. The final entry into the records of New Orange, the last written by a Dutch official in the city, stated: "On the 10th November Anno 1674, the Province of New Netherland is surrendered by Governor Colve to Governor Major Edmund Andros in behalf of His Majesty of Great Britain."

When the English had regained possession of the town, a grim ceremony was held in front of the City Hall. The public executioner broke Captain Manning's sword over his head for surrendering the city to the Dutch. But under Andros' rule, New York prospered. He ordered a dock built along Water Street from Coenties Slip to Whitehall Slip, and for nearly three quarters of a century it was the city's only quay. Public wells were drilled to improve the water supply, the colony's first insane asylum was opened and its first street lighting program inaugurated. On moonless nights every seventh house was ordered to display a lantern, with the cost of candles divided among neighboring property owners. A city-appointed chimney sweep was installed in office, and a program for the support of paupers established. New York's first welfare client, known as "Top-Knot Betty," was given three shillings a week for food and lodging.

Wheat had begun to supplant corn as the colony's most profitable crop, for there was a ready market for flour in the adjoining colonies and the West Indies. The existing process of grinding wheat to make flour and sifting it to remove impurities and packing it for shipment, or bolting, was too inefficient to meet the demand, however, and the English substituted horse-driven mills for the windmills favored by the Dutch. Because of the capital investment required for the new machinery, this concentrated the trade in the hands of a few well-to-do men. To entice them into increasing their investments, Andros gave them a monopoly on the milling and bolting of flour. Some of the same men, Nicholas Bayard (old Peter Stuyvesant's nephew), Stephanus van Cortlandt, and Frederick Philipse, among them, also received huge land grants, which gave them a stranglehold on the colony's economic and political life.

Power and privilege were completely monopolized by a new aristocracy based upon vast land holdings and trade monopolies. Wealth and status were transformed into political influence, which, in turn, was converted into privileged access to the land. For example, Philipse concentrated his huge holdings into the manor of Philipsburgh. Robert Livingston, the shrewd son of a Scottish clergyman with a keen eye for good land, soon controlled the 160,000 acres of what are now Dutchess and Columbia counties. Van Cortlandt held a patent for Van Cortlandt Manor consisting of 85,000 choice acres in the Hudson highlands.

They also benefited from trade of another kind. The harbor was filled with a forest of masts—so many that an acute observer would have noticed more ships than were needed to carry the colony's exports of flour, furs, and naval stores. Many of them appeared to be too rakish and heavily armed to be innocent trading vessels. A few hours in any of the waterfront taverns or mercantile coffeehouses would have provided a solution to the mystery. New York had become a thieves' market where pirates disposed of the loot they had taken on the high seas. Merchants willing to overlook the momentary awkwardness of a few bloodstains on goods offered for sale at bargain prices were turning huge profits.

Nicholas van Rosenvelt, by now a strapping young man, apparently saw little opportunity to better himself in this closed society of monopoly and privilege. His eye turned instead to the Hudson River Valley, which was to play such an important role in the family's history. He had watched as grizzled fur traders clad in stained buckskins paddled their canoes down the river from the wilderness with bales of furs they had bought from the Indians for a few trinkets and then sold at a substantial profit. Here was a business in which a young man without influence could prosper if he were a bold and daring fellow and was willing to accept risks. Besides, he had no ties to hold him to New York. His sisters had all made comfortable marriages and had established their own homes.

Elsje, the oldest, married Hendrick Jillesh Meyer, a cordwainer, or cobbler, in 1671 and they made their home over his shop on Pearl Street. Meyer's father, a carpenter, was one of New Amsterdam's leading craftsmen, and had been often hired by the authorities to make repairs to the fort and other civic buildings. The couple had nine children, and later in life, Meyer became an assistant alderman. Anna Margaret married Heyman Alderste Roosa, of whom nothing is known, and had six children. Christina, however, began the Roosevelt tradition of marrying up in the world by wedding Nicasius de la Montagne. Originally French Huguenots, his family included a physician who doubled as an adviser to Governor Kieft, and the master of a Latin school who was also one of the colony's leading poets. The councilor, Dr. Johannes de la Montagne, once thwarted an attempt by a disgruntled farmer to shoot Kieft by sticking his thumb in the firing pan of the assassin's pistol. Two children were born of this union. The records fail to provide any clues as to what happened to Anna, the youngest of Nicholas' sisters, who was born after their father's death.

Moving upriver to Esopus, on the west side of the Hudson, about halfway between New York and Albany, Nicholas established himself as a trapper and Indian trader. This could be a dangerous business. Only a few years before, the Indians, resent-

ing the intrusion of the Dutch, had laid siege to the town, which
was enclosed by a wooden palisade. The settlers watched helplessly as their livestock was slaughtered and their crops destroyed. Twenty-three days passed before Stuyvesant could
muster sufficient volunteers to come to the aid of the severely
frightened farmers. This raw force drove off the Indians, and
as an example, Stuyvesant ordered that a dozen captured braves
should be sold as slaves in Curaçao—a wanton decision that
stirred a demand for revenge. Not long afterward, the Indians
struck Esopus again. Twelve houses were burned to the ground
and twenty-one people killed, many of them women and children.
Stuyvesant dispatched another force up the Hudson to deal with
this menace, and the absence of these men was a contributing
factor to the weakness that forced him to surrender to the British
without a fight.

With these dangers fresh in mind, Nicholas is said to have
been a pioneer in offering humane treatment to the Indians. Not
only did it help ensure his safety as he tramped through the
woods or paddled his canoe from one Indian village to another to
bargain for pelts, it was also good business. Indian hospitality
required someone who was presented a gift to return it tenfold,
so fur traders learned to open negotiations by giving the Indians
a few cheap trinkets and reaping a harvest from their "generosity." And if Nicholas followed the practices of his fellow
traders and trappers, he was probably not above poaching a few
pelts within the bounds of the manor of Rennsalaerswyck, which
covered thousands of acres on both sides of the Hudson.

Today, the fur traders are regarded as romantic figures who
abandoned an ordered society to live among the Indians. In fact,
the trade usually brutalized both those engaged in it and the Indians as well. The primary objective of the trade was beaver
rather than luxurious furs for wraps and coats. These skins were
used for making felt hats, and "beaver" was the slang word for
hat in the seventeenth century. Most colonists wore dressed
deerskins for their ordinary clothing. Although the fur traders
had the virtue of courage, many of those who sought their fortunes in the forests were, in the words of one writer, "misfits in
civilization, psychopaths, such men as are found today in prisons,
alcoholic wards and the skid rows of the big cities." Most colonies
forbade them to give the Indians liquor and firearms in exchange

for pelts, but neither law nor considerations of public safety could prevent some traders from doing what was profitable. In their wanderings, they also transmitted diseases to the Indians, such as smallpox, to which they had little resistance, and decimated entire tribes.

Nicholas did well in the fur trade, and in 1680 was among the burghers of Esopus who petitioned that a minister be appointed to preach the gospel in the riverside town. It was also during this period that the "van" disappeared from the family name and the various spellings resulting from the illiteracy of its own members and that of various government clerks were standardized as Roosevelt. Two years later, Nicholas, now twenty-four, decided to end his solitary life and went down to New York, where he married Heyltje Jans Kunst. Although she has usually been described as the daughter of Jans Barentsen Kunst, a carpenter of mixed Dutch-German extraction, most of the existing information about Heyltje has been called into question and she remains a shadowy figure. One writer conjectures that she may have been the granddaughter or grandniece of the widow Annetje Jans, a strong-willed woman who played a prominent role in the annals of New Amsterdam and once owned the property on Wall Street now occupied by Trinity Church.

Following the wedding, the young couple returned to Esopus, where they remained for the next eight years. Like most Roosevelts, they had a large family, and four of their ten children—all but two of whom reached adulthood—were born while they lived there. After more than a decade of the harsh and precarious life of the frontier, Nicholas had achieved his goal of making enough money to go into business in New York. Leaving Esopus for good in 1690, he established himself in the highly profitable bolting trade and opened a mill for grinding wheat and corn on Stone Street, near the waterfront. For the rest of his long and eventful life, this remained the center of his operations.

Writing about the Roosevelts in the early years of the twentieth century, when one was in the White House, Mrs. Schuyler van Rensselaer took a somewhat condescending attitude toward the clan—inspired no doubt by pique that they had fared so much better than her own. "At no pre-Revolutionary period was the Roosevelt family conspicuous nor did any member of it attain distinction," she said in her *History of New York in the Seventeenth Century*. But the fact of the matter is that the Roosevelts were far more distinguished than Mrs. van Rensselaer would have us believe. Beginning the family tradition of public service, Nicholas was twice elected alderman and was among New York's leading citizens during one of the most turbulent periods in its history.

The city to which Nicholas had returned in 1690 was a bubbling cauldron of revolutionary unrest. The Glorious Revolution of 1688 which swept the Catholic King James II from the throne of England and replaced him with his Protestant daughter, Mary, and her husband, William of Orange, had been comparatively peaceful at home. In New York, however, events took a tragic and violent turn. Francis Nicholson, the acting governor, and his chief advisers, among them such magnates as Bayard, Van Cortlandt, and Philipse, who had grown rich under James's rule, stood fast for the King—or at least until they could determine which way the wind was blowing in England. But the mass of New Yorkers favored William and Mary, and a drunken threat by Nicholson to burn the town touched off a revolt.

Jacob Leisler, a German-born militia captain and merchant, seized power with the announced intention of preserving the colony for the Protestant sovereigns. Arriving in New Amsterdam as a penniless soldier in the employ of the Dutch West India Company, Leisler had married a rich widow. He had long been dissatisfied with the control of the colony maintained by the ruling clique, and voiced the demand for an end to monopolies with wider opportunities for the little fellow. It was rich against poor; aristocrats against the people. Although he was a pigheaded, anti-Catholic bigot who railed against "the Scarlet Whore of Rome" and warned of a French invasion to restore James to the throne, Leisler's twenty-one months in power had overtones of a social revolution.

Leisler tried to put an end to the worst aspects of the graft and corruption that permeated every aspect of life and to break the grip of the great landlords and wealthy merchants upon the colony. As a result, the yeomen farmers and the small businessmen considered Leisler as their champion and flocked to his standard. But the magnates, fearful of being despoiled of their wealth and influence, regarded him as a dangerous rabble-rouser.

They quietly plotted his overthrow. Emissaries were sent to London to circulate horror stories about the revolutionary excesses of Leisler's regime and to influence public opinion against him. In reality, Leisler executed no one, and not a drop of blood was shed during the upheaval, although comparing himself with Oliver Cromwell, he sometimes acted in a dictatorial manner. For two years, William and Mary were too busy putting down Jacobite rebellions in Scotland and Ireland to pay much attention to what was going on in America, giving Leisler the mistaken idea that royal recognition had been granted to his government. It was an error that was to bring him to a traitor's death—and touched off a conflict that was to dominate New York's history during the next quarter century.

Unlike most well-to-do citizens, Nicholas Roosevelt supported Leisler. As a self-made man he undoubtedly saw Leisler's reforms as providing the opportunity for men like himself to get ahead. But the tide was about to turn against Leisler. The new governor finally dispatched by William and Mary was an Irish soldier bearing the ominous name of Henry Sloughter. A small squadron of ships and two companies of regular troops under the command of Colonel Richard Ingoldesby accompanied him to his new post. Unfortunately, Sloughter was delayed by a storm and Ingoldesby, whose mind had apparently been poisoned by the anti-Leisler propaganda circulating in England, arrived ahead of him. He quickly entered an alliance with the aristocratic faction and demanded Leisler's surrender. Leisler obstinately refused to recognize Ingoldesby's authority, barricaded himself in Fort George, as it was now known, and declared that he would give up authority only to the new governor. This standoff lasted for six weeks, but hotheads on both sides eventually prevailed. During an exchange of gunfire on March 17, 1691, a redcoat was killed, sealing Leisler's fate. Two days later, Sloughter arrived and ordered Leisler and nine members of his council arrested on charges of treason and murder.

The court that tried Leisler and his associates was packed with their enemies and quickly brought in a verdict of guilty. Sloughter was reluctant to sign the death warrant, so his signature was obtained while he was drunk, a common enough condition of the new governor. On May 16, 1691, Leisler and his son-in-law, Jacob Milbourne, suffered the penalty meted out to traitors on the present site of City Hall Park, a fitting place for the execution of a man opposed to graft and corruption. Gazing out over a large crowd from the scaffold, Leisler said, "I hope my eyes shall see our Lord Jesus Christ in heaven. I am ready! I am ready!" He and Milbourne were hanged, cut down while still alive, disemboweled, and their bodies hacked into quarters. "The shrieks of the people were dreadful," reported an observer. Locks of Leisler's hair and bits of his clothing were carried away by his supporters as if they were holy relics.

Having accomplished the judicial murder of Leisler, the magnates set about dismantling all traces of his reforms. One of the first acts of Sloughter's council, packed with large landowners, was to reaffirm the legality of all existing land grants. Edicts were also issued reducing wage levels and tightening the requirements for becoming a freeman, or voter. Sloughter received his reward in the form of a special grant of funds, voted to recover unexpected "expenses" incurred in restoring law and order to New York. The Leislerians, who stood in the shadow of the scaffold, charged this was a payoff for his support of the aristocratic faction. Sloughter spent most of the time in an alcoholic haze, no doubt contemplating the riches that would soon be his. But there was to be no golden harvest for him. He died soon after taking office, supposedly from the effects of drink.

Yet Jacob Leisler's martyrdom was not in vain. By arousing the ordinary folk of New York against the aristocracy, he created a situation in which the magnates could never again secure absolute mastery of the colony—although they repeatedly tried to do so with the assistance of various royal governors. For the next generation, the electorate were divided between Leislerians and anti-Leislerians, or into popular and aristocratic parties.

Before Benjamin Fletcher, Sloughter's successor, left London, the authorities had impressed upon him the need for a policy of pacification to end the campaign of violence against Leisler's followers. But as soon as he arrived in New York, Fletcher, destined to be the colony's most corrupt and greedy governor, threw in his lot with the aristocratic faction. In return for bribes and with a stroke of his quill pen, he handed out more than a million acres of land to the grandees and created a flock of new landed families.

For example, Henry Beekman, founder of a clan that was to figure prominently in New York real estate, received a grant running twenty miles along the east bank of the Hudson "as large as a middling county in England." Fletcher also extended an enthusiastic welcome to the pirates, whose trade was a boon to the New York merchants, and he was given a share of the loot they brought to New York to be "fenced."

Having met his temporal needs, Fletcher next turned to matters of the spirit. As thunderous a Bible-thumper as any Puritan divine—he took time out twice a day for prayer—the governor was one of the organizers of Trinity Church and donated a prayer book and pew to the congregation. The building of the church coincided with the establishment of the Church of England as the colony's official religion, and was another symbol of the division of the people. For the most part, this separation was along ethnic and religious lines, with the aristocracy adopting English ways while the Leislerians were primarily Dutch and adherents of the old Reformed Church.

Nevertheless, events conspired to bring about Fletcher's downfall. The Leislerians, working in England to secure a reversal of the bill of attainder against their dead leader, spread stories about the graft and corruption rampant under his rule. He had a falling out with some of his allies. And English merchants, deprived of their profits by the volume of trade with the buccaneers, demanded his ouster. Much to the shock of the merchants, the Earl of Bellomont, appointed to replace him, turned out to be a reformer. Since the Leislerians opposed Fletcher, he allied himself with them. Symbolically, when Leisler's remains were transferred from a traitor's grave to the cemetery of the Dutch church, Bellomont led the torchlit procession. Many of Fletcher's land grants were abrogated and corrupt officials were rooted out, including Bayard and Philipse, who lost their seats on the Governor's Council.

Emboldened by this change in atmosphere, the Leislerians fielded candidates for municipal office, with Nicholas among them. In 1700 he was elected alderman from the South Ward, one of the six into which the town had been divided. It covered the area from the tip of Manhattan to Wall Street and between the Broad Way and Broad Street. The following year, Bellomont

died, and the aristocratic party saw the opportunity to regain its
power. The municipal elections of 1701 became a contest for supremacy between the two factions.

Although New York now had a population of nearly five thousand people, only a handful were eligible to cast ballots, and
there was a tumultuous campaign for their votes. In the South
Ward, Nicholas was opposed by Brandt Schuyler, member of a
family that had arrived in America shortly before the Roosevelts,
who had once held the seat for the aristocratic party. The election had an outcome that was to become increasingly familiar to
New Yorkers over the years—the Leislerians made a barefaced attempt to steal it.

The election returns gave Schuyler a majority of 41 to 37 votes
for Nicholas in the South Ward, and in two of the other wards
the Leislerian candidates had also apparently gone down to defeat. Fifteen days after the election, on October 14, 1701, Thomas
Noell, an English merchant and standard-bearer of the aristocratic party, was inaugurated as mayor by the acting governor,
John Nanfan. Proceeding to the City Hall, he summoned the vic-
tors in the municipal election to be sworn in. Before he could
administer the oath, however, Nicholas and the other Leislerian
candidates contended that the opposition had won by fraud, and
said they had already taken the oath from Noell's predecessor,
who was conveniently a member of their own party. The aristocratic faction immediately challenged these claims, and it looked
as if the meeting would erupt into a brawl. "The ferment and uproar rose to such a height that a general conflict was impending,"
states an old account, "and the mayor rose and dissolved the
meeting upon which the multitude dispersed."

With both sides claiming victory, the harassed Noell first ascer-
tained that he, not the previous mayor, had the right to swear in
the new aldermen. Next, he appointed a commission, equally
divided between the parties, to investigate the balloting in the
contested wards and to come up with a decision on who should
sit. The Leislerians refused to participate in the inquiry, however,
either because they thought Noell might not be impartial or,
more likely, because they fully realized their claims might not
withstand close inspection. In the end, the commission upheld
the right of Schuyler to the seat, and Nicholas was ousted. Later,

the Roosevelts and Schuylers were reconciled through marriage.
And in 1719 Nicholas again ran for alderman, this time from the
East Ward, and was elected handily.

New York's troubles were not over, however. In the summer of
1702, the town was gripped by heat, and the mosquitoes which
made the nights miserable seemed worse than years gone by.
They seemed to be most numerous near the low swampy land to
the east and around the ponds. Perhaps they would go away
when it got cooler. Soon, however, people began to be taken sick.
They had fever and chills, their eyes, necks, and chests were
faintly tinged with yellow, and they vomited a black bilelike sub-
stance. And they soon died. It was the *vomito*—the dreaded yellow fever. Terror-stricken citizens abandoned Manhattan for the
countryside. The roads were crowded with carts and wagons and
people on foot, fleeing an enemy that was even more terrible because it was invisible. In a few weeks, more than five hundred
New Yorkers had died, or about 10 percent of the population.

To some, the ravages of yellow fever seemed divine retribution
for the sins of the city—and particularly those of the new governor, Edward Hyde, Lord Cornbury. Undoubtedly the most bizarre character to serve as a royal governor anywhere, Cornbury
was a transvestite who delighted in flouncing about before the as-
tonished citizenry in women's clothing. He was frequently seen
at night strolling the ramparts of Fort George, while wearing a
voluminous hoop skirt, elaborate headdress, and flourishing a fan.
He apparently fancied that this feminine finery enhanced his resemblance to his royal cousin, Queen Anne.

Cornbury was married, and his wife also created a strong impression upon New Yorkers. According to one story, Cornbury
had married her because of a fetishistic infatuation with one of
her ears. There came a time when the ear no longer pleased
him and he refused to give her any money. Lady Cornbury then
took up begging and stealing to make up for the missing funds.
Furs, gowns, and jewelry were borrowed and never returned.
When her coach was heard approaching, society ladies hid their
valuables, because if her ladyship saw anything she liked, she
was certain to send for it the next day—and that would be the last
the owner would see of it.

Greedy and avaricious, Cornbury looted the public treasury

and in exchange for "special grants" aligned himself with the aristocratic party. Finally, even he went too far. During one of the periodic war scares with France, it was found that he had embezzled funds earmarked for the colony's defense, leaving it open to enemy attack. Panic swept the city. Cursing the governor, the burghers, with Nicholas and his sons probably among them, sweated with pick and shovel to throw up earthworks to defend their homes. When the scare was over, the Common Council took steps to prevent Cornbury from again getting his hands on public funds. They appointed a treasurer answerable only to themselves, much to the governor's anger. The authorities in London approved this action, which marked the beginning of responsible government in America. Before being dismissed from his post, Cornbury made an indirect contribution to the family history of the Roosevelts, however. To show his gratitude for a large land grant in Dutchess County on the east bank of the Hudson, the recipient named it Hyde Park in honor of the governor.

By the early part of the eighteenth century, New York was America's third largest city, ranking after Philadelphia and Boston in size, but rapidly gaining on the latter. "The nobleness of the town surprised more than the fertile appearance of the country," wrote an officer of the Royal Navy upon first seeing New York. "I had no idea of finding a place in America, consisting of nearly 2,000 houses, elegantly built of brick, raised on an eminence and the streets paved and spacious, furnished with commodious keys [quays] and warehouses, and employing some hundreds of vessels in its foreign trade and fisheries—but such is this city that very few in England can rival its show."

Along with this growing prosperity came an increased demand for slaves. By 1700 New York had more blacks among its population than any city north of the Chesapeake, and a slave market was opened at the eastern end of Wall Street. But unlike the southern colonies where most blacks were owned by large landholders who used them to till their plantations, those in New York usually belonged to small holders who owned only one or two slaves. For the most part, they were employed as domestic servants, in shipbuilding, and as coopers, tailors, bakers, masons, and weavers. Some slaves were hired out by their masters who pocketed their wages, arousing considerable bitterness among the white working class because the practice undercut the wages of free laborers. Like most of their class, the Roosevelts owned slaves who labored in their various enterprises, but the exact number is not known.

New Yorkers usually followed the Dutch tradition of kind treatment of their slaves in contrast to conditions often prevailing in the South. As the slave population increased to about 20 percent of the total, however, the whites were haunted by the possibility of a revolt, and severe restrictions were placed on the activities and movements of blacks. In 1702 it was decreed that if three or more slaves gathered together, they could be flogged. Blacks were not permitted to drink or gamble and were forbidden "from playing publickly in the streets on Sunday." Fire was always the great fear of New Yorkers, and with blacks coming and going freely, the opportunity for arson was thought to be great. When such cases occurred, blacks were usually suspected and the penalty was death. In 1708 four slaves—two black men, a black woman, and an Indian—were either hanged or burned at the stake on Long Island on charges of having murdered their master, pregnant mistress, and four children. They were executed with "all the torment possible" as an example to the others.

But this cruelty only created a desire for revenge among some blacks for the "hard usage they apprehended to have received from their masters" and to secure their freedom. They plotted to massacre all the whites in New York in one fell swoop. Believing they had been made invisible by a secret powder that a sorcerer had sprinkled over them, about two dozen blacks, armed with guns, knives, axes, and clubs, gathered in an orchard off Maiden Lane shortly after midnight on April 6, 1712. Among them was a slave named Tom, the property of old Nicholas Roosevelt. Two of the group with a grudge against their master went to his home and set it afire. Then they rejoined their comrades who were lying in wait ready to murder any whites who came to put out the fire. In the eerie light of the flames, nine persons were killed, including one man shot by Nicholas Roosevelt's slave, and another seven were wounded.

Panic raced through New York like fire in a ship's rigging, and it was feared that the entire slave population had revolted. Alarm guns were fired at the fort and drums rattled. Volunteers were armed and troops dispatched to the troubled area to restore order; sentries took up posts at strategic points to prevent the blacks from escaping from Manhattan. They fled into the woods and marshes but were soon flushed from cover. Some shot themselves or slit their own throats to prevent capture and to avoid the terrible fate awaiting them. Retribution was swift and merciless. Although the forms of due process were observed, "the cards were stacked against the defendants," says one authority.

In all, twenty-five blacks were condemned to death, of whom eighteen were actually executed. Of these, thirteen were quickly hanged; one was hung in chains until he died of starvation, and another was broken on the wheel, which meant that he was spread-eagled on a cartwheel while the executioner proceeded to smash each of his limbs with a sledgehammer before finally crushing his chest. Three were burned to death, with Tom, the Roosevelt slave, suffering the most horrible fate of all. He was condemned to be roasted alive over a slow fire, with the agonizing process taking more than eight hours. Under existing law, the owners of each of the executed slaves were given twenty-five pounds in compensation for their loss.

Throughout this succession of upheavals and epidemics, Nicholas Roosevelt continued to prosper. Successful in business and politics, he became a "burgher of the major right," which meant that he was numbered among the town's leading citizens. Living until 1742 when he died in his eighty-fourth year, he was also the patriarch of a large and increasingly influential family. In his old age, he could take pride in his three sons, Nicholas, Johannes, and Jacobus, who were doing well on their own, and his five daughters had continued the family tradition of good marriages. Respected by his neighbors and often called in to settle disputes among them, he maintained a zest for life and the lively sense of humor that has been a hallmark of most members of the family.

One day a group of men idling in front of a blacksmith shop were unexpectedly treated to a sudden swish of brightly colored petticoat and a momentary glimpse of a trim ankle. They belonged to Nicholas' wife, Heyltje. Someone, probably a political enemy, complained of this wanton spectacle, and Heyltje was hauled up before a magistrate on charges of violating the sumptuary laws regulating dress and displaying her ankles "in an unseemly fashion to the scandal of the community." Nicholas not only accompanied his wife to court but also conducted her defense so ably that the charges were dismissed. Pausing only long enough to file suit for slander against the busybody who had instituted the proceedings, he then accompanied Heyltje to the nearest cloth merchant. He ordered a roll of even richer and gayer brocade and told her to have a petticoat made from it.

This story may be too good to be true—a similar tale is told about Annetje Jans, who may or may not have been related to Heyltje. But then, again, it could have happened. It is pleasant to think so.

Chapter IV
A FAMILY IN FERMENT

Musing in 1901 on the reasons for his family's continued vitality while most of New York's old Dutch families had long since sunk into oblivion, Franklin Roosevelt credited it to their "progressiveness and true democratic spirit." In a thesis written during his sophomore year at Harvard* which traced the clan's rise, he said:

> One reason—perhaps the chief—of the virility of the Roosevelts is this very democratic spirit. They have never felt that because they were born in a good position they could put their hands in their pockets and succeed. They have felt, rather, that being born in a good position, there was no excuse for them if they did not do their duty by the community. . . .

No one could accuse Nicholas Roosevelt's two most prominent sons, Johannes, born in 1689 while the family was still living at Esopus, and Jacobus, three years younger and born following the move to New York, of standing idly by with their hands in their pockets. In fact, if some contemporary accounts are to be believed, the Roosevelt boys sometimes had their hands in someone else's pocket. Shrewd, sharp, and perhaps a bit unscrupulous when it came to business, they were forerunners of a distinctive American type: the "go-getter."

Between them, they established the two separate—and often

---

* This paper, written in longhand, is in the files of the Roosevelt Library. Based largely on entries in the old family Bible upon which FDR took the oath as President four times, it was graded "O.K." by Hiram Bingham, a young history instructor and later discoverer of the lost Inca city of Machu Picchu.

rival—Roosevelt lines that have come down to our own time. Johannes, who with the increasing anglicization of New York was often known as John in legal documents, was the founder of the Oyster Bay branch of the family, which produced Theodore Roosevelt and his niece, Eleanor. Jacobus, often called James, was the progenitor of the Hyde Park branch, which produced Franklin Roosevelt. Franklin and Eleanor were fifth cousins, and when they married in 1905, Eleanor's Uncle Ted, who gave the bride away, told the bridegroom in his high-pitched voice: "Well, Franklin, there's nothing like keeping the name in the family."

The two brothers had their fingers in many pies. While almost nothing is known of their older brother, Nicholas, who died sometime about 1718 at the age of thirty or so, they were active in commerce and politics. Not only did they take part in the family flour-milling business but they also manufactured linseed oil, which was used in the making of paint, operated leather tanneries, engaged in real estate speculation and building construction, and had shares in a mine. Perhaps to further their business interests as well as serving the community, they participated in politics and both were alderman or assistant alderman at various times. Not yet of the aristocracy, the Roosevelts were in the first rank of the commercial gentry and were considered among the colony's "better sort." As one writer has noted, they were at this time probably richer than the Adamses of Boston and the Biddles of Philadelphia.

Although the Roosevelt brothers often worked hand in hand, Johannes spread his net wider. Undoubtedly as a result of his political influence, he secured from the General Assembly a ten-year monopoly on the production of linseed oil for the entire colony. With New York rapidly becoming a shipbuilding center— a vessel could be built in America for half its cost in Britain— there was a heavy demand for this foul-smelling product. Orders poured into his flaxseed mill on Maiden Lane near the waterfront, and Johannes was on his way to becoming the first wealthy Roosevelt. But he was not a man to be satisfied with success in a single field. He branched out into the manufacture of chocolate and flour and then into street repair and building construction. Along with Philip van Cortlandt, he secured in 1720 a contract for the repair of the sidewalks along Wall Street, which may have been another political plum. The fact that a Roosevelt and a Van Cortlandt were business partners is clear evidence that the bitter animosities of the Leisler era had faded away.

Johannes was one of four commissioners appointed to oversee the rebuilding of the fortifications after a fire swept Fort George and destroyed several of the structures within its walls. He was given a contract to rebuild the secretary's office at a cost of 260 pounds. Located in the fort's east garden, the one-story brick building was to have two fireplaces, a shingled roof, painted woodwork, four windows, and a writing desk and benches. The contractor was to "finish both the outside and the inside work-manlike to the turning of the key." Johannes must have done his work well, for the colonial authorities soon gave him a contract for the construction of a battery of eight guns on Long Island. He was also placed in charge of maintaining a group of French prisoners of war and purchased considerable gunpowder for the colony's account. For Johannes, good business and good citizenship went hand in hand.

Acting with a syndicate composed of himself, Frederick Philipse, and John Chambers, Johannes, in effect, became one of New York's first sports impresarios. They took up a nine-year lease in 1734 on a plot of ground "lying at the lower end of the Broad Way fronting to the Fort . . . to be enclosed to make a Bowling Green thereof with walks therein, for the beauty and ornament of said street as well as for the decoration and delight of the inhabitants of the city." A yearly rental of one peppercorn was set, the charge usually established for a transaction deemed to be in the public interest. When the lease expired, it was not renewed, but the area had gotten its name and it has remained a park ever since.

Johannes showed an artistic side that was rare for the family. In 1731, when a new charter was presented to the city by Governor John Montgomerie, he was given the honor of making an elaborate metal container in which it was to be kept. The fact that he was "a political henchman" of Mayor Richard Lurting no doubt had much to do with the choice. Amid the ringing of church bells, the governor handed over the charter to the waiting Common Council on the steps of the new City Hall on Wall Street, where Federal Hall now stands. Among those who received it was Alderman Jacobus Roosevelt. Johannes soon joined him on the council. With his growing wealth, Johannes widened his cultural horizons. He imported paintings and furnishings for his home from Holland and it became something of a show-place. "His home was viewed as a wonderland by his less enterprising fellow-citizens," says one old account. Johannes was also a member of a Committee of Five that helped found what became the New York Society Library.

Jacobus Roosevelt was the first of the family to take the plunge into New York real estate in a big way. In 1723 he and several other prominent citizens secured a grant "of the lots of land . . . fronting Hudson's River to low water mark to the Green Trees near the English church." This site is now bounded by Battery and Rector streets, on the Lower West Side. Five years later, Jacobus began the speculations that were the foundations of his fortune. He secured title to ten lots, each measuring 25 by 120 feet in the Beekman Swamp for a total of one hundred pounds. Adjacent to what is now City Hall Park, this low-lying area covers the ground presently encompassed by Frankfort, Spruce, Gold, and Cliff streets.

Although the land was marshy and covered with tangled briars, Jacobus immediately grasped the possibilities of the area. He persuaded his brother to join him in the investment and to-gether they bought the entire swamp. There had been a rising tide of complaints about the cluster of malodorous tanneries and slaughterhouses that had grown up at the bottom of Wall Street, and on October 11, 1720, the Common Council, in what may have been the first environmental cease-and-desist order in Amer-ican history, had called the slaughterhouses "a public Nuisance" [which] Ought in A short time to be removed." Jacobus per-suaded the owners of the offending industries to set up shop in the Beekman Swamp, where he built several buildings for their use. He also convinced the authorities to cut a street through the area, which became Ferry Street and added to its value. Vast mounds of tan accumulated in the area, and the neighborhood boys fought mimic battles from behind redoubts of the stuff. Long after the tanneries and slaughterhouses had been displaced by the encroaching city, the area remained the center of the leather trade. More than a century later, the Beekman Swamp property was still in the hands of the Roosevelt family, and formed a part of the bequest that established the Roosevelt Hospital. Incidentally, one of the buildings constructed by Jacobus in 1725 remained standing until 1946. The wreckers who pulled it down found that the hand-hewn oak beams were sound and the structure was still habitable.

Neglecting no attractive opportunity, the Roosevelt brothers secured land in Westchester County as well. Old records state that they were joint owners "of undivided land lying between Rye and Byrom River and blind brooke"—now prime suburban acreage. Some of their dealings inspired mutterings about political favoritism that finally exploded into charges of outright corruption. In 1748 Johannes, Jacobus, and three other prominent citizens, among them Leonard Lispenard, a member of the Common Council, petitioned the aldermen for the use of waterfront lots along the East River adjacent to some property that the group already owned. They apparently intended to build a pier on the lots in question for the unloading of skins that were being shipped to the Beekman Swamp tanneries. The council quickly acceded to the request, undoubtedly influenced by the fact that Lispenard was one of their colleagues and Jacobus had previously been a member.

Little notice was taken of this transaction until five years later when a gossipy sheet called *The Independent Reflector* raised serious questions about its propriety. "The astonishing Propositions made by the Petitioners" have become "a common Coffee-House Topic, and the subject of almost every Conversation," stated an unsigned letter to the editor which appeared on February 1, 1753. It was charged that the group had obtained control of the lots in question without payment for rent for twenty years, and they proposed to pay only ninepence a foot after that date. This was denounced as one of the most blatant land grabs in the history of the colony, to be viewed with "universal Detestation and Abhorrence."

Warming to the subject, the anonymous letter writer estimated that if the lots were held for the full twenty-year period, they would be worth no less than 6,000 pounds—dropping a tidy fortune into the laps of the Roosevelts and their friends. He pointed out that a few years before, a Colonel Moore—more than likely one of those who had been complaining about the deal in the coffeehouses—had paid eighteen pence a foot for other water lots, or a total of 1,400 pounds, and had not been given a twenty-year period of grace. Others had paid a shilling and ninepence a foot for similar land. "These Gentlemen, it seems, were no Adepts in the Art of cajoling Corporations out of their Lands. . . . Nay, they were totally ignorant of the modern Refinement of claiming without Title, and buying without paying." The letter writer and William Livingston, editor of *The Independent Reflector*—who may have been one and the same—joined in demanding that the lots be sold at public auction. "That a Majority of so conspicuous a Body, as the Corporation of this City, should join in so iniquitous a Concession is utterly incredible," Livingston declared in an accompanying editorial. Less than two months later, however, the council brushed off these demands and the Roosevelts and their partners kept the land.

The reaction of the Roosevelt brothers to these charges of shady operations is unknown, but if past performance is any clue, Jacobus, for one, must have exploded. He had a notoriously short fuse and at least once it landed him in the courts to face a suit for slander. In 1718 a goldsmith named Benjamin Wincope, who had made a tankard for Jacobus, sued him for two hundred pounds in damages, a substantial sum at the time, claiming that Roosevelt had deprived him "of his good name" and had "hurt and prejudiced him" in the eyes of "his Neighbours & other faithfull Subjects of our Said . . . Lord the King."

Wincope claimed in papers filed in the Mayor's Court on April 26, 1718, that Jacobus had accosted him on the waterfront two weeks before and during an argument had angrily shouted in Dutch: "I will prove that you are a perjured person and that you have taken a false oath!" By this, Wincope said he meant that Roosevelt had accused him of being "a person that hath been convicted of Perjury and is publickly known and esteemed for Such a person." Inasmuch as the witnesses to this incident understood Dutch, Wincope alleged he was "greatly prejudiced and disgraced" and had undergone "great labours and Expences for the putting a Stop the false Rumours" which stemmed from it. There is no record of Jacobus' answer or whether he had to pay damages for the alleged slur.

Johannes Roosevelt's involvement with the legal system was far grimmer. He played a prominent role during the New York Conspiracy trials of 1741—which surpassed the Salem witch trials in hysteria and savagery. In all, more than 120 blacks and 20 whites were charged with conspiring to burn and loot the town, rape the women, and kill the men. Before this unreasoning terror subsided, 13 blacks were burned at the stake, 16 were hanged along with 4 whites, and 77 whites and blacks were banished to the West Indies. Quack, one of the blacks burned at the stake on charges of having set a fire at Fort George which destroyed the governor's residence and most of the buildings, was the property of Johannes Roosevelt.

Ever since the slave insurrection of 1712, New Yorkers had feared another uprising, and with Britain at war with Spain, tension was high. The city now had a population of some 9,000 white people and 2,000 slaves. Despite the harsh and repressive measures instituted for controlling the blacks following the earlier incident, the whites were convinced that at any moment they might have their throats cut while they lay in their beds. "What they have done, they may at one time or other act over again," said one, expressing the popular opinion. To add to the unease, New York was also just emerging from the effects of the most severe winter in the memory of its inhabitants, food was short and prices high. The city had also experienced an economic recession and workingmen found jobs scarce because, they said, of the competition of slave labor.

Early in 1741, New York was struck by a wave of burglaries which the authorities attributed to a gang of blacks who frequented a cheap tavern operated by a white man named John Hughson, at what is now the corner of Greenwich and Thames streets. Hughson had a reputation as a "fence" for stolen goods, but a search of the premises failed to turn up any of the loot. But Mary Burton, a sixteen-year-old white indentured servant who worked for the tavern keeper, told a friend that her master had received silver and linen taken in one of the robberies. The friend hastened to the authorities with this information and Mary Burton was arrested. Promised her freedom if she talked, the girl implicated Hughson, his wife, a prostitute named Peggy Kerry (Carey?), and several blacks who patronized the tavern, in the burglaries. All were taken into custody and Hughson now admitted having received some of the stolen property.

In the midst of this excitement, a series of mysterious fires was reported, climaxed on March 18, 1741, by a blaze at Fort George, which destroyed the governor's residence and several other buildings. Although the lieutenant governor, George Clarke, blamed the fire on the carelessness of a worker soldering a gutter, muttering mounted against the blacks. As one of the fires burned, a white woman claimed to have overheard a slave chanting: "Fire, Fire, Scorch, Scorch, a little, damn it, by-and-by." The following day, there were four fires in various parts of the town. Whites were convinced that the blazes were set by blacks, and when Cuffee, a slave belonging to Adolph Philipse, was seen fleeing from the scene of a fire, the cry went up "that the negroes were rising." Cuffee was arrested and charged with arson.

Swept forward like litter on a rushing stream, the Common Council met to consider the situation and concluded that "the fires were set on foot by some villainous confederacy of latent enemies among us." Rewards were offered for information and little Mary Burton stepped forward to claim them. She spouted charges that a gang of blacks often met at Hughson's tavern, where they plotted to burn and loot the city. A grand jury which included Johannes Roosevelt, who is called John in the old records, handed down a sheaf of indictments. Large numbers of terror-stricken blacks were arrested and to save their own skins hysterically accused each other of crimes. Among those taken into custody was Johannes' slave, Quack, who was said by some of the prisoners to have set fire to the governor's residence. No one seemed to remember that Lieutenant Governor Clarke had surmised the fire was accidental. To add to the hysteria, several fires were reported in Hackensack, New Jersey, across the Hudson, where two blacks accused of arson were burned at the stake. And a dispatch was received from Governor James Oglethorpe, of Georgia, warning that he had received information from Florida that "the Spaniards [have] employed emissaries to burn all the magazines and considerable towns in English North-America."

In this nightmare atmosphere, Hughson, his wife, Peggy Kerry, and a handful of blacks were tried and hanged for receiving stolen goods, and Quack and Cuffee were sentenced to be burned alive for having been involved in the conspiracy to burn New York. Johannes Roosevelt and one of his sons made an attempt to save Quack from the flames by testifying:

Quack was employed most part of that morning the fort was fired, from the time they got up, in cutting away the ice out of the yard;

that he was hardly ever out of their sight all that morning, but a small time while they were at breakfast; and that they could not think he could that morning have been from their home so far as the fort.

When this failed, Johannes had one final card to play—a last-minute confession made at the stake might win the slave a reprieve. As a large crowd gathered in what is now City Hall Park demanding the immediate execution of Quack and Cuffee, he told the terror-stricken Quack there was only one way to save himself. Chained to the stake and with the fagots already piled about him, the black man babbled the tale that the whites wished to hear. Everything that Mary Burton had said was true and Hughson had originated the plot. He confessed to having set fire to the governor's residence at the innkeeper's orders by planting a lighted brand in the roof shingles near the gutter the night before. The badly frightened Cuffee also gave a similar confession to a Mr. Moore, the colony's deputy secretary.

Moore suggested to the sheriff that the execution be halted and the prisoners be removed to jail while he reported the confessions to Clarke. Before he could return with the reprieves, however, the bloodthirsty crowd prevented the sheriff from removing the prisoners to safety. Roaring in protest and brandishing clubs and stones, the mob cried that it had come to see the villainous blacks burn—and burn they must. The fagots were lit and Quack and Cuffee perished in the flames. The "evidence" they had supplied in their dying declarations was used to implicate other slaves in the plot who were duly executed. One of the condemned saved his life by betraying the names of others whom he claimed were involved, and they, too, soon became victims of the white man's vengeance. This vicious circle widened as one of these unfortunates escaped death by giving the names of still more blacks, who were rounded up and executed. The terror continued unabated until August 29, 1741, when the last of the victims was hanged. And then like a summer storm, the madness subsided as suddenly as it had begun. Johannes Roosevelt got the contract to rebuild the structures at Fort George that had allegedly been put to the torch by his slave.

Notwithstanding the pressures of commerce and politics, Johannes and Jacobus were good family men. Both married young and between them they produced twenty-four sons and daughters, most of whom survived the many sicknesses to which children were prone in that era. Johannes wed Heyltje Sjoerts, daughter of the well-to-do Captain Olfert Sjoerts in 1708. Five years later, Jacobus married Catharina Hardenbroeck, who came from a well-established family in New Jersey. This was another step upward for the Roosevelts because Catharina's family was allied with the aristocratic Philipse clan. The eldest Roosevelt, Nicholas, who died about 1718, left three children, including a son who became the third Nicholas in the family. Not long after the death of her husband, Sara Fulman Roosevelt married Philip Schuyler, thereby creating an alliance with that family. And Rachel Roosevelt, old Nicholas' youngest daughter, married into the well-to-do Low family.

Jacobus was also a pillar of the Dutch Reformed Church. In his old age he was its senior elder, and on July 2, 1767, was given the honor of laying the cornerstone of a new church being erected at what is now the corner of Fulton and William streets. Old age was no bar to an open mind in his case and he was receptive to new ideas. Such flexibility was nowhere more evident than in his leadership of the church during a period of great change. In the century since Holland had lost control of the colony, many of the old customs and traditions had been replaced by English practices. Eventually, the winds of change began to rattle even the stained-glass windows of the church, the last bastion of tradition, where services were still conducted in Dutch. No longer regarding themselves as transplanted Dutchmen as their fathers had done, many of the younger members of the old families eagerly embraced Anglicization, not only changing their names but abandoning the Reformed Church for the Church of England.

Realizing that if the trend continued the Dutch church would disappear, Jacobus Roosevelt and Philip Livingston launched a campaign of modernization to make its practices more attractive to the younger generation. In 1762 they petitioned the other elders, who included men with names such as Beekman, Brevoort, and De Peyster, for approval of the hiring of an English-speaking minister and for sermons to be given in English. The request touched off a bitter controversy and several stormy meetings of the deacons were held before approval for the changes was forthcoming. The Reverend Archibald Laidlie, who held a pulpit at Flushing, on Long Island, was given the call and he turned out to be an eloquent preacher. "Ah, Dominie, we offered up many an earnest prayer in Dutch for your coming among us," one of the English-speaking advocates is said to have remarked, "and truly the Lord has heard us in English." While the Dutch church never regained its former prominence, some of the defectors returned, and preserved by Jacobus Roosevelt's efforts, it still thrives in New York. Ironically, the descendants of Jacobus joined the exodus to the Anglicans, while those of Johannes, who was less interested in religious matters, remained faithful to the old church much longer.

Until now, the Roosevelts, with the exception of old Nicholas' days as a fur trader, had produced only businessmen and merchants—conservative and level-headed fellows—but the line took an interesting turn with Nicholas Roosevelt III. Nicholas, whose mother had married into the Schuyler clan after the death of her husband, was one of the eighteenth century's finest gold and silversmiths. Refining the artistic taste that had been shown by his uncle Johannes in his selection of furniture and paintings for his home, he produced work in gold and silver that has been described by connoisseurs as "indicative of the highest skill."

Born in 1715, Nicholas was apparently apprenticed to Cornelius Wincope, the son of old Benjamin Wincope, who had sued Jacobus for slander. By the time he was twenty-four he had established himself as a goldsmith and had been made a freeman. He had a shop on Thames Street fronting on the Hudson River, where he produced severe-looking tankards, bowls, spoons, and gaily decorated smaller objects. He married twice, and a son of the second union, also named Nicholas, who was born in 1758, later moved to Stillwater in upstate New York where he founded another branch of the family in addition to the Hyde Park and Oyster Bay lines. His descendants were restless and some moved as far away as Missouri. As a result, said Franklin Roosevelt in his Harvard thesis, "there are scattered all over the country families of Roosevelts whose origin is quite obscure, either people who had adopted the name or have lost all trace of their ancestors."

Like his grandfather and uncles, Nicholas was interested in politics and was elected assistant alderman from the West Ward in 1748. He served in this post until 1763 when he was elected alderman, an office he held for another five years until forced to step aside because of poor health. Nicholas seems to have been diligent in conducting the public business because the records of the Common Council show that he missed only a few meetings during his twenty years of service. Probably his political prominence was no hindrance when it came time for the council to choose an official goldsmith for the city, and Nicholas fulfilled several commissions for his fellow aldermen.

He produced six gold boxes engraved with the arms of the city which were presented by the authorities to various English dignitaries who either governed the colony or served there in a military capacity. None of these boxes has ever been found—one expert theorizes that they were taken back to England, where they remain in the families of the recipients. Twenty-two examples of his craftsmanship in silver still exist, however, in museums and other collections around the country, where they are highly valued possessions. Among them is a pair of beakers made for a Dutch church in Brooklyn, which were engraved with sound counsel: "Speak what is true; Eat what is well prepared, and Drink what is pure." The sole surviving example of his work in gold is a baby's rattle produced about 1760 and now in the Metropolitan Museum of Art in New York. In contrast to the severity of Nicholas' other known work, it is exuberantly decorated.

With the failure of his health, Nicholas not only abandoned politics but closed up his shop and put his home up for rental. In an advertisement placed in the New York *Gazette and Weekly Mercury* of January 30, 1769, he states that the house is "roomy and convenient . . . with seven fireplaces, a large yard in which is a pump and cistern, and a garden and grass-plot."

> Also to be sold by said Roosevelt, a parcel of ready made silver, large and small, Viz. Silver teapots and tea-spoons, silver hilted swords, sauce-boats, salts and shovels, soup-spoons both scallep'd and plain, table spoons, tea-tongs, punch ladles and strainers, milk-pots, snuff-boxes, and sundry other small articles, both gold and silver . . . which he will sell very reasonable. . . .

Nicholas apparently moved to New Jersey where he owned property near Hackensack, but he did not long survive in retirement. He died about the middle of 1769 at the age of fifty-four. His uncle Johannes had preceded him, but Jacobus carried on until 1776, a momentous year in the history of the nation—and of the Roosevelts.

Chapter V
RESISTANCE AND REVOLUTION

Looking at Gilbert Stuart's portrait of Isaac Roosevelt which hangs in the comfortably informal library-living room of his great-great-grandson Franklin's home at Hyde Park, it is difficult to conceive of him as a revolutionary. He is an aristocrat down to the fine lace at his throat and wrists. Long-faced and with shrewd eyes that peer out from under arched brows, this is the face of a man obviously not to be trifled with. Yet, in the family annals, Isaac Roosevelt is known as "The Patriot" and he was an ardent fighter for the cause of American independence.

Until Theodore Roosevelt charged up San Juan Hill into the White House, Isaac was the first Roosevelt of real renown. Banker, businessman, politician, and member through marriage of the Hudson River aristocracy, he openly risked his neck and fortune for the cause of liberty in contrast to many members of his class who remained loyal to King George III. Perhaps this was due to the Roosevelts' "democratic spirit"—although more than likely it is attributable to complex economic, political, and social factors. But no matter what his reasons, Isaac was dedicated to the Patriot cause.

To him, the pledge of "our Lives, our Fortunes and our sacred Honor" of the Declaration of Independence was more than idle words. Lacking the radical persistence of an Adams or the eloquence of a Jefferson, he was not in the first rank of the founding fathers, but performed the day-to-day labors that made independence a reality. He served in the New York Provincial Congress, which took over the reins of government in 1775, and was one of the city's first two members of the State Senate. Forced by the British to abandon his home and business, he joined the colonial militia at the age of fifty. Because of his skill in commercial matters, a better use was found for his talents and he was called upon to help finance the war. And after independence was won, he was an outspoken supporter of the Constitution and a leader of the fight for ratification.

When Franklin Roosevelt was under attack for riding roughshod over the Constitution, he sought support in his ancestor's reputation for selfless patriotism. Speaking in Poughkeepsie during the closing days of the 1936 presidential campaign, he recalled Isaac's labors in behalf of that document:

> About a block from where I stand, up there on the corner of Main Street, there was a little old stone building and in the year 1788 there was held there the constitutional convention of the State of New York. My great-great-grandfather was a member of that convention. . . . And so you will see that not only in my person but also by inheritance I know something about the Constitution of the United States, but also the Bill of Rights.

He had already used Isaac's activities as the basis for his application for membership in the Sons of the American Revolution.

Isaac Roosevelt's prominence must have surprised his family, for it was not planned. Born on December 19, 1726, he was the fifth surviving son and seventh child of Jacobus and Catharina Roosevelt. The role of family favorite appears to have been reserved for his eldest brother, Johannes, his senior by eleven years. Johannes was the first Roosevelt to be sent to college. Despite the family's later affinity for Harvard, he attended Yale, graduating in 1735. Instead of adopting one of the learned professions such as doctor, lawyer, or minister like most college graduates of the day, he entered the profitable trade of merchant-grocer. In keeping with the family commitment to public service, Johannes served as an assistant alderman from 1748 to 1767. In one respect, however, he broke with family tradition. He and his wife, Annetje Luquier, daughter of a family that had come over from France by way of Holland to settle on Long Island, had only one child in contrast to the large broods favored by most of the early Roosevelts.

60 THE ROOSEVELT CHRONICLES

Young Isaac grew up in his father's house on Queen (now Pearl) Street, which was crowded with children who romped and quarreled and enjoyed themselves. He probably attended one of the Latin schools in the city and unlike his oldest brother was put to work on one or another of his father's various enterprises to learn the rudiments of bookkeeping and to keep track of correspondence. In summers, when New York was subject to various sicknesses, Jacobus' children were packed off up the Hudson to Esopus, now renamed Kingston, where the family had had connections since old Nicholas Roosevelt's days as a fur trader. Among their friends was Colonel Martinus Hoffman, who owned vast tracts of land on both sides of the river in Ulster and Dutchess counties. He also had a daughter named Cornelia, four years younger than Isaac.

In August 1752 Isaac and Cornelia were married in the Dutch Church at Rhinebeck. Whether their union was a love match or had been arranged by their parents is unknown, but in any case it was a classic example of what was then called "a good marriage." Today, when young people live together with or without benefit of clergy and parents consider themselves lucky if they are informed ex post facto, such an arrangement seems hopelessly quaint. But it was through such "good" marriages that the old families maintained their identities and vigor—and in the case of the Roosevelts, bettered themselves.

Through his alliance with Cornelia, Isaac entered what one writer has called the "patroonocracy" which dominated upstate New York just as the "plantocracy" dominated Maryland, Virginia, and the southern colonies. The Hoffmans were minor members, to be sure—descendants of a Finnish soldier who had been in the Swedish service before emigrating to New Netherland—but the marriage raised Isaac from the respectable commercial class into the rarefied atmosphere of the Hudson Valley landed gentry. The teachings of the French physiocrats, who held that all wealth was ultimately derived from ownership of the soil, had a strong influence on eighteenth-century Americans, as did their memories of the high land values prevailing in Europe. Thus, social prestige was automatically bestowed upon the owners of broad acres.

Although he could have passed the rest of his life as a country gentleman managing his father-in-law's ample estate and ten

slaves, Isaac chose to make his fortune in the rough-and-tumble
of trade in New York. Having grown to 18,000 inhabitants and
expanded beyond the tip of Manhattan, the town had at last
surpassed Boston as America's second city, but still lagged behind Philadelphia. It had also lost much of its Dutch look. While
some houses built of colored Flemish brick and with steplike gables still remained from Dutch days despite the ravages of periodic fires, more and more structures were built in the English
mode. They had the gambrel roof, equally spaced windows, and
classical doorways already familiar in Georgian London. The
spire of St. Paul's Church patterned after Sir Christopher Wren's
graceful St. Martia's in the Fields in London dominated the sky-
line. Visitors praised the cleanliness of the streets and commented on the richness of the attire of the well-to-do and the
liveliness of city life. Feasting, music, dancing, and the theater
were all popular.

But New York was already a city of vivid contrasts. In the al-
leys, or straggling out along Warren Street, were clusters of ram-
shackle wooden houses crowded with the poor. Only a few blocks
away were the homes of the merchant princes, with the mansion
of William Walton, on fashionable St. George's Square, the
grandest of all. Three stories high, with a portico crowned by the
Walton arms and with gardens running down to the East River,
the house was topped by a balustraded roof from which its
master could watch as his ships entered and left the harbor. Walton was a lavish host and his entertainments were among the
most elaborate in prerevolutionary America. As a sign of the rising status of the Roosevelts, Isaac's bachelor brother, Jacobus,
five years his senior, lived across Queen Street from the Walton
mansion.

Sugar, molasses, and rum, traded for flour, pork, and corn,
were the staples of New York's lucrative commerce with the
West Indies, but there were only a few sugar refineries in the
city. Sensing the opportunity for profit, Isaac went into partnership with his brother-in-law, Andrew Barclay, a prominent merchant who had married his sister, Helena, the family belle, and
they opened a refinery of their own. Soon, Isaac owned the largest sugar house in New York. Established in a stone building off
Wall Street, it was connected by an alley with the rear of his
home which faced onto the west side of Queen Street, near

Franklin Square. "Double, middling and single refined loaf sugars, clarified, muscovado and other molasses" as well as several types of rum were to be had at his establishment, according to a surviving advertisement.

Isaac quickly joined the ranks of New York's most prosperous businessmen, and was one of the founding members of the Chamber of Commerce. In civic affairs he was among the leaders of a campaign to improve the quality of the city's fire protection, and was also active in charitable and church work. In 1770 he was one of the incorporators of New York's first hospital, and served as a deacon of the Dutch church in which his father was an elder. For a man who did not own vast estates in his own right or have a flotilla of merchant ships flying his house flag, Isaac did well socially. He was often in attendance at the gala evenings at the Walton mansion where the colonial aristocracy and their wives—the De Lanceys, Livingston, Schuylers, and Van Cortlandts—intermingled with British officers in glittering regimentals and other representatives of the Crown. While not close to William Walton, he was an intimate friend of Andrew Walton, the old man's nephew. When his brother Jacobus died in 1771, Isaac quickly moved into his house, just across the street from the Waltons.

Incidentally, nothing that Jacobus accomplished in life caused as much comment as the macabre circumstances surrounding his passing, for on August 12, 1771, the *Gazette and Weekly Recorder* reported:

> On Tuesday last Mr. Jacobus Roosevelt, of this city being in Health, no otherways heated than by the Weather, which was extremely hot, drank pretty freely of the cold Water from the Well in his Sugar House Yard. He was presently seiz'd with Pain in the Stomach and Aching in the Bones, which obliged him to go to Bed; Physicians were sent for, and proper Medicines administered, but his Illness continued till next day at 11 o'clock when he grew better and the Doctors had hopes of his Recovery—But about 12 o'clock he was seiz'd with violent Pains as before, and in a very short Times expired; soon after which his Flesh turn'd yellow. . . .

Yet for all his prominence, Isaac was not the family patriarch that his grandfather, the first Nicholas, had been. After more than a century in America, the Roosevelts had become far too numerous and the relationship too extended for anyone to play such a role. Not only were there the various branches in New York—all with members named Jacobus, Johannes, and Nicholas, making it nearly impossible to sort them out today—but trade and ambition had carried others as far away as the West Indies, where they became planters and merchants.

In addition to Isaac's sister Helena, who had become the bride of Andrew Barclay, for whom Barclay Street was named, other female relations married well in the Roosevelt tradition. Margreta Roosevelt, his uncle Johannes' eldest child, married into the distinguished De Peyster clan. Helena Roosevelt Low, his Aunt Rachel's daughter, became the wife of Henry Kip, whose family gave its name to the Kip's Bay area around Thirty-fourth Street and the East River. Another niece, Catharina, the daughter of Nicholas II, married Steenwyck de Riemer, son of Isaac de Riemer, who had been mayor of New York. Others married into the equally prominent Duryea, Crommelin, De Witt, and Lispenard families. Through such alliances, observed Franklin Roosevelt in his Harvard thesis, "the stock [was] kept virile and abreast of the times."

Isaac's own private life had tragic overtones. A year after his marriage, he had the melancholy task of inscribing the following in the family Bible:

August 18. Monday morning, one o'clock, our first son was born in Wednesday, ye 15th of August was baptized and named Abraham. Having for his Godfather and Godmother Jacobus Roosevelt and Catharina Roosevelt, who being his grandfather and mother.

This our first son dies in the Lord on Tuesday afternoon at four o'clock the second day of October in the same year, being seven weeks and one day old, and interred in the family vault in the New Dutch Church Yard.

The following year, the grieving father noted the death of his second son, Martinus, named after his wife's father, who died at the age of eleven months. Not until 1760, after the birth of two daughters, did Isaac and Cornelia have a blessedly robust son to carry on the family name. He was christened Jacobus for his grandfather, but became known as James.

While Isaac was prospering, relations between Britain and her colonies were beginning the long slide toward the American Revolution. Paradoxically, the roots of the breakup of the British Empire lay in Britain's victory in 1763 in the last of the great wars for empire with France, known in America as the French and Indian War. The Union Jack now flew without a rival from Hudson's Bay to the Florida Keys and from the Atlantic shore to the Mississippi. But this vast new empire had to be defended against any attempt by the French to regain control of it. Financially drained by the long struggle, Britain felt she could not assume the sole financial burden of maintaining the 10,000 men required to defend the colonies.

Resolving that the Americans should bear the cost of their own defense, the cool and appraising eye of George Grenville, the Prime Minister, fell upon the Acts of Trade and Navigation. It was a fatal mistake. First enacted in the mid-seventeenth century, these laws were aimed at subordinating the economic interests of the colonies to those of the mother country by tying their trade to Britain. Before 1763, there had been little opposition to them in the colonies because the Americans were prosperous and enforcement was lax. Under Sir Robert Walpole, Prime Minister from 1721 to 1742, and his successors, Britain's colonial policy had been one of "salutary neglect." He believed that an unrestricted flow of trade would bring more gold into Britain's coffers than taxes and customs duties which would only create angry opposition. For example, the Molasses Act of 1733, which restricted the lucrative trade between the British colonies and the French, Spanish, and Dutch islands in the Caribbean, had long been blithely ignored by sugar merchants like Isaac Roosevelt. Smuggling and avoidance of customs duties had become a way of life in America, and this left-handed form of free trade was the foundation for many of the largest fortunes of Boston, Newport, New York, and Philadelphia.

To put an end to this widespread evasion of customs duties in the colonies—it cost the British government an estimated 8,000 pounds yearly to collect 2,000 pounds—Grenville beefed up the notoriously corrupt Revenue Service and ordered the Royal Navy to enforce the Navigation Acts. There was an immediate howl of protest from the Yankees. As long as the French and their Indian allies had terrorized frontier settlements, there were no more loyal subjects of the Crown than the American colonists. But with the French no longer a threat to their safety, they expected less interference from Britain in their affairs—not more. "Discontent was painted in every man's face and the distress of the people was very great," observed one businessman when the news of Grenville's measures reached New York.

When increased vigilance failed to produce the needed revenue, the Prime Minister resorted to other means. The Sugar Act, first of these measures, lowered the existing duty on molasses but raised it on sugar, much to the ire of Isaac Roosevelt and his fellow refiners. They were placed in a quandary. Those who paid the new duties were undersold by trade rivals because smuggled sugar was still available at cheaper prices; those who engaged in smuggling risked confiscation of their ships and cargoes if captured by the Royal Navy.

The Stamp Act that followed created an even greater outcry. Effective on November 1, 1765, it acquired stamps valued at from twopence to ten pounds to be affixed to all legal documents, publications, and commercial paper. Most Americans, from the humblest artisan to the richest merchant, regarded the Stamp Act as an infringement of their rights as freeborn Englishmen. It was not so much the cost or inconvenience of the stamps that riled the colonists as the fact that it was the first direct tax imposed in America by a Parliament, in which they contended they had no representation. Such levies had usually been imposed by the colonial assemblies chosen by the freemen themselves, and they regarded the Stamp Act as the entering wedge for other measures that would abridge their rights.

In New York more than two hundred merchants—probably including Isaac Roosevelt and other members of the family—met at the City Arms Tavern to pledge themselves to boycott British goods until the offending measures were rescinded. Tension mounted as the effective date for the Stamp Act neared. Passionate denunciations of the British government and threats of violence filled the air. On November 1 church bells tolled, some citizens wore mourning, and even the backgammon boxes and dice at the Merchants Coffee House were draped in black on this day of "lamentation and woe." With the coming of darkness, the long-smoldering anger bubbled over into the streets.

Brandishing blazing torches, clubs, and a few firearms, a mob of several thousand persons—laborers, artisans, shopkeepers, sailors, apprentice boys, and frolicking blacks—led by Isaac Sears, a roughhewn shipmaster and former privateersman, swarmed down Broadway from the Common at the present site of City Hall Park to Fort George. Trampling down the iron fence about the Bowling Green, these self-styled Sons of Liberty frightened Cadwallader Colden, the elderly lieutenant governor, into seeking refuge on one of the British ships in the harbor. Deprived of their intended victim, they put the torch to his gilded coach and forced the officer in charge of distributing the stamps to burn them. And then, amid cheers and shouted obscenities, "King" Sears led the mob back uptown to the elaborate home of Major Thomas James, of the Royal Regiment of Artillery and commander of the garrison. They had a score to settle with him, for James had blustered that he would "cram the Stamp Act down the peoples' throats." Having wrecked his house and looted his wine cellar, the rabble trooped off with the Royal Regiment's colors at the fore.

Isaac Roosevelt was no Son of Liberty and far too distinguished a person to have participated in such open defiance of the law, but undoubtedly he sympathized with the demonstrators. But neither rioting in the streets nor the angry denunciations of "taxation without representation" in the coffeehouses brought about an end to the Stamp Act. When the merchants of London and Bristol began to feel the pinch of the colonial boycott on their pockets resulting from a 25 percent drop in trade, they pressured Parliament into rescinding the measure. This news was hailed with jubilation throughout the colonies. In New York, for example, an equestrian statue of King George III was erected on the Bowling Green. But amid the rejoicing, the Yankees ignored a Declaratory Act passed at the same time that the Stamp Act was repealed which reaffirmed Parliament's right to impose direct taxes in America.

By the summer of 1770, however, most of the outstanding grievances between Britain and her colonies appeared to be on their way to a peaceful resolution. A new ministry headed by

Isaac Roosevelt (1726–94), by Gilbert Stuart. Courtesy, Franklin
D. Roosevelt Library.

James Roosevelt (1760–1847). Courte[
Franklin D. Roosevelt Library.

Home of James Roosevelt on Bleecker Street, New York City.
Courtesy, Franklin D. Roosevelt Library.

Dr. Isaac Roosevelt (1790–1863). Courtesy, Franklin D. Roosevelt Library.

Cornelius Van Schaack Roosevelt (1?
1871). Courtesy, Theodore Roose
Collection, Harvard College Library

Roosevelt and Son, 94 Maiden Lane. Courtesy, Theodore Roosevelt
Collection, Harvard College Library.

Thee, Theodore Roosevelt, Sr. (1831–78). Courtesy, Theodore
Roosevelt Collection, Harvard College Library.

Mittie, Martha Bulloch Roosevelt (1
84). Courtesy, Theodore Roosevelt
lection, Harvard College Library.

Robert Barnwell Roosevelt (1829–1906).
Courtesy, Theodore Roosevelt Collection, Harvard College Library.

Teedie, Theodore Roosevelt (aged five). Courtesy, Theodore Roosevelt Collection, Harvard College Library.

The funeral procession of Abraham Lincoln passing in front of the home of Cornelius V. S. Roosevelt at Union Square and Broadway on April 25, 1865. Theodore and Elliott Roosevelt are at the second-floor side window. Courtesy, Theodore Roosevelt Collection, Harvard College Library.

Lord North removed most of the obnoxious restrictions placed upon colonial commerce with the exception of a modest three-pence-a-pound tax on tea which was kept as much for symbolic reasons as for revenue. Food shortages in Europe created a demand for American corn and wheat and trade rebounded with the end of the ban on the importation of British goods. Soon it was even safe again for Redcoats to stroll along the Battery at the tip of Manhattan with their girls on their arms. In London the easygoing and good-humored Lord North spent many contented hours dozing in his seat in the Commons, prompting one agitated member to wish the Prime Minister had "someone at his elbow to pull him every now and then by the ear . . . to keep him awake to the affairs of America."

The lull in the struggle between Britain and her colonists was warmly welcomed in New York, where the proffered olive branch was eagerly grasped by the wealthy merchants and other leading citizens. While they had strongly opposed any assault by Parliament upon the rights of the local government which was under their control, they also feared mob rule by "King" Sears and the Sons of Liberty, which bore within it the seeds of radical social upheaval. Besides, hostilities with Britain could lead to a blockade by the Royal Navy, which would drive their ships from the seas and cause the loss of lucrative markets in the British West Indies. Thus, when it came to choosing between King and country, most of the New York merchants—with the conspicuous example of the Roosevelts and a few others—supported the Crown.

For three years, however, the craft of the radicals lay becalmed. The lull was not broken until 1773, when Parliament, to keep the East India Company from bankruptcy resulting from the incompetence of its own directors—in much the same way the Congress has since supported certain defense industries—granted it a monopoly for supplying tea to the American colonies. The problem lay in the refusal of Americans to buy British tea because it was taxed. Instead, they drank an immense quantity of smuggled Dutch tea, depriving the company and the Crown of revenue. Believing that the colonists would prefer cheap tea to principle, Lord North, awakened momentarily from his slumbers, gave the company the right to sell its product directly to the consumer, cutting out the middleman. This made the price of tea in America lower than that charged by the smugglers, even with the threepenny tax on each pound. But it soon became clear that the radicals were more interested in brewing trouble than tea.

The tea monopoly succeeded in uniting the smugglers, the wealthy merchants, and the Sons of Liberty. The smugglers were afraid of being driven out of business by cheap tea; the lawful businessmen feared that the East India Company's monopoly might be extended to other goods; and the radicals regarded the tea tax as one more violation of their rights as freeborn British citizens. Tea became the symbol of London's mismanagement and domination of colonial affairs. Word that the tea was on the way created considerable consternation in America and meetings were held up and down the coast to determine what should be done when it arrived. In some ports it was not even permitted ashore and in others it was allowed to rot in damp cellars. In New York, where the ship carrying the first tea chests was delayed by bad weather, discussions were still being held when word was received of the Boston Tea Party. On December 16, 1773, a band of men sketchily described as Mohawk Indians had boarded three tea ships and unceremoniously emptied the chests into the harbor.

Despite an earnest desire to play down the American problem, the British government could not tamely ignore this outrage. "The dye is now cast," George III told Lord North, the Prime Minister. "The Colonies must either submit or triumph." North ordered the port of Boston closed until the tea had been paid for, and military government was imposed upon the city. Pleas for help went out from Boston, including a demand for another boycott of British goods and other strong measures. In New York merchants such as Isaac Roosevelt were faced with the question of just how far they wanted to go in opposing the Crown. While they wished to help the Bostonians in their plight, they had no desire to see "King" Sears and the radicals restored to positions of control in the colony. Such families as the De Lanceys, Van Cortlandts, and De Peysters decided to join the revolution in order to direct it into safe channels.

Both sides nominated candidates for a Committee of Fifty-one that was to replace an existing Committee of Correspondence and coordinate New York's resistance to the usurpations of the British. The moderates scored the first victory when Isaac Low, a leading merchant and a Roosevelt relative, was chosen as chairman. On May 19, 1774, the list of nominees—including Isaac Roosevelt—was presented to "a great concourse" of people massed before the Merchants Coffee House. Watching from a balcony, an observer reported that "on my right hand were ranged all the people of property, with some poor dependents, and on the other all the tradesmen, &c. who thought it worth their while to leave daily labour for the good of the country." With a plea from Low for unity ringing in their ears, many of the ordinary folk voted for the representatives nominated by the well-to-do, Isaac Roosevelt among them. The conservatives were euphoric because cool and prudent men now controlled the committee rather than Sears and the radicals. But they failed to take into account the stupidity of the British government.

The Coercive Acts promulgated by Parliament to bring the Bostonians to heel succeeded instead in stampeding the rest of the colonists to the side of the radicals. To prevent them from gaining control of the Committee of Fifty-one, the moderates were forced to accept a call for a Continental Congress designed to organize a common front to British oppression. Isaac Roosevelt was not among those chosen by the committee to represent New York at the meeting in Philadelphia, but the four men selected, Isaac Low, John Jay, John Alsop, and Peter Livingston, were moderates like himself. Wishing to protect American rights without breaking with England, they had no thought of "independency."

But to prevent "violent men" like Massachusetts' Samuel Adams from getting control of the Congress, they were forced to accept an embargo on the importation of British goods that was to go into effect on December 1, 1774, unless Parliament acceded to American demands. Low, for one, resisted the imposition of economic sanctions, no doubt speaking for Isaac Roosevelt and the other New York merchants when he argued that cutting off West Indian sugar, molasses, and rum would be disastrous. The prevailing view, however, was that once Britain's pocketbook began to hurt, she would be brought to reason, as had happened a decade earlier. And so, on this optimistic note, the Congress adjourned, after the delegates had agreed to return to Philadelphia on May 10, 1775.

Torn between moderates and conservatives, the Committee of Fifty-one found it increasingly difficult to hold to its middle course. Its members had either to endorse the economic sanctions against Britain or be branded as Tories and Loyalists. A Committee of Sixty, in which the radicals played a larger role, took its place. Isaac Roosevelt maintained his membership, unlike some of his fellow merchants. Two centuries later, it is impossible to fathom his motives, but certain elements appear paramount in his decision—and psychological factors may well have been as important as economic and political reasons.

Like most merchants, Isaac had seen his sugar refinery and other business interests suffer because of the gross mismanagement by the Crown and its minions of its relations with America. But this in itself was not enough to turn him into an adversary of the British government. Others, like the De Lanceys and Philipses, faced the same problems and remained loyal to the King. What made Roosevelt different? While the Tory aristocrats regarded themselves as Englishmen, Isaac Roosevelt may have considered himself a New Yorker, an American and a Dutchman, instead of an Englishman. He had not a drop of English blood in his veins, had never visited England, and was a prominent member of the Dutch Church rather than the Anglican communion. Nevertheless, the break could not have been easy. He must have paced the floor of his handsome house on Queen Street through many a long and lonely night before making his decision.

While Isaac pondered, some Americans prepared for open warfare. In New England the Yankees hoarded arms and powder and with the coming of spring 1775, practiced military exercises and sharpshooting on their village greens. Even the children played, not at hunting Indians as was their usual game, but at mowing down columns of Redcoats. In New York a visitor reported seeing "nothing but rubbing up arms, enlisting, exercising and every other preparation denoting a vigorous resolution in the people to defend themselves against all oppressors to the very last."

Despite these ominous signs, the New York Assembly, elected back in 1769 and under the control of the conservatives, refused to enforce the embargo against British goods decreed by Congress and to appoint delegates to a new Congress. As a result, in the coffee shops, taverns, and on the street corners, the Committee of Sixty was increasingly regarded as the colony's legitimate legislative body. "Are we to permit this handful of Tories to prevent New York from joining with the other colonies in the common cause?" was the question on everyone's lips.

An answer was not long in coming. In spite of the objections of the conservatives, a recommendation by the Committee of Sixty that a Provincial Convention be called to take over the colony's government was shouted through. This was followed by a vote empowering the committee to choose New York's delegates for the upcoming Congress. On April 20, 1775, Isaac Roosevelt and his fellow members met to take this historic step which placed New York in line with her sister colonies.

Unknown to them, two days before, General Thomas Gage, commander of the British troops at Boston, having learned that sizable quantities of arms and powder were being stockpiled by the Yankees outside Boston, had given orders for a raid. Shortly after ten o'clock on the night of April 18, about seven hundred men secretly pushed off in longboats from the foot of Boston Common. They were rowed across the black waters of the Charles River with muffled oars, and waded ashore near Cambridge. Early the next morning, the troops, tired and chilled, their feet sloshing in their boots, were off on the road to Lexington and Concord.

Chapter VI
FOUNDING A NEW NATION

War! War with the British! War!

Isaac Roosevelt, like many New Yorkers, was probably on his way to church on Sunday morning, April 23, 1775, when a travel-stained horseman galloped into the city from the north. Racing down Broadway, he reined in his mount only long enough to shout to clusters of startled citizens that Yankee Minutemen and Redcoats had fought a series of bloody skirmishes at Lexington and Concord four days before. Licking their wounds, the British had retreated back to Boston, where, protected by fortifications and the guns of the Royal Navy, they sullenly awaited relief.

The city was thrown into an uproar. Church bells that had been solemnly summoning the faithful to prayer now agitatedly pealed an alarm. Crowds gathered on street corners to read copies of a dispatch brought by the rider. Militiamen turned out with their muskets and leaving wives anxiously twisting their aprons, hastened to the waterfront to prevent two vessels from sailing with supplies for the British in Boston. The tiny British garrison—only five companies strong—prudently remained within the walls of Fort George, and an angry crowd broke into the armory at City Hall, carrying off kegs of powder and some six hundred muskets. For three days and nights, there were parades and bonfires and fireworks—as if a war had ended rather than just begun. There was much drumbeating and milling about as militiamen swaggered around the city with little to do except frighten suspected Tories with threats of tar and feathers. "The taverns filled with Politicians at Night—Little Business done in the Day," remarked an observer.

Faced with the option of the sword or submission, the Americans chose to fight. "Independency" was still merely a gleam in the eye of the most militant of radicals, but for all practical purposes the break with Britain had come. While many Americans flinched from taking the final step, regarding themselves as loyal subjects of the Crown who were fighting the tyranny of a corrupt and evil ministry, they were inexorably carried along by the dynamics of the revolution itself. They were forced to assume control of the various colonies by default as British officials abandoned their posts and fled to the safety of the King's ships.

In New York, where Governor William Tryon had been away on a year-long visit to England, steps were immediately taken to organize a new government. On April 26 the Committee of Sixty unanimously voted itself out of business. Because of "the commotion occasioned by the sanguinary measures pursued by the British ministry," it proposed that a more widely representative Committee of One Hundred be installed in its place and that delegates be elected to a Provincial Congress to take over the reins of government from the discredited assembly. With his long association with the cause of liberty, Isaac Roosevelt was an obvious candidate for the new committee and was chosen as one of the city's twenty delegates to the Provincial Congress. One of the numerous Nicholas Roosevelts was also named to the Committee of One Hundred.

Six days after the news of the fighting outside Boston was received, an estimated seven thousand persons—probably the largest crowd in New York's history—massed at the Liberty Pole in what is now City Hall Park to pledge themselves to resist British tyranny. Read by Isaac Low, this "General Association" declared:

We, the freemen, freeholders and the inhabitants of the city and county of New York . . . shocked by the bloody scene now acting in the Massachusetts Bay, do, in the most solemn manner resolve, never to become slaves; and do associate under all the ties of religion, honour and love to our country to adopt and endeavour to carry into execution whatever measures may be recommended by the Continental Congress, or resolved upon by our Provincial Convention for the purpose of preserving our Constitution, and opposing the execution of the arbitrary and oppressive acts of the British Parliament. . . .

When he had finished, Low placed the document on a table and solemnly affixed his signature to it. One by one, the members of the Committee of One Hundred came forward to follow his example, Isaac Roosevelt among them. Copies of the "Association" were printed and posted at the polling places so all the citizens could add their names.

Slowly, over the next several weeks, delegates from the upstate counties joined the city members of the Provincial Congress meeting at the Merchant's Exchange on Wall Street, and the body evolved into a State Legislature. Establishing a new government was no easy task, however. It required long hours, exhaustive and exhausting debates, endless conferences, and hard bargaining between radicals like Isaac Sears, who were gaining the upper hand, and conservatives such as Abraham Walton and John De Lancey, still hoping that reconciliation with Britain was possible.

The major problem facing the Provincial Congress was the vulnerability of New York to British attack. Although the Royal Navy's ships on the North American Station were few, undermanned, and in poor repair, it controlled the coastal waters and could spearhead an invasion from Boston or Halifax at any moment. Or, British troops might be sent down from Canada by way of Lake Champlain and the Hudson to attack the city from the rear. The citizens were urged to procure arms and "to perfect themselves in the military art." Militia companies sprang up everywhere and the British garrison commander noted uneasily that "in every corner of the town you see parties drilling and learning their exercises."

The militia got their chance to make a brave show on June 25, when they were turned out to welcome General George Washington as he passed through the city on his way to take command of the troops outside Boston. Nicholas Roosevelt, Jr., son of the goldsmith, served as first lieutenant of a socially elect company who called themselves the Corsicans. Proudly, he joined Captain Thomas Fleming in inspecting their men. The company's elite standing was confirmed by the fact that Fleming, a former British officer, was a member of the De Lancey clan by marriage.

Among the most eager troopers was an ambitious young college student named Alexander Hamilton, who had recently arrived in the city from the West Indies.

The Corsicans may not have known much about soldiering but they were smartly turned out. They wore short green jackets to which were pinned on the left breast a red tin heart emblazoned "God and Right." Low-crowned hats worn with one side jauntily turned up and bearing a ribbon reading "Liberty or Death" topped off their outfit. Not to be outdone, John Roosevelt, Isaac's older brother, had at the age of sixty become captain of a militia company called the Oswego Rangers, who were dashing in blue coats and white britches. Because of his prominence, John was chosen as the company's spokesman when they petitioned the Provincial Congress to place them on active duty.

Before leaving the city, Washington urged the authorities to send troops to reinforce the motley collection of New Englanders who were holding the Redcoats at bay. The Continental Congress had assigned a quota to each colony, with New York being called upon to raise four regiments of ten companies each, or about three thousand officers and men. Legend has it that every American was a patriot who abandoned the plow or the shop to take musket in hand and answer the clarion call of liberty. In truth, however, probably more Americans remained loyal to the Crown or indifferent to the cause than supported it. One need look no further than the efforts to obtain men to fill New York's quota of troops to see the truth of this observation.

Although the term of enlistment for this first levy for the Continental Army was brief—only until December 1, 1775—few men were eager to serve away from their homes. It was one thing to join the militia and parade on the Common to the cheers of relatives and friends; it was another to march off in the dust of the Post Road to Boston to face the uncertainties of military life. Difficulties also resulted from a high-minded attempt by the Provincial Congress to break with the tried-and-true method of obtaining soldiers, such as plying prospects with liquor. But when quotas remained unmet, these scruples were forgotten; funds were allocated to "entertain" likely-looking young fellows, and several popular taverns were designated as recruiting stations.

Obtaining officers turned out to be equally difficult. It had been expected that the sons of the better families would eagerly

volunteer for commissions in the new regiments, but they proved
to be singularly reluctant to do so. Because of their wide contacts, Isaac Roosevelt and Abraham Walton were appointed to a
special committee charged with trying to persuade likely prospects to seek commissions. In many cases, they found that if prospective candidates joined any armed force at all, it was likely to
be the British Army. There was a sprinkling of aristocratic names,
but most of the officers of the New York regiments came from
families identified with the radical cause. Nevertheless, enough
officers and men were eventually found to form the first of the
units that were to be New York's contribution to the revolutionary cause, and to get them off to join General Washington's
army. Alexander McDougall, one of Sears's closest associates, was
given a commission as the regiment's colonel.

Roosevelt and Walton had other problems, even when they
found officers and men. Where were the arms, munitions, uniforms, tents, and blankets to outfit them? Where was the barest
organization for feeding and training the men? Not even the
most rudimentary preparations had been made to receive re-
cruits. Barracks and camps were lacking. Powder was so short
that the army besieging Boston dared not fire salutes out of fear
of provoking a barrage from the British that could not be answered. In fact, Benjamin Franklin suggested that the troops be
armed with bows and arrows, noting that a man could fire four
arrows in the time it took to fire a musket just once.

The town was scoured for fowling pieces, and any firearm that
could shoot was borrowed or bought by Roosevelt and Walton.
The Provincial Congress wrote to gunsmiths in England offering
free passage to America, and almost every blacksmith was put to
work making gun barrels and bayonets. Isaac Roosevelt even
gave the lead sash weights from the windows of his home to be
cast into bullets. Foundries and powder mills were established
and a special premium well above the going price was offered for
powder produced within the colony. Agents were also sent to
Europe and the West Indies to purchase arms and powder or to
trade wheat and other produce from them. New York picked up
an unexpected bonus when several cartloads of munitions were
stolen from the British as the last handful of troops were being
evacuated to the ships in the harbor. For several days afterward,
the townspeople held their breaths, expecting the vessels to let

loose a barrage of destruction upon them in revenge. Eventually, however, the ships hoisted sail and headed for the open sea, leaving New York under the complete control of the Americans.

General Washington was convinced that the British would soon return because New York's strategic position made it an ideal base for conducting offensive operations in America. Control of the city provided access to the Hudson River, it was centrally located for mounting an invasion of either New England or New Jersey, and its harbor could provide unsurpassed shelter for the entire British fleet. Besides, a sizable proportion of the city's population had Loyalist sympathies, particularly the merchants and other well-to-do citizens. So, even before the British abandoned Boston for Halifax in March 1776, Washington decided to fortify New York. The task of preparing the almost defenseless city to meet the expected British onslaught was given to General Charles Lee, who arrived early in February.

Lee, a strange and enigmatic man, had served in the British Army and as a soldier of fortune had fought in Poland's wars of liberation from Russian dominance. Although he possessed a certain technical expertise, Lee was quarrelsome and quirky. New Yorkers were struck by his unkempt appearance and the pack of dogs that accompanied him everywhere. The task before him was a difficult one. "What to do with this city . . . puzzles me," said Lee. "It is so encircled with deep navigable waters that whoever commands the sea must command the town."

Finding quarters for the sudden flood of soldiers pouring into the town from the north after the British abandoned Boston was a major problem. As more and more men arrived, quickly overflowing the barracks that had been used by the Redcoats, the Provincial Congress appointed Isaac Roosevelt and two other members "to examine the lists of empty houses . . . and to ascertain such as they may think proper for use of the troops." Isaac and his associates were instructed to choose buildings "least liable to be injured by the troops" and the brunt fell upon the houses abandoned by wealthy Tories. Soon, the paneled rooms of some of the city's finest mansions were crowded with soldiers none too respectful of the property of their departed owners. "Oh, the houses in New York, if you could but see the insides of them, occupied by the dirtiest people on the continent!" lamented a citizen. "If the owners ever get possession again, I am sure that they must be years in cleaning them."

Captain John Roosevelt of the Oswego Rangers was given the not always easy task of serving as liaison between the Provincial Congress and the newly arrived Continentals. As in any place where large numbers of soldiers are suddenly introduced, he was soon saddled with myriad complaints about the drunken carousing and other vices of the troops. Prostitutes and gamblers followed the army, and to the north of the city, at the present site of Washingon Square, there was a squatter's camp of tents and huts inhabited by whores and pimps. It was dubbed the Holy Ground. Continental officers had, on the other hand, just as many complaints about the poor food, bad water, and insufficient hospitals provided by the local authorities. When Isaac Roosevelt's committee ran out of abandoned houses in which to quarter the troops, they were billeted in barns, sheds, and tents. Smallpox and other diseases were rampant, killing far more men than the enemy.

To prevent the British from using their fleet to envelop the exposed American flanks with amphibious attacks, Washington, who had assumed command at New York, built forts on both sides of the Hudson and took up positions on Brooklyn Heights, across the East River from Lower Manhattan. Redoubts and trenches were dug, trees were cut down and dragged into place to obstruct the main streets, and batteries were erected at key points. Many of the inhabitants, expecting New York to soon become a battleground, fled to safety, and the roads were crowded with refugees leaving the city and columns of troops entering it. "Picture to yourself the once flourishing city evacuated by most of its members, especially the fair," wrote one officer. "Business of every kind [is] stagnated."

And then, on June 29, the British returned. Lookouts stationed at Sandy Hook sighted a cloud of sails coming up over the horizon . . . ten . . . twenty . . . thirty ships . . . and still the sails continued to appear. When the last vessel dropped anchor, there were 52 warships and 427 transports rising and falling on the swells in the lower harbor. Within a few nights, the campfires of 34,000 troops—a large part of them German mercenaries—twinkled on Staten Island within sight of the anxious Yankees.

As the British gathered their might, the final barriers to independence were falling in Philadelphia. Ten years of conflict had at last dissolved the bonds of affection Americans had for the mother country, and the need for French recognition in order to achieve victory finally forced them to take this long-dreaded step. On July 2, 1776, the atmosphere within the Pennsylvania State House was stifling and horseflies buzzed through the open windows from a nearby livery stable, no doubt hastening a vote on the issue before the Continental Congress: "*Resolved,* That these United Colonies are, and, of right, ought to be, Free and Independent States. . . ." Two days later, a Declaration of Independence drafted for the most part by Thomas Jefferson was adopted with the approval of all the delegations except that of New York, which had not yet received instructions from the Provincial Congress.

On July 9, that body, meeting in White Plains, where it had moved to be away from the threat of British guns, finally put New York wholeheartedly into the Revolution. Even though his father, old Jacobus Roosevelt, had died two months before, on May 5, at the age of eighty-four, Isaac Roosevelt was there to vote in favor of a resolution supporting independence and creating the State of New York. That same day, General Washington ordered that the Declaration of Independence be read to all units of the Army. The troops were drawn up at dusk in a hollow square on the Common, with Washington and his aides mounted on horseback in the center, while a leather-lunged officer read the document in the fading light. It was greeted with cheers, but because of the proximity of the British, there were no bonfires, pealing of church bells, or salutes as in other towns. Such a demonstration might have been mistaken for the signal that the British were attacking. A crowd of soldiers and civilians drifted away to the Bowling Green, where the massive gilt statue of King George III had stood since the repeal of the Stamp Act. Breaking down the iron fence about it, workmen fastened ropes to the figure of horse and rider and pulled it crashing to the ground. The fragments were carted away to be cast into bullets.

Nevertheless, as Charles Lee had pointed out, New York was indefensible as long as the British controlled the surrounding waters and could outflank the Americans on Manhattan. The island was also too long to be defended by the force that Washington could muster, and the British were able to make amphibious landings along its shores wherever they wished. Most analysts believe that the best strategy would have been for the Americans to put the city to the torch and to abandon the ruins to the British, but Congress would not permit such a drastic step. So, in little more than two months after the Declaration of Independence, Washington's army was driven from New York with heavy losses, and once again, the Union Jack was unfurled over the city, where it was to fly until 1783.

For Isaac Roosevelt, the cost of patriotism was high. He was forced to abandon all his property, his sugar refinery, and his fine house to the not-so-tender mercies of the Tories who flocked into the town and made it their capital. Among them was Abraham Walton, who remained behind in New York and like many of the successful merchants, took the oath of allegiance to King George —carrying on business as usual. Isaac Roosevelt sought refuge at his wife's old family home at Rhinebeck, with his brood, which now included two sons and five daughters. Although he was over fifty years of age, he volunteered as a private in the Sixth Regiment of the Dutchess County militia. Shouldering a musket on the green with the local farmers, he practiced the rudiments of close order drill, and learned how to ram powder and shot down the barrel of his weapon and to prime and fire it on command.

Although he may have enjoyed the drills and periodic calls to arms, better use was soon found for his talents. While the Provincial Congress was in adjournment, Isaac was commissioned by the Committee of Safety to arrange for an emission of paper money to pay for supplies for New York's troops. He worked out procedures for the issuance of 55,000 pounds in 213,400 bills, ranging in value from one eighth of a dollar to ten dollars. To prevent the currency issue from aggravating the cancer of inflation, already gnawing at the vitals of the American cause, a sinking fund was established to redeem the bills over a three-year period beginning in 1779. All this was to prove valuable experience when Isaac became one of New York's leading bankers after the war.

Other members of the Roosevelt family also supported the revolutionary cause, even though it was at low ebb. James Roosevelt, old Johannes' son who had run a hardware store which did a profitable business with the East River shipyards, had avoided public life almost as assiduously as his cousin, Isaac, had pursued it, preferring to tend to his business and his garden. When the British occupied New York, he fled with his family to Kingston, where at the age of fifty-one he joined the militia. His son, James I Roosevelt (the old Dutch families preferred not to use Junior), was only seventeen but he went into the army, too, serving in the Commissary, or Quartermaster, Department for the entire war, reportedly without pay. And Cornelius Roosevelt, the elder James's brother, an alderman before the war and forty-five years old when hostilities began, didn't let that stop him from enlisting in the colonial forces. He ended the war as an ensign in the First New York Regiment.

Because of the ever-present danger of British raids, the Provincial Congress was constantly on the move and Isaac Roosevelt traveled with it, a none-too-pleasurable experience for a man of his years, considering the state of the roads. The delegates met at Fishkill, Kingston, Poughkeepsie, and Albany, as circumstances and safety required. Isaac was on hand in Kingston in April 1777, when a convention hammered out a new constitution for the state of New York. Read to the public by John Jay, its principal author who stood on a barrel head on the courthouse steps, this document was the result of a compromise between conservatives and radicals. It was not designed to produce a democratic government; if anything, it was intended to prevent too much democracy, for democracy was identified with license and disorder. Although the suffrage was widened, it was graduated on the basis of wealth. Only the well-to-do were permitted to vote for the governor and state senators, while the franchise of the small property holders was limited to choosing members of the assembly. Religious freedom and trial by jury were guaranteed and slavery was continued. All in all, the new constitution protected the interests of property owners rather than those of the tenant farmer and the mechanic.

Yet. when it came time to choose New York's first governor, the aristocratic Philip Schuyler was defeated by George Clinton, who had made his mark in politics by appealing to the commonfolk. The election was a clear sign that despite attempts to maintain the old order in power, the future belonged to the politician who could win the support of the mass of voters. Isaac Roosevelt was elected to the State Senate without difficulty and served throughout the remainder of the war. It was an office far more important then than now. Clinton appointed him a member of his council and he was one of the war governor's closest advisers. Besides his many legislative duties, he also assumed several other tasks, including the issuance of letters of marque that licensed privateers to prey upon British shipping.

Despite his part-time military service and full schedule of political duties, Isaac's thoughts were often of the life that had been interrupted by the war and of his sugar refinery now in British hands. As he told Clinton upon one occasion, he longed for the day "when it may please God that I can set my house at work again." The war and his forced exodus from New York had also saddled him with a wearying load of family troubles. While his oldest son, James, graduated from the New Jersey College at Princeton in 1780 at the age of twenty, Isaac's second son, Martin, died while in attendance at the school. Once again, the grieving father opened the old family Bible to record the passing of one of his children: "1781. Sept. 19 on Wednesday night at 11 o'clock this my son departed this life after a lingrin illness of about 2 months when at Colledge at Princeton. . . . being 16 years 3 months and 14 days old." Three years before, his second daughter, twenty-three-year-old Sarah, had died at the family's Dutchess County home.

As the executor of his father's will, Isaac also bore the responsibility for distribution of Jacobus' considerable estate, estimated at some 16,000 pounds in "bonds and mortgages, monies and plate," as well as considerable real property. He was constantly being importuned by the heirs for a settlement, but as he exasperatedly pointed out upon one occasion, "the Circumstances of the War rendered Compliance with the directions of the Will respecting the Legacy impossible." In many cases, Isaac was forced to advance money from his own pocket to poverty-stricken relatives. When a building belonging to one member of the family caught fire after having been seized by the British and used as a barracks, he wrote Sir Henry Clinton, the British commander, seeking a settlement on behalf of his relative's children. They "have no other support save what they get from me," he said, and expressed concern that the "orphans may in the end be deprived of their rights without benefit to King or Country." Clinton did not deign to answer this plea for justice.

The American Revolution ended with the surrender of Cornwallis at Yorktown on October 19, 1781. "Oh God! It is all over!" Lord North had cried upon learning the news. But the British did not evacuate New York, their last foothold in their former colony, until November 25, 1783. By mutual agreement, the last of the Redcoats were rowed out to their waiting ships as George Washington entered the city at the head of his troops. Escorted by tootling fifes and drums and jangling squadrons of cavalry, the general rode slowly down the Bowery Road past cheering crowds on a fine bay gelding, nodding ever so slightly—now to the right and then to the left. The Stars and Stripes were quickly broken out over the fort despite an attempt by the British to delay it by removing the halyards and greasing the staff.

Isaac Roosevelt and his son James were among those who cheered as a thirteen-gun salute boomed out as the last British soldier shoved off from the foot of Whitehall Slip. The elder Roosevelt was in charge of the arrangements for a dinner given by Governor Clinton in Washington's honor that night at Fraunce's Tavern. It must have been a merry affair for the bill for 156 pounds submitted by Isaac included the following items:

120 dinners
135 bottles of Madeira
36 bottles of port
60 bottles of English beer
30 bowls of punch
60 wine glasses broken
8 cut decanters broken

The city to which the Roosevelts returned was far different from what it had been seven years before. Two disastrous fires had leveled more than a quarter of the town, and the steeple of Trinity Church, the most prominent landmark, had crashed to the ground in ruins along with several hundred homes, shops, and warehouses. Others had been commandeered for barracks and stables—including the three Dutch churches. Streets were in such disrepair that many were all but impassable, trees had been cut for firewood, and gardens had become jungles of weeds. The houses of patriots had been stripped. But Isaac was lucky. He found his home on Queen Street—now called Pearl Street as in Dutch times—in relatively good condition, and the sugar refinery behind it had emerged almost unscathed from the occupation. The Rhinelanders, his major rivals, were not so fortunate. Their building had been seized by the British and converted into one of the city's more notorious military prisons.

As soon as the British and most of their Tory allies were gone—with the exception of a handful like Abraham Walton who chose to remain behind—work began on rebuilding the town. Soon, scaffolding and the sounds of construction were everywhere as a new city emerged from the ruins of the old. Immigrants poured in—among them a twenty-one-year-old butcher's boy named John Jacob Astor, who came from the hamlet of Waldorf in Germany. Young James Roosevelt, who had read law in the Poughkeepsie office of his relative, Egbert Benson, but never practiced, was taken into the sugar business. Isaac placed several newspaper advertisements announcing the reopening of the firm, now known as Isaac Roosevelt & Son, located at 159 Pearl Street. Old James Roosevelt, his cousin, had also returned safely from the war and along with his son, James I Roosevelt, reopened his hardware store.

Despite his new responsibilities in the sugar trade, James Roosevelt also found time to be something of a man about town. Writing to a college chum, he provided a spirited account of his adventures in New York:

We were together at Mr. N. B——d's—You saw his Daughter—Did you ever see a Countenance expressive of so much Goodness? But you were with her only a moment and I have since passed two days with her—& for more than three days after her image was ever present to my Mind—I cannot express my Ideas of her—She is not to be ranked among *Women*—She is a superior Being. . . .

Come then among us & I will endeavour to make New York agreeable to you—Our Girls begin to grow more amiable—they are losing their British & Acquiring American Ideas—& when they become perfect Americans they will not be excelled by any Women on the Continent.

James was not to be ensnared by Miss B——d, however. His bride turned out to be the girl next door—or at least from across the street. In 1786 he married Mary Eliza Walton, the daughter of Abraham Walton, who had been a childhood playmate. They set up housekeeping at their new home at 18 South Street, not far from the sugar house.

At about the time of James's marriage, Isaac and his wife probably noticed that a distinguished New Yorker named Richard Varick was becoming a frequent caller at their home. Varick had been an aide to General Washington during the war and had been named recorder of the new city government. Although he ostensibly came to Pearl Street to discuss politics and business with Isaac, Mr. and Mrs. Roosevelt were amused to note that he spent an increasing amount of his time with Maria, their twenty-three-year-old daughter. So it must have come as no surprise to Isaac when he received a letter from Varick concerning "a subject of interesting Importance to myself, and which tho' new I trust is not altogether unexpected to you."

> Ever solicitous that my Conduct in private as well as public life, should be guided by the Strict rules of Honor and Properiety [wrote Varick], I feel some Degree of Compunction at the Liberties I have lately taken in repeated visits to your family, without announcing to You, Sir, the Views by which my Conduct was actuated lest it be considered in an unfavorable Point of Light.
>
> Influenced by an Independence of Sentiment and Action, which I hope will ever form a Part of my Character, and impelled by Respect to You, Sir, and Mrs. Rosevelt, as well as by affection for the Amiable Person who is the Subject of my present address,—I am now induced to adopt this Mode of Communicating to You, that, at an early Period after an intimate acquaintance with your daughter *Mary*, I became attached to her. . . .
>
> It will afford me great Pleasure to be informed, Sir, that my past Attentions have not been considered as improper, and Your Obliging Answer will dictate a Line of Conduct for my future Pursuit.

Isaac must have encouraged Varick in his "future Pursuit," for not long afterward, he asked Maria to marry him. She accepted,

but for reasons that have not come down to us, requested a delay
in the ceremony. Varick was soon anxiously writing his "dear
Maria":

> Altho' I feel a little embarrassed at the necessity of this Step and
> anticipate same in You on the Receipt hereof, I am bound, as well,
> by Motives founded in the most pure Esteem and Affection for You,
> as by my Duty to myself to take my Pen to ask a Decision on my
> several applications to you soliciting that the Period for the final
> Consummation of our mutual Wishes may not for any trivial
> Causes, be unnecessarily protracted. . . .
> I find it indispensible to lay down, to myself at least, an Alterna-
> tive Line of Conduct, on the Subject. . . . This I will in Candour
> communicate to you when your Reply which I hope, nay expect, to
> receive, the first Moment I can have the pleasure of seeing you—
> Fully persuaded that your Answer will be dictated by Reason and
> Good Sense; that your Conduct ever will be the Result of candid
> and deliberate Reflections, and that you are, on this occasion, ut-
> terly incapable of being influenced by Considerations which can in
> any Degree diminish those exalted Sentiments I ever entertain of
> you—I shall cheerfully attend to you at the first moment of Leisure
> to receive a hint to my own Conduct. . . .

Varick's plea was successful and the couple were married less
than two months later, on May 8, 1786. Although they had no
children, the Varicks remained together for forty-five years, until
Richard's death in 1831. Maria survived him for another decade.
Even though their union was obviously a love match, it was in
the Roosevelt tradition of a "good" marriage that improved the
family's standing. Varick became Speaker of the New York State
Assembly, State attorney general, and served as mayor of New
York for twelve years.

In the hectic period following the Revolution, Isaac Roosevelt
and his fellow businessmen saw the need to bring some sort of
order out of the financial chaos resulting from the war. Congress
and the various states had issued a flood tide of paper currency
which was now worthless and had driven hard money out of circulation. Alexander Hamilton, at twenty-seven already recognized as one of the cleverest lawyers in New York, had long advocated the creation of a bank to stabilize the currency and

restore business confidence. With the Bank of North America opened by Robert Morris in Philadelphia at the end of 1781 as his model, he provided the guiding hand for the Bank of New York formed with a capital of $500,000 in hard cash. Isaac Roosevelt was among the bank's organizers and first thirteen directors.

The Bank of New York opened its offices on June 9, 1784, in the front parlor of what had been the Walton mansion across Pearl Street from the Roosevelt sugar house. General Alexander McDougall was elected its first president, but two years after the institution's founding, Isaac took over as president. Writing of Isaac Roosevelt a half century later, Philip Hone, the eminent diarist, observed that the "president and directors of a bank were other sort of people from those of the present day. Proud and aristocratical, they were the only nobility we had . . . powerful in the controlling influence they possessed over the commercial operations of the city, men could not stand straight in their presence. . . ."

Dividing his time between the sugar business and the bank, Isaac began his day at the refinery by conferring with his son, James, who was now his partner. Then he would cross the street and be at the bank well before it opened its doors at 10 A.M. It remained open until 1 P.M., closed for two hours so the clerks could balance their books, and reopened from 3 to 5 P.M. Bills and notes were discounted at 6 percent, and although the rules said "money lodged at the bank may be re-drawn at pleasure," overdrafts were not permitted. Under Isaac's direction, annual dividends paid the shareholders increased from 3 to 7 percent over five years.

Like most of the Roosevelts, he had an eye for a good piece of real estate and his eye wandered as far afield as the rapidly growing port of Baltimore, when he inquired about buying land in the Fells Point area. In New York he added to the extensive holdings left him by his late father and owned properties on the New Slip, Old Slip, Front Street, Jacob Street, Water Street, Cherry Street, Peck Slip, Batavia Lane, and Wall Street, as well as his home and refinery on Pearl Street.

Isaac's duties at the bank brought him into close contact with Hamilton, and he absorbed much of the brilliant young man's thinking about the need for a strong federal government.

Through his marriage into the aristocratic and influential Schuyler clan, Hamilton had been elected to the postwar Congress, which met in New York, where he observed at first hand the inadequacies of the new nation's weak and divided government. For eight years, from 1781 until 1789, the United States was not so much governed as maintained in a sort of caretaker status under the loosely drawn Articles of Confederation. Congress functioned as little more than a council of ambassadors of an uneasy league of thirteen more or less sovereign republics. Hamilton blamed the "imbecility" of the Confederation on the "rage for liberty" that seemed to possess the American people. Having thrown off the British yoke, the Americans had purposely established a weak government in order to prevent the reinstatement of tyranny. Chaos, confusion, and governmental paralysis reigned. Shaking his head at the sight of his chosen country floundering in disorder, Hamilton declared: "A nation without a national government, is in my view, an awful spectacle."

By 1787 Hamilton's views were shared by enough merchants, shipowners, budding industrialists, moneylenders, and large landowners in all the states to produce the Constitution. Intended to provide a stable government, this document was, as one historian has written, "democratic enough to be adopted but not so democratic as to constitute any menace to upper-class control." The Constitution would not become the law of the land, however, until nine states had ratified it, and ratification was no easy problem, particularly in New York, where Governor Clinton led the predominately rural opposition. These Anti-Federalists were opposed to a strong central government and claimed that the Constitution, which lacked a Bill of Rights, would benefit only the rich, rather than the small farmer, the urban laborer, or the debtor.

Isaac Roosevelt, as strong a Federalist as he had been a Patriot during the war, was elected along with Hamilton, John Jay, and Robert R. Livingston as Federalist members of the New York City delegation to the State Convention called to ratify the Constitution. Before sailing up the Hudson to Poughkeepsie, where the convention was to be held, the Federalist delegates were given a exuberant send-off, including a thirteen-gun salute. But when they took their seats, their spirits sagged, for only about nineteen of the sixty-five delegates favored ratification. The debate raged for forty days and nights, with Hamilton, as the only member at the convention who had signed the Constitution, providing the arguments for ratification. He warned that if the document was not approved, New York City might secede and join the Union as a separate state. Despite his flights of oratory and threats, the Anti-Federalists stood firm. They would not even budge when word was received that New Hampshire had become the ninth state to ratify the Constitution, making it the law of the land. "Since nine states have acceded to it, let them make the experiment," declared one opponent of ratification. New York would go it alone, he said.

As Hamilton parried and thrust on the convention floor, Isaac Roosevelt and the other Federalists worked behind the scenes to reach a compromise. The Anti-Federalists agreed to accept the Constitution if it were amended to suit their demands, and on July 26, 1788, New York became the eleventh state to ratify it, Virginia having done so a few days before. Of the fifty-seven members voting, thirty were for ratification and twenty-seven were opposed. Two votes cast the other way could have meant disaster for the new nation. Isaac Roosevelt had helped provide that margin of victory—and it may well have been the greatest contribution he made to his country in his long career.

On the morning of April 30, 1789, George Washington stepped out on the balcony of what had been the New York City Hall on Wall Street and with his right hand on an open Bible, took the oath: "I do solemnly swear that I will faithfully execute the office of President of the United States and will, to the best of my ability, preserve, protect and defend the Constitution of the United States." He leaned down to kiss the Bible, and as he straightened up, he murmured: "So help me God!" Inauguration day had dawned cloudy and overcast, but the sky soon brightened—which was regarded as a good omen for the future. As a state senator and a leading Federalist, Isaac Roosevelt had a prominent place during the ceremonies. Like most businessmen, he was gratified when Hamilton, his colleague and friend, was named Secretary of the Treasury and given the opportunity to put his plans for restoring the nation's financial health into practice.

New York was chosen as the capital of the United States, and the city took on all the brilliance of a republican court. Dinners, balls, card parties, and receptions were held every night and one grande dame breathlessly asked: "When shall I get spirit to pay all the social debts I owe?" The President held a levee, or reception, at his rented home at 39 Broadway, one of the city's grandest mansions, on Tuesday from three to four in the afternoon to which all ladies and gentlemen of fashion were invited. On Friday evenings, Mrs. Washington gave a reception, which was considered somewhat formal and stuffy but all the right people were in attendance. The President usually came, looking grave and staying until 9 P.M. Full dress was obligatory.

Isaac Roosevelt took only a peripheral interest in the social whirl because his wife, Cornelia, who was in poor health, died on November 13, 1789, at the age of fifty-five. Her death provided Washington with an opportunity to establish some of the ceremonial limitations of his office. Writing in his diary the following day, the President noted:

Received an invitation to attend the funeral of Mrs. Roosevelt (the wife of a Senator of this State), but declined complying with it, first because the propriety of accepting an invitation of this sort appeared to be very questionable, and secondly (though to do it in this instance might not be improper), because it might be difficult to discriminate in cases which might thereafter happen.

The city's moment of glory was soon over, for Hamilton traded the site of the capital to the South in return for southern votes for his financial schemes. In 1800 the central government was to move to a malarial marsh beside the Potomac River not far from Washington's beloved Mount Vernon, and until then was to be in Philadelphia. The change meant little to Isaac, for in 1791, at the age of sixty-five he decided to retire from business. He resigned as president of the Bank of New York and turned over sole management of the sugar house to his son, James. Of all his offices and titles, he kept only the presidency of the New York Hospital Society and that of the newly organized New York Dispensary, which was designed to minister to the poor and sick "unable to procure medical aid at their own dwellings" and "so circumscribed as not to be proper objects for the Alms House or Hospital." Isaac's long and active life was drawing to a close and he died on October 15, 1794, having accomplished much for himself, his family, and his country. He was, said the Chamber of Commerce in a memorial notice, "beloved and honored as a tried, true and constant patriot."

Chapter VII
STEAMBOAT 'ROUND THE BEND

Under a star-spangled arch of flags and bunting, a large and boisterous crowd gathered on the levee at New Orleans on the morning of January 10, 1812. Ladies and gentlemen in their finery,
frontiersmen in buckskins, soberly dressed shopkeepers, and a
cluster of black dock wallopers all kept their eyes fixed up the
Mississippi. Suddenly, a plume of smoke was sighted above a ragged line of trees and a strange-looking craft glided into view.
Puffing along without the aid of sails, oars, or poles and with only
the brown water churned up by her paddle wheels disturbing the
peace of the river, the vessel eased toward the wharf. To let off
steam, an engineer opened the safety valve, drowning out the
cheers of the crowd—and the *New Orleans*, first steamboat to sail
down the Mississippi, had completed her maiden voyage. Standing at the rail savoring his triumph was her proud builder, Nicholas J. Roosevelt, son of James Roosevelt, the New York hardware
merchant, and his wife, Lydia. Nestled in her arms was their son,
Henry, who had been born on the adventurous voyage from
Pittsburgh.

The steamer's arrival symbolized the fresh and invigorating
spirit sweeping the United States in the opening years of the
nineteenth century. Legend has it that in those days there was a
southern congressman who sometimes amused himself and his
colleagues by turning a somersault or two on the floor of the
House of Representatives while proclaiming that "America is a
great country! America is a great country!" This was, of course,
carrying exuberance a bit far, but the nation was indeed entering

a period of tremendous growth. With the continent fairly oozing wealth, the road to riches lay open—and the Roosevelts were ready to take full advantage of the opportunities that lay so readily to hand.

Following the death of Isaac Roosevelt, his son, James, a wealthy man through his inheritance of the sugar refinery and extensive real estate, steadily increased his holdings as New York City overflowed its old boundaries. Soon, he owned property all over the island, including a sizable chunk of Harlem to the north of the city. Undoubtedly, James agreed with John Jacob Astor, who shortly before his death declared: "Could I begin again, knowing what I know now, I would buy every foot of land on the island of Manhattan."

The other major branch of the Roosevelt family, although not as wealthy or as socially distinguished, was improving its position, too. James I Roosevelt had taken over his father's hardware shop at 94 Maiden Lane and, more imaginative than the old man, had broadened the stock to include imported European glass and other building materials with a ready market in the booming city. His younger brother, Nicholas, shunned the hardware business, however, and in a startling departure for a family that had shown little technological bent, became one of the leading engineers of the day. Although Nicholas has been slighted by history, every Roosevelt is convinced that he invented the steamboat. The point is arguable, but Nicholas *did* help make steam navigation commercially feasible in the United States. His reward was frustration and disappointment.

Born in New York in 1767, Nicholas was taken with the rest of his family to Kingston when the British occupied the city, and boarded with a farmer named Joseph Oosterhaudt. An inquisitive lad with a passion for mechanical gadgets, young Nicholas spent much of the time at Oosterhaudt's work bench. He tinkered with the machinery of a mill on the property and when he was fourteen or fifteen experimented with a model boat propelled by paddle wheels over each side. Fitted with pieces of shingle that served as paddles, these wheels were turned by hickory and whalebone springs that were activated by the unwinding of a cord that had been tightly wound around a central axle. This arrangement powered the model across a pond near the Oosterhaudt farmhouse at a good rate of speed.

When the war ended, Nicholas returned to New York, and re-suming his education, pushed the novel means of propulsion which he had discovered to the back of his mind. His brother, James, wished him to start work in the family hardware business when he finished school, but Nicholas made it clear that he had no intention of settling down behind a counter to sell glass and nails. Instead, he served an apprenticeship in a forge and iron-working shop, and by the time he turned twenty-one was a skilled craftsman capable of supervising and directing the work of others.

During this period, his thoughts may have turned again to his experiments on Joe Oosterhaudt's pond. In 1788 a Philadelphia jack-of-all-trades named John Fitch successfully demonstrated a steamboat on the Delaware River that was propelled by a bank of oars on each side, which looked to some observers like a band of Indians rowing a canoe. At about the same time, James Rum-sey, carrying out experiments on the Potomac River in western Virginia, used a steam-operated pump that drew in water at the bow of a boat and expelled it at the stern to force the craft along. Word of these experiments spread rapidly among the handful of engineers in America, and according to one account, Nicholas Roosevelt commented to friends that the only really efficient means of propelling a steamboat was through the use of paddle wheels over the side. But he made no effort to renew his experi-ments or to interest potential investors such as his wealthy cousin Isaac Roosevelt in the project.

Reports of Nicholas' competence quickly spread, and he was sought out by a syndicate that planned to reopen the abandoned Schuyler copper mines in New Jersey which had become flooded, and in 1793 he became a director of the New Jersey Copper Mine Association. Finding an outmoded steam-operated pump on the scene, Nicholas succeeded in getting it working, but the project proved unprofitable and the mine was again abandoned after eighteen months. Nicholas had, however, become fascinated by steam engines and decided to open a shop to produce them. Some of his associates from the mining venture put up the money to purchase land on the Passaic River, near what is now Belle-ville, New Jersey, and he opened a foundry and machine shop. He called it the Soho works after the establishment operated by

James Watt, the developer of the steam engine, in Birmingham, England.

The Soho plant was the first of its kind in America, and Nicholas became the nation's leading steam engine builder. He constructed engines for many purposes, including a set of massive pumps long used by the Philadelphia waterworks to bring water from the Schuylkill River to the city's reservoirs. He also built a rolling mill to supply the newly organized U. S. Navy with copper sheathing for the bottoms of six 74-gun ships of the line that were ordered by the administration of President John Adams. But he had never forgotten his youthful experiments and often talked of building a steam-powered vessel that would be independent of wind and current.

In December 1797, Nicholas received a letter from Robert R. Livingston, the aristocratic chancellor of the state of New York and an amateur inventor, that was to bring him both exhilaration and heartbreak. It read:

> Mr. [John] Stevens mentioned to me your desire to apply the steam machine to a boat. Every attempt of this kind having failed, I have constructed a boat on perfectly new principles which, both in the model and on a large scale have exceeded my expectations. I was about writing to England for a steam machine, but hearing of your wish, I was willing to treat with you on terms which I believe you will find advantageous. . . .

Through his extensive political influence, Livingston had received a twenty-year monopoly of steam navigation on the Hudson from the New York legislature provided he could produce a vessel within a year that was of at least twenty tons capacity that would move against the river's current at a rate of not less than four miles an hour. Nicholas entered into a contract with Livingston and Stevens, the chancellor's brother-in-law, to produce such a craft and received a 12 percent interest. Almost from the very beginning of the project, he probably regretted having joined it. A careful inspection of Livingston's plan disclosed that it was the impractical work of a dilettante. It called for the steam engine to force water through a box, or "well," at the stern of the craft with such velocity that the jet would turn a wheel in the box, which would propel the boat forward. Nicholas and one of his assistants, who had worked with Watt, pointed out that most of the energy generated would be wasted against the sides of the box but to no avail.

Not only could Livingston not be persuaded to alter his plans—rich people "are not used to hear the truth," commented Nicholas' assistant—he deluged the engineers with last-minute inspirations and changes. Chancing upon a book on water resistance, he discovered that he had neglected this factor and blithely told Nicholas to construct the vessel of the lightest timber possible so that it would draw only a foot of water. "How can an engine be kept in order when every part of the boat gives?" Nicholas disgustedly wrote on the back of the letter. And so it went, with the chancellor alternating demands for alterations with complaints about the slowness in completing the craft.

By August 1798 all was at last ready for a test. Nicholas fired up the boiler and although his engine produced a creditable forty to forty-five strokes a minute, it was incapable of turning Livingston's stern wheel because of water resistance. Angered at the suggestion that his wheel was to blame for the failure, the chancellor contended that the engine was not up to specifications and threatened not to pay for it. An outside expert confirmed Nicholas' diagnosis of the problem and said only a more powerful engine would turn the wheel. While setting to work to build such an engine, Nicholas made a historic suggestion. Recalling the paddle wheels with which he had experimented as a boy, he wrote Livingston on September 6: "I would recommend that we throw two wheels of wood over the sides . . . and that we navigate the vessel with these until we can procure an engine of proper size."

Having received no reply, he wrote to the chancellor again two weeks later, saying, "I hope to hear your opinion of throwing wheels over the sides." Livingston's answer when it came was blunt. "I say nothing on the subject of wheels over the sides, as I am perfectly convinced from a variety of experiments of the superiority of those who have adopted." With this door slammed in his face, Nicholas went back to work on Livingston's steam wheel. With the chancellor's grudging permission, he made alterations which permitted the boat at least to move.

On October 21 Nicholas reported that the Spanish minister, who had visited the shop to order a steam engine, "was on board the day we made the last experiment. . . . During our sail he, at the time the wind and tide favored us, supposed we went at the rate of 6 miles an hour, but I think the delight he felt expressed by the novelty of the voyage caused his mistake. My report to you was 3 miles in still water which I have reason to believe was accurate." Faced with the requirement for a boat that would do four miles an hour if he were to keep his monopoly of steam navigation on the Hudson, Livingston tried to persuade Nicholas to say that the Spaniard had been correct in assessing the boat's speed. Eventually, however, even he could no longer avoid facing the fact that despite continued tinkering the boat was a failure. The partners then went their own separate ways.

Nicholas soon had other worries than the development of the steamboat, for the election of Thomas Jefferson to the presidency in 1800 had a disastrous effect upon his business. Believing that a navy was wasteful and a spur to foreign adventures, Jefferson immediately halted all work on the warships that had been ordered by Adams, thus canceling the contract for copper sheathing. Nicholas was left holding the bag for the sizable expenditures he had made in building his rolling mill and was almost thrown into bankruptcy. He was rescued from his creditors by the offer of a job by Benjamin H. Latrobe, an English-born architect and engineer who was building the Philadelphia waterworks and other projects, including the U. S. Capitol, in Washington. In 1808 he married Latrobe's daughter, Lydia.

Livingston fared much better under the new administration. Jefferson appointed him as minister to France, and he negotiated the Louisiana Purchase. While in Paris, he made the acquaintance of Robert Fulton, an American painter and inveterate tinkerer. Fulton was trying to interest the French government in a submarine that he designed which he claimed would destroy the British squadrons blockading French ports. Fulton's submarine, the *Nautilus*, passed its tests with flying colors but he sank no British ships. When the French withdrew their financial support, Livingston, who had persuaded the pliable New York Assembly to extend his monopoly of steam navigation on the Hudson, convinced the disappointed inventor to turn his attention to steamboats.

Beguiled by the financial rewards dangled before him by Livingston, Fulton began work on an experimental craft. His chosen means of propulsion—a complicated contraption consisting of an endless chain and floats—was unsuccessful and Livingston suggested that a different method be tried. If Nicholas Roosevelt was present on August 7, 1807, when Fulton's vessel, later named the *Clermont*, glided up the Hudson River to Albany, he must have been in for a surprise. She was propelled by a pair of paddle wheels over the side, just as he had suggested to Livingston nearly a decade before. Obviously, the aristocratic promoter had "borrowed" the invention that he had so vehemently rejected. Whether Fulton knew that Nicholas had first proposed "wheels over the side" is not known. Nevertheless, he was credited with the invention of the steamboat and reaped its financial rewards while Nicholas gained neither renown nor money.

Fulton was awarded a patent for the vertical paddle wheel in 1809, but Nicholas, with remarkable charity, did not carry a grudge against Livingston and Fulton. In that same year, he and his father-in-law, Benjamin Latrobe, joined them in a plan to build and operate steamboats on the Mississippi between Natchez and New Orleans. As a result of his role in the purchase of Louisiana, Livingston had substantial political clout in the area, and easily obtained a monopoly on steam navigation. During the preliminary discussion, Latrobe found himself alone one day with Fulton, and asked him why he had secured a patent for what was plainly his son-in-law's idea. Fulton, he said in an affidavit made public later, claimed that he had not signed the application for the patent himself—indicating that Livingston had put his name to it.

I have no pretensions to be the first inventor of the steamboat [Fulton was quoted as saying]. Hundreds of others have tried it and failed. . . . That to which I claim an exclusive right is the so proportioning the boat to the power of the engine and the velocity with which the wheels of the boat, or both, move with the maximum velocity attainable by the power, and the construction of the whole machine. . . . As to Mr. Roosevelt, I regard him as a noble-minded, intelligent man, and would do anything to serve him that I could.

Before commencing construction of a new steamer at Pittsburgh, Nicholas decided to make a personal survey of the area in order to study the currents and chart the bars and snags in some of the world's most treacherous waters. He built a large flatboat with a boxlike cabin divided into a comfortable bedroom and dining room for his bride and himself and quarters for the pilot, cook, and three-man crew. The top of the cabin was flat and fitted with seats and an awning. Over the next six months, the Roosevelts leisurely drifted down the Ohio and Mississippi. During the day, Nicholas and two or three of the men ventured out in a large rowboat to scout ahead, while each evening, the flatboat was tied up to shore. One night, as Lydia Roosevelt later recalled, several Indians clambered aboard and entered the bedroom with a demand for whiskey. They would not leave until Nicholas had gotten up and gave them some liquor.

At Cincinnati, Louisville, and Natchez, the only major towns along the shore, the travelers were courteously received, but the townspeople shook their heads when told of Roosevelt's mission. A steamboat might get down the river to New Orleans, they declared, but it would be unable to fight its way back against the strong current. Nicholas' confidence was not shaken, however, and he was determined to carry on with the project. He was so confident that a steamer would be successful on the western waters that when he found coal deposits on the shores of the Ohio, he not only bought the land but ordered supplies of fuel to be stockpiled at various points for the day when his steamboat would pass this way.

At Natchez, their voyage of exploration over, the Roosevelts abandoned the flatboat and proceeded to New Orleans by rowboat. The pilot, who had spent all his life upon the Mississippi, assured them that there would be no difficulty in securing lodgings ashore at night. But as it turned out, travelers had abused the hospitality of the people who lived along the river and they refused to provide shelter. As Lydia wrote:

A pouring rain came up one evening and we tried to reach Baton Rouge, which we did at nine at night. It was a miserable place at that time, with one wretched public house; yet we felt thankful that we had found a shelter from the storm. But when I was shown into our sleeping room, I wished myself on board the boat. It was a forlorn little place opening out of the bar room, which was filled with tipsy men looking like cutthroats. The room had one window opening into a stable yard, but which had neither shutters nor fastenings. Its furniture was a single chair and a dirty bed. We threw our cloaks on the bed and laid down, to rest, but not to sleep, for the fighting and noise in the bar room prevented that. We rose at the dawn of day and reached the boat, feeling thankful we had not been murdered in the night. It is many, many years ago; but I can still recall that night of fright.

After this experience with southern hospitality, the party spent its nights in the boat or on sandy beaches when it could find them. Sometimes, with the boat drawn partly out of the water, they could hear alligators that had mistaken the craft for a log, scratching themselves on its sides. "A knock with a cane would alarm them, and they would splash down into the water," Mrs. Roosevelt said. The voyage from New Orleans to New York was little better. Yellow fever broke out and the captain and several passengers came down with it. Some died before Nicholas and Lydia were taken off the vessel by a pilot boat and landed at Old Point Comfort in Virginia. They completed the rest of the journey by stage, reaching New York in January 1810, after an absence of nine months.

Nicholas reported his findings to his partners, and after sufficient capital had been raised, returned to Pittsburgh the following year with Lydia to begin work on a steamboat. Fulton had given him the plans for a vessel of 116 feet in length and 20 feet in beam that was propelled by paddle wheels driven by an engine with a 34-inch cylinder. She cost in the neighborhood of $38,000 and was called the New Orleans. Nicholas established his headquarters under a bluff called Boyd's Hill on the Monongahela, about a mile from where the river joined the Ohio. Over the years, shipbuilders had denuded the surrounding forests of suitable timber, and he had to send his men considerable distance in order to find it. While this force cut and trimmed trees for ribs, knees, beams, and planking, mechanics sent from New York as-

ache, made no effort to press his claims during the life of his patent. In 1827, just as it was about to expire, Delacy turned up in
the office of John H. B. Latrobe, Lydia's younger brother, now a
struggling Baltimore attorney. He suggested that Latrobe obtain
an extension of Nicholas' patent and in the meantime instructed
him to institute suit for patent infringement "against every
steamboat owner in the United States" beginning with one operating out of Baltimore on Chesapeake Bay. Not overwhelmed
with clients, Latrobe agreed to take the case. His first step was to
obtain an opinion on its merits from Roger Brooke Taney, one of
Baltimore's leading attorneys and later Chief Justice of the
United States. When Taney expressed the opinion that the
Roosevelt patent was valid, Latrobe pressed ahead.

Later, he began to have doubts. Old Delacy, a cheerfully lar-
cenous spirit, ran up a sizable bill with one of the town's leading
tailors and was imprisoned for debt. And neither he nor Latrobe
had the hundred dollars required to continue the investigation
and it was not forthcoming from Nicholas. Some writers have
asked why wealthier Roosevelts, such as Nicholas' brother, did
not put up the cash in view of the possibility that a successful
suit for patent infringement would be worth a large amount of
money. The answer may lie in the fact that Latrobe, after careful
investigation, realized that every steamboat company in the
country would join in opposing the suit he was preparing
against the Baltimore steamship line. "I tied up my papers . . .
and placed them in a pigeon-hole," he wrote nearly a half century later.

Loss of his patent seems to have had no effect upon Nicholas,
who was living at Skaneatles, in upstate New York, with Lydia
and their nine children. He had apparently given up any hope of
getting money or recognition out of his labors to make steamboats come true. He died in 1854, at the age of eighty-six, having
survived all but three of his children. Writing of him nearly a
century later, another Nicholas Roosevelt said: "He belongs
among the pioneers of the industrial revolution, combining the
capacity to imagine with the ability to create. . . . Had he possessed in a higher degree the acquisitive instinct so strong in
others of his tribe, he might have become a powerful figure in the
industrialization of America."

Chapter VIII
REAPING THE HARVEST

With its cupola gleaming in the sun, New York's graceful City
Hall was the town's most impressive building in the opening
years of the nineteenth century. But visitors were surprised to
find that only the eastern, southern, and western sides had been
faced with marble. Certain that the town would never grow
north of City Hall Park and the building's rear "would be out of
sight of all the world," the city fathers had ordered this side
finished with brownstone, thereby saving $15,000. It was a false
economy. In a generation, the metropolis marched up Fifth Avenue to Gramercy Park and rows of houses were being built as far
north as once-remote Forty-second Street. Following the opening
of the Erie Canal in 1825, business boomed, real estate values
skyrocketed, and as Dr. Oliver Wendell Holmes noted, "New
York City is the tongue that is lapping up the cream of commerce
and finance of a continent."

The simple agrarian economy of the age of Jefferson was giving way to the Industrial Revolution. Through the acquisition of
Florida and the Louisiana Purchase, the nation had more than
doubled in size, and from 1800 to 1830, the population tripled to
nearly 13 million people. Hundreds of miles of turnpike were
being built, canals were being dug, and rights of way were being
cleared for the first steam railroads. Cotton and woolen mills
were opened and smoke billowed from countless factory chimneys. Thousands of Americans were crossing the Appalachians
each year to establish homes on a frontier that was being pushed
ever westward. Each year, new states were added to the Union.

In New York, the last traces of the old Dutch town had long since been submerged under a mass of brownstone and brick. Already, the city had adopted the strange custom of tearing down and rebuilding itself every decade or so. "Brickbats, rafters, and slates were showering in every direction," wrote Philip Hone, the diarist. Underwater lots on both the east and west sides owned by the Roosevelts, the Astors, and others had been filled in and Manhattan was taking on its present shape. The streets of Lower Manhattan were still narrow and crooked, but farther uptown they had been laid out in a rigid grid. The Broadway hills had been graded—the dirt was shoveled into the Collect, the freshwater pond on the Lower West Side, by unemployed sailors in one of the first make-work projects—and it was no longer possible to see down the Upper Bay to the Narrows. Broadway itself was a wonder to visitors. Averaging eighty feet in width and lined with poplars, it was built up as far as about Twenty-third Street and was the city's fashionable promenade. New Yorkers compared Broadway to Regent Street in London, and although most foreigners did not go that far, some visitors found the shops "but little inferior to those of London and Paris." Many of them were fitted with plate-glass windows furnished by Roosevelt & Son, of Maiden Lane, now the city's chief supplier.

In the midst of this hurly-burly, the Roosevelts continued to make their way, although they did not become robber barons or amass fortunes to rival those of dour John Jacob Astor or Cornelius Vanderbilt, the bare-knuckled Staten Island ferryboat skipper who was becoming America's richest man. As Franklin Roosevelt later wrote of his ancestors, "None were poor, yet none were ever exceptionally rich or founded great fortunes." Nevertheless, in the century and a half that the family had been in America, it had developed a peculiar character of its own with both a public and a private face.

To the public, the Roosevelts were faithful to the spirit of the first Nicholas, common ancestor of both major branches, and appeared for the most part to be stolid and solid Dutch burghers. Unimaginative, God-fearing fellows, they were, with few exceptions, businessmen and merchants. Even the college-educated Roosevelts opted for the countinghouse rather than the learned professions. They usually married young, often to girls of substantial family, were faithful husbands and indulgent fathers of the Papa-knows-best school to large broods of children. The Roosevelt women were dutiful daughters who consistently married upward on the social scale. Reflecting this public face, one mid-nineteenth-century chronicler said, "no family shines more honorably in the ancient Dutch annals of this province than the Roosevelts—venerated burgomasters of the day."

The Roosevelts' private face was rather different, however. Although they appeared on the surface to be among the most conformist of old Knickerbocker families, they possessed an independent spirit that surfaced periodically. Among themselves, the Roosevelts were "as voluble as they were energetic," says one of them. "Whenever two or more Roosevelts met, each talked vociferously and ceaselessly, paying no attention to what anyone else tried to say." Most family gatherings had the tendency to "develop into a symphony of concurrent monologues, in which stout lungs [were] at a premium." The family's two major branches each had a dominant figure—James Roosevelt, old Isaac's son, and Cornelius Van Schaack Roosevelt, oldest son of James I Roosevelt, the revolutionary soldier and hardware merchant. James set his side of the family on the road to Hyde Park, while C.V.S., as he was known, became the clan's first millionaire and originated the attachment of his branch to Oyster Bay.

"A gentleman of the old school" were the words usually applied to James Roosevelt by his contemporaries. There is a Dickensian quality about the face that peers from his portrait, painted in old age, which hangs opposite that of his father in the living room of the house at Hyde Park. Steel-rimmed spectacles give James an austere look at first glance, but there are signs that he may have been more benevolent and less autocratic than Isaac the Patriot. Gerald W. Johnson, one of Franklin Roosevelt's biographers, may well have James in mind when he wrote of the President's ancestors: "They were simple worthy people, intelligent without genius, decent without saintliness, educated without erudition, not slothful in business, but not titans of industry—in short, admirable, but not inspiring."

Like his father before him, James devoted himself to the family sugar refinery, expanding and managing his real estate holdings, and to the Bank of New York—but he lacked the acquisitiveness and vision of the old man. A member of the bank's Board of Directors for many years, he was never president and his fortune was not as great as that amassed by his cousin, C. V. S. Roosevelt, who started with less. James also had little interest in politics and public service, although he served as a Federalist member of the State Assembly from 1796 to 1797 and was a city alderman in 1809. Even so, he was the last member of his branch of the family to hold elective office until his great-grandson Franklin went to the State Senate a century later.

James lived a pleasant and rather prosaic life with his wife, the former Maria Eliza Walton, dividing his time between his town house at 18 South Street and his estate in Harlem. They had eleven children, of whom eight survived to maturity. Their eldest son, named Isaac for his grandfather, was born on April 21, 1790. James seems to have had two passions—reading and a love of country life. The charging-out ledger of the New York Society Library for 1789 shows that he borrowed the following books that year:

Gordon's History of the American War, three volumes; Tour through France; Bachelor of Salamancha, two volumes; Smyths' Tour in the United States, two volumes; Hayley's plays; Hume's History of England, eight volumes; Cotton Mather's works; Emmeline, two volumes; Arundel, two volumes; Brydone's Tour through Sicily and Malta; Political magazine, five volumes; Fair Syrian, two volumes; Caroline of Litchfield, two volumes; Modern times or Gabriel outcast; Cook's Voyages, four volumes; Life of Putnam; Hawkesworth's Voyages, two volumes; Johnson's Anecdotes; Henriade; Zoriada; Lady Luxborough's Letters to Shenstone; Beauties of magazines; Pliny's Epistles; Emma Corbett; Temple's works; Wilson's Pelew Islands; Herring's letters; Power of Sympathy, two volumes; Marriage Act, two volumes; Row's Callipaedia; Cotton's works; Smith's Universalist.

There is no guarantee that James read them all, but if he did he must have been a rapid reader. He was never called upon to pay the one-penny-a-day fine levied by the Society for books kept out over a week. James's thriftiness carried over into the management of the Harlem estate, which covered some four hundred acres that are now bounded by the East River, 110th Street, Fifth Avenue, and 125th Street. The tract had been covered by forest when he purchased it and he cut the trees for lumber and fuel which were sold at a profit. The soil proved to be rocky and the drainage was poor, so James used the estate primarily as a breeding farm for horses. Insulated from the noise and pressures of Lower Manhattan, he busied himself in his stables with the bloodlines of his animals and the pleasures and problems of the gentleman farmer. When the roads were in good condition, his fastest horses could take his carriage downtown in an hour.

Maria died in March 1810, after a quarter century of marriage. "In her death her husband and children have sustained irreparable loss," it was said. "They have cause long—very long to mourn the most affectionate and best of wives and most tender of mothers." But James did not long remain a widower, for he married Catherine Eliza Barclay three years later. She was twenty-three years younger than her husband, and like his first wife, a member of a family that had remained loyal to the King during the Revolution. Catherine's father had served in the British Army and been captured by the rebels along with some other Tories and imprisoned at Trenton. Two children were born of this marriage, which ended after less than three years when the second Mrs. Roosevelt died.

For some time, James had considered disposing of the Harlem estate and returning to Dutchess County, where he had spent his youth. Now that he was alone again, he sold the farm to John Jacob Astor for $25,000—today it would be worth millions—and accompanied by his son, Isaac, toured the area near Poughkeepsie, where he had read law nearly forty years before. His eye fell on a hilltop at the northern limits of the town, which he purchased in December 1818 and called Mount Hope. Located on the east side of the Albany Post Road, the estate is now the Hudson State Hospital, and James's large and comfortable house, which had a majestic view of the Hudson River, stood near the present site of the institution's main building. James spent his summers there amid the last patroons while Isaac, a bachelor, lived at Mount Hope the year round.

The second Isaac was an anomaly for the family—a shy and retiring Roosevelt. Although he physically resembled his grandfather and namesake, he did not have his strength and sparkle. Graduating from Princeton at eighteen, young Isaac attended the College of Physicians and Surgeons in New York from which he obtained a medical degree in 1812. Why he chose a medical career is a mystery, because he was not cut out for it. Instead of

opening a practice, he continued his studies under Dr. David
Hosack, one of the town's leading physicians and Alexander
Hamilton's doctor at the fatal duel with Aaron Burr. Dr. Hosack
was also a leading botanist and had an extensive garden on
what is now the site of Rockefeller Center. "Though well educated in his profession and fond of its literature, its practise was
distasteful . . . and being removed from the necessity of practise,
he never engaged in it, chosing rural enjoyments and agricultural
pursuits," said his brother-in-law, Dr. Guy Carleton Bayley. "He
was of a delicate constitution and refined tastes." In fact, it has
been said, Dr. Isaac's tastes were so refined that he couldn't stand
the sight of blood.

Early in 1821, James Roosevelt married for the third time, this
time to Harriet Howland, a descendant of John Howland, a
Mayflower passenger who had distinguished himself by falling
overboard and nearly drowning. The Howlands had abandoned
New England for New York, where Harriet's brothers, Gardiner
G. and Samuel Howland, were prominent merchants and shipowners. She was thirty-seven; James was sixty-one. Writing to his
son, the ebullient bridegroom said:

> I have now the happiness to tell you that I have become the Hus-
> band of HH . . . I can most sincerely tell you that I find Mrs. R all
> that Woman ought to be & all that my Heart can desire. I hope
> most devotedly that one day you will meet with a woman who will
> make you equally happy. . . . My Harriet sends her best wishes to
> you. I will be made very happy in having a visit from you. . . .

South Street had become too commercialized and heavily
trafficked, so James sold the home in which he had lived with his
two previous wives and joined the move uptown to Greenwich
Village. He built a two-story red brick house at 64 Bleecker
Street on the corner of Crosby Street, two blocks south of Washington Square, already one of the city's better addresses. Next
door lived John Aspinwall, another leading merchant and ship-
owner, who had married into the Howland family. James divided
his time between Bleecker Street and Mount Hope, spending his
summers on the Hudson and winters in Manhattan. The marriage
seems to have had no visible effect on Dr. Isaac's living arrangements, for he continued his languorous existence as a full-time

resident at Mount Hope. Almost a recluse, he rarely left the place, and divided his time between management of the estate, the study of botany, and the building of an enviable collection of books on the history of medicine.

It appeared as if the enormous vitality of the Roosevelts had waned in James and completely played itself out in his feckless and hypochondriacal eldest son. They seemed content to merely enjoy the benefits of what their ancestors had amassed, rather than to add to the family's renown and resources. Alexis de Tocqueville, who visited the United States about this time, seemed to be writing of Dr. Isaac when he observed in *Democracy in America:* "In America the aristocratic element has always been feeble from its birth; and if at the present day it is not actually destroyed, it is at any rate so completely disabled that we can scarcely assign to it any degree of influence in the course of affairs."

And then, in 1827, Dr. Isaac surprised everyone by taking a wife at the age of thirty-seven. His bride was nineteen-year-old Mary Rebecca Aspinwall, the daughter of James's next-door neighbor on Bleecker Street, and his third wife's niece. This marriage brought about an alliance between the Roosevelts and one of America's most vibrant families. Unlike James and Isaac, who were satisfied with husbanding what they had inherited or to marry money, the Aspinwalls were merchant princes who sent their ships around the world in search of wealth and owned shipyards along the East River and warehouses in many ports. The Aspinwalls, among the founders of Brookline, Massachusetts, first called Muddy Waters, were originally seamen, whalers, and privateersmen. Dr. William Aspinwall had fought at Lexington, was a military surgeon during the Revolution, and pioneered in the use of inoculation against smallpox.

The most successful of the Aspinwalls was Mary Rebecca's older brother, William Henry. Apprenticed to the countinghouse of his uncles, the Howlands, he was eventually made a partner in the firm which had a profitable trade with the Mediterranean, Britain, and Mexico. When the Howland brothers retired, they turned the business over to young Aspinwall and his cousin, William E. Howland, and it became known as Howland & Aspinwall. Broadening their operations, they sent ships to Latin America and around Cape Horn to China. They built the clipper

Rainbow, first of these speedy craft to be launched in New York, and she startled the maritime world by making a round-trip voyage to Canton in the time usually required to merely reach that port. A man of vision, Aspinwall helped organize the Pacific Mail Steamship Company in 1847 which had a contract to carry the mail to settlers in Oregon by way of Panama, and then began building a railroad across Panama.

According to a story told by Franklin Roosevelt, Aspinwall had borrowed $10 million for railroad construction and needed another $2.5 million to complete the last eighteen miles of track. But the dissatisfied bondholders refused to put up further funds and he went to his office one morning expecting to be forced into bankruptcy. "The morning paper carried the sensational story of the discovery of gold in California," Roosevelt continued. "Aspinwall went to New York not to face ruin, but to be met by smiling creditors who readily subscribed the necessary funds." The eastern terminus of the railroad, now Colon, was originally known as Aspinwall. Soon one of the richest men in New York, Aspinwall had an elaborate mansion on University Place and a showplace on the Hudson at Barrytown, just above Rhinebeck. After dining with the Aspinwalls, Philip Hone remarked that he had never seen "a more beautiful and commodious mansion, or in better taste on every particular."

Dr. Isaac's first son, named James after his father, to continue the family pattern of James-Isaac-James-Isaac-James, was born at Mount Hope in 1828. Now blessed with a family, Dr. Isaac decided the time had come to establish his own home and purchased property just to the north of Mount Hope on the west side of the Post Road and south of the village of Hyde Park and built a house heavily shrouded by trees. He called the place Rosedale. In the meantime, old James remained active and broadened his investments to include the newly opened Delaware & Hudson Railroad. On the eve of his seventy-sixth birthday, on January 9, 1836, he wrote his son and daughter-in-law with evident satisfaction that the stock had taken "a sudden rise" and he had sold five hundred shares at a considerable profit. In this same letter, he reflected upon his long life:

When I think I shall have seen three score & sixteen years—six years more than the alloted life of man—I have great cause to bless &

thank God not only for my continuance in life but that I am permitted at my advanced age when many are bowed down with their
Infirmities & Life a burden to live in the enjoyment of Health & Activity of body & to take pleasure in the Society of Friends. But in
the course of nature the remaining period of my life must come, & it
may be soon—pray with me *then* that I may hopefully & thus fully
resign my spirit to him who has graciously protected & prospered
me from my birth to the present time. . . .

Despite this foreboding, James still had almost another dozen
years to live, and celebrated the birth of a second grandson, John
Aspinwall Roosevelt in 1840. He died at his Bleecker Street home
in his eighty-eighth year shortly after suffering a paralyzing
stroke. The Poughkeepsie *Journal* noted that "Mr. Roosevelt
spent his summers at his country seat in our vicinity and our citizens will not soon forget his erect and venerable form, moving
among us with all the sprightliness of youth. His was indeed 'a
green old age' and to the very day at which he was summoned
from the earth exhibited few of the infirmities of age." Dr. Isaac
inherited Mount Hope and spent the remaining years of his life
somberly puttering about the adjoining estates. Upon his death in
1863, Rosedale passed to John A. Roosevelt and Mount Hope
went to James Roosevelt, who nineteen years later became the father of Franklin D. Roosevelt.

While James and Isaac Roosevelt were happy to live graciously
on wealth accumulated by others, Cornelius Van Schaack Roosevelt was a far more ambitious fellow. Born in 1794, he was the
oldest of the six children of James I Roosevelt, the hardware merchant, and his wife, Maria Van Schaack. "My grandfather on my
father's side was of almost purely Dutch blood," his grandson,
Theodore, later recalled. "When he was young he still spoke some
Dutch, and Dutch was last used in the services of the Dutch
Reformed Church in New York when he was a small boy." C.V.S.
appears to have been a spirited lad, for his grandson repeated the
following tale:

In *his* boyhood Sunday was as dismal a day for small Calvinistic
children of Dutch descent as if they had been of Puritan or Scotch
Covenanting or French Huguenot descent. . . . One summer after-

noon, after listening to an unusually long Dutch Reformed sermon for the second time that day, my grandfather, a small boy, running home before the congregation had dispersed, ran into a party of pigs, which then wandered free in New York's streets. He promptly mounted a big boar, which no less promptly bolted and carried him at full speed through the midst of the outraged congregation.

Increasingly prosperous as a result of the building boom and the need for hardware and glass, James I could afford to send his son to college and C.V.S. enrolled at Columbia. Already intending to enter the family business, the young man considered college a waste of time and left without graduating. He took over management of his father's business and placing greater emphasis on the importation of glass, created a near monopoly for Roosevelt & Son. Work was C.V.S.'s passion and getting rich his ambition. He even found it difficult to break away long enough to be with his fiancée, Margaret Barnhill, of Philadelphia, whose Quaker ancestors had come over with William Penn. "Business calls me with its imperious beckoning," he wrote. "Oh could I tear myself from that absorber of every gentle feeling." Such doubts were quickly dismissed, however, for a month later, he declared: "Economy is my doctrine at all times—at all events till I become, if it is to be so, *a man of fortune.*"

This single-minded devotion to economy was reflected in the young man's plans for the couple's future home. "You know that I hate extravagance in young folks," he told Margaret, "and the only things in which I shall be extravagant will be carpets for the two lower rooms, a sideboard and a sofa. *Our* chairs will not be mahogany. My idea is that of little or nothing for ornament alone, but of that which is useful to be also ornamental if possible." Prudently, he waited until after the wedding, in 1821, to buy the family silver. When he had examined the gifts they had received and determined what was still needed, he gave his bride the money to make the purchase.

But for all his businesslike manner, C.V.S. adored his wife, to whom he had written reams of poetry during their engagement. She bore him six sons, of whom five survived—Silas Weir, James Alfred, Cornelius, Robert Barnhill and Theodore. The mansion that he built at the southwest corner of Broadway and Fourteenth Street across from the south side of Union Square re-

sounded to their cries and laughter. It had a large hall with an
inlaid black and white marble floor and a wide staircase which
ran around the sides of the hall that made it ideal for games and
for hiding. Theodore, the youngest and the father of the future
President, was born in 1831. Thriftily, the Roosevelts handed
down clothing from one son to the next, and Theodore, much to
his embarrassment, wore whatever the others had outgrown.
Once, he burst into tears when he heard his parents discussing
the next set of hand-me-downs that he was to wear. The boys did
not attend school but were taught at home by a Mr. McMillan, a
private tutor, who must have been hard-pressed to control his
boisterous charges. "There goes that lovely Mrs. Roosevelt with
those five *horrid* boys!" was a comment often heard among family
friends and neighbors.

Over the years, C.V.S.'s somewhat strange figure became more
prominent in the countinghouses of Lower Manhattan. He was a
short, red-haired man with a head that seemed too large for his
body and shrewd eyes framed by square little spectacles. "His appearance always suggested to me a Hindoo idol, roughly carved
in red porphry," said one acquaintance. The Panic of 1837 gave
him his chance to fulfill his ambition to become "a man of fortune." Resulting from the collapse of a wild speculative boom in
western lands, manufacturing, transportation, and banking, the
crash plunged the nation into a four-year-long depression. Farm
prices sank, banks failed, businesses closed their doors, and job-
less workers rioted for bread in the streets of New York.

Confident that sooner or later the country would pull out of
this economic tailspin, C.V.S., following the classic business practice of buying when everyone else is selling, purchased real estate
all over Manhattan at bargain prices. Then he sat back and
waited for the inevitable increase in value. The success of his
scheme can be gauged by the fact that in 1842, he was estimated
to be worth about $250,000, most of it inherited from his father,
who had died two years before. Three years later, his fortune had
doubled to more than $500,000. The average worker earned then
from fifty to seventy-five cents a day. In 1844 he was one of the
organizers and a member of the Board of the Chemical National
Bank, which achieved renown by making all its payments in gold,
even during the Civil War.* Three years before his death in 1871,

* A Roosevelt served on the Board of Directors until 1969.

C.V.S. was included along with an Astor, a Rhinelander, and a Lorillard among the ten largest owners of taxable property in the city, with holdings worth in excess of $1.3 million. His total fortune was considerably greater, and he was thought to be one of the five richest men in New York—as well as the wealthiest Roosevelt by far.

C.V.S. was an indulgent parent, and those who knew him only in his office would have been surprised to see this usually austere man romping with his sons. Everyone seemed to talk at once and a visitor may have found it difficult "to comprehend the various styles of manner and peculiar dialects in use among us," Silas Weir Roosevelt, the eldest son, once observed. "This . . . requires a great deal of versatility, for a stranger must be somewhat bewildered by the sudden fits we take of irony, cordiality, conceit, affection, nonsense and sense; which succeed each other without apparent connection or warning approach." The one time in which C.V.S. insisted on decorum was at Sunday "lunch," at which waffles were usually served and only Dutch was spoken at the table. It was a family tradition that had probably come down from his father as a means of preserving the ancestral language.

Theodore Roosevelt recalled his grandmother, Margaret, as "a woman of singular sweetness and strength." Although of English-Welsh descent—in fact, she was the first non-Dutch woman to marry into this branch of the family—she learned to speak the language. "It was she who taught me the only Dutch I ever knew, a baby song of which the first line ran, 'Trippe troppa tronjes,'" he wrote in his *Autobiography*. "I always remembered this, and when I was in East Africa it proved a bond of union between me and the Boer settlers, not a few of whom knew it, although at first they always had difficulty in understanding my pronunciation—at which I do not wonder."

C.V.S. and Margaret were firm believers in the benefits of summer vacations in the country for growing children and the family "migrated, usually en masse," to the newly fashionable Jersey shore or up the Hudson. They stayed in boardinghouses mostly, but one summer C.V.S. chose a "Water Cure Establishment." Some of the family cheerfully called it "the Lunatic Asylum." Following the Civil War, C.V.S. began the practice of summering near the village of Oyster Bay, about thirty miles from Manhattan on the north shore of Long Island. Reaching the area was something of an adventure in those days, requiring a trip by train and carriage or by boat from the East River piers. The beaches were mostly pebbles and the water sometimes chilly, but the Roosevelt brood, now including several grandchildren, found Oyster Bay delightful. C.V.S. established his summer residence there overlooking the water, and his branch of the family has been associated with it ever since.

Margaret Roosevelt had died in 1861, and after forty years, C.V.S. was alone. Unlike his cousin James Roosevelt, he did not remarry. Once again, he began writing poetry, most of it dedicated to his late wife. A poem, which he called "Alone," dated January 27, 1863, is typical:

> Alone, alone, that word Alone:
> Its melancholy toll
> Echoes its notes of sadness through
> The chambers of the Soul.
> Alone, alone: where e'er I go
> I feel myself alone.
> There's nothing now to speed my steps
> No loved one now I own. . . .

With his children grown and with families of their own, C.V.S. lived by himself in the house on Union Square for ten years before his death in 1871. Memorialized as "a highly respectable old landmark and a millionaire"—not quite the same as a gentleman of the old school—he was as much a family founder as old Isaac Roosevelt. Although his side of the family had not yet risen to the social heights of the Hudson River Roosevelts, they now far exceeded them in wealth. And he had the satisfaction of seeing his sons firmly established in business, politics, and charitable work as well as on the social ladder. Greatness lay just over the horizon.

Chapter IX
SAINTS AND SINNERS

Every family has its share of muted scandals and skeletons tucked away in closets and the Roosevelts are no exception. Although the family tree boasts of a link to the first American-born Catholic saint and several other members who devoted themselves to good works, it also includes, as one Roosevelt cheerfully notes, "poets, parasites and even a few alcoholics." There is even a mystery woman who violated the firm dictate of old Knickerbocker society that a lady's name should appear in print only upon three occasions: to announce her birth, her marriage, and her death. In fact, the story of Janet Roosevelt fills an entire chapter of a curious chronicle called *The Old Merchants of New York*. The book's title makes it sound like another high-Victorian celebration of wealth, but behind this staid facade, Walter Barrett, the pseudonymous author, retailed gossip and scandals involving Little Old New York's leading families.

The strange story of Janet Roosevelt begins with Barrett claiming that upon reading the *Morning Chronicle* one day in January 1806, his eye fell on the following item:

$1000 reward will be paid for any information that can be given of a nurse named Milly Seymour, who in the year 1805 lived for several months in the upper part of a two story brick house in Maiden lane; two doors below Nassau street, on the south side; or of a male child named Rupert, then a babe; or of her husband, William Seymour. Apply to Mrs. I., at 22 Courtlandt street.

"It struck me as funny. I read it a dozen times. I took a Directory of 1805, and went through the I.'s until I found Inderwick, widow Janet." Although he had discovered this clue, Barrett put the incident aside until he saw the name again in the July 25, 1812, issue of a weekly newspaper, the *Museum*, which carried the following item:

Died—On Wednesday morning last, after a long and weary illness, which she bore with Christian fortitude, Mrs. Janet Inderwick, widow of the late Jansen Inderwick. She was aged thirty-four years.

Curiosity aroused, Barrett hunted up the old advertisement. "I found it in all the journals of 1809. Again I found it in the New York *Gazette* of 1810. After her death I again found the same advertisement; but instead of applying to Mrs. Inderwick, it was to 'Robert Jones, counsellor-at-law, Nassau street.' Still, I did not take up the subject in earnest until I found the same advertisement in the New York *Herald* of July 10, 1856, but with a different lawyer." Now, stated the writer, he launched a zealous search for the facts behind these mysterious notices. This is what he said he came up with:

Jansen Inderwick was a member of an old Dutch family that had come to New Amsterdam in 1623, and "at one time owned one-tenth of the island of Manhattan." In 1795 he married a Miss Janet Roosevelt. Although Barrett does not tell us anything of her background or from which branch of the Roosevelt family the bride came, he states that "she was an extremely lovely person, as her portrait, still in existence, shows that she must have been. I will not attempt to describe her charms. She must have abounded in these to have secured the affection, as well as the hand, of the gifted, the handsome, and the wealthy descendant of an ancient Dutch family."

For eight years they lived together, dividing their time between Inderwick's twenty-acre country estate in what is now midtown Manhattan and the town house on Courtlandt Street. Janet "was much admired by everyone, and was the belle among the leading families of this city," but the couple had no children. Inderwick became "morose, dejected, and, it was said, almost cruel to his wife." In September 1803, Janet, "to the surprise of everyone," packed two trunks and moved to a boardinghouse on lower Broadway. From that day until Inderwick's death two years later, the couple never spoke to each other again. Yet, he dispatched a carriage to the boardinghouse for her use every day, and when she needed money, she sent her black servant girl to Inderwick with a request for a stated sum. "Whether it was $100 or $500, he sent the amount required back to her in Bank of New York notes," says Barrett.

The strangest part of the story is still to come. Upper-crust New Yorkers of the day took turns entertaining each other at dinners and evening parties and Janet and Jansen were invited out as if nothing had happened to their marriage. They would attend parties as a couple but would leave without having exchanged a word. Inderwick gave such affairs as often as anyone, at Courtlandt Street, and Janet attended. "When she was in her husband's house . . . [she] acted in all respects as the mistress—the servants obeyed her as such—still she did not speak to her husband, or he to her."

In October 1804 a merchant named Richard Rupert took up residence in the boardinghouse in rooms adjoining Janet's. "Frequently Mrs. Inderwick used to be seen conversing with him in the parlor," Barrett continues. "They appeared to grow more intimate. Ere three months had passed, she used to send notes to him at his store in Pearl Street. It was observed that he answered these notes in person, and boldly entered her private apartments. Still her husband took no notice of these proceedings. After six months from the time of Mr. Rupert's arrival she did not come into the parlor at all. She frequently went out riding in her carriage" and was always accompanied by him. And then, without any explanation, Janet and her black servant suddenly moved to Sussex County, in New Jersey.

"She was gone two months, and it was reported that she had the typhus fever, and came very near dying. When she returned to her boarding house, she was very much emaciated. Her husband sent every day to inquire after her health." Following Janet's return, Barrett states somewhat archly, "she seemed to have a new subject of interest." Almost every day, her maid went to a house on Maiden Lane, where a young couple named William and Milly Seymour, who had just arrived from the country, occupied the upper floor. The couple had two children—a girl and a boy named Rupert Roosevelt Seymour, who was the recipient of lavish gifts from Janet, although she carefully refrained from visiting the house.

When the child was about a year old, Inderwick died, and Janet, as his widow, gained control of an extensive estate. She returned to Courtlandt Street, and less than a week after her husband's death, paid her first visit to the Seymour home. She petted and cuddled the little boy, and mistakenly became convinced that he was being mistreated. An argument flared, and in her anger, she struck Milly. The following day Janet returned, not as might be expected to take Rupert away, but to apologize to Milly and to give her a new silk dress that she had bought as a gift. Both the nurse and baby were gone. The house was empty and no one could tell her what had become of the Seymours. She never saw Milly or the baby again, despite repeated efforts to find them. Janet died in 1812, having according to Barrett, "probably left a dying declaration that the child was hers," and "evidently" made a will leaving him the "vast property" accumulated by Jansen Inderwick. Writing sixty years later, he said no one had ever stepped forward to claim the fortune.

Barrett has given us a fascinating tale—worthy of one of Edith Wharton's intricate novels of gaslight New York. There is one problem, however. It may never have happened. None of the existing Roosevelt family genealogies list a Janet Roosevelt, and a search of the publications cited by Barrett that are currently available at the Library of Congress fails to turn up even one of the notices which he reproduces. Thus, the story of Janet Roosevelt Inderwick and the missing heir appears to be a product of Barrett's fertile imagination. Except for one thing. Why did he use the Roosevelt name in his tale? After all, at the time the book appeared they were one of New York's most distinguished families, and likely to not only take umbrage at such use of their name but powerful enough to do something about it.

Unless, of course, there might be a kernel of truth in the story.

Philip Hone was dining out with friends, mostly conservative Whigs like himself, one evening in the winter of 1831. The ladies had excused themselves, leaving the gentlemen to smoke their Havanas and to pass the Madeira around the table. Having exhausted as a topic of conversation the latest atrocities of the Democratic President, Andrew Jackson, and his local allies in

Tammany Hall, one guest produced a visiting card which he said he had just received from Paris and circulated it among the company with a broad grin. The elegantly engraved pasteboard was greeted with laughter as it moved from hand to hand. It read:

James J. Roosevelt
Membre du Conseil de New York
et
Attaché à l'Embassade des États Unis

Hone, who detested James J. Roosevelt, a political rival and younger brother of C. V. S. Roosevelt, was caustic. "This foolish piece of vanity" was "one way of bringing a New York *assistant alderman* into notice, and transforming a minister plenipotentiary into an ambassador," he confided to his diary. If James J. had been privileged to peek into that famous series of volumes—in which he was described as "a small man, very conceited, and inferior"—he would probably have guffawed and gone on his merry way. Raffish and fun-loving, one can visualize him strolling up Broadway in a bright waistcoat, puffing on a big cigar and with his tall hat tilted at a rakish angle. His middle initial "J" was meant to show that he was the son of James I Roosevelt, the hardware merchant, but he sometimes insisted on calling himself James I. Roosevelt. Asked what the "I" stood for, he would cry, "It stands for I—me!"

Unlike his older brother, five years his senior, James J. had no interest in the hardware and glass business. Following his graduation from Columbia in 1815, he studied law and became the partner of Peter A. Jay, son of John Jay. Making up for his branch of the family's disinterest in public affairs, he began to dabble in politics. As an admirer of Andrew Jackson and an ardent Democrat, he soon became a power in Tammany Hall and was rewarded with election to the City Council. This is ironic in view of the fact that later Roosevelts began their political careers as reformers, vowing to do battle with the dragon of political corruption as represented by Tammany.

Originally founded by Aaron Burr, the Society of St. Tammany was as old as the Constitution itself, having been formed three weeks before that document went into effect. The original aim of the organization was to give the common folk of New York City a

124 THE ROOSEVELT CHRONICLES

greater voice in the process of government. Following the elimi-
nation of property qualifications for voting and the growth in the
size of the electorate over the next half century, it produced political professionals who had the technical skills to get out the
voters and to make certain that they cast their ballots correctly.
Tammany's power rested on its ability to mobilize the immigrant
vote—an ever increasing factor in elections, particularly in large
cities such as New York. Tammany offered the confused new-
comer advice, helped him locate a place to live, aided him in
finding a job, and assisted him in becoming naturalized. All it
required in turn for its services was the newly minted citizen's
vote.

Tammany's leaders sought patronage and jobs as a reward for
their political efforts. Upon displacing the representatives of the
upper class at the levers of power, they quickly developed sophisticated techniques for manipulating these positions for plunder.
As early as 1838, it was estimated that as much as $600,000 a year
was extorted from gambling dens, houses of prostitution, and assorted dives. Once Tammany was firmly in control of New York,
most of the city's leading businessmen eagerly accommodated
themselves to its ways. Some of the same men who loudly trumpeted the cause of reform worked in tandem with Tammany to
line their own pockets. According to Gustavus Myers' *History of
Tammany Hall*, James J. Roosevelt was an important link between the organization and the business community.

In 1830 James J. decided upon a change of scenery and took
himself off to Paris, where Louis Philippe, who had lived in the
United States, had just become King of the French. He was
armed with a letter of introduction from Richard Riker, a prominent New Yorker, to the aged Marquis de Lafayette.

This will be handed to you by James I. Roosevelt Jr. Esquire [the
letter read] one of the most respectable Counsellors of the New
York Bar, and a member of the City Council of the City of New
York. To which I may add that Mr. Roosevelt, in common with the
great body of American Citizens, is devoted to our free and republican Institutions.
Mr. Roosevelt . . . cannot deny himself the pleasure of seeing You &
the good City of Paris. . . . I pray you, My Dear General, to afford
him all the facilities in your power. . . .

James J. was also close to his fellow Jacksonian, William C. Rives, the American minister to France, who put him on the legation staff, giving the visitor a double entrée into Paris society—and producing the visiting card that so angered Philip Hone. While in Paris, James J. fell in love with the glamorous and beautiful Cornelia Van Ness, whose father, Cornelius P. Van Ness, had been governor and senator from Vermont and was currently minister to Spain. While living in Washington, in a house designed by Benjamin H. Latrobe, father-in-law of James J. Roosevelt's uncle, Cornelia had been the belle of capital society. James J. and Cornelia were married on May 30, 1831, at the home of the American minister, and the bride was given away by Lafayette, a close friend of her father.

The couple returned to New York, and between 1831 and 1852, became the parents of eleven children of whom only four lived to maturity. Cornelia, one of the city's queens of society, was said to be "noted for her fascinating social qualities, her exquisite beauty, grace, sprightliness and elegance of style." She also seems to have been rather sly. Although James J. inherited $150,000 from his father and amassed a fortune of his own, he balked at her extravagance. There is a family tradition that she worked out an arrangement with A. T. Stewart's department store in which her requests for petty cash were added to her husband's bills. He suspected nothing—and Cornelia amassed $30,000 for her needs.

James J. was elected to the State Legislature in 1835, 1839, and 1840. Election fraud and ballot-box stuffing were commonplace in those days with Tammany mustering an army of repeaters, floaters,* and unnaturalized aliens, so the Whigs introduced a bill providing for strict voter registration in New York City. It quickly passed the State Senate, but ran afoul of the Democratic delegates in the Assembly led by Roosevelt, who attacked the measure as unnecessary, inefficient, and a restriction on the liberties of the citizens of the city. Dipping his pen in venom, the angry Hone wrote in his diary: "James J. Roosevelt, the leader of the blackguards, in whose person, as its representative, our poor city is disgraced, takes the lead in opposition to the law, and resorts to every species of vile, disgraceful conduct and language,

* Floaters sold their votes to the highest bidder with five dollars the going rate; repeaters voted as many times as they could get away with.

in which he is supported by the whole pack. Order [and] decency . . . are openly condemned."

In return for his labors, Tammany sent James J. to Washington in 1841 as a congressman—making him the first member of the family to serve in that body. Returning to the scene of past triumphs, Cornelia was in her glory. Even President John Tyler came to the Roosevelts to play cards and former President John Quincy Adams, now a fellow congressman, was also a regular. His contribution to Cornelia's guest book was a translation of a poem that had been written there by Victor Hugo in 1831:

> La Poésie, inspiré lorsque de la terre ignore,
> Ressemble à les grandes monts que la nouvelle aurore
> Dore avant nous a son reveille.

Old John Q. attached leaden feet to Hugo's high-flying sonorities, by rendering this verse as:

> The bard is like yon hilltop high,
> At sunrise shining to the sky
> While darkness reigns below.

Politics had evidently begun to bore James J., and when his term was up, he declined renomination and certain reelection. Instead, he and Cornelia set out for Europe, where he observed the judicial and legal systems of Britain, France, and his ancestral Holland at close range. Walter Barrett claims to have encountered Roosevelt in Rotterdam "and trotted him all about during a great 'Kermis' [or Fair] to ascertain whether the New York Dutch he spoke was the same as spoken in Holland." The locals understood little of what he said. James J. resumed the private practice of law upon his return, but in 1851 accepted appointment to the New York Supreme Court. Eight years later, he resigned the judgeship to become U.S. district attorney for the Southern District of New York for a year, although he liked to be called "Judge Roosevelt."

Philip Hone had died but another diarist, George Templeton Strong, was on hand to castigate him. "Judge Roosevelt is making a special ass of himself in the matter of Central Park," Strong wrote upon one occasion. No doubt James J. was making certain that Tammany Hall got its share of the plunder resulting from the creation of the park. In 1860 James J. retired and until his death fifteen years later at the age of eighty, made his home in Paris and New York. He literally starved to death after a fall which so affected his stomach that he refused to eat. Cornelia died in Paris the following year.

None of the couple's children made much of a mark, but one son, Charles Yates Roosevelt, who was born in 1846, had some interesting descendants. He married Cornelia Livingston Talbot, a member of the Livingston family, and had a daughter who was named after her mother and grandmother. Like many upper-class girls of the late nineteenth century, this Cornelia married a member of the European aristocracy, in her case Baron Clemens von Zedlitz, of Berlin. The baron met an end almost as macabre as that of Judge Roosevelt. He was drowned in 1901 when his yacht collided with that of Kaiser Wilhelm II.

Clinton Roosevelt was ranged on the opposite side from his cousin James J. Roosevelt in the great party battles of the Jacksonian era. Born in 1804, he was the son of Elbert Roosevelt, in whose office Isaac Roosevelt's son, James, had read law, and was a radical economic and political reformer. Although his father left him a fortune estimated at nearly $1 million, Clinton hated bankers, blaming them for most of society's ills, and was the leading theorist of the Equal Rights or Locofoco movement, the left-wing Democrats opposed to Tammany. Often, he was in direct conflict with James J. Roosevelt, as the reformers tried to wrest control of the party from the bosses. It was during one such battle that the Locofocos received their name. At a meeting in Tammany Hall on October 29, 1835, the reformers seized control of the city caucus from the party regulars by producing candles and lighting them with locofoco matches, after their opponents had tried to force an adjournment of the meeting by turning off the gas. In derision, the newspapers called them the Locofoco party.

Described by a contemporary as "an honest politician of considerable talent and some eccentricity," Clinton was elected to the State Assembly in 1836 as a Locofoco candidate. At Albany he led the fight against giving valuable filled-in land along the Harlem River to a group of large property holders with good political contacts, a fight that led to his defeat the following year.

What James and C. V. S. Roosevelt, who both had important banking and real estate interests, thought of their cousin can only be surmised. No doubt they considered him "a traitor to his class" —words that were to be used against later Roosevelts in politics.

In some ways, Clinton was an early New Dealer with his demands for "a reformation of the banking system," and he first used the "rubber dollar" phrase which was picked up a century later by Franklin Roosevelt. The most widely read of his many books and tracts was *The Science of Government*, published in 1841. Written in the form of a Socratic dialogue between the "Author" and the "Producer," or workingman, it denounced the influence of bankers on the economic system and argued that prices could be controlled by regulation of the amount of currency in circulation. "The great banker, like the robber by the sword, men consider good society while the honest man of value to his fellow men is held base, ignoble, vulgar and looked down upon with scorn," Clinton declared. In another of his works, he advocated the creation of what was, in effect, a national planning board to oversee the redistribution of the national wealth and to prevent the cycles of boom and bust which he attributed to overindulgence "in that stimulant, bank paper."

Taking time out from his other projects, Clinton, noting in 1835 that there was a possibility of war between the United States and France, produced plans for an armored man-of-war which he called an "Invulnerable Steam Battery." Long and narrow and covered with iron plate, the craft was to be propelled by two 100-horsepower steam engines that would drive a pair of paddle wheels to be placed on the center line for protection. It was to be armed with a spar torpedo which exploded on contact, mortars throwing fireballs as well as a broadside of heavy guns. As an added feature, one of the steam engines was designed to throw a column of water of "six to nine inches in diameter" which would douse an enemy vessel, making the guns useless and sinking her. In summation, Roosevelt's steam battery was designed to torpedo an enemy, set him afire, pound him with gunfire, and then sink him with the equivalent of a high-pressure fire hose. Clinton volunteered to demonstrate the vessel by sinking any target in the face of protecting gunfire. The proposal was submitted to Congress but nothing was done about it, and the plans for the craft were filed and forgotten until found in the National Archives 125 years later.

In middle life, Clinton abandoned politics and resumed the practice of law, a profession in which he was remarkably successful. During the Crimean War, he found himself in Russia, and as a neutral, offered his services to the various belligerents to help end the fighting. His offer was accepted and he served as a diplomatic courier between St. Petersburg, Paris, and London in the delicate negotiations which brought about an end to the bloody conflict. Unlike most Roosevelts, he remained a bachelor, and died August 8, 1898, at the age of ninety-four. Born in the administration of Thomas Jefferson, he lived to see Theodore Roosevelt charge up San Juan Hill. But he had also outlived his contemporaries, and his obituaries consisted of only a few lines that did not even mention his books.

Hilborne Lewis Roosevelt, a grandson of C. V. S. Roosevelt and son of S. Weir Roosevelt, pioneered in the development of the electric organ and built the finest instruments seen in the United States until that time. He may have inherited his artistic instincts from his mother's family, the Wests of Philadelphia, whose most distinguished representative was Benjamin West, the painter. His father, Weir, became a lawyer following his graduation, in 1841, from Columbia. Nicholas Roosevelt, Weir's grandson, calls him "a merry soul, full of fun and whimsy, and ever ready to twist a phrase or win a smile." He was a respected poet and a persistent writer of letters to the editor. In 1854 he led the alumni of Columbia in revolt against the trustees when they refused to appoint Professor Wolcott Gibbs to a chair in chemistry because he was a Unitarian. Weir's spirited denunciation of the trustees for making religion a test of fitness to teach chemistry was supported by the alumni and the press. Appointed a member of the New York City Board of Education shortly before the end of the Civil War, he made the post almost a full-time job. Until a crippling illness confined him to his home, he made it a point to visit all the schools to better observe the problems of the system and to find solutions.

The Roosevelts of the Victorian era looked with askance at young Hilborne's interest in acoustics and organs. A half century had passed since his great-uncle, Nicholas J. Roosevelt, had cho-

sen the machine shop over the hardware counter and the line between gentlemen and mechanic was more rigidly drawn than it
had been. In fact, the firm of Roosevelt & Son was no longer in
"trade," for the family glass business had been transformed by
James Alfred Roosevelt, Weir's brother, into a Wall Street investment banking house with offices at 30 Pine Street. Brushing off
the protests of his family, Hilborne apprenticed himself to the
New York organ makers, Hall & Labagh. When he had learned
all that he could from them, he made several trips to Europe to
study the finer points of organ construction.

Correctly reasoning that the steadiness of the electrical current
would produce tonal effects that were impossible to achieve with
hand-pumped instruments, Hilborne was in the forefront in the
application of electrical devices to organs. In 1869, at the age of
twenty, he received the first patent for an electric organ action,
and three years later opened a factory on Eighteenth Street in
New York. Unlike Nicholas J. Roosevelt, he was a shrewd businessman, and with his patents secure, prospered in his new business. The instrument he constructed for the Philadelphia Centennial Exhibition of 1876 was said to be the first electric-action
organ built in America. Experts were amazed at its tone and it
produced increased orders for the firm. By 1881 Hilborne had become so successful that he had to move to a larger factory to keep
up with the demand and opened plants in Philadelphia and Baltimore as well. He manufactured some of the largest church organs
yet heard in America, among them the notable instruments in the
Protestant Episcopal Cathedral in Garden City, Long Island, and
Grace Church in New York, each of which contained over twenty
miles of electrical wires.

Not content solely with a reputation as America's finest organ
builder, Hilborne continued his electrical experiments and became interested in the newly developed telephone. Working with
the Bell Telephone Company, he produced several devices, including the automatic switch hook, which increased the
efficiency of the primitive instrument. At the height of his success, he died in 1886 at the tragically young age of thirty-seven.
His younger brother, Frank H. Roosevelt, enlarged and continued the organ business until 1893, when he sold the patents to a
rival firm. Summing up Hilborne's accomplishments, one expert

has said, "The impetus of all subsequent improvements in American organ building is largely due" to his work.

While Hilborne was making a fortune, his brother Cornelius, two years his senior, became the family's black sheep. Kicked out of the Troy Polytechnic Institute, he returned to New York City and was a man-about-town until he wore out his welcome.† He went to Paris, where he established a branch of the family known as the "Paris penal colony" but still managed to scandalize the staid Oyster Bay Roosevelts. "Have just received a letter telling me that Cornelius has distinguished himself by marrying a French actress!" his first cousin Theodore, then a Harvard student, wrote in his journal in 1878. "He is a disgrace to the family —the vulgar brute." The family took legal action to bar Cornelius from sharing in his grandfather's sizable estate, but sent him enough money to keep him from returning to New York to plague them. He lived until 1902, having "happily survived the frigid blasts of family disapproval" on borrowed money which he never repaid.

André Roosevelt, Cornelius' son, followed in the old man's footsteps. Writing of him, cousin Nicholas says his "extramarital relations added to the populations of four continents and [his] business ventures were largely at the expense of new acquaintances hypnotized by his name, his dreams and his promises." Like Cornelius, "it was hard to tell whether his success in dunning his friends and relatives or his pagan enjoyment of life gave greater offense to the 'family,' who viewed his every appearance in New York with apprehension." André, a pioneer pilot and filmmaker, helped popularize Bali as a tourist attraction, photographed volcanoes from the air, fished for sharks, and climbed Andean mountains—all with a zest for life that lasted eighty-three years. He died in 1962 in Haiti, where he was manager of a luxury hotel. The New York *Times*, in its obituary, gave his occupation as "world adventurer."

James Henry Roosevelt led an entirely different kind of life. Stricken with polio when little more than twenty—exactly a century before the same disease crippled Franklin Roosevelt—he refused to give way to despair, and amassed a fortune which he left

† Cornelius liked to amuse his friends by opening his mouth wide enough to hold a billiard ball. Once it got stuck.

for the founding of Roosevelt Hospital. He was born in 1800, the
grandson of Isaac the Patriot's younger brother, Christopher.
James Henry was a bright lad and everyone forecast a brilliant
future for him. He did well at Columbia, graduating with honors
in 1819, and decided to study law. While at school, he met Julia
Maria Boardman, a member of another old New York family, and
they fell in love. The young couple decided to marry as soon as
James Henry had established his practice, but tragedy intervened.

Little more than a month after James Henry was admitted to
the bar, he was crippled by infantile paralysis and unable to walk
without crutches. Unlike Franklin Roosevelt, however, he decided that his infirmity barred him from leading a normal life. He
and his fiancée agreed that marriage was impossible and he abandoned his plans to establish a law office. For the rest of his life,
James Henry remained at home, skillfully adding to the estate
left him by his father, which included some of the family's original holdings in the Beekman Swamp. Julia never married and
they remained close friends—a relationship that lasted for forty
years.

When James Henry died in 1863, he had lived a quiet life in
seclusion for so long that few of his fellow New Yorkers knew of
his financial operations, and his will created a sensation when
published. Except for establishing a trust fund with a $4,000 an-
nual income for Julia, who served as his executrix, and a few
small bequests, he left his stocks and bonds to the people of New
York for the establishment of a hospital "for the reception and relief of sick and diseased persons." The gift, one of the first large
philanthropic bequests made to the city, no doubt resulted from
James Henry's own sufferings which inspired sympathy for the
plight of others less able to obtain medical care than himself. He
had bequeathed the bulk of his real estate holdings, which were
primarily in New York City and Westchester County, to a
nephew, James Roosevelt Brown. When Brown died forty days
after James Henry, he willed the property to the institution en-
dowed by his uncle. The total amount received by the hospital
was in excess of $1 million—a sizable sum in those days.

Roosevelt Hospital, bounded by Fifty-eighth and Fifty-ninth
streets and Ninth and Tenth avenues, opened its doors on November 2, 1871, and is still in operation. Its founder is memori-

alized by a tablet placed on one of its walls inscribed: "To the memory of James Henry Roosevelt, a true son of New York, the generous founder of this hospital, a man upright in his aims, simple in his life and sublime in his benefaction." Throughout its long history, Roosevelt has been one of the city's leading hospitals. In 1978 it had a capacity of 583 beds and enjoyed a national reputation in the field of pediatric surgery and was a teaching facility for Columbia University's College of Physicians and Surgeons. To meet the spiraling cost of health care, it was to be merged with St. Luke's Hospital on the Upper West Side, although Roosevelt would retain its own buildings and identity.

Sometimes, when Franklin Roosevelt wished to tease his mother—"who took the ancestor business too seriously," according to his son, James—he would playfully refer to "my great aunt, Mother Seton" or her nephew, James Roosevelt Bayley, Catholic bishop of Newark and Archbishop of Baltimore. The old lady never seemed to realize that her leg was being pulled "and always rewarded him with the reaction he was striving for—an explosively reproachful exclamation of 'Oh, Franklin!'"

In point of fact the relationship between the Roosevelts and Elizabeth Ann Bayley Seton, canonized as St. Elizabeth Ann Seton by Pope Paul VI on September 14, 1975, is more tenuous than FDR would admit, but this link with the first American-born saint is something of an irony for a family considered the quintessence of the Protestant establishment.

Elizabeth Ann Bayley was born in 1774, the daughter of Dr. Richard Bayley and Catharine Charlton, whose father was an Episcopal clergyman. Dr. Bayley espoused the Loyalist cause at the time of the Revolution and served in the British army as a surgeon. When the British evacuated New York, he remained behind, and probably because of his skill as a physician was grudgingly accepted by his neighbors. He was named professor of anatomy and surgery at Columbia and was a pioneer pathologist. Later he became the first health officer of the Port of New York and almost single-handedly established a quarantine station on Staten Island. Little more than a year after the death of his first wife, in 1777, he married Charlotte Amelia Barclay, the daughter of Andrew Barclay and Isaac the Patriot's sister, Helena Roosevelt. Seven children were born to the couple, including a son named Guy Carleton in honor of his father's former commander.

In the meantime, Betsey Bayley, as the doctor's second daughter by his first wife was known, had become one of the city's most sought after young ladies. Rich, pretty, and protected, she led a gay life. Franklin Roosevelt once told an aide that his greatgrandfather, the much-wed James Roosevelt, had been in love with her. In 1794 she married William M. Seton, a wealthy young merchant with musical interests. He is said to have brought home from a lengthy European grand tour the first Stradivarius violin seen in the United States.‡ Betsey Seton had five children, but this did not keep her from being one of New York's liveliest hostesses and from taking up charity work. In 1797 she was one of the founders of the first charitable organization in the new nation, the Society for the Relief of Poor Widows and Small Children.

This life came to an end in 1803, when both her husband's health and business collapsed. The couple went to Italy, where William hoped to regain his strength, but he died soon after their arrival in Pisa. Family friends tried to persuade his widow to convert to Catholicism, but she resisted, saying, "I am laughing with God" at the attempts. Nevertheless, soon after her return to New York, Betsey joined the Roman Catholic Church, making her profession of faith in St. Peter's Church on Barclay Street on March 14, 1805. Her upper-class friends and relatives were aghast. Be a Quaker, be a Methodist, be anything but "a dirty, red-faced Catholic," one of them said. Anti-Catholic feeling was high in New York, and during the following year, a rioting mob broke into St. Peter's.

Abandoned by family and friends and after several efforts to support herself had failed, Mother Seton accepted an invitation from Archbishop John Carroll to come to Baltimore to open a school for girls. She conducted classes in a small house on Paca Street, and early in 1809, with four companions, formed a community called the Sisters of Charity of St. Joseph's, the first native American Catholic order. Later that year, they moved to Emmitsburg in western Maryland, where Mother Seton operated a school. Sixteen people crowded into a small stone house—their mattresses were secured in a cupboard during the day—but de-

‡ The Stradivarius was lost when a descendant left it on a train.

spite her poverty and other handicaps, she created a successful religious community. Today, it conducts a nationwide system of charitable and educational institutions, and has provided a rich legacy of social service. Although Mother Seton described herself as sometimes "petulant, restless and moody," she was compassionate and sympathetic. She died at Emmitsburg at the age of forty-six from tuberculosis. "I see death grinning in the pot every morning . . . and I grin back," she said. Following Mother Seton's death, her reputation for sanctity grew, and in 1907 her Cause for Canonization was introduced.

Mother Seton's vision had great influence on her nephew, James Roosevelt Bayley. He was the son of Dr. Guy Carleton Bayley, Mother Seton's half brother, who had turned to his mother's family when he sought a bride. He married Grace Roosevelt, James Roosevelt's daughter, and their first child, born in 1814, was christened at Trinity Church, with his grandfather, for whom he was named, serving as one of the witnesses. Dr. Bayley moved to Westchester soon after his son's birth, and the boy grew up in a house overlooking Long Island Sound. Like the young Roosevelts of later generations, he developed a love of the sea and at one time considered becoming a midshipman in the U. S. Navy. Later, he changed his mind, and entered Trinity College in Hartford, Connecticut, where he studied for the Episcopal priesthood.

Ordained in 1835 at the age of twenty-one, he was made rector of a parish church in Harlem, where his grandfather had had his farm. With his intelligence and family background, he was destined for advancement. But this was a period of upheaval in the Anglican communion. Inspired by the tracts of John Henry Newman and the example of his late aunt, the young man gave up the Episcopal Church in 1841 and went to Rome. A year later, he was received into the Catholic Church and like Newman, who had also been an Anglican churchman, became a priest. He always credited the prayers of Mother Seton for his conversion. Although most of his family accepted his conversion, his grandfather was so bitter that he cut Bayley out of his will, adding a codicil which read:

Whereas the said James R. Bayley, once a minister of the Gospel of the Protestant Church, has renounced the faith of his father, and is

now a priest in the Roman Church, and as I deem it neither just nor
right that any part of the property should be instrumental in building up a faith which I think erroneous and unholy, I do therefore
. . . annul and make void the aforesaid bequest and bequeath the
portion so given him by my last will and testament to the Union
Theological Seminary in the City of New York.

Father Bayley filed suit to have the codicil set aside but the
courts upheld it—and the $70,000 that would have been his share
of his grandfather's estate went instead to a Protestant seminary.

Meanwhile, his rise in the Catholic Church was as fast as it
probably would have been in the Anglican. Upon his return to
the United States he was named vice-president of the seminary at
Fordham, and in 1853, after less than a decade as a priest, was
consecrated first bishop of Newark. For twenty-eight years, he
served as spiritual leader of this diocese, which because of its
proximity to the Port of New York and the flood tide of German
and Irish immigrants, had begun to loom large in the affairs of
the Church. Throwing himself into his work, he built churches,
schools, and seminaries to meet the needs of his ever-increasing
flock.

In 1872 Bayley was named eighth Archbishop of Baltimore,
the primal see in the United States, and there was speculation
that he would soon receive the red hat of a cardinal. Commenting on these reports, the New York *Herald* remarked that it
would be "poetic fitness" if the first American cardinal should be
a Roosevelt. The archbishop had an imperial manner, it was said,
and the paper noted that while "his face is young compared with
that of many of his brethren in the episcopacy . . . it is full of
character and genius, the face of a bishop and a ruler—firm, kind,
strong, with a large head and an overhanging brow. . . ."

But his years in Baltimore were not happy ones. The major ac-
complishment of the period was the liquidation of the debt burdening the city's cathedral and its consecration. Interestingly
enough, this building was the work of Benjamin Latrobe, Nicholas J. Roosevelt's father-in-law. Nikolaus Pevsner, the architec-
tural historian, has called it a "bold and imaginative" structure
and "North America's most beautiful church." Archbishop
Bayley's health began to fail and Bishop James Gibbons of
Richmond was appointed coadjutor. Later, as Cardinal Gibbons,

he was a good friend of Theodore Roosevelt, and was well known to Franklin Roosevelt when he was in Washington as Assistant Secretary of the Navy. Franklin recalled that upon one occasion shortly after the cardinal had just returned from a visit to Rome, someone asked if he still believed in the infallibility of the Pope. "'Yes,' said His Eminence, with a twinkle in his eye, 'of course I believe in the infallibility of the Pope . . . I may say, however, that I saw the Holy Father many times and each time he called me Jibbons.'"

Archbishop Bayley retired to Newark, where he had spent his most productive years, and died there in 1877. He asked to be buried in Emmitsburg near his aunt, Mother Seton. They lie together in the vault of a little chapel in the oak-shaded cemetery—perhaps the most curious sprigs of the Roosevelt family tree.

Chapter X
MITTIE AND THEE

Christmas was still three days away but the Bulloch mansion at Roswell in the uplands of Georgia had already taken on a festive air. Gaily dressed women in swirling hoopskirts and men in swallowtail coats crowded the white-columned house for the social event of 1853—the marriage of Martha Bulloch to a handsome New Yorker named Theodore Roosevelt, father of the future President. Excited by the prospect of the wedding of "Miz Mittie," grinning black slaves jostled for position at the doors and windows. Just as evening fell, the bride, gravely radiant in a gown of white satin, descended the curving staircase carrying a small white prayer book given her by the groom. With a measured step, she entered the dining room, where an altar had been set up, and amid candlelight and flowers, the young couple were wed.

The courtship of Thee Roosevelt and Mittie Bulloch is the stuff of which romance is made. It began one night in 1850, when the youngest son of C. V. S. Roosevelt attended a dinner at the home of his oldest brother, Silas Weir Roosevelt. Among those present was Dr. Hilborne West, whose sister was Weir's wife. Dr. West had just returned from Roswell, where he had visited the family of his wife, the former Susan Elliott, the daughter of Mrs. James S. Bulloch by a previous marriage, and he entertained the company with stories about the plantation. Entranced by these romantic tales of a feudal way of life straight out of Sir Walter Scott's novels—a land of moonlight and magnolias and of chival-

Theodore Roosevelt (about twenty-two). Courtesy, Franklin D. Roosevelt Library.

Alice Lee Roosevelt (1861–84). Courtesy, Theodore Roosevelt Collection, Harvard College Library.

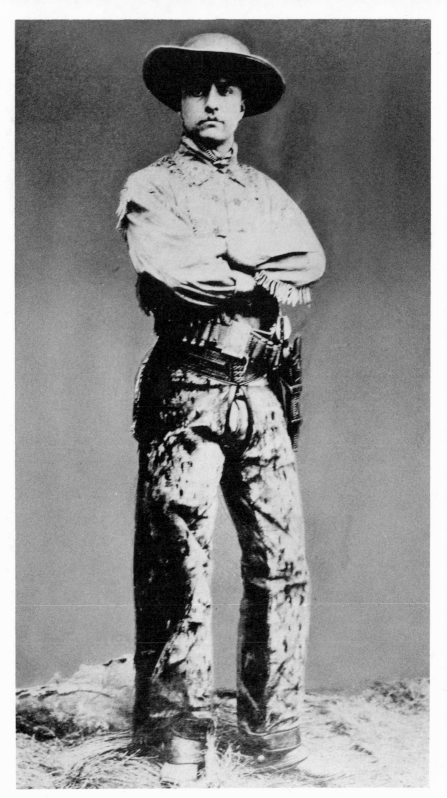

Theodore Roosevelt in the Badlands. Courtesy, Theodore Roosevelt Collection, Harvard College Library.

James Roosevelt (1828–1902). Courtesy, Franklin D. Roosevelt Library.

Rebecca Howland Roosevelt (1831–76).
Courtesy, Franklin D. Roosevelt Library.

)elano Roosevelt (1854–1941) as a
girl. Courtesy, Franklin D. Roose-
ibrary.

Franklin Roosevelt (aged five) with his mother. Courtesy, Franklin D. Roosevelt Library.

Harvard man. Franklin D. Roosevelt (1882–1945), aged twenty-one. Courtesy, Franklin D. Roosevelt Library.

Bamie Anna Roosevelt Cowles (1855–1931). Courtesy, Franklin D. Roosevelt Library.

rous men and beautiful women—Theodore asked Dr. West if he could arrange for him to visit the Bullochs.

The necessary invitations were secured, and later that year the young man set out for the South. At nineteen, Theodore Roosevelt was already a striking figure. Tall and with a leonine head, he had the natural grace of an athlete and the beginnings of a blond beard. Contemporaries credited him with all the best qualities of his family. Warm, humorous, and affectionate, he had a capacity for tenderness for those less fortunate than himself, which was to show itself in philanthropic and charity work. "No one in the world ever combined the same characteristics to the same degree," said his daughter, Anna, who like all his children, worshipped him. "He was a splendid business man, the most delightful, gay, young-hearted companion, the most stern as well as most loving of parents, and with an intense feeling of responsibility to mankind." Although he lacked a formal education, Theodore possessed intellectual curiosity, was an avid reader, and surrounded himself with stimulating people. He was an active partner in Roosevelt & Son, the thriving family glass-importing business now operated by his grimly serious brother, James Alfred, and like another brother, Rob, was interested in public affairs and philanthropy.

Theodore's appearance at Roswell created something of a stir. The letter announcing his intended date of arrival had gone astray and he appeared unexpectedly at the door one night. "The whole household was aroused by the ringing of the front doorbell," Anna recalled having been told by her mother. "All the negroes were off on a corn shucking at a neighbor's plantation" except for a child, "who having answered the doorbell, appeared before the startled group upstairs with a formal visiting card. All was immediately hospitable bustle, and he was made to feel more than welcome, and passed a most enchanting two weeks."

The Bullochs ranked among Georgia's first families. The founder of the line in America was Alexander Stobo, the Scots parson who along with his wife, Elizabeth, had survived the disastrous attempt to found a colony in Panama and had settled in Charleston, South Carolina. Their daughter, Jean, had married the Reverend James Bulloch and moved to Savannah. The most prominent of their descendants was Archibald Bulloch, a dele-

gate to the Continental Congress in 1775–76, and "president" or
governor of Georgia until his death in 1777. Not content with
civil leadership, he led the state's troops on a successful raid
against a British and Tory base on Tybee Island. His grandson,
James Stephens Bulloch, Mittie's father, was a planter, banker,
militia officer, investor in the company which built the *Savannah*,
the first steamship to cross the Atlantic, and deputy collector of
the Port of Savannah.

In 1840 he had moved to Roswell in the Georgia highlands,
about nineteen miles from what was to become the city of
Atlanta. Bulloch seems to have been propelled on his way by a
scandal. As a young man, he had courted a girl named Martha
Stewart, but teased by her friends about him and unsure of her
feelings, she put him off. Believing the rebuff final, Bulloch married Hester Elliott, the daughter of U. S. Senator John Elliott. A
week later, Martha Stewart married the senator, whom her father
wished her to wed, making her the stepmother-in-law of her former suitor. Senator Elliott died in 1827 and Hester not long afterward. In 1832 James Bulloch and Martha Stewart were finally
married—but the union offended the staid society of Savannah
and the couple eventually moved to Roswell to avoid gossip.
James built a handsome Greek Revival mansion on a hilltop,
which he called Bulloch Hall, where they entertained in lavish
style. In 1849, however, James died, leaving Martha with the care
of the plantation and a large brood of children. She had a son
and two daughters by her first husband; James had had a son in
his previous marriage, James D. Bulloch, an officer in the U. S.
Navy and later captain of a mail steamer owned by Howland &
Aspinwall; and together they had a son and two daughters—the
youngest of which was Mittie.

Young Theodore found life at Roswell enchanting. During the
day, he went riding across the plantation's broad acres or hunting, and at night there was a round of parties, dinners, dances,
and amateur theatricals. Sometimes the family gathered for a
musical evening which was later described by Anna Roosevelt:
"Aunt Annie Gracie and Mother sang together. Mother was a
charming alto and Auntie the soprano. Uncle Stewart played the
flute, and our uncle, Captain Bulloch, the violin. . . . None of
them had any particular education, but all of them had the most

delightful gifts. They were all good-looking, and all had entranc-
ingly stormy love affairs." Theodore found himself paying more
and more attention to Mittie, a vivacious fifteen-year-old blue-
eyed brunet with skin that "was the purest and most delicate
white, more moonlight-white than cream-white." She was a
spirited horsewoman and they often went riding together. When
he departed for New York, he took with him as a keepsake, a
gold thimble which she had given him. Behind him, he had left
his heart.

They did not see each other again until May 1853, when Mittie
visited the home of her half sister, Susan Elliott West, in Philadelphia, and Theodore stopped there upon returning from a business trip to Europe. Mittie also went to New York to stay with
Weir Roosevelt's family, and as Theodore later said, "those sofas
up at Mary's" became "almost sacred" because of the time he had
spent there with her. By the time Mittie returned to Georgia the
following month, Theodore had proposed and she had accepted
him. Separated by a thousand miles, the couple tried to draw
closer to each other through a steady stream of letters, the main
theme of which is a growing affection and devotion. Following a
brief visit to Roswell by Theodore when their engagement was
announced, Mittie wrote:

Thee, dearest Thee,
I promised to tell you if I cried when you left me. I had determined
not to do so if possible, but when the dreadful feeling came over me
that you were, indeed, gone, I could not help my tears from springing and had to rush away to be alone with myself. Everything now
seems associated with you. Even when I run up the stairs going to
my own room, I feel as if you were near, and turn involuntarily to
kiss my hand to you. I feel, dear Thee, as though you were part of
my existence, and that I only live in your being, for now I am
confident of my own deep love. . . .

Theodore, who was in the store on Maiden Lane when he received this letter, immediately pushed aside his work to answer:

I felt, as you recalled so vividly to my mind the last morning of our
parting, the blood rush to my temples and I had . . . to lay [your
letter] down for a few moments to regain command over myself. I
had been hoping against hope to receive a letter from you, but such

a letter. O, Mittie, how deeply, how devotedly I love; do continue to return my love as ardently as you do now, if possible learn to love me more; I know my love for you merits such a return. . . .

Following the wedding ceremony and a honeymoon trip, the young couple returned to New York to live in a high-stepped, solid-looking brownstone at 28 East Twentieth Street, just off Fifth Avenue near Gramercy Park. The gift of C. V. S. Roosevelt, it was six blocks north of his own mansion on Union Square, and in an area of measured affluence. Now restored to the way it appeared more than a century ago, the house has, despite the heavy brocade draperies, busy wallpaper, and horsehair sofas, an air of simplicity and serene gentility. C.V.S. had presented each of his sons a similar home upon their marriages, and Theodore's brother, Rob, lived next door in a house that was a duplicate of his own.

Robert Barnwell Roosevelt—he was actually christened Barnhill after his mother's family but the newspapers insisted on giving him a new middle name which he philosophically accepted—bounded into the carefully ordered world of the Oyster Bay Roosevelts like a star-spangled circus acrobat.* Flamboyant and energetic, he took life with a gusto that often astounded—and sometimes embarrassed—his relatives. Two years older than Theodore, he had studied law and had a successful practice but his interests ranged far beyond narrow legal precedents and dusty lawbooks. "Vigorous, lusty, vital, he was an Elizabethan survival in the Victorian era," observed his grandnephew, Nicholas Roosevelt. "Uncle Rob . . . cared little for the conventional and broadcast his thoughts to all who would read or listen to them."

Like an increasing number of sons of well-to-do families who did not have to work for a living, Rob followed the example set by the British upper class and devoted himself to public service. At one time or another—and usually at the same time—he was a sportsman, attorney, social reformer, political gadfly, congressman, diplomat, essayist, novelist, and conservationist. Although he is all but forgotten today, he was the founder of the

* According to a family tradition, Rob adopted a new middle name while still young because his friends teased him about being called "Barnhill."

American environmental movement and as the author of the legislation creating the U. S. Fisheries Commission, was considered
the American Izaak Walton. Until the advent on the national
scene, of his nephew Theodore, who very much resembled him in
style and thought, he was the most prominent Roosevelt of the
nineteenth century.

Partial owner and editor of the New York *Citizen*, the organ of
the reformist Citizens' Association, he helped lead the fight
against the Tweed Ring that had a stranglehold on the city in the
years immediately following the Civil War. Like most of the family, who had been Democrats before the war, Rob supported
Abraham Lincoln's efforts to preserve the Union, and served for a
few months in Washington with a New York Volunteer Regiment. He was a founder of the Loyal National League and of the
Union League Club, both of which performed important propaganda tasks for the war effort. Following Appomattox, however,
he had returned to the Democratic fold along with the Dutchess
County Roosevelts while most Oyster Bay Roosevelts remained
Republicans. But he was no loyal Tammanyite, for almost immediately he launched an unrelenting attack on the boodlers who
had control of the Hall and the city government.

If any American city ever belonged to one man, it was New
York during the heyday of William Marcy Tweed. Just how
much the Boss and his minions stole during their reign will probably never be known. Estimates range from a low of $20 million
to a high of $200 million, if fraudulent bonds are included. Under
Tweed's stewardship, the city's debt nearly tripled, from $34.4
million as of the end of 1869 to $97.2 million in September 1871.
During virtually the same period, the federal debt actually
declined by about $212 million.

Standing a hair under six-feet tall and weighing nearly three
hundred pounds, Big Bill Tweed commanded respect by his imperial presence. He sparkled and gleamed as he moved about,
weighed down with numerous diamonds and pieces of gold jewelry. Thomas Nast used his most prominent features, an egg-
shaped head and a long nose, to brilliantly caricature him as a
buzzard in the *Harper's Weekly*. The other members of the Ring
were Peter B. Sweeny, whose name was often printed in anti-
Tweed newspapers as "$weeny"; Abraham Oakey Hall, the "Ele-
gant Oakey" as he was known because of the magnificence of his

attire and manner; and "Slippery Dick" Connolly, who was so quick at figures that within a few years he ran the city comptroller's modest salary into a $6 million fortune.

To the Ring belongs the distinction of putting corruption on an orderly and businesslike basis. Before the rise of Tweed, municipal graft was hit or miss, but he rationalized the system. Everyone who wanted a contract with the city had to "kite" his bills by a fixed percentage and pay to the Ring the difference between what the job actually cost and the amount paid by the city. At first, the amount that these bills were to be padded was 55 percent. This was raised to 60 percent, and then to 65 percent. Tweed and his fellow Ring members were generous with charity, which, considering the amount of loot that they were reaping, they could well afford. During the savage winter of 1870, for example, when women and children were starving in the streets of New York, Tweed donated $50,000 to buy food for the poor. Others bought coal, although critics sniffed that few of the poor had cellars in which to put it. And long before Franklin Roosevelt created the New Deal, Tammany had its own social welfare programs. Hospitals, orphanages, homes for the aged, and religious institutions of all faiths participated in the Ring's largess. Over a three-year-period, the Catholic charities and schools received $1.4 million from the city's coffers; those of the Episcopal Church about $57,000; the Jews got $25,800; and the Methodists, $7,300.

But even if Tweed and his merry men stole from the rich and gave to the poor, they stole even more from the poor. A few dollars' worth of Christmas groceries or a bushel of coal did nothing to alleviate the condition of the poor. In fact, they suffered more from the plundering of the city than the rich. Foul, rat-infested slums, rotting, rickety tenements, garbage-filled streets, and crime and violence were of little concern to Tammany. Money appropriated for city services was plundered, and inspectors whose job it was to prevent such conditions were paid off.

Big-business men also did their share of bribing and corrupting city officials to get what they wanted. When Commodore Cornelius Vanderbilt, as the ex-ferryboat skipper now styled himself, wanted a traction franchise for a line running from the Battery to Forty-second Street, he was there with cash in hand. When William B. Astor wanted land he owned that was under water to be filled in by the city, he was also on Tweed's doorstep. They found it easy to do business with the Boss. With him in control, they had only to pay one large bribe and not a host of small ones. He suited their definition of an honest politician: When he was bought, he stayed bought. Recently some writers have challenged the conventional view of Tweed's activities, claiming that corruption was little worse than usual. They say reform politicians and former allies such as Samuel J. Tilden multiplied the Boss's sins to win control of the city and the state for themselves. There may be some truth in this, but there was still plenty to inspire geysers of indignation from Rob Roosevelt and his fellow reformers.

Tweed's masterpiece was the old New York County Courthouse in City Hall Park. When plans for the building were originally announced in 1858, the respectable sum of $250,000 was earmarked for the job. When finished in 1871, it had cost a phenomenal $13 million, enough to buy all of Alaska almost twice over. Carpets and shades alone cost $675,534.44 and thermometers, $7,500. The bills rendered by the contractors were, in Rob's words, "not merely monstrous, they are manifestly fabulous." In the end, these excesses helped destroy the Ring. During the summer of 1871, a disgruntled Tammanyite secretly copied all of the records regarding the construction of the courthouse and dropped these documents in the lap of Tweed's great enemy, the New York *Times*, which splashed them across its front page.

Supplied at last with documentary evidence of the Ring's depredations, the reformers called a mass meeting at the Cooper Union on the evening of September 4. As soon as the doors were opened, the hall was immediately packed by a dense throng, and thousands who were unable to get in milled about outside. They were whipped up into a frenzy by Rob Roosevelt and other speakers. Not only had the Ring looted the city treasury, it had "pulled away the very keystone of the arch of liberty," he declared. "If the public money is stolen, why not the public liberty, too?" Another speaker asked the rhetorical question, "What are we going to do about these men?" and the shouted answer came back: "Hang them! Hang them!"

Rob was appointed a member of the high-powered Committee of Seventy which broke the Ring's power and hounded Tweed from office in disgrace. He managed the successful mayoral campaign of William F. Havemeyer, the reform candidate, and himself went off to Washington as a reform congressman. There he helped expose the machinations of Alexander R. Shepherd, the head of a corrupt ring which had driven a horse and wagon through the treasury of the District of Columbia, ending popularly elected government for a century. But reform had little staying power. Reformers are "only morning glories," said George Washington Pluckett, a Tammany leader. Although they attacked corruption, the reformers did not provide a remedy that appealed to the average American. They were convinced that good government could be provided only by the "best" people—men like themselves—which left no place for the ordinary citizen. Havemeyer was defeated after one term—and in Washington the short-memoried citizens eventually erected a statue of Shepherd not far from the White House.

Rob Roosevelt's greatest contribution was in the field of conservation of the nation's natural resources. Today, when almost everyone is aware of the necessity to preserve the environment, it is difficult to envision the controversy that was aroused a century ago by any attempt to limit development or prevent the decimation of fish and wildlife. Since colonial times, Americans had been "boomers," who regarded the immediate and unlimited exploitation of natural resources as their democratic right. Rob was led by his early interest in hunting, fishing, and outdoor life to realize that if this policy of unrestrained growth was allowed to continue, it would result in the eventual destruction of certain species of game and fish by greedy and careless hunters and fishermen. Beginning in 1862, he wrote three books which attracted public attention to the cause: *Game Fish of the Northern States of America and British Provinces, Superior Fishing,* and *The Game Birds of the Coasts and Lakes of the Northern States of America.* These books launched the tradition of the hunter-naturalist, best personified by Rob's nephew, Theodore.

Almost single-handedly, Roosevelt persuaded the New York Legislature to create in 1867 a three-member State Fisheries Commission, the first of its kind in the nation. Because his fellow members were generally occupied with other tasks, he had for twenty years almost a free hand to put his theories into operation. Early settlers had found an abundance of shad and other fish in the Hudson River, but in recent years indiscriminate

fishing and the dumping of sewage and mill wastes had all but
depopulated it. Rob established hatcheries for the artificial prop-
agation of fish and tried to reduce water pollution. Not only did
he have to battle city officials and mill owners who took a public-
be-damned attitude, but he also ran up against the shad fishermen, who did not understand that his programs would be
beneficial to them in the long run.

To increase their catch, they used fine-mesh nets that prevented mature fish from ascending the river to their spawning
beds, endangering the species. Rob lobbied a bill through the
Legislature requiring wider mesh and for traps to be left open on
weekends during the spawning season, which angered the fishermen who felt the measure was depriving them of their livelihood.
His difficulties were compounded when the man placed in charge
of restocking the river announced that the program was aimed at
"making fish cheap" for the consumer. Hatching boxes began to
be mysteriously destroyed in the night and men hired to place
pans of impregnated spawn in the water often seemed to stumble
at the wrong moment, thereby ruining the operation. Moving
quickly to combat this guerrilla campaign, Rob won the fishermen over to his side by embarking on a tour of the river towns in
which he answered their questions, calmed their fears, and emphasized that an increased supply of fish would augment their in-
comes. Soon, his success was noticed in other states and in England, France, and Germany as well, which copied his methods.
When the British minister asked for information about the conservation program, Hamilton Fish, the Secretary of State, referred him to Rob, whom he jocularly called "the Father of all the
fishes."

Political reform may have failed to produce the changes that
Rob had hoped, but this did not cause him to abandon public
life. "Up guards and at 'em!" was his motto, and throughout his
long life—he died in 1906—he was always in the news. In 1879 he
was appointed one of the commissioners overseeing the construction of the Brooklyn Bridge, a post he held until 1881, when
he resigned with a blast against the mismanagement and delays
in completing the project. This was followed by a term as
member of the Board of Aldermen in which he secured passage
of a pure-food ordinance. He was an ardent supporter of Grover
Cleveland, and when the latter became the first Democrat to be

elected President since the Civil War, he offered Rob the office of subtreasurer. Roosevelt gratefully declined, but later accepted appointment as minister to Holland, serving at The Hague from 1888 to 1889.

During the Spanish-American War, he was still on the offensive against corruption in all its forms. Amid widespread reports that grafting contractors had supplied the troops with contaminated food and defective arms, he helped create a citizens' committee to search out the guilty parties and to make certain that they were punished after the war. Writing to the New York *Times,* he said:

> We all personally know of cases of the grossest neglect. I can quote several among my own friends or family. . . . In one case a Lieutenant Colonel [undoubtedly his nephew, Theodore] writes me that he has had nothing but hard tack and bacon since he has been before Santiago. Finally, he walked ten miles to get a package of rice and beans, but did not eat a grain of either. When he returned and saw how much more his men needed it than he did he divided it up among them. . . . If we cannot hang [the contractors responsible] let us expose them to public execration and send their names down through all time as the synonyms of infamy.

Somehow, Rob found the time to write sixteen books and tracts on a variety of subjects, to be a patron of the arts and music even though he was so tone deaf as to be unable to distinguish between "The Wearing of the Green" and "God Save the Queen." He was also something of a ladies' man and usually presented his conquests with a pair of green gloves. He is said to have bought them by the gross. Much sought after as a dinner speaker, he was said to possess "a surpassing command of irony, sarcasm and vitriolic inventive, combined with a powerfully paternal method of appealing to one's better nature." He was president of the Holland Society and vice-president of the Sons of the American Revolution, as well as treasurer of the Democratic National Committee and an often-mentioned presidential possibility.

And he was a champion letter writer, in an age in which letter writing was an art. Presidents, generals, admirals, politicians, editors, authors, poets, and actors were included among his wide circle of correspondents. Distinguished foreign visitors to New York

usually found a welcoming note from him at their hotel upon
their arrival along with a small gift. Even Oscar Wilde, who
delighted in poking fun at his American hosts, responded gracefully to Roosevelt's overtures.

Nevertheless, for all his success, Rob was denied the thing that
would have delighted him most—election as mayor of New York.
Tammany Hall would never support him because of his zeal for
reform, and the Republicans would not back him because he was
too loyal a Democrat. Although he was critical of the Republi-
canism of his nephew, who so resembled him in many other respects, he followed his career closely and journeyed to Washington to see him inaugurated in 1905. Shortly afterward, the
President wrote his "Dear Uncle Rob":

> It was peculiarly pleasant having you here. How I wish Father
> could have lived to see it too! You stood to me for him and for all
> that generation, and so you may imagine how proud I was to have
> you here.

Rob reciprocated by suggesting that the Democrats nominate
Theodore for President in 1908.

For a well-to-do young couple like Theodore and Mittie Roosevelt, life in midcentury New York was a pleasant round of calls
and parties. Still, Mittie was new to the city and the adjustment
may have been difficult after the free and easy life of Roswell,
but girls of her generation were expected to accept the unexpected without too much fuss. Besides, she was soon pregnant,
and the Roosevelt's first child, a daughter christened Anna, was
born January 7, 1885. She was known as Bamie, short for *bam-
bina*, and later as Bye because she was already on the move, but
she did not remain a child for long. Almost from birth, she
suffered "spinal trouble" which family tradition ascribed to her
having been dropped in the bath by a nurse. In reality, she may
have been the victim of an undiagnosed case of polio.

Bamie's earliest memories were of being carried in her father's
arms from the nursery to lie all day on a sofa in the rear room on
the second floor of the Twentieth Street house which had been
converted into a wisteria-covered open piazza. Although

harnessed in a "terrible instrument," she recalled this as "a period of great happiness." Each day she lay on the sofa, waiting for her father to return from work. "I would hear the click in the front door of his key, his quick, light step running up the stairs, and immediately into my room." He always brought ice cream or fruit or a trinket for his invalid daughter "and would frequently sit with me until I had my supper, and would then, with his very strong arms, quietly carry me into the nursery where I slept." Bamie's ordeal lasted until she was about four years old, when Theodore heard of a young physician named Dr. Charles F. Taylor, who had radical theories about orthopedics. He prescribed special exercises for the child and devised a lighter harness for her. Soon she was up and about, romping like any other playful young girl, and lived a remarkably active life. Although she always gave the impression of being slightly hunchbacked, her beautiful eyes and vivacity made everyone forget her handicap.

The affliction suffered by his firstborn had a profound effect upon Theodore. Writing to his wife of a visit to church while away on one of his many trips for the family business, he said: "A little child sat in our pew this morning that had lost one of its eyes. A person, evidently the father, was with it, and it was almost painful to see the way in which he took care of it. I could not help thinking all the time that this might be in store for us, too. Poor little thing, I never think of Bamie without pain." His daughter's suffering aroused his feeling of compassion for the unfortunate and channeled it in a direction that was to benefit mankind in general.

Experiments and research in orthopedics had developed in a haphazard fashion over the years and there was need for a place where sufferers could be treated and discoveries coordinated. Theodore decided that New York needed a hospital specializing in such cases and devoted all his efforts toward its founding. In the beginning, he could stir little interest among the city's affluent citizens. One afternoon he invited a number of friends to what was described as "a purely social reception," but once he had gathered them together, he unveiled the true purpose of the meeting. He had quietly brought a number of poor children suffering from orthopedic problems from their slum homes so his guests could see the graphic nature of the problem themselves. As his youngest daughter, Corinne, later recalled:

> The little sufferers were . . . laid upon our dining room table, with the steel appliances which could help them back to normal . . . on their backs and legs, thus ready to visualize to New York citizens how these stricken little people might be cured. He placed me by the table where the children lay, and explained to me how I could show the appliances and what they were supposed to achieve; and I can still hear the voice of Mrs. John Jacob Astor, as she leaned over one fragile-looking child and turning to my father, said, 'Theodore, you are right; these children must be restored and made into active citizens again, and I for one will help you in your work.' That very day, enough money was donated to start the first Orthopedic Hospital, in East 59th Street.

Over the years, Theodore's strong personal sense of obligation to society increased and ranged far afield. He was a founder of the Children's Aid Society, the State Charities Aid Association, and was a guiding force in the affairs of the YMCA. When he realized that the streets of New York were filled with abandoned and homeless children, he helped organize the Newsboys' Lodging House on West Eighteenth Street. He not only provided financial support and persuaded his friends to contribute—"All right, Theodore, how much is it this time?" they would say as he approached with a certain look in his eye—even more important he gave his time to counseling the boys and listening to their problems. As one friend said, "He literally went about doing good." He found foster homes for those that he could and dug into his own pocket to provide railroad fares home for runaways or for others to get a fresh start in the West. One lad who later became governor of Alaska observed that Theodore had picked him up "in the streets of New York, a waif and an orphan, and sent me to a Western family, paying for my transportation and early care. Years passed and I was able to repay the money which had given me my start in life, but I can never repay what he did for me. . . ."

One would have thought that these activities, along with his active role in Roosevelt & Son, would have been enough for any man, but Theodore was also a founder, trustee, and contributor to the Metropolitan Museum of Art and the Museum of Natural History. A convivial man who liked parties, balls, and pretty women, he and Mittie led a gay and active social life, and were known among Knickerbocker society for their open-handed generosity. There was nothing of the professional "do-gooder" about him, for he loved life and transmitted his infectious enthusiasm to all about him. "I can see him now," wrote a friend, "in full evening dress, serving a most generous supper to his newsboys in the Lodging House, and later dashing off to an evening party in Fifth Avenue." Bamie said that he was an excellent dancer who stayed on at balls so late that he was usually swept out with the debris. And his son, Theodore, remembered him as a "sport" who liked to drive a four-in-hand team with a verve that sometimes approached recklessness, and with the long tail of his linen duster bagging behind him like a balloon.

Theodore's philosophy seemed to be summed up in a letter written to Corinne on her birthday: "Remember that almost everyone will be kind to you and love you if you are willing to receive their love and are unselfish. This, you know, is the virtue that I put above all others and, while it increases so much the enjoyment of those about you, it adds infinitely to your own pleasure." How well he measured up to this precept can be judged by the comment of his famous son. "My father," he declared, "was the best man I ever knew."

Chapter XI
"WE THREE"

One evening in 1905, a group of friends were dining with Theodore Roosevelt, and the talk eventually turned to a discussion of which of them had known the President longest. The prize went to Morris K. Jesup, a New York banker and philanthropist, according to Henny Pringle, a Roosevelt biographer. He had visited the house on Twentieth Street a day or two after Roosevelt's birth on October 27, 1858, and had been taken into the nursery by the President's father. "You were in your bassinet making a good deal of fuss and noise for a youngster of your age," Jesup told Roosevelt. "Your father, however, lifted you out, and asked me to hold you."

"Was he hard to hold?" asked Elihu Root, the Secretary of State, amid a burst of good-natured laughter.

Unfortunately, young Theodore was probably all too easy to hold. The originator of the strenuous life was a delicate child, afflicted with terrifying attacks of asthma, poor eyesight, and a puny body. The story of his life is a struggle against physical infirmity—and this struggle had much to do with the making of his personality. Often, he would awaken in the middle of the night, struggling for breath. "One of my memories is of my father walking up and down the room with me in his arms," he wrote in his *Autobiography*, "and of sitting up in bed gasping, with my mother and father trying to help me." Sometimes a horse and rig were hastily summoned from a nearby livery stable, and young Theodore, wrapped in blankets and cradled on his father's lap, would be driven at a nightmare pace through empty city streets with the hope of forcing air into his straining lungs. He grew into a pale and wan boy, with prominent teeth and nearsighted blue eyes.

Yet, despite his poor health, Teedie, as he was known, was a happy, chattering, and curious child with an infectious grin. Soon he and Bamie were joined by a brother, Elliott, born in 1860, and a sister, Corinne, who was two years younger. Like the other Roosevelt children, they quickly received nicknames and were called Ellie and Conie. Corinne also suffered from asthma, so Elliott, as the huskiest and healthiest of the younger children, or "We Three" as they called themselves, became their natural leader. But Teedie managed to hold his own. Intellectually precocious, he was an avid reader, quickly developing a keen interest in natural history, and was a skillful storyteller and originator of exciting games. "We used to sit, Elliott and I, on two little chairs, near the higher chair which was his, and drink in these tales of endless variety," recalled Corinne. Usually, they were serials "which never flagged in interest for us, though sometimes [they] continued from week to week, or even from month to month."

Theodore Roosevelt, Sr., was the center of his children's world. "We used to wait in the library in the evening until we could hear the key rattling in the latch of the front hall, and then rush out to greet him," said his oldest son. "We would troop into his room while he was dressing, to stay there as long as we were permitted, eagerly examining anything which came out of his pockets which could be regarded as an attractive novelty." Morning prayers were a daily ritual and the three youngest children sat with their father on the sofa while he conducted the reading. Vying among each other, they sought the place between the elder Roosevelt and the sofa arm which was called the "cubbyhole" and was regarded as the seat of favor.

"We had a glorious childhood," wrote Bamie many years later, and much of the excitement was provided by Uncle Rob's wife, Aunt Lizzie, who lived next door. She kept "a perfect menagerie —guinea pigs, chickens, pigeons, everything under the sun that ought not to have been kept in a house." When she decided she wanted a cow in the backyard, "the cow with great effort was persuaded down the basement steps, through the hall, and out into the yard. Of course, it had no sooner arrived than the entire neighborhood rose in arms and had them threatened with legal action unless the cow was at once removed. This proved an almost impossible deed to accomplish, for the frightened creature refused absolutely to enter the house again, and finally it had to have its legs bound partly together and its eyes blindfolded, and then be dragged out."

Aunt Lizzie also kept a monkey named Topsy, which she insisted on dressing as if it were a child, down to a shirt with studs and trousers. Topsy bit Bamie one day, and escaping his pursuers, climbed atop a wardrobe and tore off all his garments in a rage and threw them on the floor, except for his trousers. Unable to pull his tail through them, the monkey angrily tore at them in frustration. "I can remember as if it were yesterday lying on the bed and ceasing to feel my wounds while giggling with laughter at the appearance of Topsy dancing up and down trying to get his tail out of his trousers," said Bamie.

Upon one occasion, Teedie imitated the monkey, biting Bamie on the arm—and receiving his first and only spanking. Ordinarily, the senior Roosevelt did not have to resort to threats or physical punishment to keep his high-spirited brood in order; a word of caution or a stern glance was usually enough. "Perfectly conscious that I had committed a crime," Teedie sought security under a kitchen table. When his father reached under it to drag him out, the panic-stricken child grabbed a handful of bread dough from the tabletop and hurled it at him. He was halfway up the stairs when he was caught and given the punishment that the crime deserved, despite Bamie's pleas for Papa to desist because the bite hadn't really hurt her.

Just as contemporary small boys are excited by outer space, children of the Victorian age, inspired by the discoveries of Darwin, were fascinated by natural history and zoology. Teedie's interest in the subject began when he was seven years old. Sent to buy strawberries for the family breakfast at a market on Broadway, he found a seal that had been killed in New York Harbor laid out on display. "The seal filled me with every possible feeling of romance and adventure," he recalled. Having already read a few books for boys on natural history, he haunted the market until the seal was removed. He made careful measurements of the corpse and was given the seal's skull, which became the centerpiece of what "We Three" called the "Roosevelt Museum of

Natural History." Teedie also embarked on a natural history of his own, "written down in blank books in simplified spelling." The collection was first kept in his room, but following a rebellion by a chambermaid, was removed to a bookcase in a rear hall.

Encouraged by his mother and father in his new interest—"as they always did in anything that could give me wholesome pleasure or help develop me"—Teedie expanded his zoological activities and took up taxidermy, adding formaldehyde and arsenic to the melange which terrified the servants. He was also given a small-caliber gun and on the family's trips to the country tried to bag animals and birds for his collection. This led to the discovery of his nearsightedness. Finding that his companions often took aim at targets that he couldn't even see, "I spoke of this to my father, and soon afterwards, got my first pair of spectacles, which literally opened up an entirely new world to me," he said. "I had no idea how beautiful the world was until I got those spectacles."

The coming of the Civil War cast a dark shadow over this happy family circle. Like the nation, the residents of the Twentieth Street house were divided. Following the birth of her children, Mittie's health, never robust, wilted into a languid though decorative decline. She found it impossible to manage money and developed a perpetual tardiness that made her late for everything. Her mother and sister, Anna, came to New York to manage the household and stayed on through the war, with Anna serving as the children's tutor. The three Georgia-born women formed a united front of staunch Confederate sympathizers among the Roosevelts, who supported the Union. Like most New York businessmen who had commercial contacts in the South, Theodore had deplored the drift toward war, but once it came, he and his family loyally supported the Union. With her brother and two stepbrothers fighting for the South—James and Irvine Bulloch served in the Confederate Navy and Stewart Elliott fought with Lee's army—Mittie refused to attend the regular Saturday night dinners and other affairs held at the home of her father-in-law on Fourteenth Street, where pro-Union sentiment was strong.

The younger children were oblivious to their mother's anxieties. In fact, Teedie paraded up and down the nursery in a miniature uniform of the New York Zouaves to triumphantly celebrate

Union victories. Bamie, however, was old enough to sense that something was amiss and later told a friend how unhappy those years had been for her mother. "I know the Roosevelts and I should hate to have married into them at that time unless I had been one with them in thought," she said. "They think they are just, but they are hard in a way."

Influenced by his wife's protestations that it would kill her if he joined the Union Army and fought against her brothers, Theodore agreed, against his better judgment, not to volunteer for military service. "Always afterward," reported Bamie, "he felt he had done a wrong thing in not having put every other feeling aside to join the fighting forces." There is evidence that in later years, young Theodore felt that in this one case his beloved father had let him down. Corinne believed that his own determination to make a military reputation was "in part compensation for an unspoken disappointment in his father's course in 1861." None of the Roosevelt brothers joined the Army, although all were of military age. Instead, like many well-to-do men, they paid substitutes to shoulder muskets in their place.

The only member of the family who appears to have actually experienced combat was George Washington Roosevelt, a cousin from an obscure Pennsylvania branch, who enlisted in the Union Army at the age of seventeen. He lost a leg at Gettysburg, was promoted from sergeant to captain, and was given the Congressional Medal—a decoration more commonly awarded then than now. Unable to return to the front because of his wounds, Cousin George helped raise and train a fresh company of volunteers. Following the war, he received a political sinecure in the consular service and was consul at Auckland, New Zealand, Matanzas, Cuba, and Bordeaux, France. As consul general in Brussels, where he died in 1907, he became an intimate friend of King Leopold, who was fascinated by the old soldier's inexhaustible fund of Civil War tales.

In his relief work in the slums, Theodore discovered that the rapid mobilization of the Union Army had left many of the soldiers' families destitute because no arrangement had been made for them to receive part of the serviceman's pay. Quickly devising a scheme for voluntary allotments, he went to Washington to lobby for passage of the enabling legislation. Through the influence of his friend, John Hay, one of President Lincoln's secretaries, he secured the support of the administration and became a friend of the President and Mrs. Lincoln. The First Lady, who spelled his name "Rosevalt," often invited him to go riding with her in the countryside around Washington and even sought his opinion when she went to buy new bonnets.

Obtaining congressional support for the allotment plan was far more difficult. It required considerable skill on Theodore's part to persuade the suspicious members that he sought no gain from the proposal and it was being put forward solely for the benefit of the troops and their families. Finally, after several months of persuasion, the law was passed and Theodore was appointed one of three allotment commissioners designated to administer the plan and persuade the soldiers to join it. This proved to be far more difficult than it sounded. The troops were suspicious and there was strong opposition from the sutlers, who had purchased licenses to operate the modern equivalent of post exchanges—which included saloons and sometimes brothels.

For the next year, Theodore spent most of his time away from home, visiting divisions, regiments, companies, and platoons, mostly on horseback and in the worst weather, and serving without pay. He probably saw more of army life than many of the men actually in the service. Through constant practice, he developed a sales pitch designed to persuade men to sign up. "I had three companies formed into the three sides of a square and used all my eloquence," he wrote to Mittie of one appeal. "When I had finished, they cheered me vociferously. I told them I would be better able to judge who meant their cheers by seeing which company made the most allotments, and raised a spirit of competition in this way that made the rolls the best we had taken during the day."

Out in the field one night, taking down by candlelight the names of the men who had agreed to make allotments, he wrote: "I could not help thinking what a pretty subject for a painting it would make, as I stood out there in the dark night surrounded by the men with one candle just showing glimpses of their faces, the tents all around us in the woods. One man, after putting down $5.00 a month, said, 'My old woman has always been good to me and if you please, change it to $10.00.' In a minute, half a dozen others followed his example and doubled theirs."

Theodore referred only rarely to the differences between himself and his wife. On New Year's Day 1862, he wrote: "I do not want you not to miss me but remember that I would never have felt satisfied with myself after this war is over if I had done nothing, and that I do feel now that I am doing my duty. I know you will not regret having me do what is right, and I do not believe you will love me any the less for it." For her part, Mittie kept her anxieties to herself, and her letters are filled with details of life at home. "Teedie came down stairs this morning looking rather sad, and said 'I feel badly—I have a tooth ache in my stomach. . . .' He is the most affectionate and endearing little creature."

Wisely, Mittie did not tell him that she and her sister and mother, although surrounded by Yankees, covertly kept up their contacts with the Confederacy. Periodically, they prepared parcels of medicine, clothing, and money that were smuggled to their friends in the South. Teedie or Bamie would be taken on a picnic in Central Park, where the parcels would be turned over to couriers who had no trouble in running the blockade. There were also meetings arranged through innocent-seeming newspaper advertisements with mysterious strangers who brought letters from Uncle Jimmie and other relations. "One of my most vivid memories were the days of hushed and thrilling excitement, which only occurred when Father was away," said Bamie. "Grandmother, Mother and Aunt Annie would pack a box, while . . . Theodore and I helped, not knowing at all what it was about, except that it was a mystery and that the box was going to run the blockade. Our favorite game for years afterward, needless to say instigated by Theodore, was one of 'running the blockade' over the bridge in Central Park, in which I was the blockade runner, and he was the Government boat that caught me."

James D. Bulloch was the chief of the Confederate Secret Service in Europe—but there was little that was secret about his mission. Immediately after he landed in England, it was widely known that his task was to either purchase or build Confederate commerce raiders. A bold and skillful manipulator, he played a game of cat and mouse with Charles Francis Adams, the American minister in London. The most famous of these raiders was the *Alabama.* To prevent Adams from having the vessel seized by the British authorities while she was under construction, Bulloch registered her as the merchantman *Enrica*, and at the end of July 1862, took her to sea on what was to be a trial run. A gay party of ladies and gentlemen were invited to see her put through her paces—and then were brought back to Liverpool on a tender while Bulloch sailed the vessel to the Azores for a rendezvous with a supply ship carrying cannon and other equipment. Most of the preliminary work required to fit her with her armament had already been made, such as the cutting of gunports and the placing of heavy ring bolts in the deck, so the work of turning her into a warship was completed in a few days. On August 24, 1862, Captain Raphael Semmes raised the Confederate flag over his new command and placed her in commission as the *Alabama*.

Bulloch, who had returned to England, had done his work well. Manned by a crew of hard-bitten English and Irish seamen led by southern officers, including sixteen-year-old Irvine Bulloch who served as a midshipman, the *Alabama* ranged over the high seas for nearly two years. She played havoc with Yankee commerce, appearing ghostlike off the Newfoundland Banks, in the Caribbean, off the Cape of Good Hope, and in East Asian waters. In the course of her rovings, she captured sixty-five merchant vessels, valued at over $5 million, and sank a Yankee gunboat in the Gulf of Mexico. The *Alabama* received many courtesies from friendly officials in English ports around the world, a fact that was galling to Yankee skippers sent in pursuit of the raider and stuck in the memory of the American people. After the war, Britain had to pay $15.5 million to settle claims arising from the damage done by the various British-built cruisers.

The *Alabama* was finally brought to bay in the English Channel off Cherbourg, France, on June 19, 1864, and sunk after a desperate duel with the U.S.S. *Kearsarge*. Irvine Bulloch was said to have fired the raider's last, defiant shot before her crew abandoned her. Along with Captain Semmes, he was picked up by the *Deerhound*, an English yacht that had crossed the Channel to watch the fight, and they were spirited off to safety in Britain. Forgetting his own pro-Union sympathies, Theodore Roosevelt was to turn this incident into a political asset when he campaigned through the South forty years later. "One would suppose that the President, himself, fired the last two shots from the *Alabama* instead of his uncle," wrote a Washington *Star* reporter. "Mr. Roosevelt's relationship with a Confederate officer is accepted as practically equal with having fought for the cause, himself."

The elder Roosevelt, having completed his work as an allotment commissioner—and having received the thanks of the New York Legislature for his work—stayed closer to home but did not cease his good works. He helped organize the Protective War Claims Association which saved the families of soldiers with claims against the government millions of dollars in fees which grasping agents tried to extract from them. And when the war was over, he aided crippled veterans in finding work through a Soldier's Employment Bureau. This organization, said one observer, did "more, and vastly better, work than all the Soldiers' Homes combined." Theodore also began to take his children on his round of charitable visits to the Newsboys' Lodging Home, Miss Slattery's Night School for Italian children, and various hospitals in which he had an interest and they were required to lend a helping hand.

Life was hectic in the Roosevelt household. "Generally . . . Saturdays commenced by a ride on horseback in the Park, followed instantly . . . by a visit of inspection to both the Art Museum and the Museum of Natural History, and then to some one of the Children's Aid Society schools," according to Bamie. "We would get home for lunch very late, and as a rule would find whoever was most interesting of the moment in New York lunching with us. By the time that was over, we either drove in the Park, or visited a hospital." Inspired by his father's example, young Theodore taught a mission class for three years before going to Harvard and for all four years he was in college. "I do not think I made much of a success of it," he acknowledged later on.

Along with Confederate President Jefferson Davis, James and Irvine Bulloch were among the few southerners who were not granted amnesty following the Civil War, and they took refuge in England. Mittie, whose mother had died in 1864 at about the time that the family plantation at Roswell was sacked by Sherman's army on its march through Georgia,* longed to see her

---

* Bulloch Hall survived, however, and in 1978, the restored mansion, now owned by the city of Roswell, was opened to the public. Local legend has it that Margaret Mitchell, who visited the place as a newspaper reporter, used it as a model for Tara in Gone With the Wind.

brothers, and in 1869, persuaded her husband to take the family abroad. The trip was also designed to provide a change of atmosphere for Teedie, still wracked by chronic asthma—"asmer" as he put it in his own version of phonetic spelling—and to find a suitable finishing school for fifteen-year-old Bamie.

Besides visiting England for the family reunion, the Roosevelts went on a year-long Grand Tour of Europe which took them to Scotland, Belgium, Holland, France, where Mittie and Bamie explored the shops of Paris, and on to Switzerland, Germany, and Italy, where they spent Christmas amid the grandeur of Rome. For "We Three," however, the trip was a bore. They missed their usual summer vacation in the country and were not interested in museums and cathedrals. "I did not think I gained anything from this particular trip abroad," Teedie later wrote. "I cordially hated it, as did my brother and sister." Nevertheless, according to a letter to a playmate, Edith Kermit Carow, he seemed to have had a marvelous time making an ascent of Vesuvius in which "the smoke nearly suffacated [sic] us." After careful inquiry, Theodore left Bamie at a school operated by Marie Souvestre, a remarkable Frenchwoman, at Fontainebleau, outside Paris, and the rest of the family returned home.

When Teedie's asthma continued unabated, his father took him aside one day for a man-to-man talk and said: "Theodore, you have the mind but you have not the body, and without the help of the body the mind cannot go as far as it should. You must *make* your body." And as Corinne reported, her eleven-year-old brother looked up and "with a flash . . . of white teeth" accepted the challenge. "*I'll make my body,*" he replied earnestly. The porch off the nursery was converted into a gymnasium complete with all kinds of athletic equipment and Teedie's sister wrote that "for many years one of my most vivid recollections is seeing him between horizontal bars, widening his chest by regular, monotonous motion—drudgery indeed—but drudgery which eventuated his being not only the apostle but the exponent of the strenuous life." Already, life was an unrelieved if joyous struggle.

Tutored at home, first by his Aunt Annie and then by a French governess, Teedie was spared the taunts of other youngsters because of his spindly appearance and his studious manner. One summer, however, having suffered a severe attack of asthma, he was sent to a camp at Moosehead Lake in the Adirondacks. On the stagecoach ride, he encountered two boys of his own age "but very much more competent and also much more mischievous." They proceeded to make life miserable for him and when he finally decided to fight them, "I discovered either one singly could not only handle me with easy contempt but handle me so as not to hurt me much." With his pride injured, Teedie resolved not to let this happen again. When he returned to New York, he persuaded his father to allow him to take boxing lessons. He worked out with John Long, an ex-prizefighter known to the elder Roosevelt, and although he regarded himself as a "painfully slow and awkward pupil," developed what Carleton Putnam, has described in his first-rate biography "the fighting instincts which were to dominate his character."

In 1871 the firm of Roosevelt & Son fulfilled the last of its large contracts—the replacement of the plate glass destroyed by the Chicago fire with W. Emlen Roosevelt being sent there to represent the firm—and faced with domestic competition went out of the glass importing business. Under the shrewd direction of Theodore Roosevelt's older brother, James Alfred Roosevelt, it became a leader in investment banking, particularly in selling the bonds of expanding American industries in the European market. James Alfred helped finance the transatlantic cable and was a close friend and business associate of James J. Hill, the railroad magnate, a tie that was to prove paradoxical when his nephew, Theodore, became President, and attacked the trusts created by Hill. James Alfred was selective in his clientele, however, and is said to have personally thrown the Mephistophelian Jay Gould bodily out of his office at 30 Pine Street. While his brothers Rob and Theodore were active in politics and philanthropy, James Alfred lived for business. He succeeded his father, C. V. S. Roosevelt, on the Board of Directors of the Chemical Bank; served as president of the Broadway Improvement Company, the family real estate holding company, and was a director of the New York Life Insurance Company and the Delaware and Hudson Canal Company, whose vice-president was another James Roosevelt, this one Dr. Isaac Roosevelt's oldest son.†

Having finished with the Chicago glass project and been appointed American commissioner to the Vienna Exposition of

† James Alfred Roosevelt was the ultimate commuter. In 1898 he died on the 4:32 Long Island train to Oyster Bay.

1873, Theodore Roosevelt again took his family abroad to await the completion of a new home at 6 West Fifty-seventh Street. The area around the house of Twentieth Street was rapidly going commercial and the old house was too small, so with a characteristic Rooseveltian eye on future real estate values, he chose a site for his new house north of the current center of fashion. The tour began with a houseboat voyage of about six hundred miles up the Nile, and Teedie was enchanted by the experience. "I think I have enjoyed myself this winter more than ever before," he wrote Edith Carow.

His health had improved dramatically, his asthma attacks were less frequent, and even his father was amazed at his energy as they tramped along the riverbank hunting specimens for the "Roosevelt Museum." "He is the most enthusiastic sportsman and infused some of his spirit into me," said the elder Roosevelt, who was hard put to keep up with his energetic fourteen-year-old son. Throughout the rest of the trip which took the family to the Holy Land, Turkey, and Hungary before their arrival in Vienna, Teedie was absorbed in skinning and stuffing his bag. Elliott, who roomed with him, complained in vain about having to share quarters with partly dissected specimens and noxious chemicals that almost poisoned him. Finding a snake under his brother's bed, Elliott drew a chalk line down the center of the room and declared no trespassing beyond it would be allowed.

Teedie, Elliott, and Corinne spoke French but did not know German, so their parents decided to leave them for a few months with a family in Dresden so they could pick up the language while the finishing touches were put on their new home. Theodore returned to New York to help steer the family business safely through the financial panic of 1873, while Mittie took the waters at Carlsbad. Along with a handful of other homesick expatriate children, "We Three" organized the Dresden Literary American Club, where they read stories and poetry which they had written when the boys were not battering each other with boxing gloves their father had sent them. Teedie cultivated the look of a German student, wearing his blond hair long, and as he put it, "learned a good deal of German . . . in spite of myself." He also came away with a favorable impression of the German people which lasted until World War I.

Bamie returned with them to the house on Fifty-Seventh Street after several years of absorbing Mademoiselle Souvestre's courses in history, politics, and literature. Because of the increasing vagueness of their mother, she took over the management of the household. Mittie now found it almost impossible to keep appointments. Invited out to tea or other social events, she would sometimes spend so much time trying to make up her mind what to wear that it was too late to go. Often, a carriage would be summoned and then left standing in the street for hours until it had to be dismissed. Mittie also developed a phobia about cleanliness and had everything draped with sheets. Nevertheless, her husband and children accepted the foibles of their "dear little Motherling" in an affectionately protective way.

In addition to moving to the new house in town, Theodore also decided to join the family colony at Oyster Bay, and rented the same house overlooking Long Island Sound that his father had rented. To the amusement of his friends, he called it "Tranquillity" because its white-pillared portico reminded him of the Bulloch house at Roswell. "Anything less tranquil than that happy home . . . could hardly be imagined," said Corinne, who dubbed Oyster Bay "The Happy Land of Woods and Waters." Overrun with friends and cousins, the place was always bubbling with activity. The children swam and rowed, hunted and explored the woods and shoreline on foot and horseback—and as usual, Teedie was the leader. Sometimes he went up to the crest of Sagamore Hill, named for the Indian chief Sagamore Mohannis, and declaimed poetry into the wind at the top of his voice. Looking back on those days from old age, a friend said that the characteristic she most remembered about him "was the unquenchable gaiety which seemed to emanate from his whole personality. . . . As a young girl I remember dreading to sit next to him at any formal dinner lest I become so convulsed with laughter at his whispered sallies as to disgrace myself and be forced to leave the room."

When Teedie turned sixteen, his father decided that unlike himself, his eldest son should attend college, and breaking with the family tradition that Roosevelts attended Princeton or Columbia, earmarked him for Harvard. Teedie's education, however, had been spotty. Although he was an acknowledged expert in natural history, spoke French and German, and his mind was a storehouse for an enormous collection of facts that he had picked

up in his omnivorous reading, he couldn't spell and was abysmal
at any sort of mathematical reasoning. So a tutor named Arthur
Cutler was secured, and for the next two years, Teedie divided
his time between improving his body and his mind. In September
1876 he entered Harvard, a tanned young man with long sideburns and a spindly frame that belied his vigor and zest for life.

Harvard Yard was unprepared for Theodore Roosevelt, Jr., as
he styled himself. With a student body of 821, the college prided
itself on its languor. Undergraduates favored a "Harvard drawl"
that was almost a yawn, walked in a "Harvard swing" that
resembled a shamble, and professed disdain of any form of enthusiasm. Henry Adams, who resigned as a history instructor the
year after Roosevelt's arrival at Cambridge, described his students as "ignorant of all that men had ever thought and hoped,"
although he grudgingly acknowledged "their minds burst open
like flowers at the sunlight of a suggestion." One of the few
places where Harvard men allowed their reserve to slip was in
raucous behavior at the "girlie" shows at the Globe Theater. Arriving in Cincinnati after a harrowing stand in Boston, the head
of one troupe of dancers is supposed to have nervously inquired:
"Is there a university here?"

Young Theodore—he was only called Teddy by the family
when a young man—was so buoyant that in the beginning he was
regarded by his classmates as something of an eccentric, a view
compounded by his odd, squeaky voice and thick glasses. "It was
not considered good form to move at more than a walk, [but]
Roosevelt was always running," said one Harvard contemporary.
Foreshadowing the President who regarded the White House as
"a bully pulpit," he already loved to argue and exhort. "He used
to stop men in the Yard or call them to him," according to another friend. "Then he would block the narrow gravel path and
soon make sparks from an argument fly. He was so enthusiastic
and had such a startling array of deeply rooted interests that we
all thought he would make a great journalist." In class, Theodore
had a tendency to interrupt professors with questions, especially
in natural history, which was his favorite course. Upon one occasion, the lecturer became so exasperated that he cried: "Now look
here, Roosevelt, let me talk! I'm running this course!"

When he enrolled at Harvard, Theodore had the vague notion

of becoming a naturalist. Pointing out that such a career would be ill paid, his father offered to support him in this ambition *"if I intended to do the very best work there was in me;* but I must not dream of taking it up as a dilettante. Harvard emphasized laboratory work while Theodore was more interested in field work, so over the years he gradually lost interest in making science his career. Still, Theodore enjoyed himself at Cambridge. "What a royally good time I am having," he confided to his diary during his junior year. In those subjects that interested him—natural history, history, political economy, and literature—he did well and was tapped for Phi Beta Kappa when he graduated in 1880. Having become interested in the naval side of the War of 1812, and finding no adequate book on the subject, he had with characteristic vigor started work on one of his own.

Theodore served as editor of the *Advocate,* one of the student publications, was a nonsinging member of the Glee Club, and active in the Natural History and Finance clubs, although his knowledge of economics remained shaky throughout his life. Too light for football or crew, he became known as a boxer, reaching the finals in the lightweight division during his junior year. Asthma was less of a problem and during vacations he went on rugged camping trips and mountain-climbing expeditions. When his fellows learned to take his eccentricities in stride, he did rather well socially, too. He was secretary of the Hasty Pudding Club, and a member of Porcellian, the most exclusive of Harvard's clubs. As a New York aristocrat, he had ready access to the best homes of Boston and suburban Chestnut Hill, and became a familiar figure at dinner parties, dances, and picnics given for the younger set. "He danced just as you'd expect him to dance if you knew him," said one debutante. "He hopped."

Later, Theodore was critical of the education that he had received at Cambridge. "There was very little in my actual studies which helped me in after-life," he declared. "There was almost no teaching of the need for collective action, and of the fact that in addition to, not as a substitute for individual responsibility, there is a collective responsibility." His education had exalted the individual who had no duty "to join with others in trying to make things better for the many by curbing the abnormal and excessive development of individualism in a few." The result was "acquiescence in a riot of lawless business individualism which would be quite as destructive to real civilization as the lawless military individualism of the Dark Ages." It is doubtful, however, that such liberal views coincided with his thinking when he was a student at Harvard.

In the meantime, Elliott had been sent at his request to boarding school at St. Paul's in Concord, New Hampshire, where at first he did well. "I think all my teachers are satisfied with me," he wrote his father in September 1875. But soon, he began to complain of excruciating head pains which led to his withdrawal from school. No cause could be found. Some doctors suspected epilepsy but there was no family history of such attacks; others have since suggested that the illness may have been psychosomatic because the seizures occurred when Elliott was faced with challenges he believed he could not meet. Convinced that physical infirmities could be overcome by an active outdoor life, the elder Roosevelt sent Elliott to stay with one of his friends, an officer at the army post at Fort McKivett in the Texas hill country. There, he rode, shot, and hunted, and his head pains disappeared. But all plans for the boy to follow a systematic program of reading and study also vanished with them.

The senior Roosevelt's own life also underwent a change. For the first time, he accepted an active role in politics. Like many men of his class, he had always regarded politics as "a dirty business," but he overcame his misgivings to help further the cause of civil service reform. Today, when the civil service at all levels is under attack for gross inefficiency and a lack of responsiveness, it is difficult to recall the incandescent passions stirred a century ago by the fight for reform and the simple faith of liberals in its all-encompassing benefits. With an evangelical fervor worthy of the medieval crusaders, they believed that politics would be purified and the temptations of office removed by merely ending the spoils system. The cause of civil service reform took on some of the abolitionist zeal of the previous generation, and among its most surprising supporters was President Rutherford B. Hayes. Known to detractors as "Rutherfraud," he had come to power in 1877 as a result of what may well have been the first stolen presidential election in American history.

One of the bitterest political struggles of the Gilded Age was touched off when Hayes moved to take control of the New York

Customs House, which had long been a cornucopia of graft. The President had two reasons for this action: Businessmen had steadily complained about the scandalous conditions there and it was a way of striking back at Senator Roscoe Conkling, New York's Republican boss, who controlled patronage at the Customs House and had failed to support Hayes during the election. The President demanded the resignation of Chester A. Arthur, one of Conkling's lieutenants, and nominated Theodore Roosevelt, Sr., as collector in his place. Undaunted, "Lord Roscoe" took up the challenge and the nation was treated to the spectacle of a leading Republican senator fighting an appointment made by his own party's President. Theodore was caught in the middle in this battle of titans. Through senatorial courtesy, which customarily gives a senator a veto over federal appointments in his state, Conkling eventually managed to block Roosevelt's nomination.

Before his name could be resubmitted, Theodore was dead. Taken sick with what was later diagnosed as intestinal cancer, he died on February 10, 1878. He was only forty-six years old, and the family believed his illness was aggravated by the political rebuff. The seriousness of his father's illness was kept from the younger Theodore so as not to interfere with his studies, and the burden fell upon Elliott. For weeks, he hardly left his father's room. "Elliott gave unstintingly a devotion which was so tender that it was more like that of a woman and his young strength was poured out to help his father's condition," wrote Corinne. Throughout the rest of his life, Elliott was haunted by his father's agonized "cries for ether" and the mercy of "a chloroform sleep." When the news that he was dying spread, the street in front of the Roosevelt home was crowded with silent men, women, and children. "Newsboys from the West Side Lodging House, little Italian girls from his Sunday-school class, sat for hours on the stone steps," Corinne recalled. And almost the entire city joined in mourning the man described by the New York *World* as "Eyes to the Blind, Feet to the Lame, Good to All."

Young Theodore, his father's favorite, was overcome with grief. "I feel that if it were not for the certainty . . . that 'he is not dead but gone before,' I should almost perish," he wrote in his diary. "With the help of my God I will try to lead such a life as he would have wished."

Chapter XII
SALLIE AND JAMES

High on the bluffs just south of the village of Hyde Park where
the lordly Hudson River makes a slight bend to the east known as
Crum Elbow, there stood in 1880 a large red clapboard house
with scrollwork porches, tinted windows, and a three-story tower.
Early on the morning of May 7, James Roosevelt, master of the
manor of Springwood, was impatiently pacing his veranda. Periodically, he took out his gold watch, consulted it, and then
snapped the case closed. Normally unruffled, James, a poised and
urbane widower of fifty-two, was awaiting the arrival of guests
that included Mrs. Theodore Roosevelt and her daughters, Bamie
and Corinne. But James's thoughts were probably riveted on another member of the party, the regally attractive Miss Sara
Delano.

They had been invited to visit Springwood by James, the son
of Dr. Isaac Roosevelt, a few evenings before while he was having dinner at the Roosevelt home on West Fifty-seventh Street.
Young Theodore was preparing for his graduation from Harvard
and Elliott was planning one of the hunting trips that took up
most of his time since the abortive end of his formal education, so
the company had included only the widowed Mittie, her daughters, and a few friends, among them Sara Delano, known to everyone as Sallie. Although James had a grown son, he was still
considered a good catch, particularly in a family with marriage-
able daughters. The two branches of the Roosevelt family were
more intimate than they were to become, and in the four years
since his wife had died, he had been considered a possible suitor

for Bamie's hand. But that independent-minded young lady had quickly rejected any idea of an arranged marriage with a man old enough to be her father. Besides, James had eyes only for her friend, Sallie. "He talked to her the whole time," Mittie noted with some amusement after her guests had gone. "He never took his eyes off her!"

And Sallie Delano was well worth looking at. Tall and stately, she had dark eyes, an abundance of auburn hair, and classic features marred ever so slightly by a strong chin. A few years later, she might have served as a model for Charles Dana Gibson's coolly elegant idealization of the American girl. While James and Sallie were sixth cousins, they had never met before, but he was acquainted with her father, Warren Delano, through joint service on various corporation boards and membership in the same clubs. From the tower room of Springwood, James could look twenty miles down the other side of the Hudson to Algonac, the Delano home just above Newburgh. As an active participant in New York's gay society of ballroom and paddock, James had undoubtedly heard of the five beautiful Delano girls, of whom Sallie, at twenty-five, was next to youngest. What passed between them beside the usual dinner party pleasantries is unknown, but she was impressed enough by James's courtly manner and good humor to accept his invitation to visit Springwood.

In later years, Sallie regarded her arrival at James's home for a week-long visit as one of the most important events in her life. "If I had not come then, I should now be 'old Miss Delano' after a rather sad life!" she once told her son. It was through no lack of suitors that she faced the prospect of spinsterhood, however. There was "an avalanche of young men in the evening," according to her father, but none of them seemed to meet the high standards he had established and all were dismissed sooner or later. Warren Delano was a father in the classic Victorian mold— and to him the men who wanted to marry his daughter were not quite good enough for her. They were either too young or too old, or lacked social standing, or character, or were obvious fortune hunters, for she stood to inherit a million dollars upon his death. And Sallie, very much the dutiful daughter, lowered her eyes and did as her father suggested. Except in the case of James Roosevelt.

Springwood was in its full floral glory when she arrived and

James and his guests must have enjoyed themselves strolling on the green, clipped lawns which were fresh and beautiful before the summer heat and riding over the forested trails of the estate. When the week was over, it was obvious that James and Sallie had reached an understanding. Even though he was twice her age and had a son as old as she, Sallie accepted him—perhaps because he seemed to remind her of her father.

James became a frequent visitor to Algonac, with various family diaries commenting: "Mr. Roosevelt from Hyde Park about 11 A.M." or "Mr. Roosevelt left for Hyde Park on the five o'clock train." At first, Warren Delano thought the visitor came to see him. They saw eye to eye on most things, except politics. Delano was a rock-ribbed Republican; James had returned to the Democratic faith of his fathers following the Civil War. This was not because he sympathized with liberalism—there was little to tell the parties apart on that score—but because his views coincided with those of the southern landed gentry that had led the party before the great conflict. As for Delano, he was fond of saying that while all Democrats were not horse thieves, it seemed to him that all horse thieves were Democrats.

Taken aback when James announced his intention to propose marriage to his daughter, Delano could object only on grounds of the prospective bridegroom's age, for Roosevelt certainly met all the qualifications he had established for a future son-in-law. He was solid, sensible, socially acceptable, and comfortably well off. Besides, he liked James personally. As he once told Sallie, James Roosevelt had convinced him of the heretofore unlikely possibility that a Democrat might also be a gentleman. These factors and his daughter's determination to marry James finally forced Delano to reluctantly give his blessing to the couple.

Four months later, on October 7, 1880, Sara Delano and James Roosevelt were married at Algonac before 125 guests, "the best representatives of New York society," according to the New York *World*. With her high-necked wedding gown, the bride wore a five-strand pearl necklace that James had given her as a wedding present. "At 4:20 P.M.," her father recorded in his diary, "the married pair left the house in our Victoria, drawn by 'Meg' and 'Pet' and driven by French, taking the road north to Milton." At Milton, halfway between Algonac and Springwood, the bridal couple were met by the Roosevelt carriage. As soon as they had transferred to it, James took the reins from the coachman and drove his bride to her new home.

James Roosevelt was hardly the kind of man to ask a woman to marry him after knowing her only a few days. While he fancied the role of country gentleman and sportsman, he was the first Roosevelt to graduate from Harvard Law School and was prominent in the management of railroads and coal companies. Steadiness and deliberation were the hallmarks of his business career, although as a young man he had shown a streak of Byronic romanticism. The oldest of the two sons of Dr. Isaac and Rebecca Aspinwall Roosevelt, he was born in 1828 at Mount Hope, but spent most of his early life at Rosedale, the gloomy, tree-shrouded house which his father built on the river side of the Albany Post Road.

For twelve years, James was an only child and consequently his life was probably a lonely one, considering his father's determination to avoid contact with his neighbors. Dr. Isaac may have had good reasons for this besides his own morbid temperament. Evidence has recently been discovered that Rosedale may have been a way station on the underground railroad along which runaway slaves were smuggled from the South to Canada. On the side of the house facing the Hudson a secret cellar has been discovered, which would have been ideal for such use. "Dr. Isaac's peculiar psychology would have enabled him to engage in the alleged activity without ever saying a word about it to anyone," suggests Kenneth S. Davis, a Roosevelt biographer.

In 1840 a second son was born to the Roosevelts who was named John Aspinwall Roosevelt, but his arrival probably came too late to have had meant much change for James. Besides, he was sent off to school the following year in Lee, Massachusetts—the first time that the boy had been away from home for an extended time. Somber letters poured in from his father advising him: "Repent, believe in the Lord Jesus and lead a life of holy obedience to his commands. Strive to correct your faults—in your intercourse with your companions be gentle and mild—obtain the command of your temper." Writing to the school's headmaster, Dr. Isaac hoped that his son's outside reading be directed toward instructive books rather than novels unless they had a moral or religious tone. Almost never venturing into New York City himself, he was alarmed two years later by James's decision to attend New York University. He feared that the lad would become corrupted, "a Dandy and will walk Broadway with a cane. . . . You know you were created for better things. We live for God—for the good of our fellow men—for duty—for usefulness," he added, oblivious to his own reclusive life in Dutchess County.

James had learned, however, to disregard his father's tremulous forebodings and entered NYU anyway. He remained there for a semester, living at his grandfather's home on Bleecker Street, and seemed to have emerged from the experience unscathed. A conscientious student, he joined the college debating society and won a gold medal. Transferring to Union College in Schenectady, James was graduated in 1847 at the age of nineteen. Sustained by his mother, he overcame Dr. Isaac's objections and toured Europe during the revolutionary year of 1848. His passport describes the bearer as five-feet, eight inches tall, with a round forehead, thin face, hazel eyes, dark hair, and straight nose, and a round chin. In Italy, according to a traditional family legend, James joined Giuseppe Garibaldi's Red Shirts, who were struggling for the unification of Italy. As his son later told the story, he had become close friends with a mendicant priest with whom he spoke only Latin, and together they had gone on a walking tour of Italy. "They came to Naples and found the city beseiged by Garibaldi's army," Franklin Roosevelt related. "They both enlisted in the army, wore a red shirt for a month or so, and tiring of it, as there seemed to be little action, went to Garibaldi's tent and asked if they could receive their discharge. Garibaldi thanked the old priest and my father and the walking tour was resumed by them."*

Adventuring done, James entered Harvard Law School upon his return home and was graduated in 1851. He joined the New York law firm of Benjamin Silliman, who was responsible for creating many of the large corporations that were coming into vogue as the United States entered the Industrial Revolution. One of the firms created by Silliman was the Consolidated Coal Company which had extensive holdings in western Maryland, and

* James's descendants were to put this service to good political use. Dedicating a plaque in Verrazano Park in New York City in 1965, Franklin D. Roosevelt, Jr., observed: "I feel a close affinity to all Italians here and in Italy because my grandfather, James Roosevelt, fought as a member of Garibaldi's army in his fight for the unification and independence of Italy."

James became one of its directors. Soon, like his grandfather and namesake, he abandoned his law practice to devote himself completely to business, although his legal training was an asset in this career. James took no role in the Civil War even though he was only thirty-two years old—and unlike the elder Theodore Roosevelt, his conscience was untroubled.

Following the war James put his inheritance—Dr. Isaac having died in 1863—to work in several speculative schemes that, had they succeeded, would have given him a firm place among America's financial giants. Politicians of both parties still prattled about the glories of the free market and competition, but businessmen knew better. The technological revolution had concentrated unparalleled power in an ever-decreasing number of hands as big business became monopoly; monopolies became trusts; trusts became supertrusts. "Individualism is gone," declared John D. Rockefeller, who "rationalized" the tumultuous oil business by destroying his competitors and raising prices. James was quick to grasp the available opportunities.

Joining with his uncle, William Henry Aspinwall, he helped organize the Consolidation Coal Company, the largest bituminous coal combination in the nation, which had a monopoly on the Cumberland coal fields. At the same time James and his associates were striving to extend their sway over an even larger part of the nation's coal supply, he was engaged with other financial adventurers in an attempt to secure control of the railroads of the reconstructed southern states through a holding company called the Southern Railway Security Company.

The key man in the scheme was Thomas A. Scott, vice-president of the Pennsylvania Railroad and an experienced and skillful railroad manipulator. A disarmingly amiable man with a set of muttonchop whiskers that gave him the benign look of a successful clergyman, he knew what he wanted—and how to get it. Upon one occasion, after he had pressured the Pennsylvania legislature into passing several bills that his railroad wanted, a weary lawmaker had asked, "Mr. President, may we now go Scott free?" Now Scott's attention was focused on the creation of a transcontinental railroad to rival the recently completed Union Pacific. Rather than follow the central route chosen by that road, Scott favored a southern route. James Roosevelt was elected president of the Southern Railway Security Company and under his direction it obtained control of most of the railroads south of the Potomac and extending into Georgia and Tennessee. But the Panic of 1873 intervened and both the coal and railroad enterprises collapsed with heavy losses for the investors, including James Roosevelt.

Fifteen years later, James made another stab at financial renown. He was among a group of investors who organized the Maritime Canal Company which proposed to build an interocean canal through Nicaragua. Concessions were obtained from the Central American nation and James, a friend of President Cleveland, helped lobby an act of incorporation through Congress. He became chairman of the organization's executive committee, and under his direction, fund-raising and preliminary construction got under way. Before much work could be accomplished, however, the nation was wracked by another economic depression and investment capital dried up. Work on the Nicaraguan waterway was halted and when the isthmusian canal was finally built it was constructed not in Nicaragua but in Panama—and by another Roosevelt.

Most of James's business life was devoted to more mundane business pursuits, however, with emphasis on railroads and coal. He was a member of the Board of the Delaware and Hudson Canal Company along with his future father-in-law, Warren Delano, J. P. Morgan, and a Vanderbilt, and served as vice-president. The company controlled large reserves of anthracite coal and consistently paid dividends of 10 percent. James also served as president of the Louisville, New Albany, and Chicago Railroad, headed shipping companies which operated paddle-wheel steamers on Lake Champlain and Lake George, and owned a business block in West Superior, Wisconsin, near Duluth. Although unsuccessful in his speculative ventures, he was, nevertheless, a respected figure in railroad finance and operations. The Delaware and Hudson even named a locomotive after him.

In 1853, just as he was beginning his business career, James Roosevelt married. Following what seemed a common practice among the Dutchess County branch of the family, who married Howlands and Aspinwalls, James chose Rebecca Howland, a plump and pretty young lady of twenty-two, to be his bride. She was the daughter of Gardiner G. Howland, the family patriarch. One of her brothers, a sporting type, went to live in Paris and married a Frenchwoman, who was known as Madame Howland. Her salon is described by Marcel Proust in *Remembrance of Things Past* as much favored by the members of the Jockey Club.

Upon the death of his father, James inherited Mount Hope, but he and Rebecca were not all that happy with the place. This problem was solved for them in 1865, when the house was destroyed in a fire while its owners were on a visit to Europe and it was being rented. Most of the family papers and heirlooms were also lost in the blaze, which may have been set by a disaffected servant. James sold the property to the state of New York, which added it to the grounds of the Hudson River State Hospital—or "the Lunatic Asylum" as it was known locally. In 1867 he moved two miles up the Post Road to Hyde Park, and purchased Springwood and the surrounding 110 acres, most of it rolling and wooded and with a splendid view of the long reach of the Hudson. The house had originally been built about 1826 and the tower added in 1845. Over the years, James increased his holdings until he owned nearly 1,000 acres of prime land. The place was famous for its roses, and in the first summer there, Rebecca said they picked "thousands of roses before breakfast."

Like his father and grandfather before him, James settled into the leisured life of a gentleman farmer. He had a herd of fat Guernsey, Jersey, and Alderney dairy cows, thoroughbred driving horses and trotters, beautiful gardens, manicured lawns, fruit trees and fields of undulating grain surrounded by low, stone fences. In winter he and Rebecca lived in a town house at 15 Washington Square and, as representatives of two of New York's most prominent families, were welcome in the most exclusive society. Every year, he took the waters at a German spa, hunted in the South of France, shot grouse in Scotland, and rode to hounds with some of England's finest packs.

The year after their marriage, Rebecca gave birth to their only child. They decided to name him after his father, but James detesting the appendage "Junior," which had sometimes been affixed to his own name to distinguish him from his grandfather, named the boy James Roosevelt Roosevelt. Throughout most of his life, he was known as "Rosy" Roosevelt. "Rosy" was a tall, handsome, and intelligent youth and graduated from Columbia in

1877 with honors. He began the study of law, but never bothered to finish because he married Helen Schermerhorn Astor, daughter of *the* Mrs. Astor, who under the guidance of her social mentor, Ward McAllister, ruled New York society with an imperious hand from her mansion at 350 Fifth Avenue. McAllister established the city's social elite when he chose the four hundred guests who could be accommodated in Mrs. Astor's ballroom. Needless to say, "Rosy" Roosevelt was among them.

"English life to perfection" was the ineffable McAllister's comment when he visited Hyde Park, and no one did more to complete the illusion than James Roosevelt. Good-humored and with a hearty laugh, he took a paternalistic interest in the affairs of the village, served on the school board, was a member of the Board of Managers of the "Asylum"—"signing checks and discoursing elegantly all the while"—and although baptized in the Dutch Reformed Church, was both vestryman and warden of St. James' Episcopal Church. With his muttonchop whiskers, slightly quizzical expression, and ever-present riding crop, James seemed like a Trollopian country squire. Not everyone was enchanted, however. "He tried to pattern himself on Lord Landsdowne, sideburns and all, but what he really looked like was Landsdowne's coachman," one relative has been quoted as saying.

Twenty-three years after her marriage, Rebecca's health began to fail. In August 1876 the couple embarked on a cruise on Long Island Sound in James's yacht and it was hoped that a few days of sun and sea air would refresh her. But soon after the vessel sailed, Rebecca was stricken with a serious heart attack. She was taken to the house on Washington Square, where she died before the month was out. Following the burial of his wife in St. James' churchyard in Hyde Park and the marriage of his son "Rosy" the following year, James was at loose ends—until he met Sallie Delano.

The second Mrs. James Roosevelt often insisted that her famous son, Franklin, was "a Delano, not a Roosevelt at all," and over the years, his face took on a remarkable resemblance to his mother's. With the slightest encouragement—and sometimes to her daughter-in-law's irritation—she could recite her family's pedigree with the ease of long practice. She reached far back beyond young Philippe de la Noye, who had loved and lost Priscilla Mullins, and the passionate Thomas Delano, who had married in the shadow of his father-in-law's fowling piece, to no less than William the Conqueror. Much less was said about Isaac Allerton, "the most unpuritan of the Puritans," or Columbus Delano, who served as Secretary of the Interior in the scandal-ridden administration of President Ulysses S. Grant and was involved in widespread corruption in the Bureau of Indian Affairs.

The Delanos were a seafaring family. Whalers, merchant skippers, and privateersmen, they put out from New Bedford and nearby Fairhaven to ports in Europe and South America, and beat their way around Cape Horn to the far Pacific and China. Captain Amassa Delano sailed around the world three times, explored the South Seas, and once led an amphibious attack on Peleliu in the Carolines in 1791, on behalf of a local tribal chief who sought his help in suppressing a rebellion. While captain of a whaler in the Pacific in 1808, Delano helped solve one of the great mysteries of the sea. Having fallen in with Captain Mayhew Folger of the Nantucket sealing vessel *Topaz*, he took down the story of Folger's discovery of the lost colony of the *Bounty* mutineers on Pitcairn Island, and published the first account of this fascinating tale.

Thirsting for adventure, Amassa Delano's cousin, Captain Paul Delano, went to South America in 1818 and joined the Chileans in their struggle for independence from Spain. He commanded the fleet of transports that carried the armies of Bernardo O'Higgins and José de San Martín to Peru, where they finally destroyed Spanish power in the New World. His fifteen-year-old son, Paul H. Delano, served as a midshipman under Admiral Lord Cochrane, the dashing and daring British seaman who commanded the revolutionary navy. Young Delano was at Cochrane's side as the admiral led a boarding party that seized the Spanish flagship *Esmeralda* in Callao harbor at sword's point. Cochrane was badly wounded and Delano stood over him, cutlass in hand, to prevent the enemy from harming his commander. Both Delanos became Chilean citizens and founded a branch of the family long prominent in the affairs of the country, especially its navy.

Perhaps the strangest story in the Delano family annals is that of Adelaide Delannoy. Born in Leyden in 1792, she was living in Brussels in 1814 with her widowed mother who took in boarders

when a young English actor named Junius Brutus Booth appeared at their door. On the brink of spinsterhood, she succumbed to Booth's advances, and although he was five years
younger than she, ran away to England with him, where they
were married. The couple had a child, Richard, and Booth became a popular star. He also fell in love with a London flower girl
named Mary Ann Holmes, and abandoning his wife and son, fled
with her to the United States in 1821. Passing Mary Ann off as his
wife, Junius went to live on a farm outside Baltimore, where in
between acting engagements, bouts of madness, and battles with
the bottle, he fathered ten star-crossed children, among them
Edwin and John Wilkes Booth.

Improbable as it may seem, Adelaide knew nothing of the existence of the other Booth family in the Maryland countryside.
Junius assured her that he had gone to America solely to fulfill
theatrical engagements and he sent her funds to support herself
and their son. Mary Ann knew about Adelaide, however. In 1842
Richard Booth decided to come to the United States to seek the
father he barely remembered from childhood—and soon learned
the scandalous truth. Edmund Kean, Junius' bitter rival for the
accolade of the stage's leading tragedian, provided Adelaide with
the funds to go to America in order to embarrass his old enemy.
Following a bitter confrontation, she filed suit in Baltimore for
divorce on grounds of adultery. It was granted in 1851. Shortly
afterward, Junius and Mary Ann were married—on the thirteenth
birthday of John Wilkes Booth. A few months later, Junius was
dead, and less than six years later, Adelaide, who had remained
in Baltimore, also died. Mary Ann lived on for another thirty
years, with the numbing pain of knowing that her son had murdered Abraham Lincoln.

Warren Delano, Sallie's father, made his fortune in the China
trade. While still in his twenties, he was captain of his own ship
and by the time he turned thirty was a senior partner and resident agent of Russell, Sturgis and Company in Macao, where he
supervised the shipment of tea to the United States. Returning
home briefly, he visited his parents' home at Fairhaven and that
summer took his two sisters on a driving trip through Massachusetts. Arriving at Northampton, the travelers were introduced
to an elderly gentleman who proved to be Judge Joseph Lyman,
a member of one of the town's leading families. The judge invited

the Delanos to his home that evening where Warren fell in love with Catherine, the youngest of two pretty Lyman daughters. Undoubtedly, Sallie probably reminded her father that his bride was only eighteen years old—half his age—when she sought his approval of her engagement to James Roosevelt. Following the wedding, the couple returned to Macao, where the first of their large brood of children was born. "I suppose it was altogether terrifying to my young mother to give up her beautiful home and its peaceful security," Sallie commented many years later.

In 1846, having accumulated a sizable fortune, Delano returned to New York with the intention of enjoying his newly won wealth in the leisurely manner prescribed for gentlemen. He invested in real estate, coal, and railroads and purchased a town house on Colonnade Row on Lafayette Place, where the Delanos included John Jacob Astor and Washington Irving among their neighbors.† But neither Warren nor Catherine Delano found city life agreeable, and five years later he purchased Algonac and made the estate his permanent home. Lavishing money upon the place, he employed his neighbor and friend, Andrew Jackson Downing, America's first great landscape architect, to turn Algonac into a showplace. There, on September 21, 1854, Sara Delano was born.

"I look back upon my childhood with great happiness," Sallie recalled three quarters of a century later in a brief account of her life prepared for her grandchildren. "In those days everyone was isolated, more or less, in the country. There were no automobiles, and very few steamboats. The river always had many sailboats, forming the most lovely scene in Newburgh Bay. . . . My father had the patriarchal spirit. He cared little for outsiders, but would do anything for his own family, and for any friends in trouble. . . . Nine children lived to grow up, and as was natural among so many, there were troubles and illnesses, but my mother was always the same lovely, brave, placid spirit.

"Until I was five, we spent our winters in New York, in Lafayette Place. After that for two years at Algonac on the Hudson, all year round. But always in summer, we went in detachments to my grandfather at Fairhaven, for change of air. How

† Four of the nine graceful homes have survived into the last quarter of the twentieth century, all much the worse for wear. One of them houses part of the off-Broadway theatrical empire of Joseph Papp.

well I remember those wonderful journeys on the Fall River boat, arriving next morning early, and driving across the lovely old bridge across the Acushnet River from New Bedford to Fairhaven, and finding Grandpa and Grandmama standing at the top of the front steps to welcome us. How decidedly Grandmama ordered the manservant to take all our clothes and luggage out onto the grass, away from the house to beat and brush them before bringing them into her nice clean house!"

The financial panic of 1857 was a brutal intrusion into this charming way of life. Warren Delano's investments suffered and Algonac was put on the market but no buyer could be found. The children were unaware of the crisis, however, for as Sallie later commented, "in those days the older members of the family carefully kept away from the children all traces of sadness or trouble." The elder Delano desperately sought a means of recouping his fortune, and as his brother wrote in his diary: "Warren has various projects, mostly impractical, one of which is to go to China to do business five years and return with a fortune." And that is exactly what he did. But this time he did not deal in such a mundane product as tea. Much to his family's later embarrassment, Delano made a second—and even larger—fortune in the opium trade. In later years, when they would talk about it at all, the Delanos and Roosevelts emphasized that the Civil War had made a legitimate market for opium for medicinal purposes. On the whole, though, it was something they didn't want to discuss.

Nevertheless, Delano did so well that in two years he was able to bring his entire family out to China to join him. The four-month voyage to Hong Kong on the square-rigger *Surprise* was the high point of Sallie Delano's early life. Franklin Roosevelt never wearied of her tales of life at sea on the long voyage under canvas around the Cape of Good Hope to Hong Kong. She made friends with the sailors and long afterward still remembered their chanteys and would sing them in a rollicking voice for her son and later her grandchildren:

> Haul in the bowlin'
> The ship, she is a-rollin'
> Haul in the bowlin'
> The bowlin' haul.

"Several miles before we reached the harbor [of Hong Kong], a rowboat approached with several Chinese sailors in their white uniforms, and Papa—tall, slight, keen and dressed in white linen— sat in the stern holding the tiller," Sallie told her grandchildren. "The moment he reached the *Surprise,* and we let down the steps, he rushed up to the deck where my mother and all of us stood. He had never seen his youngest child, your Aunt Kassie, two years old. As I think of it, I can see him now, kneeling with one knee on the deck and with his arms around the beautiful baby. After a time, she returned to her nurse and said quite seriously, 'Davis, I have seen my Papa, and I think he is a very nice man.'"

Life for the Delano children was very much what it would have been had they remained in America, and the physical presence of China hardly intruded upon them. It was as if they were separated from the world about them by a transparent but impenetrable wall. The Delanos lived on a large estate called Rose Hill that was very much like Algonac and the children were taught at home in a special room fitted with straight-backed chairs so they would not slump. They had very little contact with the Chinese, except for the servants, and their father refused to permit his children to learn the language so they would not understand the servants' chatter. Warren Delano's business associates were exclusively British and they also made up the social circle in which his family moved. Apart from two trips by boat to Canton, the Delano children saw little of the country. "When we went to dine at the home of Papa's great Chinese friend," Sallie noted, "Papa told us children to pretend we liked Chinese food, though it was very strange to us."

When Sallie reached ten, after two years in China, her father decided that she and three of the other children should return home to complete their education. The rest of the family soon followed, and for the next several years, the Delanos alternated between Algonac and Europe. They lived in the glittering Paris of the Second Empire where they had an apartment overlooking the Bois, and Sallie frequently saw the Empress Eugenie riding in her carriage. Like the elder Theodore Roosevelt's children, she also spent a year in Dresden living with a German family in order to learn the language. Returning home at sixteen, a beautiful girl with soft hair, she was ready to enter the joyous society of Algonac and New York. The days were spent riding, reading, visiting the deserving poor, and entertaining a steady stream of guests and suitors. Periodically, there were visits to the city which meant dances, the theater or the opera, and dinner parties.

In 1876 the family was touched by the breath of scandal. Sallie's older brother, Warren, who had studied engineering at Harvard, had gone to live in Baltimore, where he had fallen in love with Jennie Walters, daughter of Henry Walters, a local magnate, art collector, and philanthropist. Walters, a widower, wanted the companionship of his daughter and refused to sanction the marriage. When Jennie and Warren Delano married without his permission, he disinherited his daughter, although her brother divided the estate with her upon their father's death. There is a legend in Baltimore that in his last years the old man kept a light burning day and night at the door of his mansion on Mount Vernon Place to guide his errant daughter home should she decide to leave her husband.

While tongues clacked over this juicy bit of gossip—which the Delanos never mentioned—Sallie continued to move in her regal manner through society. In fact, it was said that when she was annoyed, she became even more dignified. Bamie Roosevelt was among her closest friends and she was a frequent caller at the Roosevelt homes in the city and at Oyster Bay. Her favorite member of the family was Elliott, whom she found handsome, charming, and good fun, and gifted with the faculty of concentrating all his attention and sympathy on the person he was with. It was on one such visit to West Fifty-seventh Street that she met James Roosevelt.

On January 30, 1882, the wind whipped in off the frozen Hudson, whistled about the eaves, and rattled the shutters of Springwood. Since the evening before, Sallie Roosevelt, who was expecting a baby, had been confined to a heavy mahogany double bed in an upstairs bedroom, and now her labor pains were coming with increasing regularity. The year and a half that had followed her marriage had been idyllic. For the first month after the ceremony, Sallie and James had remained at Hyde Park, where they followed a pleasant routine. Every morning they made an inspection tour of the farm on foot and then rode through the woods, which were displaying their full autumn glory. After lunch they went walking again, perhaps to Rosedale, where James's widowed mother lived with his brother John. Sometimes they went sailing on the river. In the evening neighbors came to call, and there were simple dinners. Among the Roosevelts' guests were "Rosy" Roosevelt and his wife, Helen, who lived at the adjoining estate, which had a large dwelling called the Red House, and such Hudson River aristocrats as Archibald Rogers, one of John D. Rockefeller's lieutenants.

In November the couple went abroad on their honeymoon. They made a leisurely tour of England, France, the Riviera, Germany, Italy, and Spain, usually spending time with James's many acquaintances. The difference in their ages caused some talk, but if James and Sallie noticed it, they kept it to themselves. At Granada, where Sallie briefly fell ill, she wrote in her diary, "James [is] too devoted to me." In Amsterdam they visited a small museum which had a group of wax figures illustrating the costumes of various parts of Holland, and Sallie was startled to see a figure that bore a striking facial resemblance to Bamie—testimony to how traces of their Dutch lineage sometimes appeared among the Oyster Bay Roosevelts. They had been gone almost a year when Sallie found that she was pregnant and they returned to Springwood.

Sallie's pregnancy was not a difficult one, but the actual birth of her child was a trauma. She suffered for a full night and day, and finally the attending doctor gave her chloroform to ease the pain. But it quickly became clear that he had inadvertently overdosed her, almost killing both mother and child. Sallie sank into a coma, although her strong heart continued beating. And when the baby was born, the customary slap across the rump was not enough to set him bawling in protest. Anxiously, the doctor applied artificial respiration, breathing into the infant's mouth for what may have seemed an eternity until his skin turned from blue to pink and he uttered a lusty cry. Assured that all was well with mother and child, the relieved father wrote in his wife's diary: "At quarter to nine my Sallie had a splendid large baby boy. He weighs 10 lbs. without clothes."

Chapter XIII
SUNSHINE AND SHADOW

"See that girl? I am going to marry her. She won't have me, but I am going to have her!"

So said Theodore Roosevelt to a friend, his teeth flashing a determined grin as he pointed across the room to a fair-haired young lady with dove-gray eyes and a turned-up nose named Alice Hathaway Lee.

Theodore met Alice in October 1878, soon after he entered his junior year at Harvard. Having overcome the melancholia that had engulfed him following his father's death, he was visiting Richard Saltonstall, a classmate who lived next door to the Lee home in Chestnut Hill. He first spotted Alice, whose cheerful brightness had earned her the nickname "Sunshine," coming down a garden path and was immediately captivated. "I loved her as soon as I saw her sweet, fair, young face," he later declared. By Thanksgiving, he knew he wanted to marry her.

But Alice had other ideas. As the daughter of George Cabot Lee, the most proper of Boston bankers, she had her share of admirers, and at seventeen was in no hurry to choose one above the others. Besides, Theodore's kinetic personality was altogether different from what the gentle Alice was used to. One girl who knew Theodore at the time remembered that he was "studious, ambitious, eccentric—not the sort to appeal to at first." Often voluble on the subject of natural history, he was given to producing specimens from his pockets to illustrate a point. Rose Lee later said her sister "had no intention of marrying him—but she did."

Before succumbing to Alice's charms, Theodore's experience

with women was limited, and at twenty he was still a virgin. Taking note of the carousing of his classmates in the seamier parts of Boston, he wrote in his diary, "Thank Heaven, I am at least perfectly pure." Outside of his sisters, his closest relationship with any girl had been with Edith Carow, whom he had known since they were children. What she thought of Theodore's infatuation with Alice is unknown. Edith and Theodore appear to have reached an "understanding" about the time he had entered Harvard, but they seem to have quarreled and broken off.

With his usual tenacity, Theodore laid siege to the heart of the bewitching Alice. He rode the six miles from Cambridge to Chestnut Hill every weekend on his horse, Lightfoot, and then increasing the tempo, appeared several times a week. Alice may have had mixed feelings about her suitor but her adoring five-year-old brother enjoyed Theodore's endless fund of wild tales about bears and wolves and looked forward to his visits. In winter the young couple went skating or sleighing and read to each other in the evening before the crackling fire; in the spring there was tennis, riding, and sailing. Alice seemed both fascinated and disturbed by his ardor.

At his insistence, she was probably in the Harvard gym for the bout in which Theodore fought the defending champion for the lightweight boxing cup. He was skillfully carrying the fight to his opponent when the referee signaled the end of a round. Theodore dropped his guard, but the other fellow landed a strong blow on his nose, which spouted blood. The spectators began hissing, and Theodore raised his arm to signal for silence. "It's all right," he declared. "He didn't hear the referee." And he walked over to his opponent and shook hands. Theodore lost the fight, but this gesture of good sportsmanship was the most vividly remembered event of his college years, and his classmates were still mentioning it years later.

Shortly afterward, he appears to have proposed to Alice and she either rejected him or answered evasively. Undeterred, Theodore arranged a light schedule during his senior year so that he could devote most of his time to the pursuit of "pretty Alice." It did not go well and he was plunged into the depths of gloom, writing in his diary that "night after night I have not even gone to bed." He began to neglect his studies, and his friends became so worried that they sent for his cousin, Dr. James West Roosevelt, to help talk him out of his habit of walking despondently at night in the woods near Cambridge. And then, on January 25, 1880, an exuberant Theodore wrote in his diary:

> At last everything is settled; but it seems impossible to realize it. I am so happy that I dare not trust in my own happiness. I drove over to the Lees determined to make an end of things at last; it was nearly eight months since I had first proposed to her, and I had been nearly crazy during the past year; and after much pleading my own sweet, pretty darling consented to be my wife. . . .

The engagement was announced on Valentine's Day and an October wedding was planned, but the prospective bridegroom still had to finish college. Despite a busy round of social activities and daily visits to Chestnut Hill—"I can hardly stay a moment without holding [Alice] in my arms or kissing her"—he completed his courses with flying colors. His senior thesis was entitled "The Practicability of Equalizing Men and Women Before the Law," and as a supporter of the feminist cause, he was all for equal rights. Although his grades as a senior were down from previous years, he was twenty-first in a class of 177, graduated *cum laude*, and was awarded a Phi Beta Kappa key.

There was one cloud hanging over Theodore's happy existence, and he kept it to himself until almost the end of his life. Shortly before graduation, he had a complete checkup by the college doctor, and the physician had alarming news for him. He had detected an irregular heartbeat and told the young man to choose a sedentary occupation, even advising him to avoid running upstairs if he wished to enjoy a long life. It appeared that Theodore, in following his father's advice to build his body, had indeed helped cure his asthma and increased his endurance, but had also strained his heart. He quickly made his choice. If he had to live the kind of life prescribed by the doctor, he said he would rather die young.

As if to underscore this statement, he embarked with Elliott on a rugged six-week western hunting trip as something of a last bachelor fling. They tramped across Illinois, Iowa, and the Dakota Territory, and Theodore, out West for the first time, was fascinated by the land and the people. Although he was bitten by a snake and thrown out of a wagon on his head, he pronounced

himself "in splending walking trim. . . . [We] are travelling on
our muscle and don't give a hang for any man." Overcome with
homesickness for Alice, however, he finally abandoned the hunt
and hurried East. The marriage took place in the Unitarian
Church in Brookline on October 27, 1880—Theodore's twenty-
second birthday; Alice was nineteen.

Postponing their honeymoon, Theodore and Alice returned to
New York, where they went to live with Mittie in the house on
West Fifty-seventh Street. With a wife to support, Theodore
looked about for a career. Money was no immediate problem, for
his father had left him an inheritance of $125,000, which if
invested wisely would provide the couple with an annual income
of about $8,000—at a time when a streetcar conductor earned
only $2.75 for a fifteen-hour day. Theodore, who did not consider
himself wealthy as compared to his social equals, observed: "I
had enough to get bread. What I had to, if I wanted butter and
jam, was to provide the butter and jam." Having abandoned his
ambition to become a natural scientist, he decided to enroll at the
Columbia Law School and to read law in the office of his Uncle
Rob. He also worked on his book, *The Naval War of 1812*, which
he had begun as an undergraduate at Harvard. In addition, he
and Alice kept up a varied social schedule, and Theodore was active in the various charities launched by his father.

Briskly walking the six miles or so from the family house to the
law school on Great Jones Street and then back again every day,
Theodore had plenty of time to ponder the law and its meaning.
He quickly became disillusioned. "Some of the teaching of the
law books and of the classroom seemed to me to be against justice," he wrote in his *Autobiography*. As Carleton Putnam has
said, "he aligned the moral law and the common law and was
shocked at the discrepancy." Theodore noted that if he had not
had an income, his views might have been different, but inasmuch as moneymaking was not his primary objective, he could
afford to choose how he would earn his "butter and jam."

Consequently, he began to consider his other options and took
a fresh interest in his book. When his last class was done for the
day, he would cross Lafayette Place to the Astor Library to dig
out long-forgotten information about America's early navy. Owen
Wister, the novelist and Theodore's longtime friend, told of visit-

ing his home one evening to find the author scribbling away in the study as Alice dashed in and proclaimed: "We're dining out in twenty minutes, and Teedy's drawing little ships!"

And there was politics. In his senior year at Harvard, Theodore had told a classmate he would like "to try to do something to help the cause of better government in New York." To most of his contemporaries, this meant philanthropic good works or possibly membership on a reform committee, but Theodore, possibly inspired by the rejection by the professional politicians of his father, intended to become part of what he called "the governing class." In 1880 "a young man of my upbringing could join only the Republican party, and join it I accordingly did," he later related. But political parties were closed corporations in those days, and as a friend put it, he "had to break into the organization with a jimmy."

> The men I knew best were the men in the clubs and of social pretension and the men of cultivated taste and easy life [Theodore wrote]. When I began to make inquiries as to the whereabouts of the local Republican Association and the means of joining it, these men—and the big business men and the lawyers also—laughed at me, and told me that politics were "low"; that the organizations were not controlled by gentlemen; that I would find them run by saloon-keepers, horse-car conductors, and the like, and not by men with any of whom I would come into contact; and, moreover, they assured me that the men I met would be rough and brutal and unpleasant to deal with.

Theodore persisted, however, and was accepted with some misgivings into the Twenty-first District Republican Association, which met in a large, barnlike room over a saloon on Fifty-ninth Street. Many of the members were wary of the young aristocrat with his Harvard accent, fashionable clothes, and eyeglasses worn on a ribbon. Nevertheless, Theodore struck up a warm friendship with Joe Murray, one of the chief lieutenants of Jake Hess, the district leader, and a defector from Tammany Hall. For the most part, he spent his time trying to bridge the social gap between himself and the other members. "I went around there often enough to have the men get accustomed to me and to have me get accustomed to them, so that we began to speak the same language," he said.

Meantime, he worked on his book. Like most writers, Theodore had his barren periods when he could put nothing satisfactory on paper. "I have plenty of information now, but I can't seem to get it into words," he lamented in a letter to Bamie. In the summer of 1881, Alice and Theodore took their long-delayed honeymoon trip to Europe, and a visit to his uncle, James D. Bulloch, in Liverpool, proved to be a godsend. Uncle Jimmie, an experienced naval officer, sharpened his understanding of the realities of sea warfare and cleared up some of the technical difficulties that had stymied the author. Now the book proceeded at a rapid pace, and by the time of his return home, was just about finished.

When the couple reached Switzerland, Theodore saw another challenge—the 15,000-foot-high Matterhorn—and vowed to conquer it. The mountain had first been climbed sixteen years before by a team that had lost four of its members. The ascent had been eased by the installation of chains and ropes at critical points, but it was still a difficult climb, particularly for an amateur who had been warned by his doctor not to run upstairs. After having warmed up on a few neighboring Alpine peaks, Theodore mounted his assault accompanied only by a single guide. He reached the summit early on the morning of the second day, "after seeing a most glorious sunrise that crowned the countless snow peaks and billowy white clouds with a crimson iridescence." By late afternoon, he was having tea with Alice in Zermatt, and claiming that he was "not very tired" by all this exertion.

In searching about for a career, Theodore had deplored to Bamie the idle lives of some of his classmates, "fellows of excellent family and faultless breeding, with a fine old country place, four-in-hands, tandems, a yacht, and so on; but oh the decorous hopelessness of their lives." Just such a life seemed to be in store for Elliott. Charming, intelligent, and liked by all who met him, he was restless and unable to concentrate on a fixed goal for any length of time. If the death of their father had been a tragedy for Theodore, it was a disaster for Elliott. Deprived of the guidance and discipline of the elder Roosevelt, he drifted through life as a man about town and sportsman, a role made easy by his inheritance. By the time he was twenty, he was already drinking heavily.

Apparently feeling inadequate in the presence of his brother, who had scored a brilliant success at Harvard, and had married a beautiful girl, and was assuming the leadership of the family, Elliott departed for India on a hunting trip. He moved with ease among the British officers and native princes of Kipling's India. Writing to his mother, he was unable to account for his success, "for if ever there was a man of few resources and moderate talents I am he, yet all events and people seem to give me the best of times. . . . I am 'up' at the club and have 'dined,' 'Tiffined' and breakfasted 'out' every meal." India made him realize his lack of an education. "How I do crave after knowledge, book learning, education and a well-balanced mind," he declared in exasperation when he tried to write about his experiences. He produced several interesting sketches about hunting tigers and elephants, but lacked the staying power to flesh them out.

Returning to New York, Elliott made a fresh start—in fact, the story of his brief life is almost a story of fresh starts—and joined the family firm. He was also invited by Sallie and James Roosevelt to stand as godfather of their son at his christening. For nearly two months after his birth, the child—known only as "Baby"—had no name. As they played with him in the nursery James considered naming him after his father, thereby continuing the traditional James-Isaac cycle of that branch of the family that had begun with Jacobus Roosevelt back in 1692. But Sallie wanted to name the boy Warren Delano after her father, and as usual would have had her way, except for the objections of her brother, Warren. Warren, whose own son and namesake had recently died, said he could not bear to hear another child called by that name, so the baby was named for Sallie's Uncle Frank.

Elliott protested that he was unworthy to serve as the baby's godfather and agreed only after my "dear little mother . . . persuaded me that I should accept the high honor you offer me." And so, on March 20, 1882, Sallie wrote in her diary: "At 11 we took darling Baby to the chapel in his prettiest clothes and best behavior. Dr. Cady christened him 'Franklin Delano.' Baby was quite good and lovely so we were proud of him.*

Elliott was a frequent visitor to Springwood and Algonac, and at a house party at the Delano home, he met a pretty debutante

* FDR was christened in the chapel of St. James' Church in Hyde Park rather than the church itself, because the latter building was unheated.

named Anna Rebecca Hall. Captivated, he described Anna as "a tall slender fair-haired little beauty—just out and a great belle." At nineteen, Anna, the eldest of the four Hall sisters, was a member of a family descended from the Livingstons and the Ludlows. The marriage of her parents, Valentine G. Hall, Jr., and Mary Livingston Ludlow, had represented a union of one of New York's wealthiest mercantile families with the Hudson River aristocracy. There was a streak of instability in the family, however, which was manifested in Anna's father, in the form of religious fanaticism. Her childhood on the family estate at Tivoli on the Hudson near Rhinebeck was rigorously Gothic in marked contrast to the brightness of Elliott's early life.

Valentine Hall was a despot who ruled the lives of his wife and children with an iron hand. They were not even permitted to go shopping for their own clothes; instead, dresses were sent to the house at his order and the women were allowed to make their choice. Gaiety was considered sinful and piety encouraged. Old Mr. Hall insisted that his daughters walk with a stick across their backs that was held in place in the crook of their elbows, which gave them a regal bearing. "The proud set of the head on the shoulders was the distinctive look of the Halls," recalled a friend. Elliott was tall, handsome, fun-loving, and there was something of the dashing Guards officer about him which appealed to Anna as completely different from everything she had known. They were married in December 1882, in a ceremony described by the New York *Herald* as "one of the most brilliant social events of the season."

Upon his return from Europe, Theodore found the political opportunity he had been awaiting. Joe Murray had fallen out with Jake Hess and having decided to run his own candidate for the Twenty-first District's seat in the State Assembly, he chose Theodore. Murray reasoned that he would appeal to the so-called "better" element in a "silk stocking" district that included the brownstone mansions of Fifth Avenue. Theodore eagerly accepted the offer, even though all his relatives except Elliott advised against it. When Roosevelt won the nomination at a district caucus, Hess cheerfully backed him, too, but the campaign got off to a poor start. Accompanied by Hess and Murray, the candidate set out to call on local saloonkeepers who had considerable political clout. Let Joe Murray take up the story:

> We started in a German lager-beer saloon on Sixth Avenue. The saloon keeper's name was Carl Fischer. . . . Hess introduces T.R. to Fischer and Fischer says, "By the way, Mr. Roosevelt, I hope you will do something for us [saloonkeepers] when you get to Albany. We are taxed much out of proportion to grocers, etc., and we have to pay $200 for the privilege [of operating]."
> "Why that's not enough!" said T.R.
> After we got out on the sidewalk we came to the conclusion that we had better stop the canvass right then and there. I says, Mr. Roosevelt, you go see your personal friends. Hess and I will look after this end.

Despite the candidate's distressing tendency to speak his mind, he won the election by fifteen hundred votes, twice the usual Republican majority. "I have become a political hack," he jocularly wrote a friend.

Theodore burst upon the State Assembly with something of the same effect he had had upon his classmates at Harvard. "We almost shouted with laughter to think that the most veritable representative of the New York dude had come to the Chamber," said Isaac Hunt, a rural member, who later became one of Theodore's best friends. It was Hunt who provided the freshman delegate with the ammunition that enabled him to launch his career as a reformer. During an investigation of some insolvent insurance companies, Hunt had uncovered irregularities which indicated that Judge Theodore Westbrook of the State Supreme Court was in collusion with the receivers to milk the companies and turned the evidence over to Theodore. Digging into the matter, Roosevelt found that the judge had also conspired with Jay Gould and other financiers in a shady deal to seize control of the Manhattan Elevated Railway Company. Outraged, he demanded a legislative inquiry into Westbrook's conduct.

Before it could get off the ground, Theodore's crusade was crushed by an alliance of Republican and Democratic professionals who had cozy "arrangements" with big business. But his charges aroused the newspapers and civic leaders, and the leadership was forced to permit an investigation by a legislative committee. As expected, the committee whitewashed Westbrook—but

Theodore's reputation as a reformer was made. He was praised
by the newspapers for his courage, and reform groups honored
him at testimonials. Charles Evans Hughes, then a young law student, characterized Theodore's political debut as "a splendid
breeze blowing through the legislative halls making everyone feel
brighter and better." Thus, in his first year in Albany, As-
semblyman Roosevelt had become a figure to be reckoned with
and his reelection was assured.

The news from the literary front was also good. *The Naval
War of 1812*, published early in 1882, was well received by the
critics on both sides of the Atlantic and went through several edi-
tions. W. L. Clowes, a British naval historian who was preparing
a multivolume history of the Royal Navy, was so impressed that
he asked Theodore to write the volume on the War of 1812—an
honor for an American and recognition of the quality of his work.
A century later, it is still one of the most valuable books on the
subject.

During his second term in the Assembly, Theodore was
brought face to face for the first time with the poverty and social
injustice that existed on the dark underside of America. As a
young legislator, his economic and social views were conven-
tionally conservative—favoring low wages, low taxes, and a low
level of social services. When a bill was introduced to reduce the
working time of streetcar conductors from fifteen to twelve hours
a day, he opposed it on grounds that the measure would interfere
with the workings of the free market. As William Henry Harbaugh, one of his most perceptive biographers, has pointed out,
Theodore lacked understanding of the effect of the Industrial
Revolution on the relations between labor and capital. Sheltered
from the economic realities of the industrial age, he had no
knowledge of the growing impersonality of relations between
employer and employee, the intense competition for subsistence-
level jobs, and the grinding boredom of most unskilled work. To
him, the degradation of the workingman was a result of natural
law rather than the fruit of laissez-faire capitalism. But to his
credit, Theodore was capable of growth and understanding,
unlike some of his contemporaries.

Samuel Gompers, the English-born head of the Cigar Makers'
Union and later founder of the American Federation of Labor,
provided Theodore with his first lesson in the need for social

change. For years, reformers had denounced the manufacture of cigars in the tenements of New York by unorganized immigrants —most of them Bohemians who spoke no English—as detrimental to the health of the workers and those who smoked their products. Cigar manufacturers, on the other hand, preferred that the work be done at home to save the cost of renting factory space. Gompers succeeded in having a bill introduced in the Assembly banning the home manufacture of cigars, but opponents shunted the measure to a special committee with the expectation that it would be killed there. Theodore was appointed a member, probably because of his antilabor record. To Gompers' surprise, however, he proved to be open-minded and agreed to accompany the union leader on an inspection so he could see conditions in the slums for himself. Theodore was appalled at what he found.

"I have alway remembered one room in which two families were living," he said. ". . . There were several children, three men and two women in this room. The tobacco was stowed about everywhere, alongside foul bedding, and in a corner where there were scraps of food. The men, women and children in this room worked by day and far on into the evening, and they slept and ate there." The conditions that he saw on this visit and several others were enough to turn him into a supporter of Gompers' bill. With strong backing from Theodore, the bill passed the Assembly only to die in the Senate when a lobbyist stole it from the files in the closing hours of the session. The following year, it was passed by both houses and signed into law by Governor Grover Cleveland, only to be declared unconstitutional by the courts. Later, Theodore was to say that it was this case that first caused him to question the wisdom of a judiciary that permitted such inequities to exist on grounds that it would be denying the cigar makers their freedom of choice to forbid them to work at home. "They knew legalism, but not life," he declared.

During the latter part of his second term in the Assembly, Theodore's asthma began to bother him again. Intrigued by the West during his hunting trip with Elliott three years before, he returned to the Dakota Badlands during the autumn of 1883. He arrived at a turning point in the history of the West. The last great buffalo herd was being hunted down to make way for the Texas longhorns being driven north to stock the cattle ranches opening on the sprawling grasslands. Eager to bag a buffalo,

Theodore found the guides reluctant to accompany a tenderfoot with glasses and it took considerable persuasion before one would go with him. For several days, the hunters tracked a buffalo herd over rough country, missing several opportunities for a kill. All their food ran out except for a few biscuits, their clothes and blankets were soaked by interminable rain, and they awakened in the morning with teeth chattering. "Isn't this bully!" Theodore told the surprised guide. "By Godfrey, but this is fun!" At last he got his buffalo—and climaxed the hunt with an ecstatic Indian war dance about the carcass and a $100 bonus for the guide. He was so enthused about the West and confident of its future that before returning to New York, he invested $14,000 in the Maltese Cross cattle ranch at Chimney Butte, on the Little Missouri River.

Theodore handily won reelection to a third term in the Assembly, and with the Republicans having taken a majority of the seats, he became a candidate for the speakership. Opposed by the bosses of the Republican organization who were convinced that Roosevelt could not be controlled, he was defeated when some of his supporters defected. Still, at the age of twenty-five, he was a force to be reckoned with in the party. And with 1884, a presidential election year, he was certain to have a voice in determining the role that the key New York delegation would play at the Chicago convention the following summer.

The new year had much to offer Alice and Theodore Roosevelt besides pleasing political prospects. Alice was pregnant with their first child, which was due in mid-February, and the couple were discussing plans for a home of their own at Oyster Bay. Soon after their marriage, Theodore had taken Alice to the summit of Sagamore Hill, where as a boy he had declaimed poetry into the wind, and they decided to build their home there looking toward Long Island Sound. By the time they were ready to begin construction in 1884, Theodore had purchased ninety-five acres of land and was steadily adding to his holdings. The house, named Leeholm after Alice's family, was to be a spacious high-Victorian mixture of gables, dormers, chimneys, and porches with ten bedrooms and a large library. There, Theodore planned to live an expansive life with his beloved Alice and surrounded by many children.

Alice was being kept company during her pregnancy by Theodore's sister Corinne, now married to Douglas Robinson, a Scottish-born graduate of Oxford who was in the brokerage business. Corinne had given birth to a son, Theodore Douglas Robinson, the year before, and the third floor of the West Fifty-seventh Street house was being readied as a nursery for both children. Theodore, who was conducting an investigation of corruption in New York City, commuted from Albany on weekends. On his last visit, Alice was doing well, although his mother was in bed suffering from what was said to be a cold. He was in the legislative chamber on the morning of February 13, when a telegram arrived announcing the birth of a daughter the night before and that mother and child were doing well. His colleagues crowded around to offer their congratulations. Later that day, there was another telegram, ominously bidding him to come to New York immediately. "I shall never forget when the news came and we congratulated him on the birth of his daughter," recalled Isaac Hunt. "He was full of life and happiness—and the news came of a sudden turn and he took his departure."

Thick fog enshrouded New York as Theodore's train crept into the city at a snail's pace, arriving shortly before midnight. The streets were empty and from the river came the mournful sound of fog horns. Theodore was relieved to see a light burning in the window of Alice's third-floor bedroom, but a distraught Elliott met him at the door with words similar to those with which he had greeted Corinne: "There is a curse on this house. Mother is dying and Alice is dying, too." Alice had been stricken with Bright's disease, and Mittie was in the last stages of typhoid. The baby was alive and well, however. Theodore dashed up the steps to his wife's room on the third floor two at a time to discover that she barely recognized him.

For the next two hours, he remained with Alice, holding her in his arms as if to prevent her from slipping away from him. Someone murmured that if he wished to see his mother before she died, he should hurry down to her room on the second floor. In the stillness of the early morning, he stood with his sisters and brother at Mittie's bedside in the same room in which their father had died six years before, and he echoed Elliott's words: "There *is* a curse on this house!" Mittie died at 3 A.M. and Theodore returned to Alice's room in a daze to take her in his arms again. The sad vigil continued through the long night and into the following afternoon, when Alice died. It was St. Valentine's Day—the fourth anniversary of the announcement of their engagement.

Theodore's family and friends were concerned that the trauma might destroy him. Arthur Cutler, his old tutor, reported on the day of the double funeral that "Theodore is in a dazed, stunned state. He does not know what he says or does." Yet, within a week, he had regained enough control of himself to return to the Assembly where his fellow members stood in silent tribute as he took his seat. The newborn child, christened Alice Lee after her mother, was left in Bamie's capable arms. To a friend, who expressed condolences, he wrote, "Your words of kind sympathy were very welcome to me, and you can see I have taken up my work again; indeed I think I should go mad if I were not employed. . . ."

In later years, Theodore closed the door on his life with Alice, not mentioning her in his *Autobiography* or talking about her with anyone, even her daughter, Alice. But before shutting her away in his memory, he wrote a final tribute:

. . . She was beautiful in face and form, and lovelier still in spirit; as a flower she grew, and as a fair young flower she died. Her life had been always in the sunshine; there had never come to her a single great sorrow; and none ever knew her who did not love and revere her for her bright, sunny temper and her saintly unselfishness. Fair, pure, and joyous as a maiden; loving, tender, and happy as a young wife; when she had just become a mother, when her life seemed to be just begun, and when the years seemed so bright before her—then, by a strange and terrible fate, death came to her. And when my heart's dearest died, the light went from my life for ever.

The presidential campaign of 1884 came as a relief for Theodore, for it allowed him to submerge his grief and his energy in a fight to prevent James G. Blaine from winning the Republican nomination. If any politician embodied the values—or lack of them—of the Gilded Age, it was Jim Blaine. Member of Congress from Maine, Speaker of the House of Representatives, ranking senator, Secretary of State, and perennial presidential hopeful, the "Plumed Knight" was a dominant force in the councils of the Republican party and in the affairs of the nation. A magnetic leader with eyes that flashed sparks and a voice that hypnotized the galleries, he pursued the voters up and down the byways of the Republic for thirty years. Year after year, election after election, his name echoed over the land like a drumbeat: "Blaine! Blaine! James G. Blaine!" But he could never disabuse a majority of the voters of the conviction that he was a crook.

Regarding Blaine as "decidedly mottled," and opposed to President Chester A. Arthur who had benefited from his father's political rejection six years before, Theodore supported the dark horse candidacy of the reform-minded Senator George F. Edmunds of Vermont. He led the Edmunds forces to victory at the state party convention at Utica, but it was a different story at the Republican national convention in Chicago a few months later. The Blaine steamroller easily crushed the opposition, and the "Plumed Knight" was nominated on the fourth ballot. Reformers such as Carl Schurz, Henry Ward Beecher, and Charles Francis Adams, unable to stomach their own party's nominee, bolted to the Democratic candidate, Grover Cleveland—and expected young Roosevelt to join them.

Theodore was faced with the most agonizing dilemma of his political career. As a delegate to the national convention, he was pledged to support the party's nominee. Yet, if he did so, he would compromise his own principles and would be ostracized by his fellow reformers, or "mugwumps." And if he didn't, the party regulars, who had long memories, would make certain that he had no future in national politics. He might have quietly sat out the campaign at his ranch in the Dakota Badlands, which would have enabled him to retain his standing as a practical politician with both the reformers and party regulars. Instead, with the impetuosity that had caused one legislative colleague to say "he was the most impulsive human being I ever knew," he issued a strong statement supporting Blaine. And if that wasn't enough, he came East to campaign in his favor. Even Roscoe Conkling had refused to do that. When asked to take to the stump in Blaine's behalf, the imperious "Lord Roscoe" snapped, "No thanks, I don't engage in criminal practice."

The mugwumps were shocked and dismayed. Men who had praised Theodore as the Republican party's conscience and hope for the future now turned upon him. To make matters worse, Blaine was narrowly defeated by Cleveland because his failure to disavow a supporter's charge that the Democrats were the party of "Rum, Romanism and Rebellion" cost him New York's vital Catholic vote. Writing to his good friend Henry Cabot Lodge following the election, Theodore gloomily assessed his prospects:

> Blaine's nomination meant to me pretty sure political death if I supported him; this I realized entirely, and went in with my eyes wide open. I have won again and again; finally chance placed me where I was sure to lose whatever I did. . . . I do not believe that I shall ever be likely to come back into political life.

Having lost the support of the reformers and without the solace of national office to make up for it, Theodore returned to Dakota. He was in the wilderness both figuratively and literally.

Chapter XIV
"THE WINE OF LIFE"

Theodore Roosevelt's abrupt decision to go West had a certain logic about it. Not only did the adventurous ranch life of the Badlands provide relief from his haunting memories of Alice and time to lick his political wounds, it seemed like good business. Following the Civil War, there was an enormous demand for beef from the prosperous East, and the undulating grasslands of the northern plains, reaching down from Canada like a thumb, were viewed as a land of opportunity. One of the best-selling books of the day was *Beef Bonanza or How to Get Rich on the Plains*, and Theodore may have decided to put its teachings into practice. He steadily increased his investment in Dakota ranch land and cattle until it totaled over $52,000.* He nearly lost his buckskin shirt, but the West put its brand upon him for life. From then on, he was always associated in the public mind with the image of the cowboy.

Roosevelt's western adventures were, as one writer has said, the ultimate dream of every red-blooded American boy. Wearing a sombrero low over his eyes and packing a six-gun, he was at one time or another a cowpuncher, rancher, big-game hunter, and deputy sheriff, and was thrown together with cowboys, gamblers, guides, gunmen, peace officers, and even a few European

---

* In addition to the $125,000 he had inherited from his father, Theodore received another $62,500 upon the death of his mother. His uncle, James Alfred Roosevelt, head of Roosevelt & Son, warned him against the Dakota investment but to no avail.

aristocrats who had wandered into ranching. Looking back thirty years later, he wrote with nostalgia of an era that had long gone:

> We led a free and hardy life with horse and rifle. We worked under the scorching midsummer sun, when the wide plains shimmered and wavered in the heat; and we knew the freezing misery of riding night guard round the cattle in the late fall roundup. In the soft springtime the stars were glorious in our eyes each night before we fell asleep; and in the winter we rode through blinding blizzards, when the driven snowdust burnt our faces. . . . We knew toil and hardship and hunger and thirst; and we saw men die violent deaths as they worked among the horses and cattle, or fought in evil feuds with one another; but we felt the beat of hardy life in our veins, and ours was the glory of work and the joy of living.

Theodore was suspect in this hard-bitten company, as a dude, an easterner, and a ranch owner who had never punched cows, and he won his spurs the hard way. One night, he went into a hotel barroom to find a foul-mouthed drunk striding up and down before the cowed patrons with a cocked revolver in each hand. He had already put several shots into the face of the clock over the bar. Catching sight of the bespectacled Theodore, he called him "Four-eyes" and bellowed: "Four-eyes is going to treat!" Regarding it as a joke, Roosevelt sat down behind the stove, where he joined in the laughter at his expense, but the drunk repeated his command at pistol point. Rising from his chair as if to obey, Theodore lashed out with a fast right to the jaw, a left, and another right. The drunk sank to the floor and his guns went off harmlessly.

Such exhibitions of courage hastened Theodore's acceptance by his neighbors, but he continued to amuse them. During a roundup, he called one of his men to "Hasten forward there!" This threw everyone into paroxysms of laughter, and long afterward, Dakotans were summoning each other by calling, "Hasten forward there!" Even so, he proved himself to their satisfaction, eating his share of trail dust, capturing three horse thieves at gunpoint, and helping organize the ranchers to deal with their problems. Somehow, he found time to produce a sheaf of magazine articles, all but finish two books, and to begin work on what was to be his major literary and historical effort, the multivolumed *Winning of the West*. The effect of Roosevelt's experiences in the Badlands is stamped on almost every page of the work, and according to Frederick Jackson Turner, the historian of America's western expansion, he depicted this movement "as probably no other man of his time could have done."

Theodore also kept a sharp eye on political developments in the East. Throughout his stay in Dakota, Henry Cabot Lodge and Bamie kept him fully informed of all twists and turns in both local and national politics through a steady stream of letters and newspaper clippings. Periodically, he shuttled back and forth between the Badlands and New York. The house at Oyster Bay had been completed—at a cost of $16,675—and Theodore had reached an understanding with Bamie, who was little Alice's guardian, giving her the use of the place while he made his headquarters when he was in town at her house at 422 Madison Avenue.

Riding with the Meadowbrook hunt while on a visit to Long Island, Theodore was tossed from his horse, and despite a badly bruised face and a broken arm, insisted on remounting and was in at the kill. "I am always willing to pay the piper when I have had a good dance," he wrote Lodge, "and every now and then I like to drink the wine of life with brandy in it." This rugged life put an end to his asthma attacks and he developed the bull neck and barrel chest that characterized him for the rest of his life. But by the end of 1886, he was ready to make a permanent return to New York. Ranching in the Badlands had proven to be a poor business proposition because of drought and overstocking, and the coming winter looked as if it would be a harsh one for the stockmen. New York's Republican bosses had also offered him the party's nomination for mayor. Even more important, he had secretly become engaged to Edith Carow—and she had no intention of becoming a rancher's wife in the wilds of far-off Dakota.

Following his marriage to Alice, Theodore had maintained a casual friendship with Edith, who had attended the wedding, but Alice complained that she could not relate to Edith, claiming she was cool and distant. Perhaps, as Carleton Putnam suggests, this was because the Roosevelts' star was in the ascendancy, while Edith's was sinking. The death of her father, who had drunk up most of the family's money, left Edith, her mother and sister teetering on the brink of genteel poverty. In fact, Mrs. Carow decided to move to Europe, where living costs were less than in the United States. Following Alice's death, Edith seems to have made up her mind to land Theodore this time—and she was a very determined woman. Perhaps Theodore, still faithful to the memory of Alice, realized this, for he told Bamie that he wanted to be warned when Edith visited the Madison Avenue house so he could avoid her.

The warning system broke down—perhaps with Bamie's connivance—and Theodore and Edith confronted each other one day on the stairs in the front hallway of the house. No one knows what passed between them, but they began to see each other again and Theodore's romantic loyalty to Alice's memory weakened. "I have no constancy—*no* constancy," he angrily told a friend after pacing his room half the night. He needn't have felt so guilt-ridden, for he was only twenty-eight and very much wanted a family and a home. Edith and Theodore reached an understanding in November 1885, but to allow for a proper period of mourning for Alice, they decided to wait for a year to be married. Theodore returned to the Badlands and Edith went to London with her mother.

Less than a year later, he was back in New York as the Republican candidate for mayor. This was a dubious honor because he had been given the nomination by the bosses only because they saw no chance for their candidate to win and needed a sacrificial lamb. The situation was created by the presence in the race of Henry George, author of the widely read *Progress and Poverty*, and candidate of the United Labor party. George blamed periodic depressions and the poverty of the working class on wild speculation in land as the nation developed and espoused the "single tax"—a massive levy on the profits of increased land values—which he claimed would obviate the need for all other taxes. Needless to say, George's ideas, which were immensely popular with the working class, frightened businessmen and other respectable citizens. Seeing an opportunity to attract their votes, Richard Croker, the wily chief of Tammany Hall, secured the Democratic nomination for Abram S. Hewitt, a reform-minded millionaire, rather than the usual Tammany wheelhorse. The Republicans, expecting Hewitt to win, nominated Roosevelt as a stopgap.

Theodore was under no illusions about his chances for victory, and accepted the nomination to reestablish himself in politics. Although he campaigned with his usual energy, he was so certain of defeat that he and Bamie booked passage on a steamer to England for immediately after the election. They adopted assumed names to keep up the confidence of his supporters. As expected, Theodore was defeated—"worse even than I had feared," he wrote Lodge. He trailed Hewitt and George, winning about fifteen thousand fewer votes than Republican candidates usually received in New York. Obviously, many party members had deserted to Hewitt, out of fear of both the single-tax messiah and young Roosevelt. Taking consolation that "at least I have a better party standing than ever before," he and Bamie sailed for England. On shipboard, they met an engaging young British diplomat, named Cecil Spring-Rice, and when Theodore and Edith were married at St. George's Church, Hanover Square, on December 2, 1886, "Springy" was best man.

Brisk winds blew in off Long Island Sound, chopping white-capped V's into the gray water as a coach carrying Theodore, Edith, and little Alice drew up before the house at Oyster Bay at the end of March 1887. A day or two before, the three-year-old child, wearing her best dress and sash, had greeted her step-mother at Bamie's house with a huge bunch of pink roses in her arms. In deference to his new wife, Theodore had changed the name of the estate from Leeholm to Sagamore Hill. Edith had visited the place when Bamie was living there, but as she moved through the paneled hall lined with the mounted heads of big game shot by her husband and the rooms filled with white-shrouded furniture, she looked about her with fresh interest. Now it was her task to transform the sprawling house into a comfortable home for Theodore and their children, for she was already pregnant. While Edith busied herself with fitting the new furniture that she had bought in Europe in with the pieces already on hand, Theodore weighed his prospects—and they were far from bright.

During the previous winter, a blizzard had lashed the high plains of Dakota decimating the cattle which had been allowed to forage for themselves, and leaving some ranchers dead and most bankrupt. Theodore's own herds had been wiped out and he was faced with the loss of almost his entire investment. What was left was tied up and unavailable for support of his growing family.† At one point, his brother-in-law, Douglas Robinson, who was managing his financial affairs, warned that he was digging into his capital at a rate of $2,500 a year. There was no more heinous sin in staid Knickerbocker society than to touch capital. With the hope of increasing his income, Theodore stepped up his literary productivity while casting about for an opportunity to re-enter politics.

Meanwhile, life at Sagamore settled into a pattern. Theodore adored his golden-haired little daughter, saying she was "too sweet and good for anything." In September 1887 Alice was joined by Edith's first child, a boy whom they named Theodore, Jr. His father described him as "a very merry lovable little fellow" who crawled everywhere "just like one of Barnum's seals." Fascinated by the baby, Alice refused to allow her tiny rocking chair to be moved from beside his crib and boasted: "My little brother's a howling polly parrot." Over the next decade, the couple had four more children: Kermit, born in 1889, Ethel in 1891, Archibald in 1894, and Quentin in 1897.

Once, when the children came down with the measles, Theodore made Alice and Ted each a miniature ram and a monitor from pasteboard, and together with some toy ships from Ted's collection, reconstructed the Civil War battle of Mobile Bay. "They were, of course, absorbed spectators," he wrote. "In the battle Ted's monitor was sunk; and as soon as I left to dress, Ted began the battle over again, Alice looking on from the bed. This time Ted intended that Alice's monitor should sink while Alice was alert to see that no such variation took place.

" 'And now bang! goes a torpedo, Sisser's monitor sinks!' " declared Ted.

" 'No, it didn't sink at all!' " insisted Alice. " 'My monitor always goes to bed at seven, and now it's three minutes past!' "

Nevertheless, Alice's childhood was not unalloyed joy. Looking back over her long life on her ninetieth birthday, she said she had really been the "ugly duckling" of the family. "My brothers used to tease me about not having the same mother. They were very cruel about it and I was terribly sensitive." And, for the first several years of her life, she was an orthopedic case, suffering from

† By the time the Badlands operation was finally liquidated in 1899, Roosevelt had suffered a loss of about $20,000 on the venture.

what was later suspected to be a mild case of polio. "Every night before going to bed my good [step]mother used to stretch each foot in a steel contraption that rather resembled a medieval instrument of torture, and for several years I wore braces on each leg from ankle to knee," she wrote in her memoirs. "Even when walking on level pavement they used to catch and throw me." Alice never saw eye to eye with her stepmother and was already something of a rebel, perhaps compensating for her other problems. At nine, she decided that she didn't want to be a girl any longer and announced her intention of wearing trousers instead of skirts and of owning a pet monkey.

When the braces were taken off, Alice was able to join in the strenuous life pursued by the other children at Sagamore. Theodore often took part, enjoying nothing better than to lead a ragtag band of his own children and myriad cousins and visitors on long cross-country "scrambles" that were more obstacle course than nature walk. The outings usually ended with a picnic and overnight stay in the woods. Theodore entertained the group by telling ghost stories while they were gathered around the campfire—and would pounce on an unwary listener with a bloodcurdling yell as a fitting climax for a terrifying tale. Speaking of Theodore's joyous exuberance even after he became President, Spring-Rice dryly observed to a friend: "One thing you must always remember about Roosevelt is that he is about seven years old." Eleanor Alexander, who later married Ted, spent a summer at Oyster Bay keeping up with the Roosevelts and pronounced it "splendid training, but, while it was going on, I lost twenty-six pounds."

What was Edith Roosevelt's reaction to her sometimes outrageous husband and her unruly brood? One detects a certain ambivalence. Most of the time, she was kind and considerate, but it is said she could also be demanding and possessive. Some of Bamie's friends also claimed that she was ruthless in the way she took over Theodore's life, pushing his sister out of it. When her neuralgia was acting up, neither her spouse nor the children knew what to expect and her affection for them was tempered by a sharp tongue. During one "scramble," Theodore permitted the young participants to go swimming with their clothes on. When the company arrived home, Edith immediately sent them to bed with a dose of ginger syrup. "There's nothing I can do," the President of the United States told the protesting juveniles. "I'm lucky that she didn't give me a dose of ginger, too." Still, the marriage was a happy one and on the thirty-second anniversary of his engagement to Edith, Theodore told Quentin, "I really think I am just as much in love with her as I was then—she is so wise and good and pretty and charming."

The presidential election 1888 gave Theodore his chance to get back into politics. Tiring of life on the sidelines, he took the stump in favor of Benjamin Harrison, who succeeded in ousting Grover Cleveland in the White House. Cabot Lodge, now a force to be reckoned with in Republican politics, insisted that a post be found for his deserving friend and he was given one of the four seats on the Civil Service Commission. Theodore was delighted to accept the job, which paid $3,500 annually. Matthew F. Halloran, the commission's executive secretary, never forgot Roosevelt's arrival on the scene on May 13, 1889. There was a bustle in the outer office and then Theodore burst upon him: "I am the new Civil Service Commissioner. Have you a telephone? Call the Ebbitt House. I have an appointment with Archbishop Ireland. Say I will be there at ten o'clock."

Until Theodore's brisk advent, the Civil Service Commission had been regarded as a genteel facade behind which patronage and politics operated as usual. It had been organized in 1883 to administer the Pendleton Civil Service Act which required open competitive examinations in filling government jobs and placed about 14,000 federal workers under the merit system. Shaking down government workers for political contributions was barred, although the practice was not stamped out. Cleveland had extended Civil Service coverage to another 7,000 workers, while packing the rest of the bureaucracy with Democratic jobholders. Republican stalwarts demanded their place at the public trough, and Harrison, although he had declared in his inaugural address that he would enforce the Pendleton Act "fully and without evasion," declared open season on Democratic jobholders.

John Wanamaker, the Philadelphia merchant prince who had been named Postmaster General in reward for his skill at "frying the fat" out of businessmen as campaign finance chairman, was given the task of wielding the ax. Soon, newspaper cartoonists were portraying Wanamaker with a tape measure over his arm, calling out "Cash!" as he held a bargain sale of post office jobs. In all, he removed some 30,000 fourth-class postmasters and replaced them with job-hungry Republicans. This wholesale sweep immediately brought Theodore into collision with Wanamaker. "Offices are not the property of the politicians," he declared. "They belong to the people and should be filled only with regard to the public service." As a result, much of Harrison's term was marred by an open struggle between the two men, and almost daily Theodore expected to be dismissed by "the little gray man" in the White House. But his battle in behalf of civil service reform had again put him in the good graces of the mugwumps and Harrison hesitated to alienate them. Theodore's bipartisanship so impressed Cleveland that when he returned to the presidency in 1893, he kept Roosevelt on the commission.

Theodore's six years in Washington, which lasted until his resignation in 1895 to have a fling as a member of New York City's Board of Police Commissioners, propelled him into the national spotlight. Immediately grasping the possibilities for making propaganda inherent in his post, he had produced a flurry of speeches and magazine articles and conducted an intensive lobbying campaign to strengthen the cause of civil service reform. Newspaper coverage of his battles with the spoilsmen converted it from a worthy but dull cause to a burning issue. Under Theodore's direction, an additional 26,000 jobs were removed from the category of political plum and placed under the merit system, new tests for applicants were devised, and for the first time women were put on the same competitive level with men, which resulted in a corresponding increase in their number in government jobs. But one problem defied solution despite Roosevelt's energetic search for an answer and haunts the civil service a century later—how to promote efficiency among government workers and to make them responsive to the people they are supposed to serve.

In 1895 New York City's Police Department had just emerged from another of the periodic investigations of graft and corruption that mar its history. Touched off by the Reverend Charles H. Parkhurst, who charged that New York was "a very hotbed of knavery, debauchery and bestiality" from which the politicians and police enriched themselves, the inquiry had led to the ouster of Tammany Hall from control of the municipal government. The

reform mayor, William L. Strong, offered a seat on the newly
revamped Board of Police Commissioners to Theodore, who accepted with alacrity. Bored by the Civil Service Commission, he
was eager to get back into New York politics, and the challenge
of cleaning up the Police Department appealed to his combative
instincts. The three other board members immediately named
him its president.

As soon as he arrived at the dingy old Police Headquarters on
Mulberry Street, he grabbed the force by the scruff of its neck
and gave it a good shaking up. Superintendent Thomas Byrnes,
the city's top cop who had amassed a fortune of $300,000—
through wise investments on Wall Street, he claimed—was the
first to go. He was followed by a raft of other policemen of all
ranks who were found to be on the take from gamblers, saloonkeepers, brothel owners, confidence men, and assorted other
criminals. He pedaled to his office every morning on a bicycle
and wandered the streets late at night with a black cloak over his
evening clothes and a hat pulled down over his eyes in search of
crime or a policeman asleep on duty. Police reporters such as
Jacob Riis, who had written *How the Other Half Lives*, a vivid
account of the appalling conditions in New York's slums, and
Lincoln Steffens, the first of the muckrakers, accompanied him on
his midnight rounds and found that he made colorful copy. "We
have a real Police Commissioner," wrote Arthur Brisbane of the
World. "His teeth are big and white, his eyes are small and pierc-
ing, his voice is rasping. . . . His heart is full of reform . . .
[and] . . . he looks like a man of strength . . . a determined
man, a fighting man, an honest, conscientious man, and like the
man to reform the force."

Policemen watched nervously over their shoulders at night for
a dark-cloaked figure with blindingly white teeth, and street ped-
dlers sold whistles shaped like "Teddy's Teeth." Even if vice was
merely driven undercover rather than stamped out, newspapers
all over the country praised New York's vigorous new commissioner, and Lodge, who had become senator from Massachusetts,
began to see the presidency as a possibility for his friend. As for
Theodore, he enjoyed his job immensely. When a notorious anti-
Semitic preacher arrived from Germany and demanded police
protection while he made speeches attacking the Jews, Roosevelt

gleefully assigned a Jewish sergeant and a detail of forty Jewish policemen to guard him.

Before the laughter had died down, however, Theodore took a step that severely damaged his popularity. He decided to enforce the Raines Law which required saloons to close on Sunday, depriving the thirsty citizenry of their booze and beer. Roosevelt was no prohibitionist, but argued that failure to enforce this law set a bad precedent and was tailor-made for under-the-counter payments to the police from saloonkeepers who wanted to stay open. He felt that the wave of protest created by strict enforcement of the Sunday closing law would force the Assembly to repeal it. Instead, the protests were directed against him—particularly from among the sizable German-American population whose family custom it was to hold forth on Sunday in the city's many beer gardens. He was charged with instituting a dictatorship and styled "King Roosevelt I." The Germans held a protest parade and dared Theodore to attend, but he was on hand to join in the laughter when a coffin labeled "Teddyism" was carried by. Near the end of the parade marched an old German with thick eyeglasses who peered closely at the reviewing stand and loudly demanded:

"*Wo ist der Roosevelt?*"

"*Hier bin ich!*" the commissioner shouted back amid a wave of laughter.

Everyone agreed that Theodore had survived the ordeal better than expected, but his days as police commissioner were clearly numbered. The other three board members, jealous of his notoriety, had been trying to undercut him for some time and he had become an embarrassment to Strong's reform administration. Once again, Cabot Lodge came to the rescue, by persuading the reluctant William McKinley, the newly elected President, to name Roosevelt as Assistant Secretary of the Navy. Reform did not long survive his departure for Washington, for once again Tammany was voted back into power. And within a few years, there was another investigation of corruption in the New York Police Department.

Probably there is no greater contrast in American politics than that between Theodore Roosevelt and William McKinley. A stolid, unimaginative Republican party wheelhorse and former

Ohio congressman and governor, McKinley looked like a bronze statue searching for a pedestal. To William Allen White, the Kansas editor, he was a "kindly, dull gentleman . . . honest enough, brave enough, intelligent enough for politics—and no more." Another observer said the new president "had the art . . . of throwing a moral gloss over policies which were dubious if not actually immoral." But McKinley had one thing going for him—and that was his good friend Mark Hanna.

Marcus Alonzo Hanna was a Cleveland industrialist who had made a fortune in coal, iron, banking, and Great Lakes shipping. But he had wider ambitions. He craved power and sought it in politics—not by running for office himself but through the efficient management of others. Shrewd and cynical, he shouldered his way to becoming the closest thing to a national "boss" ever seen in American politics, and William McKinley was the instrument through which he worked.

Hanna put McKinley in the presidency in 1896 through a campaign in which the candidate was packaged and merchandised like a patent medicine. Estimates of the cost ranged upwards of $10 million—the most ever spent on a presidential election until well after World War I. To gather this huge bankroll, Hanna played upon the fears of his fellow industrialists that the election of William Jennings Bryan, the prairie Galahad and pitchman of the cheap dollar, would mean revolution. Bryan didn't have a chance, and his scalp soon hung from Hanna's belt. Under his benevolent gaze, the green light flashed for railroad mergers, industrial combinations, communities of interest, and trusts of all kinds. Tariffs were set at ridiculously high levels and big business was guaranteed protection against hostile legislation. The last thing that Hanna wanted was some wild man like Theodore Roosevelt upsetting this blissful arrangement, and guarantees were obtained from Lodge for his good behavior.

If any job had been made to order for Theodore, it was Assistant Secretary of the Navy. The basic thesis of his first book, *The Naval War of 1812*, was that America needed a strong navy to defend its interests abroad and to protect its coasts against enemy attack. He was among the first Americans to recognize the importance of the teachings of Captain Alfred Thayer Mahan, the high priest of sea power, and had written a glowing review in the *Atlantic Monthly* of Mahan's first and most important book,

The Influence of Sea Power Upon History, 1660–1783. The work appeared in 1890 as the spirit of Manifest Destiny was again in vogue, after having lain dormant since the Civil War. Latin America, the Caribbean, and the Far East were being eyed as areas where the great surpluses of America's farms and factories could be disposed of at a profit. The new imperialists did not envision colonizing these area, but wished to exploit them commercially and to bring the benefits of American civilization to the benighted natives—"the lesser breeds without the law" in the words of Theodore's good friend Rudyard Kipling.

"America must begin to look outward," advised Mahan, and businessmen and politicians echoed his ideas. Overseas trade was the key to national greatness, he maintained, citing the example of Britain, and command of the sea and a strong navy were vital to its protection. To support the great fleet he envisioned, Mahan called for bases in the Caribbean and the Far East and for a canal across Central America to facilitate commerce between the East and West and the rapid movement of the American battle line from the Atlantic to the Pacific. The new Assistant Secretary was the living embodiment of Mahan's ideas and he worked overtime at making improvements in the quality of the Navy's ships and men. His chief, the elderly John D. Long, whom Theodore called "a perfect dear," lacked the energy to oversee an expanding force and delegated considerable authority to him—much to his own delight and that of ranking naval officers who found him sympathetic to their cause.

Not content with operating from behind a desk, Roosevelt made whirlwind inspections of the navy yards and took great delight in reviewing the Navy's new battleships at sea. He worked at improving its gunnery, recommended that an experimental submarine be purchased, and as early as March 1898 suggested that the Navy look into the prospects for manned flight. Taking note of the experiments that Professor Samuel P. Langley of the Smithsonian Institution was conducting with a steam-powered model "aerodrome," he wrote Secretary Long: "The machine has worked. It seems to me worthwhile for this government to try whether it will not work on a large enough scale to be of use in event of war." The war to which Theodore was referring was brewing with Spain over the control of Cuba.

The United States had long looked upon the island with keen

interest, and much consideration had been given over the years to either buying it from the Spanish or seizing it outright. In 1895 the latest in a series of Cuban revolts against Spain had broken out, and most Americans were sympathetic to the rebel cause. Anti-Spanish feeling was fanned by the "yellow press" of William Randolph Hearst and Joseph Pulitzer, which went into "typographical paroxysms" to denounce the alleged brutalities of the Spaniards and the destruction of American property, valued at some $50 million. While both President McKinley and Mark Hanna opposed war with Spain, Roosevelt was in the vanguard of those urging intervention on the side of the Cubans. Speaking at the Naval War College, he truculently declared that "no triumph of peace is quite so great as the supreme triumph of war."

On February 15, 1898, the battleship Maine, which had been sent to Havana to protect American lives and property, was destroyed by a mysterious explosion that took the lives of 266 officers and men. Cool heads suggested that judgment be suspended until an investigation had been made into the cause of the blast, but Hearst and Pulitzer flooded the country with "war extras" blaming the Spaniards for the loss of the ship. "Intervention is a plain and imperative duty!" trumpeted Hearst's New York *Journal*. The cause of the explosion has never been conclusively determined, but Admiral H. G. Rickover theorized in 1976, on the basis of modern technical studies, that a fire resulting from spontaneous combustion in a forward coal bunker—a not uncommon occurrence on warships of the day—set off ammunition in an adjoining magazine. Be that as it may, the American people, whipped into a frenzy by the jingoistic press, was swept along to war despite the efforts of McKinley and the Spaniards to avoid a conflict. On April 19, 1898, Congress, with the clarion call "Remember the *Maine!* To hell with Spain!" ringing in its ears, approved a joint resolution that was tantamount to a declaration of war.

Although most strategists envisioned a war with Spain as being limited to the Caribbean, Theodore had laid plans not only for an intervention in Cuba but for the seizure of the Philippines. When war came, the Asiatic Squadron was to steam into Philippine waters, destroy the decrepit Spanish fleet based at Manila, and take possession of the islands. To make certain these bold plans were carried out with dispatch, he engineered the selection of

Commodore George Dewey, whose fiery temperament matched his own, to command the squadron. Wearied by the series of emergency meetings that had followed the sinking of the *Maine,* Secretary Long took the day off on February 25, 1898, leaving Theodore in charge of the Navy Department. He wasted no time in sending Dewey, then in Hong Kong, a cablegram ordering him to concentrate his scattered ships:

> Keep full of coal. In the event of declaration of war Spain, your duty will be to see that the Spanish squadron does not leave the Asiatic coast and then offensive operations in Philippine Islands.

When he heard about the orders, Long said Roosevelt had acted like "a bull in a china shop," but no attempt was made to rescind Dewey's orders. As soon as the commodore was informed of the declaration of war, his squadron stood out into the South China Sea bound for Manila Bay, some six hundred miles away, with the band of the flagship *Olympia* playing the Sousa march "El Capitan." Early on the morning of May 1, Dewey's ships opened fire on the Spaniards off Cavite, and by the time the smoke had cleared, Roosevelt's foresight had resulted in a great victory. The nation went wild, even though most Americans could have joined President McKinley in confessing that he "could not have told where those darned islands were within two thousand miles." By then, Theodore, enraptured by visions of military glory, had left the Navy Department to take a more active role in the war. Almost thirty-eight years old, with six children and a wife who was recuperating from a serious operation, he could have remained where he was, but that was not his style. "I want to go because I wouldn't feel that I had been entirely true to my beliefs and convictions, and the ideal I had set for myself," he told a friend. Perhaps he also intended to make up for his father's failure to join the Army during the Civil War.

Congress had authorized the organization of three volunteer cavalry regiments to be raised in the West, and Secretary of War Russell A. Alger offered command of one of them to Roosevelt. Wisely he declined, pointing out that his military experience, which consisted of a few years with the New York National Guard, did not qualify him for the post. Instead, he suggested that command of the regiment, the 1st United States Volunteer

Cavalry, be given to Colonel Leonard Wood, a military surgeon who had won the Medal of Honor in the campaign against the Apache chieftain Geronimo. Roosevelt accepted a commission as lieutenant colonel, and as second-in-command departed in a Brooks Brothers uniform for San Antonio, where the regiment was being mustered into the service.

A mixture of western cowboys, eastern sportsmen, and Ivy League athletes, the regiment immediately captured the attention of newsmen. They were dubbed the Rough Riders and described as "a society page, a financial column, a sports section, and a Wild West show all rolled into one." The regiment quickly won a place on the front pages of the nation's newspapers from which it was not to be dislodged. Theodore entered into his new duties with gusto. Having taken his men on a long and dusty training march, he led them upon their return into a saloon and stood treat for all the beer they could drink. "Sir, I consider myself the damnedest ass within ten miles of this camp," he contritely told Wood when it was pointed out that the Army did not usually operate in this fashion.

The campaign for Cuba began in the same lighthearted fashion in which America had entered the war with Spain. Everyone expected that the Army would have little to do because it was thought that the Navy would have little trouble in duplicating Dewey's feat in the Caribbean. But hopes of a quick victory faded when the Spanish warships which had been sent into those waters eluded the Americans and took refuge in the harbor of Santiago, under the protection of powerful shore batteries. The Navy established a blockade, but it was finally accepted that foot soldiers would have to be called in if the Spanish squadron was to be flushed from its lair.

The landing of the some 12,000 men of the U. S. Army's V Corps upon the beaches of Daiquirí and Siboney to the east of Santiago on June 22, 1898, was, according to Richard Harding Davis, who was covering the war for the New York *Herald*, one of the most bizarre episodes in the history of warfare. Looking down upon the operation from a nearby hillside, he wrote:

An army was being landed on the enemy's coast at the dead of night, but with somewhat more of cheers and shrieks and laughter than rise from the bathers in the surf at Coney Island on a hot Sunday. It was a pandemonium of noises. The men still to be landed from the "prison hulks," as they called the transports, were singing in chorus, the men already on shore were dancing naked around the camp-fires on the beach, shouting with delight as they plunged into the first bath that had offered in seven days, and those in the launches, as they were pitched headfirst at the soil of Cuba, signalized their arrival by howls of triumph. . . .

Luckily, the Spaniards did not resist the landing and had retreated to the outer defense perimeter of Santiago. Responsibility for the next move rested upon the ample shoulders of General William R. Shafter, a three-hundred-pound veteran of the Civil War. To probe the enemy's defenses, he ordered a pair of Regular Army infantry regiments to make a reconnaissance in force, while the cavalry, including the Rough Riders, who had been ordered to leave their horses in Florida before embarking for Cuba, were kept in reserve. But Shafter, remaining aboard his headquarters ship, failed to take into account the intense rivalries that existed between the various units of his army.

General Joseph Wheeler, commander of the horseless horsemen and the senior officer ashore, had different ideas as to how the campaign should be launched. "Fighting Joe" had been a dashing Confederate cavalry leader and in the three decades since Appomattox, had thirsted for renewed glory. During the War Between the States, infantry had never scouted ahead of cavalry—not even dismounted cavalry—and he saw no reason for it now. Informed by Cuban irregulars that the Spaniards had established a fortified position about three miles from Siboney, Wheeler slyly pushed the cavalry ahead of the infantry by means of a forced march.

There were two roads out of Siboney—one a narrow path that more or less paralleled the seacoast and the other, a wagon track about a mile farther inland. Having outsmarted the infantry, Wheeler ordered Colonel Wood to take some five hundred men of his regiment down the path that led to the left while an equal number of troopers from two Regular regiments, the 1st and 10th Cavalries—the latter a black unit that had gained its spurs fighting the Indians—were assigned the inland road. Like an inverted V, the trails joined at a place called Las Guasimas.

Reveille had been at three o'clock in the morning of June 24. No bugles were sounded, but the sergeants moved among the huddled forms, shaking the men out of their blankets. Shortly after daybreak, they had set out in a column of fours, but as the dense underbrush closed in, were forced to narrow down to twos, and finally to single file. A thick curtain of cactus, vines, and low trees lined both sides of the trail, hiding small, almost secret places covered with waves of tall grass. It was perfect country for an ambush.

The Rough Riders were resting on their packs beside the trail at a place where it dropped sharply into a deep ravine and then turned upward toward a long ridge topped by the crumbling ruins of a large ranch house. Suddenly, bullets kicked up dirt at their feet. Under fire for the first time, the startled men hesitated in the open. "Deploy!" shouted Wood. "Take cover!" Springing to life, the troopers darted into the dense brush, frantically batting down the almost impenetrable growth with the butts of their carbines. Several men were killed at the regiment's point, including Sergeant Hamilton Fish, Jr. The Spaniards, using smokeless powder, were almost invisible in the high grass, and the only sign of their presence was the *whit-whit* and *z-z-z-eu-u-u* of Mauser bullets. At last, the enemy was spotted, and the Rough Riders began to move forward in quick desperate rushes, dashing from one bit of cover to another. "They advanced grimly, cleaning a bush or a thicket of its occupants before charging it, and securing its cover for themselves," reported Davis, who had accompanied the troops into action. Here is Theodore's account of what happened next:

As we advanced, the cover became a little thicker and I lost touch of the main body under Wood; so I halted and we fired industriously at the ranch buildings ahead of us, some five hundred yards off. Then we heard cheering on the right, and I supposed that this meant a charge on the part of Wood's men, so I sprang up and ordered the men to rush the buildings ahead of us. They came forward with a will. . . .

A bullet struck a palm tree so close to Roosevelt's head that it filled his eyes and ears with tiny splinters; another clipped off one of Wood's gold cuff links. Yelling at the top of their lungs, the Rough Riders swept up the hill toward the ruins. At almost the same time, the 1st and 10th Cavalries, which had been heavily engaged on the right, made contact with the regiment and joined in sweeping the enemy before them. "Come on!" shouted "Fighting Joe" Wheeler. "We've got the damn Yankees on the run!"

Following the skirmish at Las Guasimas, in which sixteen men were killed and about fifty wounded, Wood was promoted to brigadier general, and in recognition of his coolness under fire, Roosevelt was made a colonel and given command of the Rough Riders. Even the Regular Army officers, who had little use for raw volunteers, reluctantly acknowledged that he had handled himself well. A further test came on July 1, 1898—probably the most exciting day in Theodore's life—when General Shafter launched his attack on the defenses of Santiago.

Barring the American advance was a line of ridges known as the San Juan hills which were topped by blockhouses and lined with entrenchments manned by a Spanish force that outnumbered the attackers. To the right of the Americans was another hill, called El Caney, which flanked their position. Shafter's plan called for the quick capture of El Caney by a brigade of Regulars before the troops would be sent across the open ground to take the Spanish positions on the ridges in front of them. But the attack on El Caney bogged down, and the men awaiting the order to assault the San Juan hills were caught under merciless enemy artillery and rifle fire. The black powder used in their guns revealed their positions, and the presence of an observation balloon sent aloft to search out the Spaniards was, in Davis' words, "an invitation to kill everything beneath it. And the enemy responded to the invitation."

For an hour and a half, the troops endured a "hell of fire and heat," the correspondent continued.

The volleys from the rifle-pits sputtered and rattled, and the bullets sang continuously like the wind through the rigging in a gale, shrapnel whined and broke, and still no order came from General Shafter. . . . The situation was desperate. Our troops could not retreat, as the trail for two miles behind them was wedged with men. They could not remain where they were for they were being shot to pieces. There was only one thing they could do—go forward and take the San Juan hills by assault.

Theodore was about to order his men to advance to the sound of the enemy's guns when orders came for the Rough Riders to move forward to support the 3d, 6th, and 9th Cavalries in an assault on one of the heights known as Kettle Hill. "The instant I received my order I sprang on my horse and then my 'crowded hour' began," he later wrote. The Rough Riders broke from the woods behind the 9th, and finding the senior officers hesitant to charge because they had received no orders, Roosevelt shouted: "If you don't want to go forward, let my men pass, please." The regiment's junior officers and black soldiers quickly sprang into line with the Rough Riders. "I waved my hat and we went up the hill with a rush," Theodore declared. Shrapnel nicked him on the elbow and troopers fell about him.

"Roosevelt, mounted high on horseback, and charging the rifle-pits at a gallop and quite alone, made you feel that you would like to cheer," said Davis. "He wore on his sombrero a blue-polka-dot handkerchief . . . which . . . floated out straight behind his head like a guidon. Afterward, the men of his regiment who followed this flag adopted a polka-dot handerchief as the badge of the Rough Riders." The correspondent, who picked up a rifle and joined in the assaults wrote:

They had no glittering bayonets, they were not massed in regular array. There were a few men in advance bunched together and creeping up a steep, sunny hill, the top of which roared and flashed with flame. The men held their guns pressed across their breasts and stepped heavily as they climbed. Behind these first few, spreading out like a fan were single lines of men, slipping and scrambling in the smooth grass, moving forward with difficulty, as though they were wading waist high through water. . . . It was much more wonderful than any swinging charge could have been. They walked to greet death at every step, many of them, as they advanced, sinking suddenly or pitching forward and disappearing in the high grass, but the others waded on. . . . The Spaniards . . . fired a last volley and fled before the swift-moving wave that leaped and sprang up after them. . . . They drove the yellow silk flags of the cavalry and the Stars and Stripes of their country into the soft earth of the trenches and looked back at the road they had climbed and swung their hats in the air.

Little more than a month later, the "splendid little war" was over, but not before Theodore, now an acting brigadier general, had gotten himself into hot water again. Some of his officers, worried that the troops were being left in Cuba during the yellow fever season, prevailed upon him to write a letter to Shafter suggesting that the army be sent home as soon as possible. Emboldened by his agreement, they also prepared a round robin which all including Theodore signed, declaring that "this army must be moved at once, or perish." When the letter was made public, there was an uproar. Shortly afterward, the volunteer troops were evacuated, but the Regular Army which remained behind never forgave Theodore for his impetuosity. And Secretary of War Alger saw to it that he did not get the Medal of Honor which he thought he deserved.

Nevertheless, even before he arrived back in New York to find himself a national hero, Roosevelt—or the Colonel, as he now liked to be called—had been all but chosen by the Republicans as their candidate for governor. Tom Platt, the state's GOP boss, was reluctant to give him the nomination, but he liked the prospect of turning the state over to the Democrats even less, for the incumbent Republican administration was deeply mired in a scandal. Platt and Roosevelt met, and the candidate agreed to consult with the "Easy Boss" on appointments and legislation if he were elected. Once again, there were anguished howls from the mugwumps that Theodore had sold them out, but he brushed off the complaints.

Seven uniformed Rough Riders accompanied the Colonel's campaign train across the state, and a bugler began each rally by sounding the charge. "You have heard the trumpet that sounded to bring you here," the candidate would begin. "I have heard it tear the tropic dawn when it summoned us to fight at Santiago." The Democratic candidate might just as well have stayed at home.

Safe in office, Theodore surprised both the mugwumps and Platt. He conferred with him about legislation and appointees as he had promised, and then proceeded to go his own way. When Theodore backed increased taxes on corporations and other reform measures and insisted on naming his own men to important state jobs, the Boss contrived in 1900 to have him kicked upstairs into the vice-presidency. Mark Hanna resisted the move to choose Roosevelt as McKinley's running mate, but the convention all but nominated him by acclamation. Hanna realized that Theodore was no radical, but regarded him as an unpredictable fellow who couldn't be relied upon to stay on the reservation. "Don't any of you realize that there's only one life between that madman and the Presidency?" he protested.

Tom Platt came to Washington for the inauguration "to see Theodore take the veil," as he gleefully told a friend. Alice, now a vivacious seventeen, who watched the parade from a window over Madame Payne's Manicure Shop at Fifteenth Street and Pennsylvania Avenue, along with the rest of the Roosevelt brood, was another interested spectator. "As I looked at President McKinley, I wondered, in the terminology of the insurance companies, what sort of a 'risk' he was," she later recalled. Theodore himself regarded the vice-presidency as a comedown after the governorship, and was convinced that his political career was finished. "The vice president . . . is really a fifth wheel to the coach," he declared. "It is not a stepping-stone to anything but oblivion." To pass the time, he contemplated resuming the study of law.

Fate intervened, however, in the guise of an anarchist with a gun. On September 6, 1901, McKinley was fatally wounded while attending the Pan-American Exposition at Buffalo. Six days later he died—and Theodore Roosevelt was sworn in as Chief Executive on September 14, 1901. "I told William McKinley it was a mistake to nominate that wild man!" cried a bitter Hanna. "Now look, that damned cowboy is President of the United States!"

Chapter XV
"A BEAUTIFUL FRAME"

"All that is within me cries out to go back to my home on the Hudson River." So said a weary Franklin Roosevelt as the burdens of World War II pressed down upon him. The happiest years of his life were spent on the sprawling acres at Hyde Park and he drew spiritual sustenance from the place. From the window of his room, he looked out over green lawns toward the slow-moving river and the purple Catskills beyond—a sight he loved above all others. Fondly recalling his childhood from the vantage point of the White House, he saw "a small boy [who] took a special delight in climbing an old tree, now unhappily gone, to pick and eat ripe sickle pears. In the spring of the year he sailed his toy boats in the surface water formed by the melting snow. In the summer with his dog he dug into woodchuck holes. And he used to lie flat between the strawberry rows and eat sun-warmed strawberries—the best in the world."

Probably no President of the United States had a happier and more secure childhood than Franklin Roosevelt. "He was brought up in a beautiful frame," a relative observed many years later. As the only child of an elderly father and a young mother who realized they would have no other children, he was adored by his parents. Following the custom of the period, James Roosevelt turned over the details of the boy's upbringing to his wife. Child psychology was unheard-of in that day, but Sallie followed a program aimed at "keeping Franklin's mind on nice things, on a high level; yet . . . in such a way that Franklin never realized that he was following any bent but his own." It seems to have worked well, for he was a happy, healthy, and tractable lad—completely unlike the wan, spindly child that his cousin Theodore had been. Except for an attack of typhoid when he was seven, he hardly ever suffered a serious illness.

Franklin was only three when his parents took him on his first of many trips to Europe, and the family's return provided him with his earliest memory. The steamer on which the Roosevelts were traveling ran into a severe storm, and as water flooded their cabin, it appeared as if the ship was sinking. Wrapping her son in her fur coat, Sallie declared: "Poor little boy. If he must go down, he is going down warm." Franklin, who was enjoying all the excitement, was more concerned about the safety of his playthings. "Mama! Mama! Save my jumping jack!" he cried as his favorite toy bobbed on the fast-rising water.

Sallie doted on her child and breast-fed him until he was nearly a year old. She kept him in shoulder-length golden curls and dresses until he was five, and then insisted on dressing him in the kilts of the Murray clan, to which she was related. Franklin was almost eight before he succeeded in persuading his mother to buy him some English sailor suits with trousers. He was almost nine before Sallie allowed him to bathe himself, and even after he was President, she insisted that he wear overshoes before going out in wet weather. Franklin, in turn, worshipped his mother, realizing at an early age that hers was the governing voice at Springwood.

But there was no rivalry between the boy's parents for his affections. Despite his strong attachment for his mother, Franklin idolized James—whom he called "Pops" and "Popsy"—and was certain of his father's love in return. Although old enough to be Franklin's grandfather, James enjoyed a close relationship with the boy, and no question was too troublesome or too unimportant for him to answer. Franklin's father "never laughed at him," Sallie wrote. "With him, yes—often." James spent a good deal of time with Franklin, and even though Sallie was overprotective of the boy, he taught him to swim, to sail, to fish, and to ride. Upon one occasion when Sallie felt the boy should be disciplined for some breach of the peace, she turned the matter over to James, who called the boy aside and said: "Consider yourself spanked." In winter they went tobogganing on a nearby slope and sailed a speedy iceboat on the frozen Hudson. Franklin was an excellent horseman and was soon given a pony of his own—with the stipulation that he was to be responsible for its care and grooming. By the time he was eight, he could ride the twenty miles from Springwood to Algonac at his father's side without tiring.

As in the case of many only children, Franklin spent much of his time in the company of grown-ups, who found him a shy but precocious child. Upon one occasion when an aunt praised him for his tact, the little boy proudly burst out: "Yes, I'm just chock full of tacks!" Although it is generally thought that Franklin Roosevelt pretty much had his own way as a child, this was not the case. He did not require strict discipline, for as Sallie said, he was "instinctively . . . a good boy," but she kept him on a tight schedule of activities. One day he rebelled against this regimen. Noting a certain sadness on his face, his mother asked why he appeared so unhappy, and was told that he longed for "freedom." Sallie allowed him to come and go as he pleased for a day except for mealtimes. She did not ask him how he spent his time, but noted that he returned home a bit dirtier and more tired than usual. "Quite out of his own accord," she observed, on the following day "he went contentedly back to his routine."

One of Franklin's most vivid memories of his childhood was the blizzard of 1888. "We were cut off," he recalled. "In those days there were few refrigerators and practically no canned goods. At the end of four days we had just about run out of food." James tried to ride up to the village for supplies, but his horse sank into the snow up to its shoulders. Fortunately, a farmer who had shoveled his way along the top of a stone wall carried some milk, eggs, and a couple of chickens to James, who managed to return safely with them. Springwood was out of touch with the rest of the world for almost a week, much to the delight of Franklin, who burrowed out tunnels in the snow.

James tried to instill in his son a sense of stewardship and good manners—of *noblesse oblige*—rather than an interest in the grubbier aspects of moneymaking. Franklin's parents hoped that he would become a country squire like his father and grandfather, content to live a quiet life along the Hudson. Franklin liked to tell a story that illustrated his father's attitude toward the new rich spawned by the industrialization of America. Upon one occasion, Sallie reported they had received a dinner invitation from the Vanderbilts who recently completed an opulent mansion just up the Hudson from Springwood. Having heard much about the place, she expressed an interest in seeing it, but James adamantly declined the invitation. "If we accept, we shall have to have these people to our home," he declared.

From his father, Franklin learned a love of the land and how to efficiently manage the estate that was his birthright. From the time he was small enough to perch on his father's shoulder, he was taken by James on his rounds of the farm and stables. Later, these inspections were conducted on horseback, and every day, they rode across the clipped lawns and meadows, down the long drive to the Post Road and access to the fields that were part of the Roosevelt holdings. Franklin was particularly interested in his father's last remaining pair of trotters, and was fascinated by James's stories about the record-breaking Gloucester, the first horse to trot a mile in less than 2 minutes, 20 seconds. James had sold Gloucester to Senator Leland Stanford before Franklin was born, when he became convinced that trotting was no longer a sport for gentlemen. But the animal never ran a race under Stanford's colors; he was killed in a train wreck while being shipped to California. Gloucester's tail later adorned a wall of the presidential bedroom in the White House.

The sea was also in Franklin's blood and tugged at him throughout his life. With rapt attention, he listened as his mother told him of her childhood voyage halfway around the world on a square-rigger and as his grandfather, Warren Delano, spun out tales of clipper ships and whalers skippered by the Delanos. When he visited the family's ancestral home at Fairhaven, Franklin pored over the old canvas-bound logs of bygone whalers that he found stowed away in the attic and spent much time on a stone wharf jutting out into the Acushnet River. Forty years later, the sight of the last vestiges of New Bedford's once great fleet of whalers, rocking gently at anchor with their tall masts soaring above the granite warehouses, was still fixed indelibly on his mind. Franklin thrilled to the adventures of the Bulloch brothers and the *Alabama*, although he noted that some of the Roosevelts still considered them "pirates." He began to dream of an appointment to Annapolis and a naval career.

Franklin was also a passionate blue-water sailor, and as Frank Freidel, one of his biographers, has noted, he could hardly be lured ashore from his father's fifty-one-foot sailing yacht, the

Half-Moon. When he was sixteen, he was given his own boat, a twenty-one-foot knockabout, the *New Moon,* in which he explored the rugged shoreline of the Bay of Fundy near the family summer place on Campobello Island. Years later, as Assistant Secretary of the Navy, he found this knowledge useful. Sailing in a destroyer to inspect naval facilities in Frenchman's Bay on the coast of Maine, Franklin suggested that since he was intimately familiar with those waters, he should pilot the vessel through a passage between Campobello and the mainland. The destroyer's skipper, Lieutenant William F. Halsey, Jr., reluctantly yielded the conn, worried that this "white-flanneled yachtsman" might pile his ships up on the rocks. He was surprised to find that Roosevelt "knew his business" and took the vessel safely through the treacherous channel.

Like Cousin Theodore, Franklin was also an enthusiastic naturalist. When he turned eleven, James gave him a small-caliber rifle and he began bagging birds for his collection. At first, the boy tried mounting the specimens himself, but unlike Theodore, he never became skilled at taxidermy and the work was turned over to a professional. Over the years, the collection grew in size and variety and James and Sallie were extremely proud of it. Later, Sallie had the glass cabinets housing the birds moved near the front door where visitors to Hyde Park can still see the collection as they enter the house. Bird watching was one of Franklin's lifelong hobbies, along with stamp collecting and gathering naval memorabilia, and as President he would sometimes rout out guests at Hyde Park at dawn to join him in the woods to search for birds. He claimed to be nearsighted, but as his wife observed, "he could always point to a bird and tell me what it was."

Franklin grew up without much companionship from children his own age. Various Roosevelt and Delano relations visited Hyde Park, including his niece and nephew, Helen and Taddy, the children of his half brother, James Roosevelt Roosevelt, but his closest friends were Archie and Edmund Rogers. Their father, Archibald Rogers, was one of John D. Rockefeller's lieutenants, and they lived a mile and a half away at an estate called Crumwold. After Archie died of diphtheria in 1889, Eddie was Franklin's dearest companion. Together, they built a tree house among the hemlocks and launched a raft which promptly sank, carrying their fishing equipment to the bottom of the Hudson. Franklin's first taste of education came in October 1888, when he was invited to join the Rogers boys in studying German under the tutelage of their governess for two hours each day at Crumwold. He had already been taught to read and write simple English words at home. Franklin picked up basic German from these classes, and his knowledge of the language was improved by a Fräulein Reinhardt, the first of a line of governesses installed at Springwood. An intense, humorless woman who later had a nervous breakdown, she was followed by Jeanne Sandoz, a young French-speaking Swiss, who proved to be Franklin's favorite teacher.

"More than anyone else, [she] laid the foundations of my education," he wrote many years later. It was not an easy task. Franklin had outgrown his shyness and like most preadolescents enjoyed playing the comedian. Posing a riddle for Mademoiselle, he asked: "What animals are always ready to travel?" Answer: "Elephants—they always have their trunks with them." He insisted on spelling his name backward and was often mischievous. She was a talented teacher, however, and succeeded in giving him a sound grounding in French and other subjects, as well as injecting a slight sense of social responsibility in her charge. A hint of it showed in a composition written about ancient Egypt, despite his breeziness. "The working people had nothing," Franklin wrote. "The kings made them work so hard and gave them so little that by wingo! they nearly starved and by jinks! they had hardly any clothes so they died in the quadrillions."*

The boy was not only an omnivorous reader but soaked up information easily. Sallie was reading aloud to him one day while Franklin lay sprawled at her feet, seemingly absorbed in his stamp collection. "I don't believe you are hearing a word I am reading," she said, with some irritation. To prove her mistaken, Franklin repeated word for word the entire last paragraph that his mother had read. When she expressed surprise, he replied, "Why, I'd be ashamed if I couldn't do at least two things at once." Franklin read the usual books for boys and then ransacked Springwood's well-stocked library. He liked books about the sea and naval affairs and read Mahan's works on sea power and his

* Mlle Sandoz left after two years to marry, and Fräulein Reinhardt entered a sanitarium, so Roosevelt often joked that he had driven one governess insane and another to matrimony.

Life of Nelson as a teenager. He was also fond of Kipling and Parkman, but his reading included a wide range of subjects, and his appetite for facts was seemingly insatiable. Sallie once discovered him propped up in bed reading his way through the Webster's Unabridged Dictionary.

Before he was fourteen, Franklin had accompanied his parents on eight trips to Europe. As James grew older and his health began to fail, the family went to the spa at Bad Nauheim with increasing frequency. In 1891 when Franklin was nine, he was enrolled at the local school for six weeks, his only experience of ordinary school life. "I go to public school with a lot of little mickies," he wrote a cousin. "We have German reading, German dictation, the history of Siegfried, and arithmetic . . . and I like it very much." The German schoolmaster reported that he was "an unusually bright young fellow" with "an engaging manner" and was "one of the most popular children in the school."

Franklin also saw far more of his own country than most boys of his age. As a president of the Louisville, New Albany, and Chicago Railroad, James was entitled to his own private rail car— the late-nineteenth-century equivalent of a corporate jet—and often took his son along on inspection trips, traveling as far as upper Wisconsin where the elder Roosevelt owned property. The high spot came in 1892 when James was appointed a New York commissioner to the Chicago World's Fair. No sooner had the family stepped down from their private car than they were met by a conspicuous figure in full coachman's livery including a tall hat and whip. "Cousin Jimmy, I am your Cousin Clinton," said the man, who turned out to be one of the upstate New York Roosevelts who had moved West. The proprietor of a large livery stable, he had the concession to provide transportation for official visitors to the fair. Cousin Clinton insisted on getting up on the box to personally drive the family to their hotel—and an aide to whom Franklin told the story guessed that the President's father enjoyed the experience more than his dignified mother.

When Franklin was five, James took him to the White House to meet his good friend, Grover Cleveland. The President had offered James the post of minister to Holland in return for his services to the Democratic party, but Roosevelt declined the appointment. Much to his satisfaction, his eldest son, James, who had made a handsome contribution to the party, was named first secretary of the American Embassy in Vienna, during Cleveland's first term. "Rosy" was rewarded with a similar post in London after making a $10,000 contribution during Cleveland's second term.† Young Franklin remembered the President as being careworn and depressed. As James and his son rose to go, Cleveland put his hand on the boy's head and said: "My little man, I am making a strange wish for you. It is that you may never be President of the United States."

Among the many Roosevelt cousins who came to Hyde Park to visit was a painfully shy little girl named Anna Eleanor Roosevelt. The daughter of Franklin's godfather, Elliott Roosevelt and his beautiful wife, Anna, she was a withdrawn child who stood bashfully in a doorway sucking on a finger, until Franklin set about entertaining her by crawling "around the nursery . . . bearing me on his back," as she later recalled. Eleanor Roosevelt —she rarely used her full name except to sign legal documents— was born on October 11, 1884, and compared to Franklin's sunlit childhood, that of his fifth cousin was Dickensian in its bleakness.

"From all accounts I must have been a more wrinkled and less attractive baby than the average," Eleanor wrote in her memoirs, which are a curious mixture of revelation and reticence. "I was a shy, solemn child even at the age of two, and I am sure that even when I danced, which I did frequently, I never smiled." She paints a self-portrait of a sensitive child, full of fears—"afraid of being scolded, afraid that other people would not like me"—hungering for praise and affection from her mother, and secure only in the company of her beloved father. "He dominated my life as long as he lived, and was the love of my life for many years after he died," she declared. But as his daughter's need for him grew, Elliott became an increasingly shadowy figure in her life.

Eleanor described her mother as "one of the most beautiful women I have ever seen" but was convinced that in Anna's eyes

† While "Rosy" was serving in London, his wife, Helen Astor, died leaving him with the care of his son and daughter, Taddy and Helen. He asked Bamie to come and help him, and she, as always when there was a family crisis, quickly responded. Intelligent, fun-loving, and gregarious, she soon had many friends in English upper-class circles, and Ambassador Thomas F. Bayard asked her to serve as the embassy's unofficial hostess. Much to the surprise and delight of her family, she married Commander William Sheffield Cowles, the U.S. naval attaché, a genial and portly man with a walrus moustache whom she called "Mr. Bearo." Despite her age and deformity, they had a healthy son, William Sheffield Cowles, Jr., who was born in 1898.

she saw disappointment in her own plainness. "You are the ugly duckling of the family," she was told by one of her mother's sisters, confirming her own feelings of inadequacy. Anna was given to headaches and for hours she would be called upon to stroke her brow, but her mother preferred her other children and showed it. Because of the little girl's grave solemnity, Anna considered her "old-fashioned" and called her "Granny." To add to her problems, Eleanor wore a very uncomfortable brace for two years that was designed to correct a spinal curvature and prevented her from bending over. "I was always disgracing my mother," she said in later years.

Curiously enough, like Franklin Roosevelt, one of her earliest memories was of a disaster at sea, but the reaction of the two children was diametrically opposite. While Franklin regarded his near brush with drowning as a great adventure, Eleanor was terrified by the experience. Not yet three, she was on her way to Europe with her mother and father, when their ship collided with another vessel and the passengers were ordered to abandon ship. "My father stood in a boat below me, and I was dangling over the side to be dropped into his arms," she recalled. "I was terrified and shrieking, and clung to those who were to drop me. Finally, I was safely in the little boat, and we transferred to the boat which had run us down in the fog, and were taken back to New York."

The accident left Eleanor with a lifelong fear of the sea, and when she tearfully refused to board another ship, was left behind in New York with relatives, the first of many desertions. By 1890 Elliott had begun to drink heavily, and the family—which now included a son, Elliott, Jr.—began to disintegrate. The elder Roosevelt spent much of his time in sanitariums seeking a cure for his alcoholism, only to have new bouts with the bottle. A second son, Hall, was born in 1891, while the family was living in Europe, a period in which six-year-old Eleanor spent many unhappy months in a convent outside Paris where she had been placed to learn French. "When people have asked how I was able to get through some of the very bad periods in my later life," she once said, "I have been able to tell them honestly that, because of all the early discipline I had, I inevitably grew into a really tough person."

Early in 1892, Elliott returned to the United States and in an effort to reconcile with his wife, promised Anna that he would take another cure and establish himself in a steady occupation. Anna, however, had heard this litany before, and stipulated a year of separation to see if Elliott could live up to his promises. Douglas Robinson, Eliott's brother-in-law, offered him a job managing his family's extensive timber and mineral holdings in southwestern Virginia, and at first he made a success of it. Eleanor missed her father desperately and understanding little of the reason for his absence, blamed her mother for the separation. She lived for Elliott's letters to his "Little Nell," and carried them around with her as a talisman. Shortly before the end of the year, Anna Roosevelt died of diphtheria at the age of twenty-nine. Eleanor's description of her reaction to her mother's death graphically illustrates the gulf separating them:

> I can remember standing by a window when Cousin Susie . . . told me that my mother was dead. She was very sweet to me, and I must have known that something terrible had happened. Death meant nothing to me, and one fact wiped out everything else—my father was back and I would see him very soon.

Elliott did return, but not to carry Eleanor away with him as she had so often fantasized. Anna had designated her mother as the children's guardian, and Mrs. Hall did not feel that Elliott could be trusted to take care of them. Eleanor, little Ellie, and Hall went to live in their grandmother's brownstone on West Thirty-seventh Street. When they had been installed there, Elliott came to see his daughter. "He was dressed all in black, looking very sad," she related. "He held out his arms and gathered me to him. In a little while he began to talk, to explain to me that my mother was gone, that she had been all the world to him, and now he had only my brothers and myself. . . . Someday I would make a home for him again, we would travel together and do many things which he painted as interesting and pleasant, to be looked forward to in the future together. . . . There started that day a feeling which never left me—that he and I were very close together, and some day we would have a life of our own together.

Eleanor's education had been neglected because of the discord in the family, and one of her aunts was horrified to learn that when she was nearly seven she could not read. Following her mother's death, the child was sent to a school for the offspring of fashionable families, and once she got over her initial fear of rejection, proved to be an excellent student. Like Franklin, she had a retentive memory, was very good at reciting poetry, and her compositions—many of them fantasies about her life with her father—were well written. She had no head for figures, however. "Mathematics, from plain arithmetic to geometry, was torture for me, and all grammar just about as bad, because both required a certain amount of reasoning, and I tried to do them entirely from memory," she said. Some of Eleanor's companions regarded her as a "grind," but the girl really strived to excel out of hope that this would ensure praise and attention.

"Very early I became conscious of the fact that there were men and women and children around me who suffered in one way or another," she said, tracing the origins of the lacerating social conscience that was to prove both a trial and a triumph. Upon one occasion when the Roosevelts were touring Italy, Eleanor was given a donkey to ride which was led by a small boy. Moved by the sight of his cut and bleeding feet, she insisted that he ride the donkey while she trotted alongside. While Elliott was still living with his family, he followed the practice initiated by his father of visiting the family charities and took Eleanor along to the Newsboys' Home and the Orthopedic Hospital. "Of course I did not really understand many of the things I saw, but I still think I gained impressions that have remained with me all my life," she said.

Ellie died a year after his mother, also of diphtheria, and Eleanor was now even more alone. All her thoughts were of her father, who had abandoned his position in Virginia and was living with his mistress in New York under an assumed name. "He rarely sent word before he arrived, but never was I in the house, even in my room two long flights of stairs above the entrance door, that I did not hear his voice the minute he entered the front door," she said. "Walking down stairs was far too slow. I slid down the banisters and usually catapulted into his arms before his hat was hung up." One of these visits ended in a shattering experience for the little girl. Accompanied by a couple of dogs, Elliott took his daughter for a walk and stopped off at his club where he deposited the dogs and his daughter with the doorman

Edith Carow Roosevelt (1861–1948). Courtesy, Theodore Roosevelt Collection, Harvard College Library.

Sagamore Hill. Courtesy, Theodore Roosevelt Collection, Harvard College Library.

Springwood (before the alteration of 1915). Courtesy, Franklin D. Roosevelt Library.

T.R. and his family at play (a photo taken by Edith in 1894).
Courtesy, Theodore Roosevelt Collection, Harvard College.

The Roosevelt family in 1907. Left to right: Kermit, Archie, T.R., Ethel, Edith, Quentin, and Ted. Alice had married Nicholas Long-worth. Courtesy, Theodore Roosevelt Collection, Harvard College Library.

"Princess Alice," Alice Roosevelt Longworth (b. 1884). Courtesy,
Franklin D. Roosevelt Library.

Archie and Quentin Roosevelt at Plattsburg, New York, under-
.going military training before American entry into World War I.
Courtesy, Underwood and Underwood.

Theodore Roosevelt, Jr., in World War II. Courtesy, Theodore
Roosevelt Collection, Harvard College Library.

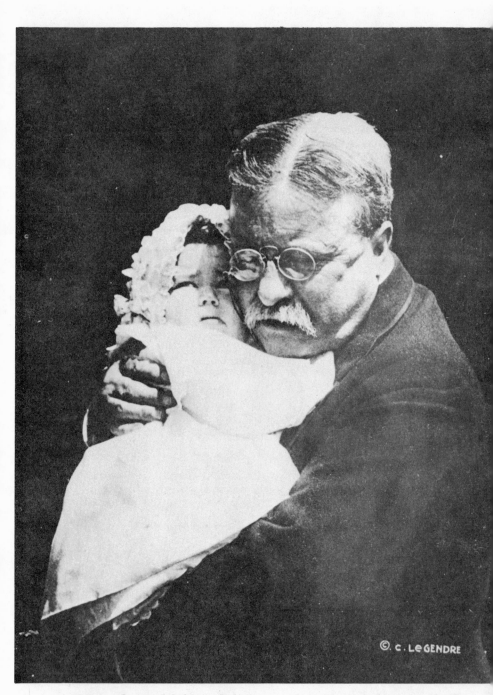

T.R. and grandchild (Edith Roosevelt Derby). Believed to be his last photograph. Courtesy, Theodore Roosevelt Collection, Harvard College Library.

while he went to the bar for a drink. For six hours she huddled forgotten on a chair in the cloakroom along with the dogs before her drunken father was carried past her. She was taken home by the doorman.

On August 14, 1894, Elliot died in a fit of delirium tremens. "I simply refused to believe it," said Eleanor, when she was told of his death by one of her aunts. "While I wept long and went to bed still weeping, I finally went to sleep and began the next day living in my dream world as usual." Mrs. Hall did not allow Eleanor or her brother to attend the funeral "so I had no tangible thing to make his death real to me. From that time on I knew in my mind that my father was dead, and yet I lived with him more closely, probably than I had when he was alive." Joseph Lash, Eleanor's friend and perceptive biographer, believes that it was probably fortunate for her that her father died when he did. "By his death Elliott made it possible for his daughter to maintain her dream-picture of him" without having to come to terms with reality.

For the next five years, until she was fifteen, Eleanor was rotated between New York and the Hall family mansion on the Hudson at Tivoli. Her grandmother was a sympathetic but strict guardian, and her sense of what was proper compounded the child's own solemnity and loneliness. Repressed and introverted, she lived "in a dream world in which I was the heroine and my father the hero." Eleanor grew up to be a tall, gawky girl with long blond hair trailing down her back. Her skirts were usually too short, and the few dresses she owned were shapeless and without style. From the first of November to the first of April, regardless of the weather, Mrs. Hall insisted that she wear long flannel underwear, black stockings, and high button shoes.

Winters were usually spent in the city on West Thirty-seventh Street, "with classes and private lessons, and for entertainment occasionally, on a Saturday afternoon, a child or two for supper or play," Eleanor recalled. Corinne Robinson, her cousin, told Lash that her mother often tried to persuade her to visit Eleanor but she was reluctant to go there. "I remember the Thirty-seventh Street home as the darkest, most desolate house I have ever seen," she said. The situation at Tivoli, where the family spent the summer, was equally grim. Valentine Hall, Jr., Eleanor's uncle, had begun to drink heavily and she was afraid of him. There were no children of her own age living nearby for her to play with, and with Uncle Vallie becoming increasingly difficult to handle, none were invited. One day Eleanor, who was visiting her Aunt Corinne, burst into tears and cried: "Auntie, I have no real home!"

Grandmother Hall tried to discourage any contact between Eleanor and her father's dynamic relatives, fearing perhaps that she and her little brother might slip out of her control. Upon one or two occasions, however, she was allowed to pay summer visits to Uncle Ted and Aunt Edith at Sagamore Hill. As a child she had sometimes played with Alice, who was closest in age of her cousins but she was "so much more sophisticated and grown-up that I was in great awe of her." Quicksilver Alice regarded Eleanor as too serious to be fun. "She was full of duty, never very gay, a frightful bore for the more frivolous people like ourselves."

But Uncle Ted's affection was genuine and gargantuan. Eleanor was his favorite niece because she was the daughter of "poor Ellie" and he felt sorry for her. Upon her arrival at Oyster Bay, he "pounced" upon her like a bear, hugging her to his chest "with such vigor that he tore all the gathers out of Eleanor's frock and both button holes out of her petticoat." When Theodore learned that the girl could not swim, he immediately set out to remedy this situation. He told her to jump off the dock, which she did with her eyes shut—her fear of displeasing him overcoming her fear of the water—and came up gasping and sputtering. He also took her on "scrambles" across the countryside in which Eleanor found it difficult to keep up with her more agile cousins. "I remember these visits as a great joy in some ways, however, for I loved chasing through the hay stacks and the barn with Uncle Ted after us, and going up to the gun room on the top floor of the Sagamore house where Uncle Ted would read aloud, chiefly poetry." Edith was very much concerned about Eleanor—but she also saw something that others didn't. "Poor little soul, she is very plain," she told Bamie. "Her mouth and teeth have no future, but . . . the ugly duckling may turn out to be a swan."

One of the few times when Eleanor saw boys of her own age was at Aunt Corinne's annual Christmas party for all branches of the family. These affairs were more pain to her than pleasure. Her cousins saw each other often and had more to talk about than she did, they were better at winter sports, and she was an awkward dancer. Mrs. Hall still insisted on dressing her in short dresses while Alice wore sophisticated long gowns. "I knew, of course, that I was different from all the other girls and if I had not known, they were frank in telling me," she observed. Upon one occasion, her handsome cousin Franklin took notice of the pathetic wallflower and asked her to dance. Forty years later she still remembered her gratitude.

Suddenly in 1899, when Eleanor was fifteen, the world opened up for her—thanks largely to Bamie. She persuaded Mrs. Hall to send the girl to Mlle Marie Souvestre's school which had done so much for her thirty years before. Following the Franco-Prussian War, Mlle Souvestre had moved her school, now called Allenswood, from outside Paris to Wimbledon near London. Under her guidance, the ugly duckling became a swan.

"I am getting along finely, both mentally and physically." So wrote fourteen-year-old Franklin Roosevelt to his mother and father from Groton in September 1896, shortly after he entered the school. Sallie had kept the boy under her wing for as long as she could, but with much forboding she was finally persuaded by James that the time had come to allow Franklin to take his place in the world. "It is very hard to leave our darling boy," she confided to her diary after she and James had left him in the care of the Reverend Endicott Peabody, the school's founder, and returned to the now strangely quiet rooms of Springwood. "James and I feel this parting very much."

It was a crisis for Franklin, too. Not only had he exchanged the love and security of Hyde Park for the casual brutalities of boarding school, he came to Groton laboring under several handicaps. His classmates in the Third Form had been together at school for two years and had created their own circles of friendship; it was difficult for a "new boy" to break in, especially when the other boys thought he spoke with an English accent. The abrupt change in living conditions must also have been a shock. At Springwood, Franklin had a large, comfortable room with a commanding view of the Hudson, while at Groton he was lodged in a spartan cubicle with only the barest essentials and a curtain across the door. The boy's biggest problem, however, was his nephew, Taddy, who was in the class ahead of him, and was regarded as "a queer sort." It did nothing for the new boy's prestige to be known as Taddy's "Uncle Frank"—but he said, "I would sooner be Uncle Frank rather than Nephew Rosy."

Punishment for a boy who deviated from what was normally accepted at Groton was swift. He was given the "bootbox"—doubled up inside a small locker by his seniors—or "pumped"—bent face upward over a lavatory trough while buckets of water were thrown over him until he felt as if he were drowning. Taddy was "bootboxed" and "pumped" but not Franklin. He managed to fit in with the majority, cultivated an acceptable accent with a disappearing "r" at the end of words, and as Sallie said, "did very well at his studies, but was very far from being a prodigy."

Peabody, who was known as the Rector, had modeled Groton on the great English public schools, and a manly Christianity was inculcated in his charges. Something of a benign despot, his presence pervaded the place from early morning chapel to the evening handshake with each of the hundred-or-so boys. "He would be an awful bully if he weren't such a terrible Christian," Averell Harriman told his father. Peabody's goal was the "moral and physical as well as the intellectual development" of the boys entrusted to him, and he preached the doctrine of service—service to God, country, and man. Athletics rather than intellectual brilliance was encouraged and as Peabody's biographer states, "Instinctively, he trusted a football player more than a non-football player, just as the boys did."

Franklin wanted very much to fit in, but he was too light for football, baseball, or crew, the only sports that mattered at Groton. Tennis and golf, at which he excelled, were not considered important. Still, to prove that he had the proper school spirit, he cheered himself hoarse at football games and accepted the thankless task of manager of the baseball team. The only place where he distinguished himself was in winning the high kick. In his second year, he won the Punctuality Prize but accumulated a sufficient number of black marks from his masters to be considered a regular fellow. He joined the Debating Society and took the affirmative on such issues as the independence of the Philippines and increasing the strength of the Navy.

Franklin and several of his schoolmates almost made their own contribution to the latter proposition. Stirred by the patriotic fervor resulting from the Spanish-American War, they laid plans to run away from school and join the Navy. The plan failed when some of the boys, including young Roosevelt, came down with scarlet fever and were placed under quarantine in the school infirmary. As soon as she heard the news, Sallie hastened to Groton. Unable to enter the sickroom, she had a tall stepladder placed under a window and there she sat for hours conversing with her son and keeping him and the other boys supplied with delicacies and games. Shortly after being elected governor of New York, Cousin Theodore who extolled the same manly virtues as the Rector, visited the school and Franklin was tremendously impressed by his remarks: "If a man has courage, goodness, and brains, no limit can be placed to the greatness of the work he may accomplish. He is the man needed today in politics."

Franklin's last year at Groton was his happiest. He was named a dormitory prefect with the task of keeping order among the new students, acted and sang in a school play, and won the Latin Prize, which consisted of a set of Shakespeare. "He was gray-eyed, cool, self-possessed, intelligent and had the warmest, most friendly and understanding smile," said one of the younger boys. To deal with his nearsightedness, he began to wear a pince-nez and adopted the habit of throwing back his head to get a better view of the person to whom he was talking. Upon his graduation at the end of June 1900, Peabody wrote that Franklin "has been a thoroughly faithful scholar & a most satisfactory member of this school throughout his course. I part with Franklin with reluctance."

Many of Franklin's classmates were to consider him a traitor to his class and to the ideals of Groton, but as he told the Rector: "More than forty years ago you said, in a sermon in the Old Chapel, something about not losing boyhood ideals in later life. Those were Groton ideals—taught by you—I try not to forget— and your words are still with me." In 1932 the old man voted for Herbert Hoover, but in 1936 and again in 1940 he was a Roosevelt man.

Franklin had wanted to enter the Naval Academy and become a naval officer, but his parents pointed out that as their only son, he would have a considerable estate to manage and other responsibilities which made such a choice impossible. Harvard and then probably the law were the prescribed path for his future. Harvard Yard had changed little over the two decades since Theodore Roosevelt had graduated, except that the student body had more than doubled and there were several new buildings. The faculty was studded with such bright names as Frederick Jackson Turner, Josiah Royce, William James, George Pierce Baker, and George Lyman Kittredge, among others. The students ranged from a few brilliant outlanders to languid aristocratic drones.

For Franklin it was pretty much a continuation of Groton. He took up residence in one of the luxurious apartments on Mount Auburn Street which was known as the "Gold Coast" and much favored by the wealthy graduates of Groton and similar schools. He had known his roommate, Lathrop Brown, at Groton, and most of his friends had also been students there. As a Roosevelt, he was immediately taken up by the hostesses of Cambridge and Beacon Hill, with some believing him to be the nephew of the dashing Theodore. Handsome and charming, he was much sought after, and there was hardly a weekend when he was not attending a dance, a dinner, or a party. "My dress-suit looked like a dream and was much admired," he wrote his mother.

Young Roosevelt majored in history and political science, with English and public speaking as his minors. He also took courses in economics, Latin, and French—a much heavier load than most Harvard men elected to carry. But Franklin was no "grind." Upon one occasion, he joined his classmates in slipping one by one out of a window and down a fire escape from one boring but nearsighted professor's lectures on English history. He studied under all the great names of Harvard, but none of them succeeded in creating a thirst for learning. In fact, he dropped out of one of Josiah Royce's philosophy courses after three weeks. Most of his grades were in the gentlemanly range of low B or C, and unlike Theodore Roosevelt did not make Phi Beta Kappa. But like Theodore, he was dissatisfied with his education at Harvard in later years—blaming it on the failure of the faculty to stimulate the students. As he told Lathrop Brown, his courses had been "like an electric lamp that hasn't any wire. You need the lamp for light but it's useless if you can't switch it on."

Athletics were also a frustration. He was six-feet one-inch tall but weighed only 146 pounds, so he was quickly cut when he went out for the freshman football team and made only one of the intramural teams. The same thing happened when he went out for the crew. He made his mark instead in extracurricular activities, particularly on the *Crimson*, the undergraduate daily. Competition was keen and the work demanding but he won one of the managing editorships. This was helped by a scoop that resulted from luck and connections. Learning that Cousin Theodore, by now Vice-President, was in Boston, Franklin telephoned to see him. Theodore let drop the word that he was coming to Harvard in a few days to lecture one of the political science classes. A year earlier, Franklin had begun his political career by joining the Harvard Republican Club, despite the Democratic leanings of his branch of the family, and had pitched in enthusiastically to help elect the Colonel and McKinley, although he was still too young to vote.

At Harvard, Franklin suffered his first social rebuff, which, according to his wife, left him with a deep psychological scar. He had hoped to be tapped for Porcellian, the most snobbish of Harvard's clubs to which Theodore had belonged, but was passed over and had to settle for Fly, the next ranking club. Eleanor Roosevelt told Frank Freidel that she believed this blow "gave him an inferiority complex and led him to become more democratic than he otherwise would have been."

What had been responsible for his rejection? Perhaps it was due to the activities of Taddy, who was using Harvard as a springboard from which to sow his wild oats. The recipient of an income of $40,000 a year from the Astor estate, he eloped with a girl named Sadie Meisinger, a frequenter of the Haymarket, generally acknowledged as New York's most prominent house of assignation, where girls were openly auctioned off to the highest bidder. The yellow press had a field day with the marriage of "Dutch Sadie" and a Roosevelt who was also a grandson of *the* Mrs. Astor. "It will be well for him to go to parts unknown . . . and begin life anew," wrote a disgusted Franklin. Taddy and his bride went to Florida, but it may not have been far enough away to preserve Franklin's social prestige in the eyes of the fastidious members of Porcellian.‡

‡ Although everyone expected the marriage to quickly break up, Taddy and Sadie returned to New York, where they lived until her death in 1940. Taddy was a recluse and lived in a garage in Forest Hills. When asked by the trustees of the Astor estate about what should be done with his income of some $60,000 a year, he told them not to bother him, writes James Roosevelt, FDR's eldest son, in his book *My Parents*. Some members of the family tried to keep in touch with him,

Perhaps his contemporaries' perception of him had something
to do with this rebuff. Some of his classmates regarded him as
"pushy," and too eager to be liked. They thought he smiled too
much and was not to be trusted. In Roosevelt's defense, it should
be pointed out that until he had entered Groton, he had had little
contact with people of his own age, and desperately wanted to be
accepted and to achieve success. If his geniality seemed a mask
for ambition it was a disguise which he believed he had to assume to achieve the goals he had established for himself. Still,
life at Harvard was pleasant despite the unsettling rejection by
Porcellian. As librarian of Fly and Hasty Pudding, he indulged
his passion for books, adding to his own collection of naval volumes and prints as well as to the clubs' libraries. And his high
spirits, vigor, and easy affability attracted many friends.

Midway in Franklin's freshman year, his father died at the age
of seventy-two. For several years, James had been suffering from
heart trouble, and all through 1900, his condition had steadily
worsened, so his passing was not unexpected. Sallie sat through
the long nights by his bedside giving him "remedies at regular intervals," but early on December 8 he breathed his last. "All is
over. At 2.20 he merely slept away," the heartbroken Sallie wrote
in her diary. "As I write these words, I wonder how I lived when
he left me." James left a $120,000 trust fund to each of his sons
which provided an annual income of about $6,000, while Spring-
wood and the residue of his estate went to his widow, who had
inherited about $1.3 million at the death of her father two years
before.

Sallie was only forty-six, and as much as she missed her husband life had to go on. "I try to keep busy, but it is hard," she
wrote. "I had all F's birds out to dust and air. . . . One day is
much like another." For twenty years, she had divided her love
between James and Franklin and now she concentrated all of it
on her son. In his will, James had stipulated that she was to be
the young man's sole guardian. "I want him under the supervi-
sion of his mother"—and she immediately took over this role. As
soon as her affairs were in order, she moved to Boston to be near
Franklin. An attractive woman with an imperious manner, she

---

but he brushed them off, too. "When he died [in 1958] they went to quite a bit
of expense to give him a fancy funeral, so it came as quite a shock when he left
his several millions to the Salvation Army." He was buried in the family plot at
St. James' Church, Hyde Park.

dominated all those about her, including her son. Young girls attracted to him by the prestige of the Roosevelt name and Franklin's broad-shouldered, square-jawed good looks were put off by his mother's influence over him. They considered him a "mama's boy" whose superficial self-assurance covered a timid conventionality, and some called him a "feather duster."

This reading of the young man's character was deceptive, however. He went along with his mother's wishes only when it suited him and brushed them aside when he desired. Rather than being frivolous, his father had instilled in him a strong sense of duty to those less fortunate than himself which was combined with a sympathy for the underdog. He worked with poor boys at the St. Andrews Boys Club in Boston and he was a leader at Harvard in raising funds for the relief of Boer women and children held in British concentration camps in South Africa. And Franklin was a hard worker when the task interested him. Thanks to advanced work he had taken at Groton, he finished the requirements for a bachelor of arts degree in three years. As a reward for his labors on the *Crimson*, he was named the paper's president—or editor in chief—a highly coveted position. But to take it, he had to remain at Cambridge for another year, so he enrolled in graduate school not with any intention of earning an advanced degree but to secure the editorship.

On Thanksgiving Day 1903, while visiting her family in Fairhaven, Sallie wrote in her diary, "Franklin gave me a quite startling announcement." "Unknown to any of us," as she put it in later years, he had fallen in love with his cousin Eleanor, and firmly announced their intention to be married as soon as possible. Sallie had been unaware of Franklin's serious interest in Eleanor—or in any other girl for that matter. As a dashing Harvard man, he had his share of dates and feminine friends, including Alice Roosevelt, with whom he exchanged bantering notes, but "he had never been in any sense a ladies man," his mother said. "I don't believe I ever remember hearing him talk about girls or even a girl.*" Immediately upon his return to Cambridge, Franklin tried to soften the blow with a soothing letter to "Dearest Mama":

* Two of FDR's sons dispute this point. Both James and Elliott Roosevelt have written that while he was at Harvard he was in love with Frances Dana, whose grandfathers were Richard Henry Dana, author of *Two Years Before the Mast*,

I know what pain I must have caused you and you know I wouldn't
do it if I really could have helped it. . . . That's all that could be
said—I know my mind, have known it for a long time, and know
that I could never think otherwise. . . . I am the happiest man just
now in the world; likewise the luckiest—And for you dear Mummy,
you know nothing can ever change what we have always been & always will be to each other—and only now you have two children to
love & love you—and Eleanor as you know will always be a daughter to you in every true way. . . .

From her future daughter-in-law, she also received a tender
letter, carefully emphasizing Franklin's suggestion that Sallie was
not losing a son but gaining another child to love her:

I know just how you feel & how hard it must be, but I do so want
you to learn to love me a little. You must know that I will always
try to do what you wish for I have grown to love you very dearly
during the past summer. It is impossible for me to tell you how I
feel toward Franklin. I can only say that my one great wish is always to prove worthy of him.

The romance between Eleanor and Franklin had begun the
previous year soon after her return from school in England. She
was on the train bound up the Hudson to Tivoli when Franklin,
on his way to Hyde Park with his mother, saw a tall, slim girl
with soft wavy hair whom he recognized as his distant cousin.
They chatted awhile and he took her into an adjoining car to
meet "Cousin Sallie," as Eleanor called her. Over the next several
months, they met at parties at various homes in New York, Boston, and along the river, and her name appeared with increasing
regularity in his diary. At the end of the year Franklin visited
Washington at the invitation of Bamie and saw much of Eleanor,
who was staying at the White House as Uncle Ted's guest. Soon,
their interest in each other broadened into love.

Eleanor Roosevelt had returned from her tutelage under Mlle

---

and Henry Wadsworth Longfellow. In fact, James flatly states that Franklin
"nearly married" her but was talked out of it by his mother, who pointed out
that Frances was a Catholic. She later married one of his classmates and FDR
remained on the best of terms with them. It is James Roosevelt's opinion that
his father would have married the young lady if he had really wanted to despite
his mother's objections.

uberant, and bubbling over with missionary zeal, he was, as Lord
Morley said, a cross between St. Paul and St. Vitus. Waving a
"big stick" abroad and promising a "square deal" at home, he
captured the popular imagination, and his dynamic personality
typified the spirit of the age.

Unlike the complaisant McKinley and his predecessors, who
had all but abdicated national leadership to the Congress, Roosevelt believed that the President should exercise the ultimate authority in government. "It was not only his right but his duty to
do anything that the needs of the nation demanded, unless such
action was forbidden by the Constitution or by the laws," the
new Chief Executive declared shortly after taking office.

With his usual enthusiasm, he embraced antitrust legislation,
child-labor laws, railroad rate reform, conservation of national resources, wildlife preserves, a moderate policy of uplift for blacks,
workmen's compensation, income and inheritance taxes, and pure
food and drug laws. Only a few of these proposals received serious consideration from a Congress dominated by big business,
and those that were approved were sometimes weakened by
Theodore's willingness to compromise. As a result, some histo-
rians have complained that his ideas were oversimplifications and
contend he never offered a completely developed plan for reform.
But this is beside the point. Roosevelt not only got more
significant legislation approved than any President since Recon-
struction, he accomplished something much more important—he
aroused the nation's conscience about the existing evils and
created a demand that something be done about them.

Theodore's elevation to the presidency coincided with a revival
of the crusading spirit which had periodically swept the nation.
Reformers and muckraking journalists were exposing what William Allen White called "the alliance between business and government for the benefit of business." From out of the plains
where once the fires of populism had brightly burned swept a
new band of insurgents who called themselves progressives.
Their target was the interlocking relationship between business
and government and they attacked the trusts and political machines. Progressivism was the most striking phenomenon of
American political and social life from Roosevelt's first term until
reform was submerged by the onrushing tide of World War I.

Believing that the country had grown too big and the people

had lost their voice in its affairs, the progressives popularized many electoral and legislative innovations in their fight against boss rule: the direct primary to replace party caucuses in selecting candidates for office; the election of U.S. senators directly by the voters rather than the state legislatures; the initiative through which citizens could enact laws; and the recall for removing unsatisfactory elected officials. But in order to cleanse politics, the progressives found it necessary to regulate big business, to end industrial feudalism that limited labor's right to organize, and to guarantee small business freedom from monopolistic control.

McKinley and Hanna had turned a blind eye as J. P. Morgan, in obvious violation of the long-dormant Sherman Anti-Trust Act, single-handedly floated the first billion-dollar trust, the United States Steel Corporation, on a flood tide of watered stock. This bold move was followed by similar combinations in utilities, shipping tobacco, railroads, food processing, and other basic industries. While the moguls paid lip service to the philosophy of rugged individualism, "America became," as Bertrand Russell noted, "an organized whole ruled for their own profit, by a handful of unprecedentally rich men."

Wall Street awaited the new President's first moves with nervous trepidation. Businessmen knew full well that he was no radical, but they worried about his reputation as a reformer, for as governor of New York, he had favored heavier taxation and government regulation of corporations. Persons close to him, including Douglas Robinson, his brother-in-law, urged Theodore to follow McKinley's pro-business policy, and in the beginning, he moved cautiously. After all, he may have reasoned, the Republican party was the party of big business and that as an accidental President, he had no mandate for change. Theodore was also fully aware that none of the Vice-Presidents who had been elevated to the presidency in the same manner as he, had been nominated for a term in his own right. Accordingly, he tried to chart a safe course between the rocks of reform and the shoals of business-as-usual.

Five months after taking office—on February 18, 1902—Theodore stunned Wall Street by moving to break up the most recent example of J. P. Morgan's organizational genius, the Northern Securities Company, a giant holding company that con-

trolled the major western railroads. The case stemmed from the
attempt by two rail barons, E. H. Harriman, of the Union Pacific,
and James J. Hill, of the Great Northern, to win a route into
Chicago. The ideal connection for each was the Burlington Railroad. Hill, who also owned the Northern Pacific, used that line to
purchase control of the Burlington. Not to be outdone, Harriman
attempted to buy enough of the Northern Pacific's shares to give
him ownership of both railroads. The price of Northern Pacific
stock soared from $100 a share to $1,000—precipitating a panic.

This was too much for old Morgan, who was serving as Hill's
financial agent. It violated his sense of order. He brought the two
men together, and in keeping with the pattern established in
founding U. S. Steel, created a community of interest designed to
end disorder in the marketplace. The Northern Securities Company which resulted from this agreement held control of the
Great Northern, the Northern Pacific, and the Burlington. Harriman was given representation on the board to bring him into
the deal. The new company was capitalized at $400 million—30
percent of it thought to be watered stock—which was estimated
as the amount railroad users would be overcharged.

Public outrage over the creation of this powerful new monopoly was unbounded. Even Mark Hanna thought Morgan had
gone too far this time. Seizing upon a popular issue, Theodore ordered Philander C. Knox, his Attorney General, to prosecute for
violation of the Sherman Act. Shortly afterward, the irate Morgan, chaperoned by Hanna, paid a visit to the White House. It
was a classic confrontation. On one side was the imperial and imperious lord of finance, with a huge fiery nose and a fixed glare
that reminded one observer of the onrushing headlight of a locomotive. On the other was the young and debonair President of
the United States, who had an undisguised contempt for money
grubbing.

Morgan began with a blunt proposal: "If we have done anything wrong, send your man [the Attorney General] to my man
[Morgan's lawyer] and they can fix it up."

Roosevelt replied that this was impossible. He did not intend
to "fix it up" but to "stop it."

"Are you going to attack my other interests, the steel trust and
the others?" asked the financier. This, he said, was the real objective of his call.

"Certainly not," replied the President, "unless we find out that
. . . they have done something that we regard as wrong."

It took two years for the courts to unravel the Northern Securities case. In March 1904 the Supreme Court ordered the dissolution of the holding company—and Theodore Roosevelt's reputation as a trust-buster was made. A typical approving comment
was that of Joseph Pulitzer: "The greatest breeder of discontent
and socialism is the . . . popular belief that the law is one thing
for the rich and another for the poor." Jim Hill knew better, however. Noting that the high court had inflicted no penalty on the
would-be monopolists, he declared that the intentions of those involved would be accomplished "in another way."

This was Theodore's major sortie into the field of trust-busting.
Throughout his administration he fulminated against the "male-
factors of great wealth" and in his second term called for several
cleverly chosen antitrust prosecutions, but he was not opposed to
trusts solely on the grounds of bigness. Unlike most progressives,
he had a more sophisticated view of the process of industrial inte-
gration. Rather than follow the progressive line that all business
combinations were by their very nature inherently evil, he divided them into "good" trusts and "bad" trusts. The distinction
was made in his own mind. "Bad" trusts were to be dissolved by
government action, while "good" trusts were to be carefully regulated. The only effective way to control the natural inclination of
businessmen to monopolize control of the market in any given industry was, he said, "federal control over all combinations engaged in interstate commerce, instead of relying on the foolish
anti-trust law. . . ."

Not long after Theodore had successfully brandished his "big
stick" under old Morgan's rubicand nose, he again intervened
decisively in the marketplace. In the spring of 1902 the United
Mine Workers called a strike of some 50,000 anthracite miners in
eastern Pennsylvania after the operators had refused their demands for a 10 to 20 percent increase in the average yearly wage
of $560, an eight-hour day, and recognition of their union. Work-
ing conditions in the mines were dangerous, wages low and hours
long, but George F. Baer, the industry's chief spokesman,
brushed off such details. "[The miners] don't suffer," he declared.
"Why, they can't even speak English." John Mitchell, the leader
of the UMW, offered to submit the miners' grievances to binding

arbitration, but Baer flatly refused to compromise and the operators shut down the mines. Public opinion sided with labor, although there were some supporters of capital such as Woodrow
Wilson, the new president of Princeton, who claimed that the
dispute was not over wages and working conditions but an attempt by the union "to win more power."

For several months the miners held out, and as winter approached, the stockpile of coal dwindled, bringing the nation
face to face with the threat of frigid homes and a complete shut-
down of rail transport and factories. Cabot Lodge warned the
President that there was a possibility of rioting in Boston if coal
did not start moving again, and ominous reports came from New
York and other large eastern cities. Because of the urgency of the
situation, Theodore sought a way to intervene in the strike, but
aides advised him that he was without such power under the
Constitution. Pronouncing himself "at wit's end," he decided to
try to get the parties together anyway, and summoned them to
the White House. Mitchell offered to accept the findings of an arbitration commission to be appointed by the President, but Baer
demanded an injunction ordering the miners back to work, using
troops if necessary. On this grim note, the meeting broke up.

Behind closed doors, the President railed against the "arrogant
stupidity" of the operators, but he had gotten an idea from the
meeting. He would send troops into Pennsylvania, all right, but
they would seize the mines under his authority to maintain public order if requested to do so by the local authorities. Feelers
were put out to the governor of Pennsylvania and Theodore
made certain that his intentions were leaked to the operators.
"What about the Constitution of the United States?" Representative James E. Watson asked the President. "What about
using private property for public purposes without due process of
law?" Roosevelt stopped suddenly, took hold of Watson's shoulder, and looking squarely into his eye fairly shouted, "The Constitution was made for the people and not the people for the Constitution!"

Threatened with the dreaded specter of "socialism," the operators caved in and agreed to accept binding arbitration by a presidential commission. The commission awarded the miners a 10
percent wage hike and reduced working hours, but did not grant
union recognition. It also recommended a 10 percent increase in

the price of coal—and the operators lost no time in taking advantage of it.

Roosevelt's actions in the coal strike established many precedents, as George E. Mowry, a leading student of his administration, has pointed out. For the first time a President had lent his good offices to obtain a negotiated settlement of a labor dispute, for the first time a President had proposed binding arbitration, and for the first time a President had threatened to use troops to seize a strike-bound industry. Theodore later claimed that his actions in settling the coal strike were aimed at ensuring "a square deal" for both capital and labor, but as Mowry says, it also opened the way for the federal government "to become a third force and partner in major labor disputes." Ironically, Franklin Roosevelt, whose father had invested heavily in coal mines, was displeased with his idol's action, saying the President's "tendency to make the executive power stronger than the Houses of Congress is bound to be a bad thing."

Theodore saw his role much differently, however. Basically a conservative, he sought to preserve the status quo by saving the masters of capital from the consequences of their own narrowness and stupidity. He was worried that their inability to see what was occurring about them would encourage the growth of radicalism and create the danger of revolution. To William Howard Taft, his good friend and successor, he wrote:

> The dull purblind folly of the very rich men; their greed and arrogance . . . and the corruption of business and politics, have tended to produce a very unhealthy condition of excitement and irritation in the popular mind, which shows itself in the great increase in socialist propaganda.

Viewing the world through the perspective of his friend and mentor, Alfred T. Mahan, now an admiral on the retired list, Theodore believed that the United States should have an influence in the world commensurate with its wealth and power. The first American President eager to take an active role in international affairs, he sought to expand the nation's influence in the Pacific and Caribbean, and favored construction of a Central American canal. The capstone of this structure was to be a strong navy. Within a few months of taking office, Theodore threw down a challenge: "The American people must either build and maintain an adequate Navy or else make up their minds definitely to accept a secondary position in international affairs. . . ."

Congress and the nation accepted this policy and in every year of Roosevelt's administration at least one new battleship was authorized, with five vessels being laid down in 1903 alone. By 1907 the United States had twenty battleships at sea. This emphasis on a big navy coincided with a dramatic change in the world balance of sea power. Imperial Germany had begun to threaten Great Britain's age-old command of the oceans, forcing the British to concentrate their ships in home waters. The resulting vacuum in the Caribbean was filled by the United States, while the Japanese, who had signed a treaty of alliance with Britain in 1902, extended their influence over Far Eastern waters. One of the most important results of this shift in international interests was a green light for the long-sought canal across Central America.

Under the terms of the Clayton-Bulwer Treaty, concluded between the United States and Britain in 1850, neither nation was to have exclusive control of an isthmian canal, which had curbed American interest in building a waterway. Following the rapprochement between the two countries, this agreement was abrogated in 1901, and the United States was free to build the canal by itself—if it could overcome the tremendous technical and medical problems that had heretofore blocked construction of a Central American waterway. Deciding that Panama, then part of Colombia, should be the site of the canal rather than a route through Nicaragua favored by the company that had been headed by James Roosevelt, Theodore opened negotiations for rights across the isthmus. In the summer of 1903 a price of $10 million plus an annual payment of $250,000 was fixed for a six-mile-wide right-of-way, but the Colombians, hoping for more, delayed ratification of the treaty at the last moment.

It was a fatal mistake. Impatient "to make dirt fly" before the 1904 presidential election, Theodore denounced the Colombians as "inefficient bandits" and threatened to seize the canal strip by force. When the desired revolution flared in Panama, he quickly dispatched the gunboat *Nashville* to Colon to "protect American interests"—and prevent the Colombians from disembarking troops to put down the insurrection. Fifteen days after the coup, newly independent Panama granted the United States control of a ten-mile-wide zone across the isthmus in perpetuity in return for the sum originally offered Colombia. Work on the canal was begun in May 1904—well in time for the election—and after the completion of the largest engineering project in history, the waterway was opened to traffic in August 1914. Brushing off charges that he had acted improperly, Theodore proudly declared: "I took the canal zone and let Congress debate, and while the debate goes on the Canal does also." His election to a full term in the White House in his own right was a foregone conclusion. "My dear, I am no longer a political accident," he told Edith on election night.

"I don't think that any family has enjoyed the White House more than we have," Theodore wrote his second son, Kermit, in 1904, soon after the boy had gone off to Groton. "I was thinking about it just the other morning when Mother and I took breakfast on the portico and afterwards walked about the lovely grounds and looked at the stately old house." Some observers wondered, however, if "the stately old house" could withstand the assaults upon it from the Roosevelts. Besides Theodore and Edith, the brood included six lively children, from four-year-old Quentin to eighteen-year-old Alice, as well as a menagerie of assorted dogs, cats, rabbits, guinea pigs, parrots, ponies, and Alice's pet green garden snake, "Emily Spinach," named for her stepmother's very thin sister Emily Carow, who lived in Italy.

Life in the Roosevelt White House resembled a three-ring circus. People were always coming and going and luncheon guests ranged from crusty old Henry Adams, who was amused by the President and called him "Theodorus I, Czar Rooseveltoff," to John L. Sullivan, the boxer, and Booker T. Washington, the black educator.* Visitors were sometimes startled by the clatter of the Roosevelt children sliding down the stairs on tin trays, and cabi-

---

* TR was the first American President to play ethnic politics on a grand scale. Long before the term was even invented, he used a family tree conveniently bedecked with ancestors from most of western Europe to win votes and influence elections. Voters with foreign-sounding names were greeted with a blinding flash of teeth, an enthusiastic handshake, and Roosevelt's assurance that he, too, was part Dutch, or Welsh, or French or German, or Scotch or whatever the occasion demanded. Such statements became so automatic that, according to one tale, the President greeted a visitor to the White House by spontaneously booming out: "Congratulations! I'm partly Jewish, too."

net members recoiled as small boys popped out of vases in the East Room. Quentin once took his Shetland pony upstairs in the elevator to visit Archie who was sick in bed, and one of the family parrots was taught to say "Hurrah for Roosevelt!" Ike Hoover the longtime chief usher, said those years were the "wildest scramble" in the history of the White House. The South Lawn was used as a baseball diamond by the chums Quentin brought home from public school, and the President sometimes joined them in games of tag. It was not unknown for an important meeting to be interrupted by a tapping on the door and the appearance of a small group of boys, whose spokesman might respectfully announce, "It's after four." "By Jove, so it is!" the President might say, and before adjourning the meeting, tell his visitor that he had promised to take the boys walking at four o'clock. "I never keep boys waiting. It's a hard trial for a boy to wait."

Theodore did not let the prestige of office interfere with his own pursuit of the strenuous life. He was the first President to go down in a submarine and up in an airplane. "I've had many a splendid day's fun in my life," he said after practicing dives in the *Plunger* in Long Island Sound, "but I can't remember ever having crowded so much of it into such a few hours." Of the airplane flight he said, "By George, it was great!" He went riding at every opportunity and becoming disturbed by reports of the poor physical condition of senior army and navy officers decreed that they would have to pass a fitness test that included a ninety mile ride in three days. To counteract grumbling by some officers, he personally led a party that rode to Warrenton, Virginia, and back, covering the hundred miles in a day. The last few miles were done in "pitch darkness and with a blizzard of sleet blowing in our faces." He also took up such pastimes as judo and fencing with broadswords and continued boxing, even though he lost the sight of his left eye in a sparring match with a military aide. Characteristically, he hid the injury, so as not to worry the young officer.

When he had nothing better to do, Theodore would go for brisk walks about Washington, usually accompanied only by a single Secret Service agent. With McKinley's fate in mind, he often packed a pistol himself, telling one friend, "I should have some chance of shooting the assassin before he could shoot me, if he were near me." One Sunday, while walking to church, he spotted two terriers attacking a kitten. He routed the dogs with an umbrella and captured the frightened kitten. Carrying it in his arms, the President inquired of the people on the neighboring porches if they knew the animal's owner, and receiving only grins and disclaimers, continued on his way. "Then I saw a very nice colored woman and little colored girl looking out the window of a small house," he wrote his daughter, Ethel. "I turned and walked up the steps and asked if they did not want the kitten. They said they did, and the little girl welcomed it lovingly. . . ."

The eventual destination of many of Theodore's strolls was Bamie's red-brick house at 1733 N Street, where he went when he wanted to get away from the pressures of the White House. Often, he sought his older sister's counsel on the issues facing him and valued her advice. "He may have made his own decisions, but talking with her seemed to clarify things for him," observed Eleanor Roosevelt, a frequent visitor to her aunt's home. Edith Roosevelt also played an important role in influencing her husband's thinking. She read the newspapers for him, calling his attention to items which he should know about, and went through the mail each morning, picking out those letters which were worthy of his personal attention. She never gave advice unless it was sought, but according to Mark Sullivan, a prominent journalist of the day, "Never, when he had his wife's judgement, did [Roosevelt] go wrong or suffer disappointment." Sometimes, Edith would put "a gentle brake" upon his impulsiveness and natural exuberance with a cautionary "'Theodore!,'" to which the President would meekly respond, "'Edie, I was only . . .'"

Although she carefully avoided the limelight, Edith directed the restoration of the White House which some of her predecessors had turned into a monument to the worst of Victorian taste. She returned the old building to the classic line and decor of the era of Adams and Jefferson that still pervades it. Edith also began the collection of portraits of First Ladies and the White House china collection.

Theodore organized his closest personal, political, and diplomatic friends into a "Tennis Cabinet," which joined him on the court behind the White House or in rambles through Rock Creek Park where streams were forded and cliffs were scaled. Jules Jus-

serand, the French ambassador, wrote a lighthearted account of
an afternoon "promenade" with Roosevelt:

I arrived at the White House punctually, in afternoon dress and silk
hat, as if we were to stroll in the Tuileries Garden. . . . To my
surprise the President soon joined me in a tramping suit. . . . Two
or three other gentlemen came and we started off at what seemed to
me a breakneck pace, which soon brought us out of the city. On
reaching the country, the President went pell-mell over the fields,
following neither road nor path, always on, on, straight ahead! I
was much winded, but I would not give in, nor ask him to slow up,
because I had the honor of *la belle France* in my heart. At last we
came to a bank of a stream, rather wide and too deep to be forded.
I sighed relief, because I thought that now we had reached our goal
and would rest a moment and catch our breath before turning
homeward. But judge of my horror when I saw the President unbut-
ton his clothes and hear him say 'We had better strip, so as not to
wet our things in the Creek.' Then I, too, for the honor of France,
removed my apparel, everything except my lavender kid gloves. The
President cast an inquiring look at these as if they, too, must come
off, but I quickly forestalled any remark by saying, 'With your permission, Mr. President, I will keep these on; otherwise it would be
embarrassing if we should meet ladies.' And so we jumped into the
water and swam across.

Fascinated with the activities of the vivacious First Family,
Americans wanted to know the most intimate details of their
lives. Reporters even tried to pry information about his father's
latest escapades from Quentin. Guardedly, the boy replied that
he saw the President occasionally, but added that he "knew nothing about his family life." Pretty, fun-loving Princess Alice, as she
was quickly dubbed by the newspapers, attracted more attention
than any member of the family except the President himself.
Alice's coming-out party at the White House in January 1902
made her the media's first superstar. Six hundred young men and
women flocked to the White House for her debut, and although
Alice complained that punch was served rather than champagne,
Aunt Corinne noted that her niece "had the time of her life" with
"men seven deep around her all the time." Cousin Franklin was
in attendance; Eleanor was still at Allenswood.
Americans could not get enough of Alice. The papers were

filled with stories about her—where she went, what she said, whom she saw, and especially what she wore. The cartwheel hats of the period seemed made to order for her haughty Gibson girl looks, and her favorite blue-gray color became known as "Alice blue." Songs were written about her and Alice became a favorite name for babies. Victorian prudery was giving way to the free and easier style of the Edwardians and it was a happy time for nonconformity. Shocking the prissy and prudish, she smoked in public, drove her small runabout at "reckless" speeds until the Washington police caught up with her, and consorted with actresses such as Ethel Barrymore. Alice fascinated Europeans as well as her own countrymen. The French Chamber of Deputies agreed to have her portrait painted, and its *Journal* noted that in a fifteen-month period she attended 407 dinners, 350 balls, 300 parties, 680 teas, and made 1,706 calls. When Owen Wister asked Theodore if he couldn't control Alice, the President replied: "I can do one of two things. I can be President of the United States, or I can control Alice. I cannot possibly do both."

Alice was seen with a variety of young men. One day Eleanor encountered her in New York and told Franklin that she "was looking well but crazier than ever. I saw her this morning in Bobbie Goelet's auto quite alone with three other men! I wonder how you would like my tearing around like that. I'm seriously thinking of taking it up." Despite the uneasiness of the relationship between Alice and Eleanor, Eleanor asked her cousin to be a bridesmaid at her wedding and Alice accepted enthusiastically. "I should love to above anything. It will be much fun. . . . Really you are a saint to ask me." Alice's own thoughts were turning toward marriage and she was seen more and more in the company of Nicholas Longworth, a Republican congressman from Ohio and fifteen years her senior. A member of a distinguished Cincinnati family, Longworth was an entertaining fellow who wore bright waistcoats and played the violin well enough to earn the praise of professionals. He could also perform with the instrument behind his back and the bow between his knees.

Both Alice and Longworth accompanied William Howard Taft, the Secretary of War, on a trip to the Far East during which Nick proposed. Although she accepted, she still harbored doubts, and at a ball in Tokyo held in honor of the visitors, Alice conversed with Lloyd Griscom, a young diplomat and friend:

"Lloyd, do you see that old, bald-headed man scratching his ear over there?" she asked.

"Do you mean Nick Longworth?"

"Can you imagine any young girl marrying a fellow like that?"

"Why, Alice, you couldn't find anybody nicer."

"I know, I know. But this is a question of marriage."

Alice's wedding to Longworth on February 17, 1906, was the most glittering social event yet held in the White House. Five hundred friends and relatives crowded into the East Room and thousands of spectators milled in the streets outside as the bride, lovely in white satin and lace that her mother had worn at her wedding, was given in marriage by her beaming father. Following the ceremony, Franklin Roosevelt, whose wife was not present because she was expecting their first child, gallantly arranged the bride's twelve-foot train for the official photographer.

Gifts had begun pouring in upon Alice as soon as her engagement had been announced, not only from at home but from abroad. From the Empress of China came eight rolls of gold brocade with the Chinese glyph for long life woven into it; Britain's King Edward VII sent a blue and gold snuffbox with his portrait on the lid; Kaiser Wilhelm II tried to top this with a miniature of himself set in a gold bracelet; France provided a Gobelin tapestry; the Japanese Emperor sent silver vases; Austria-Hungary a pearl and diamond pendant; and the Cubans, who reportedly first considered giving Alice San Juan Hill, settled upon a string of pearls valued at $25,000. Concerned by the mounting trove of what Alice called her "loot," Theodore urged her to return the gifts. She countered by saying this would be an insult to the donors. He then announced that it would be improper for his daughter to receive official presents from foreign nations. "So like him to come to that decision after the gifts were on the way," noted a sardonic Cabot Lodge.

Theodore put his personal brand on everything, including the nation's foreign policy. In the beginning, he flexed his muscles only in the Western Hemisphere. When Germany blockaded Venezuela in 1902 with the announced intention of collecting some overdue debts, he bluntly told the German ambassador that Berlin must submit the dispute to arbitration or face the U. S. Navy's battleships. "You gave that Dutchman something to think about," said an awed aide. He may have been correct, for the Germans agreed to arbitration. No nation was safe from the threat of Roosevelt's "big stick." When Britain insisted on supporting Canadian claims in a boundary dispute over her border with Alaska—claims the President considered unjust—he reinforced American forces in Alaska and threatened to have the army establish the frontier. Privately assured that Washington's claim would be upheld, he finally submitted the matter to arbitration. Faced with the rising threat of Germany, the British valued American friendship more than the territory involved, but Theodore reaped the credit for the favorable settlement.

He also promulgated the Roosevelt "corollary" to the Monroe Doctrine, giving the United States "a moral mandate" to intervene in any dispute between a Western Hemisphere and a European power. Thus, the Monroe Doctrine, originally proclaimed to prevent European interference in the New World, became a license for such interference by the United States. Over the next three decades, it served as a pretext for landing marines throughout the Caribbean and Central America and was repeatedly invoked until another Roosevelt proclaimed the Good Neighbor Policy.

Roosevelt's attention was soon drawn to the Far East where a cardinal point of his foreign policy was the maintenance of the balance of power. In 1904 war broke out between Russia and Japan with Russian interests in Manchuria and Japanese claims in Korea at stake. The key issue, however, was which of the two countries was to dominate the area. As a new Pacific power, the United States was concerned that complete victory by one side or another would upset the delicate balance then existing and create a dangerous rival in the Far East. Most Americans, including the President, cheered the surprising land and sea victories won by the Japanese, whom they had regarded as protégés since Commodore Matthew C. Perry had opened the islands to the West a half century before. Writing to Baron Kentaro Kaneko, a Harvard classmate, Theodore compared the Japanese victory over a Russian fleet at Tsushima to Trafalgar.

Having won the territory they were seeking, and near exhaustion despite their victories, the Japanese indicated to Washington that they were ready to conclude peace. Russia, teetering on the brink of revolution, was also willing to throw in the towel if she could end the war with honor. Roosevelt seized the opportunity to mediate, and his offer was accepted by both sides. The delegates gathered at Portsmouth, New Hampshire, on August 9, 1905, after having previously met at a luncheon at Oyster Bay. He cut the Gordian knot of who was to have precedence by serving a buffet from a round table and personally making the only toast allowed. The conference quickly bogged down over Japanese demands for the Russian island of Sakhalin which they had captured and for payment by the Russians of a substantial indemnity. Realizing that the Japanese were as exhausted as they were, the Russians refused to accept either proposal. "The more I see of the Czar, the Kaiser, and the Mikado the better I am content with democracy, even if we have to include the American newspaper as one of its assets," Theodore raged in private, but he dealt with the various parties with "consummate tact."

With the talks deadlocked, the President took personal control of the negotiations. Meeting privately, first with the Japanese and then with the Russians, he produced a compromise that was eventually accepted by both parties. Japan agreed to drop her demands for an indemnity, and the Russians turned over the southern half of Sakhalin. Japanese control of Korea was, in effect, ratified and she replaced Russia as the dominant foreign power in Manchuria. Still, Roosevelt, who had become worried about Japanese domination of the Far East, had managed to block them from obtaining all that they wanted at Russia's expense. The resulting Treaty of Portsmouth brought temporary peace to the Orient and international acclaim for Theodore and he was awarded the Nobel Peace Prize in 1906.† The following year, he was the guiding spirit behind the Hague Peace Conference, an early attempt at disarmament.

Although the Emperor of Japan thanked Roosevelt for his "disinterested and unremitting efforts" in bringing about the end of the war with the Russians, the Japanese soon accused the Americans of having thwarted their ambitions. Tension between the two countries was fanned by a wave of anti-Japanese feeling that swept California. In 1906 the San Francisco Board of Education ordered the segregation of all Japanese schoolchildren, which

† TR turned the $39,734.49 prize over to a foundation to promote industrial peace in the United States. The trustees could not agree on how the money should be spent, so twelve years later, the former President donated the fund, which had grown to $45,482.83, to World War I relief.

provoked anti-American rioting in Japan. With the Panama Canal still unfinished and the major elements of the U. S. Navy concentrated in the Atlantic, Roosevelt was anxious to avoid an open break with Japan. He considered the school board's action "foolish" and with considerable difficulty persuaded the Californians to rescind it in exchange for a "gentlemen's agreement" under which the Japanese government would slow the flow of emigrants to the United States.

To impress Japan as well as other nations with American power, Theodore decided to send the entire battle fleet on a voyage around the world. He wanted to find out what would happen if war broke out with Japan before the canal had been completed. With the disasters that the Russian fleet had experienced while steaming halfway around the world to its defeat at Tsushima fresh in mind, he declared, "I want all failures, blunders and shortcomings to be made apparent in time of peace and not in time of war."

Plumes of smoke billowing from tall funnels and hulls gleaming in the wintry sunshine, the sixteen battleships of the Great White Fleet sailed majestically out of Hampton Roads, Virginia, on December 16, 1907. Marine honor guards snapped to attention and bands crashed into the national anthem as the vessels passed in review before the presidential yacht, *Mayflower*. "Did you ever see such a fleet and such a day?" cried Theodore as he acknowledged the salutes with a wave of his top hat. "By George, isn't it magnificent!"

Ready for "a feast, a frolic or fight," in the words of Rear Admiral Robley D. Evans, its commander, the fleet was welcomed by enthusiastic crowds at ports along the Atlantic and Pacific coasts of South America. By the time the ships anchored off San Francisco, an invitation had been received from Japan for the fleet to come calling. Despite the bitterness between the two countries, the Japanese seemed genuinely eager to welcome the Americans. As the Yankee bluejackets paraded through the streets of Yokohama, thousands of schoolchildren waved American flags and sang "The Star-Spangled Banner" in English. The fleet sailed home by way of the Suez Canal and the Mediterranean, and arrived at the mouth of the Chesapeake on February 22, 1909, after having been away for fourteen months. It was just in time to usher out Theodore's administration in a blaze of glory.

Ten days later, Will Taft, whom he had handpicked as his successor, was sworn in as President.

After seven and a half years, the reign of Roosevelt was over. Conservatives in both parties breathed a sigh of relief, as he departed the White House to bag big game in Africa and crowned heads in Europe. J. P. Morgan expressed the hope of Wall Street that the lions would do their duty. But Theodore was still enormously popular with the mass of ordinary citizens. Had he opted for another term—a possibility he had foreclosed on election night in 1904 by saying "under no circumstances" would he be a candidate for renomination—he would have won it handily. In fact, probably no President of the United States between Andrew Jackson and Dwight D. Eisenhower was more popular at the end of his term than Theodore Roosevelt. Critics might question his sincerity and effectiveness as a reformer, but he understood that the greatest task facing any political leader is to educate the public. The White House, as he said, was "a bully pulpit." And by his example, he convinced able young men to enter politics—among them Franklin Roosevelt.

Chapter XVII
PATRICIAN IN POLITICS

Franklin Roosevelt liked to claim that his political career began when he was "kidnapped" off the streets of Poughkeepsie by some local Democratic politicos and asked to address a Dutchess County policemen's picnic. He had, however, been considering following in Cousin Theodore's footsteps for some time. Five months before marrying the President's niece, he had entered Columbia Law School and having passed the New York Bar Examination after less than three years of study, had joined the Wall Street firm of Carter, Ledyard, and Milburn. Franklin found the law boring, and was open about his political ambitions. Grenville Clark, a fellow law clerk, remembered him saying "with engaging frankness that he wasn't going to practice law forever, that he intended to run for office at the first opportunity, and that he wanted to be and thought he had a very real chance to be President."

The road to the White House that young Roosevelt mapped out for himself paralleled that traveled by his distinguished relative. He would win a seat in the State legislature, secure appointment as Assistant Secretary of the Navy, and be elected governor of New York. "'Anyone who is governor of New York has a good chance to be President with any luck,'" Franklin was quoted as saying. None of the other clerks considered his vision an idle daydream. "It seemed proper and sincere; and moreover, as he put it, entirely reasonable," said Clark.

Upon completion of his first year in law school, Eleanor and Franklin had gone on a delayed honeymoon, a three-month grand tour of Europe. The object of special attention because of their relationship to the American President, they received royal treatment—including assignment to elaborate hotel suites which Eleanor felt they could not afford. In London and Paris, Franklin indulged his passion for book and print collecting, interests that Eleanor did not share, and in the Dolomites he went mountain climbing while she stayed behind. They visited friends in Scotland and among those invited to luncheon one day were a "Mr. and Mrs. Webb" of whom Eleanor said "they write books on sociology." Making conversation, Franklin discussed "the servant problem" with the founders of Fabian socialism. On the passage across the Atlantic, Eleanor had discovered that her husband walked in his sleep and in Scotland found that he was sometimes subject to nightmares. "One night . . . I was awakened by wild shrieks in the neighboring bed," she said. Franklin sat bolt upright pointing up at the ceiling. "Don't you see it?" he cried. "Don't you see the revolving beam?"

The most memorable part of the trip was Venice, where Eleanor reported they had "a delightful gondolier who looked like a benevolent bandit and kept us out on the canals a good part of the nights. . . . I fed the birds in the Piazza San Marco, as I remembered doing as a little girl. We glided through some of the smaller canals to look through grilled entrances at what looked like fascinating gardens beyond the stately palace fronts. . . . We saw churches until my husband would look no more. "Franklin began to call her Babs, and he used this nickname for the rest of their lives together. He had to be back in New York before the end of September for the start of law school, and the voyage home was miserable for Eleanor, always a poor sailor. When her illness persisted, she went to see a doctor, who told her she was pregnant. "It was quite a relief," she said, "for little idiot that I was, I had been seriously troubled for fear that I would never have any children." Sexually naïve, she once confessed that she had not even kissed Franklin until they were married and told her daughter that "sex was an ordeal to be borne."

The young couple found that in their absence, Franklin's mother had rented a house for them at 125 East Thirty-sixth Street, about three blocks from her own home at 200 Madison Avenue. Without consulting them, she had decorated and furnished the place and even chose the servants. Sallie had pretty much run her son's life before his marriage and she obviously intended to go on doing so. One of the few times he disobeyed her wishes was when he had become engaged to Eleanor. Eleanor and Franklin were too young to marry, she had claimed, and urged them to wait until he established himself in the legal profession. Sallie acted not out of any dislike for "dear, sweet Eleanor," but probably because she wanted her son's companionship for herself. In an attempt to get his mind off Eleanor, she took him on a Caribbean cruise, but Franklin returned no less determined to marry his cousin. Having lost a battle, Sallie made a strategic retreat and took over the direction of both their lives, following the marriage to which she had given her reluctant consent.

Knowing little about how to run a household or to efficiently manage servants, Eleanor was helpless and dependent, just as Sallie desired her to be. "For the first year of my married life, I was completely taken care of," she said. "My mother-in-law did everything for me." Every day, she went walking with Sallie and took at least one meal a day with her. In the meantime, Eleanor nervously awaited the birth of her first child. Following a difficult pregnancy, the baby was born on May 3, 1906, and christened Anna Eleanor after her mother and maternal grandmother. Over the next ten years, Eleanor "was always getting over a baby or having one." Anna was followed by James in 1907; the first Franklin, Jr., who was born in March 1909 and died before the year was out; Elliott in 1910; the second Franklin, Jr., in 1914; and John in 1916. "I had never had any interest in dolls or in little children, and I knew absolutely nothing about handling or feeding a baby," Eleanor said. "I was completely unprepared to be a practical housekeeper, wife or mother." Sallie assumed responsibility for the care of the children as well as almost everything else in the household.

Jimmy Roosevelt recalled that "one of the hazards of life during the period for Anna, Elliott, Franklin, Jr., and me—Johnny escaped it by virtue of his tender years—was the procession of proper English nannies foisted on our household by well-meaning Granny." As a result, Eleanor's children had a childhood that in some ways resembled her own. The constant stream of nurses meant that affection was offered and withdrawn in a capricious

Elliott, played no role in her husband's decision. "I listened to all his plans with a great deal of interest," she said. "It never occurred to me that I had any part to play. I felt I must acquiesce in whatever he might decide and be willing to go to Albany." Before taking the final plunge, however, Franklin asked Bamie to find out if Cousin Theodore, who had returned from his African safari, would speak in Dutchess County against his candidacy because that would be fatal to it. "Franklin ought to go into politics without the least regard as to where I speak or don't speak," Theodore wrote his sister. He added that Franklin was "a fine fellow," although he regretted that he was not a Republican like Joseph Alsop, who had married his other niece, Corinne Robinson, and was active in Connecticut politics.

Despite his slim chance of winning, Franklin entered the race with a Rooseveltian zest. "I accept this nomination with absolute independence," he said in his acceptance speech a month before the election. "I am pledged to no man; I am influenced by no special interests, and so I shall remain. . . . In the coming campaign, I need not tell you that I do not intend to sit still. We are going to have a strenuous month." True to his word, Franklin startled everyone by campaigning in a red Maxwell touring car bedecked with flags, the first time that an automobile had been used in a local election. Some of his supporters worried that the vehicle, which reached the daring speed of twenty miles an hour, would frighten farmers' horses, but it permitted the candidate to cover every part of the sprawling district. In his zeal, he once overshot the New York state line and harangued voters in Connecticut. Tailoring his campaign to the area's rural interests, Franklin denounced the big-city bosses of both parties and damned the high tariff imposed by the Taft Administration which farmers claimed forced them to sell their produce cheaply and buy finished goods at high prices. And he subtly emphasized his link to the popular ex-President by interlarding his speeches with the word "bully." Sometimes, he was even more direct. "I am not Teddy," he told one rally, amid laughter. "A little shaver said to me the other day that he knew I wasn't Teddy—I asked him 'why' and he replied: 'Because you don't show your teeth.'"

Franklin could not have chosen a better year to run than 1910, for the Republicans were deeply divided on both the state and national levels. Theodore, as was to be expected, was at the center of the fight. Only fifty-two when he returned from his triumphant overseas tour, the Colonel was anxious to resume an active role in politics and was convinced that Taft had betrayed his policies. Well meaning, placid, and conservative, he believed the time had come to relax the pressures that Roosevelt had kept on big business. In place of the vigorous and dedicated reformers that Theodore had attracted to government, Taft relied upon the representatives of corporate wealth to fill his administration. Nowhere had the Rooseveltian gospel been more effective than in the conservation of America's great natural resources. Reversing the old policy that had placed the public lands at the mercy of private developers who plundered them for their own profit, Theodore had ordered thousands of acres of coal, mineral, and timber lands placed in the public trust. And it was here that Taft had chosen to make a clean break with the policies of his predecessor, appointing officials committed to the immediate exploitation of the nation's natural resources. An open split between Taft and Roosevelt soon followed.

Franklin turned the split among the Republicans to his own advantage. Making a basically nonpartisan pitch to the voters of the district, he managed to attract support from progressive Republicans as well as Democrats by identifying his opponent with the bosses opposed to the policies and programs of Theodore Roosevelt. It worked so well that he scored an upset, winning by a margin of 1,140 votes out of some 30,000 cast. His victory was part of a national tide of protest against the hapless Taft, with the Democrats winning control of the House of Representatives and more than half the governorships, including New Jersey, where Woodrow Wilson, the president of Princeton, was elected. Critics claimed that young Roosevelt had merely been lucky, but as Frank Freidel has pointed out, he "anticipated his luck with careful groundwork, and, when fortuitous opportunity came his way, capitalized upon it to the utmost."

Franklin was just shy of twenty-nine when he made his debut in Albany in January 1911. "With his handsome face, and his form of supple strength he could make his fortune on the stage and set the matinee girl's heart throbbing," wrote one reporter. Big Tim Sullivan, one of the Tammany bosses, cast a considerably less admiring glance his way, however, as he watched the young man stride across a hotel lobby. "You know these Roosevelts," he said to a fellow politico. "This fellow is still young. Wouldn't it be safer to drown him before he grows up?" Not long afterward, Sullivan probably wished he had taken his own suggestion seriously.

Before the ratification of the Seventeenth Amendment in 1913, state legislatures chose United States senators, and Tammany selected William F. ("Blue-eyed Billy") Sheehan, an unsavory Buffalo politico turned utilities magnate, to fill a vacancy. All that was required was the approval of Sheehan by the Democratic caucus and the legislature would rubberstamp the appointment. Unhappy with this undemocratic procedure, Franklin decided to oppose the choice of Sheehan, and found himself leading a small group of Democrats who had their own candidate for senator. The rebels refused to attend the caucus, leaving the Tammany candidate short of a majority. "There is nothing I love so much as a good fight," Roosevelt told a newsman with evident glee.

Making their headquarters in the house that the Roosevelts had rented, the insurgents met nightly to plot strategy. These councils of war also marked the start of Eleanor's political education. In the beginning "the rights and wrongs of the fight meant very little to me," she said, but soon she began to hover in the background and learned how politics really worked. Just as Uncle Ted's legislative battle for reform thirty years before had propelled him into the limelight, this fight did the same for her husband. People were already talking of "the second coming of a Roosevelt," and reporters began calling at the house, among them Louis McHenry Howe, the gnomelike and knowledgeable Albany correspondent of the New York *Herald*. After ten weeks, both sides finally agreed to compromise, and with the withdrawal of Sheehan's name, an organization man named James A. O'Gorman, who was acceptable to all parties, got the nomination. The Republicans jeered that the reformers had been outfoxed by Tammany, but Franklin put the best face on the deal that he could as he cast his ballot for O'Gorman. "We are Democrats— not irregulars, but regulars," he declared.

For the most part, his service in the State Senate was far less spectacular than the duel with Tammany.* Deeply interested in

* Even so, Franklin's legislative career was more distinguished than that of Theodore Douglas Robinson, son of Eleanor's Aunt Corinne and a Republican

conservation, he was chairman of the Forest, Fish and Game Committee and a protector of the agrarian interest of his rural constituents. Frances Perkins, who for twelve years served as his Secretary of Labor and was then in Albany as a representative of the National Consumers' League, was not much impressed by Franklin, saying he seemed to have little, if any, concern with social reform. She was certain that "he really didn't like people very much" and was deaf "to the hopes, fears, and aspirations which are the common lot. The marvel is that these handicaps were washed out of him by life, experience, punishment and his capacity to grow." After he had become President, Roosevelt once told Miss Perkins, "You know, I was an awfully mean cuss when I first went into politics."

Nevertheless, after some equivocation, Franklin supported women's suffrage, which required political courage. Although Vassar College, a hotbed of feminism, was in his district, most of his constituents were conservative and opposed to votes for women. It also shocked Eleanor. "I had never given the question really serious thought, for I took it for granted that men were superior creatures and still knew more about politics than women," she said. "While I realized that if my husband were a suffragist I probably must be, too, I cannot claim to have been a feminist in those early days."

On the national scene, the rift between Theodore Roosevelt and President Taft was widening. The Colonel's supporters flocked to Sagamore "like iron filings mobilizing to the pull of a revitalized magnet," urging him to seek the Republican presidential nomination. Early in 1912, he gave his answer—and added another memorable phrase to the political lexicon by declaring: "My hat is in the ring." What had begun as a personal misunderstanding between friends had developed into a bitter struggle for the leadership of the Republican party and the presidency.

With the Taft forces in control of the party machinery, the only way for Theodore to win delegates to the nominating convention scheduled for mid-June in Chicago was to contest each of

member of the State Senate. Highlights of his three terms were proposals to license cats and build a movable sidewalk between the Senate and Assembly chambers.

the primaries and persuade other states to hold them. The debate became increasingly acrimonious with Roosevelt referring to his successor as a "fathead" while Taft called his predecessor "a demagogue" and "a man who can't tell the truth." Roosevelt won a clear victory in the primaries—278 delegates to 48 for Taft and garnered nearly double the popular vote, reinforcing his claim to be the choice of the party's rank and file. Nevertheless, as a result of their control of the state conventions, the Taft forces had a razor-thin majority of the 1,078 delegates who filtered into Chicago.

The key to the nomination rested on possession of 254 contested seats and Finley Peter Dunne's Mr. Dooley forecast that the convention would be "a combination iv th' Chicago fire, Saint Bartholomew's massacre, th' battle iv the Boyne, th' life iv Jesse James, an' th' night iv the big wind." It was a fair prediction. The National Committee, safe in the hands of Taft's supporters, ruled as expected in his favor on most of the contested seats, awarding 235 to Taft and only 19 to Theodore. Unless Roosevelt could overturn these rulings, the President would be nominated on the first ballot. The insurgents tried to elect a convention chairman favorable to their cause, but Elihu Root, who had remained loyal to Taft, was chosen by a narrow margin. Roosevelt's chances of being nominated vanished with Root's victory; his former friend ruled implacably in favor of Taft in all matters that came before him. Most authorities now agree that Roosevelt was robbed of enough delegates to have at least deadlocked the convention which in all probability would have eventually turned to him rather than Taft. Angrily shouting "Thou shalt not steal!" and promising revenge, the Colonel's supporters bolted and met two months later to organize the Progressive party.

Exuberantly proclaiming himself "as strong as a bull moose," Theodore appeared before the 15,000 red-bandanna-waving delegates who cheered him for more than fifty minutes to accept the new party's presidential nomination. When the crowd had finally quieted, he unveiled what George Mowry has described as the most sweeping charter for reform ever presented by a major presidential candidate. It embraced direct election of U.S. senators, preferential primaries in presidential years, initiative, referendum, and recall, votes for women, a strict corrupt practices act, a federal securities commission, the regulation of trusts, reduced tariffs, unemployment insurance, old-age pensions, abolition of child labor, and pure food laws. "Our cause is based on the eternal principle of righteousness; and even though we who now lead may for the time fail, in the end the cause itself shall triumph," Roosevelt thundered. "We stand at Armageddon and we battle for the Lord!"

One of those who might have been expected to stand at Armageddon with the Bull Moose candidate was Franklin Roosevelt, but he had found a new idol in Woodrow Wilson. Like other progressive Democrats, he made the pilgrimage to Trenton, where the former university president had installed a reformist regime that attracted nationwide attention. Impressed and somewhat in awe of Wilson's intellectual brilliance, Franklin agreed to work for his nomination. For the first time, as Frances Perkins has said, he had come in contact with someone who "arrived at convictions by intellectual rather than emotional processes." Franklin was not a member of the New York delegation to the raucous Democratic convention that met in the stifling heat of a Baltimore summer, but worked for Wilson behind the scenes. As a result, he came to the attention of national party leaders, particularly Josephus Daniels, the North Carolina editor who was handling Wilson's public relations. It was "love at first sight," as Daniels later put it. Wilson was finally nominated on the forty-sixth ballot, and Franklin, who had climbed on the bandwagon early, could hope for reward in the likely event of a Wilson victory over the bitterly divided Republicans in November. Franklin's support of Wilson placed Eleanor in a quandary. She was a devoted admirer of Uncle Ted, and it is a measure of her support of her husband that she accompanied him to the convention.

Franklin was up for reelection to the State Senate, but while visiting Campobello with his wife and children before the campaign got under way, he came down with typhoid. Eleanor nursed him as best she could until felled with a 102° temperature. She was soon up on her feet again, but her husband "was still in bed and feeling miserable and looking like Robert Louis Stevenson at Vailima." As Franklin lay helplessly in bed, he could see his bright political future fading away. If he could not campaign, he would not be reelected and would lose his chance to obtain a place in the new Democratic administration in Washington. Twisting and turning in frustration, he suddenly remembered Louis Howe.

Wizened, barely five feet tall, and periodically wracked with asthmatic coughing that was aggravated by chain smoking, Howe looked more like the dragon than St. George—but he saved young Roosevelt's political career. For years, Howe had been searching for a man to whom he could offer his political knowledge, experience, and talent and make him into the leader he would have liked to be himself. Watching Franklin Roosevelt from the press gallery in Albany, he sensed that this handsome and ambitious young aristocrat possessed the qualities that he was seeking. When news of Franklin's success at Baltimore reached him, Howe had written him a jocular letter of congratulations that began, "Beloved and Revered Future President."

As soon as a telegram from Eleanor reached him, Howe raced to Franklin's bedside and began unfolding strategy for a campaign without a candidate. Eleanor took an immediate dislike to Howe, who smoked constantly and appeared dirty and disheveled. "I felt that his smoking spoiled the fresh air that my husband should have in his bedroom, and I was very disapproving whenever he came down to report on the campaign," she confessed. "I lost sight entirely of the fact that he was winning the campaign, and that without him my husband would have . . . probably lost the election. I simply made a nuisance of myself over those visits and his cigarettes. I often wonder how they bore with me in those days." Placed on the Roosevelt payroll at fifty dollars a week, Howe flooded the district with "personal" letters from Franklin, ran full-page advertisements in the newspapers playing up his candidate's accomplishments, and promises of more if reelected and launched an attack on his Republican rival. It all worked so well that Franklin ran ahead of Woodrow Wilson in the district without having made a single campaign appearance.

While Franklin lay flat on his back, the national campaign developed into a two-man fight between Theodore Roosevelt and Wilson as they both ignored the hapless Taft. Realistically but privately, the Colonel predicted that although he would run well ahead of Taft, Wilson would win. But this did not dampen his ardor and he crisscrossed the country. As he prepared to speak in Milwaukee on October 14, an anti-third-term fanatic shot him in the chest. The bullet tore through his overcoat, spectacles case, and the folded manuscript of his speech before lodging just beyond the ribs. He staggered for a moment, coughed to see if he would spit up blood, and stood up again. "Stand back! Don't hurt that man!" he shouted as the crowd started to lynch his assailant. Brushing off the protests of doctors and aides, he insisted on speaking. "It takes more than that to kill a Bull Moose," he told his stunned audience and continued for over an hour before consenting to being taken to a hospital. Admiration for Theodore's courage was widespread, but cheers were no substitute for votes, and the election turned out as he had predicted. Wilson piled up 6,301,254 votes to Roosevelt's 4,127,788, while Taft trailed badly with 3,485,831. Among the casualties of the debacle was Roosevelt's son-in-law, Nicholas Longworth, who had remained loyal to Taft, his fellow Cincinnatian and lost his Ohio congressional seat. "May I suggest to any of you who may have ambitions to go to Congress, to see to it that, in the same campaign your most eminent constituent is not contesting the presidency with your father-in-law," he later joked to one group.

Franklin Roosevelt's reward for his early support of Wilson was soon forthcoming. Josephus Daniels, who had been named Secretary of the Navy, asked if he was interested in becoming Assistant Secretary. The young man's face "beamed with pleasure," Daniels later recalled, and he quoted him as saying: "'How would I like it? I'd like it bully well. It would please me better than anything in the world. . . . All my life I have loved ships and have been a student of the Navy, and the assistant secretaryship is the one place, above all others, I would love to hold.'" The desired appointment was approved by President Wilson, and March 17, 1913—the eighth anniversary of his marriage to Eleanor—found him at Theodore Roosevelt's old desk for the first time. He had been in politics less than three years.

"I am baptized, confirmed, sworn in, vaccinated—and somewhat at sea," Franklin wrote his mother shortly after taking over his new duties, but he was "not at sea" very long. During his seven and a half years as Assistant Secretary of the Navy, he performed ably and efficiently, helping prepare the Navy for war and to win the victory at sea when it came. Like Cousin Theodore, who sent him a congratulatory note when he heard of

Franklin's appointment, he was soon popping up everywhere to inspect ships and shore facilities. Glorying in the crash of the seventeen-gun salute to which he was entitled, he added to the panoply by designing an Assistant Secretary's flag and made certain that it was to be broken out upon his appearance.

The Wilson years were stormy ones for the Navy—and at the center of the uproar was Josephus Daniels. A small-town editor with radical agrarian and pacifist views, he was suspicious of the Navy's hierarchy and a hopeless landlubber. Franklin once described him as "the funniest looking hill-billy I have ever seen" but he had a warm affection for his chief. Daniels angered the admirals almost immediately after taking office by rejecting their request for 20,000 additional men, but Franklin, a long-time disciple of Mahan and a "big navy" man, was popular with them. Sometimes they would wait until Daniels was safely out of town, and then come to him for a signature or a decision. Cocky and ambitious, young Roosevelt was often impatient with his superior, but the two men complemented each other. Franklin compensated for Daniels' ignorance of the Navy and its ways while the older man was a past master of the art of shepherding appropriations through a tight-fisted Congress.

Franklin's responsibilities included procurement, patronage negotiation of contracts and labor relations which gave him the opportunity to make his peace with Tammany—unglamorous matters but providing sound experience in administration and dealing with the bureaucracy.† "I get my fingers into about everything [where] there's no law against it," he declared. One of his first moves was to summon Louis Howe to Washington with a "Dear Ludwig" letter and install him in the Navy Department as his secretary at a salary of $2,000 a year. Actually, Howe served as a troubleshooter, cutting through red tape and violating precedent if needed to accomplish the tasks assigned him. Intensely loyal to Roosevelt, he both promoted and guarded his chief's reputation and almost completely identified with him.‡ "Howe lived

† It was during this period that Franklin persuaded his mother to have Springwood remodeled and supervised its transformation into its present appearance. The tower was removed, a large library-living room was added to the ground floor and over the new section, bedrooms for Sallie and Eleanor were laid out with Franklin's between them. In effect, the old Victorian house was encased in a Georgian mansion.
‡ For example, Howe made certain that FDR was out of town when the teetotaling Daniels issued an order banning the officers' wine mess as of July 1, 1914.

through Roosevelt—his life had practically no meaning for him apart from Roosevelt," according to Kenneth S. Davis, one of Franklin's biographers. It was Howe who insisted that the Assistant Secretary involve himself directly in contract negotiations with the leaders of the Navy's civilian labor force, which helped fill a gap in his education and proved useful in the future. Franklin's labor policies seemed to work, for he could later boast that there was no strike in any of the navy yards during the entire period he was in office.

The Washington of Woodrow Wilson was an exciting place and it had a maturing effect on Franklin. Riding a flood tide of progressive sentiment, Wilson reformed the nation's financial operations by establishing the Federal Reserve System, reduced the tariff to improve the flow of trade, took steps to regulate trusts and monopolies, persuaded Congress to pass child labor and workmen's compensation laws, and most important, secured enactment of a federal income tax. Franklin met such established figures as Oliver Wendell Holmes, Louis D. Brandeis, and Newton D. Baker, the Secretary of War, who had considerable intellectual and political influence upon him, as well as younger men, like Felix Frankfurter, Cordell Hull, and others with whom he was to work in the future. Although he had little personal contact with the President and as Frank Freidel says, "stood in relation to him as to a sort of super-schoolmaster, another Rector Peabody," he greatly admired Wilson. Franklin preferred to sop up information by talking to people than by reading documents, which prompted Newton Baker to tell Frances Perkins: "Young Roosevelt is very promising, but I should think he'd wear himself out in the promiscuous and extended contacts he maintains with people. But as I have observed him, he seems to clarify his ideas and teach himself as he goes along by that very conversational method."

Franklin's position carried heavy social obligations which were patiently shared by Eleanor. "I was really well schooled now, and

---

The rum ration for enlisted men had been abolished in 1862. Wherever the Navy's ships lay, there were raucous farewell parties for John Barleycorn on the eve of Prohibition as existing stocks were drunk up before the deadline. Midway during the bedlam on the *North Dakota,* one officer appeared in the wardroom wearing a baseball catcher's mask and proclaimed a toast. "Here's to Josephus Daniels," he declared—and was promptly bombarded with anything handy.

it never occurred to me to question where we were to go or what we were to do or how we were to do it," she said. "I simply knew that what we had to do we did, and that my job was to make it easy." The Roosevelts rented Bamie's old house at 1733 N Street, within walking distance of the State, War and Navy Building, next to the White House (now the Executive Office Building) where Franklin had his office. Small by the standards of official Washington, the house was a pleasant place with a postage stamp lawn in front and a little garden in the back where the family often dined in the heat of summer. Sallie continued her efforts to dominate the couple's life, however.* "Dined at 1733 N Street," she noted in her diary after her first visit to Washington. "Moved chairs and tables and began to feel at home."

The lives of the Roosevelt children orbited around their father. Anna described him as "the handsomest, strongest, most glamorous, vigorous, physical father in the world," and he joined the children in pillow fights, picnics, and games of hounds and hares. Like his own father, Franklin was not much of a disciplinarian, even when the children dropped paper sacks full of water on arriving guests. Sometimes he took them along with him to the Navy Department, where the boys were fascinated by the elaborate ship models lining the halls. "There is only one thing that interferes with their perfect enjoyment," Franklin said, "and that is my inability to take the boats out of the 'windows,' as they call the glass cases, and sail them in the bathtub or the river." Yet for all the liveliness of the Roosevelts, shadows fell across the relationship between the children and their father. Increasingly busy as his political star ascended, Franklin was often away, and when at home was usually too preoccupied to deal with his children on their own terms or to discuss their hidden fears and hopes.

Before coming to Washington, Eleanor had sought the advice of Bamie, whose husband had retired from the Navy as an admiral, as to what was expected of her as the wife of the Assistant Secretary. While impressing upon her niece the necessity of fol-

---

* Eleanor was beginning to show signs of rebellion, however. When Franklin's half brother, James Roosevelt Roosevelt, announced his intention of marrying his longtime companion, an Englishwoman named Elizabeth Riley, Sallie was shocked and tried to enlist Eleanor in a campaign against the marriage, but her daughter-in-law refused. Franklin was fond of his stepsister-in-law and saw to it that she was invited to family functions. Later, Betty Roosevelt became a close friend of Sallie's and often accompanied her on her queen-motherly progressions.

lowing the Navy's strict protocol, including the endless round of duty calls, she also had some other advice: "'You will find that many of the young officers' wives have a hard time because they must keep up their positions on very small pay. You can do a great deal to make life pleasant for them when they are in Washington, and that's what you should do.'" Eleanor was faced with luncheons, teas, receptions, and dinners—and through it all she went to house after house dropping off her card and repeating the formula, "'I am Mrs. Franklin D. Roosevelt. My husband has just come as Assistant Secretary of the Navy.'" If nothing else, it forced her to overcome her shyness. At first, she tried to make do without a social secretary, but her obligations were so heavy that she finally hired a young lady to help her three mornings a week. Her name was Lucy Page Mercer.

"These are history-making days," Franklin Roosevelt observed on August 1, 1914, as Europe plunged into the fiery cataclysm of World War I. "It will be the greatest war in the world's history." Although President Wilson espoused a policy of strict neutrality, Franklin, from almost the onset of the conflict, believed that the United States would be drawn into the struggle and urged Daniels to take immediate steps to make the Navy ready for any eventuality. Like Theodore Roosevelt, aroused again at the thought of action, he pleaded for preparedness to the point of insubordination in the face of the idealistic devotion to peace and pacifism of Wilson and Daniels.

Soon after the 1912 election, the Colonel had gone to Brazil on a lecture trip and learned of an uncharted Amazonian stream known as the River of Doubt, which he wanted to explore. "I have to go!" he proclaimed. "It's my last chance to be a boy!" The Brazilian government organized an expedition led by Theodore and his son Kermit, but things went badly almost as soon as the explorers reached the interior. Men disappeared in the jungle, boats capsized, and supplies were lost. Theodore injured his leg and it became infected; he was stricken with malaria and dysentery and with a temperature of 105°, became delirious, repeating over and over again, "In Xanadu did Kubla Khan a stately pleasure dome decree." He begged the others to leave him and considered suicide to keep from becoming a burden. Two months after the expedition had begun, what was left of the party reached

Manaus, where they learned they had been given up for lost. They had mapped the River of Doubt, now named by the Brazilians in honor of the ex-President. Theodore returned home to find that the Wilson administration had agreed to a treaty with Colombia that expressed "sincere regret" for the way the United States had acquired the Panama Canal Zone and provided for a payment of $25 million. "I regard the proposed treaty as a crime," he raged—and never forgave Wilson for the insult.

Although the United States was officially neutral, huge British and French arms purchases which lifted the country out of a recession, the financial stake of Wall Street in an Allied victory, a skillful propaganda campaign, and German ineptness all helped crystallize American public opinion against Germany. Following the sinking of the British liner *Lusitania* in May 1915 by a submarine, with the loss of 1,198 lives—128 of them Americans—an outraged Theodore Roosevelt declared that it was "inconceivable that we can refrain from taking action . . . for we owe it not only to humanity but to our own national respect." Privately, Wilson was just as angered, but he was determined to keep out of the fighting and sent Berlin a series of protest notes. Eventually, the Germans paid an indemnity for the loss of American lives and ordered U-boat skippers to spare large liners. Visiting her father at Sagamore one day, Alice Longworth told him that Wilson had dispatched another note to Germany. "Did you notice what its serial number was?" he asked. "I fear I have lost track myself, but I am inclined to think it is No. 11,785, Series B."

The conflict bogged down into a bloody stalemate on land, and the Germans, in a desperate attempt to starve Britain into submission, resumed unrestricted submarine warfare in February 1917. They fully understood that this move would probably bring the United States into the war on the side of the Allies, but gambled on scoring a decisive victory before America could mobilize its vast resources. Within a few weeks several American merchantmen were torpedoed with loss of life, and Wilson, who had just been re-elected with the campaign slogan "He Kept Us out of War," asked Congress for a declaration of hostilities. On April 6, 1917, the American people took up arms to make the world "safe for democracy."

Franklin was now in his element. Seemingly everywhere, he gave orders for the enlistment of large numbers of men, opened "boot" camps, let contracts for new ships and for mounds of supplies, and gave advice whether it was sought or not. "I have loved every minute of it," he declared. He moved so fast in purchasing supplies that the Navy cornered the market in some items, and Wilson had to order him to share his trove with the Army. The war at sea was at the crisis stage. Allied merchantmen were being sunk faster than they could be built, and Britain had only a three-week supply of grain on hand. The cry from across the sea was for destroyers and more destroyers, and within a month of the declaration of war, the first six American vessels arrived to join the hunt for enemy U-boats. More followed as soon as they could be readied.

Like Theodore Roosevelt in 1898, Franklin wanted to resign and accept a commission, but both Wilson and Daniels persuaded him that he was more valuable where he was. As for the Colonel, with the first sound of the bugle, he began bombarding the White House and the War Department for permission to organize a division and take it to France. But Regular Army officers still remembered the round robin after Santiago, and Wilson was bitter about the attacks of his policies. "I really think the best way to treat Mr. Roosevelt is to take no notice of him," the President coldly told an aide. "That breaks his heart and is the best punishment that can be administered." This refusal fanned Theodore's already raging hatred of Wilson. Unable to fight himself, the old lion sent his cubs to do battle. Ted, Jr., was wounded and gassed; Archie was wounded so badly that he was declared completely disabled and both were decorated; Kermit did not wait for the United States to enter war and joined the British Army, earning the Military Cross; and Quentin teamed up with Hall Roosevelt to memorize an eye examination chart so they could join the fledgling air service. Ted's wife, the "other" Eleanor, was the first woman sent by the YMCA into the fighting area and Ethel worked in a hospital in France along with her husband, Dr. Richard Derby. "It's rather up to us to practice what father preaches," said Quentin.

Meanwhile, the Navy was trying to find ways to deal with the U-boat menace. To meet the immediate need for antisubmarine craft while new destroyers were being built, Franklin pushed through the construction of 110-foot wooden-hulled submarine chasers. Officered and manned by reservists, the "splinter fleet" played an important role in making the seas safe for Allied shipping. He also fathered the North Sea Barrage, a wall of some 70,000 mines, extending 240 miles across the North Sea from Scotland to Norway athwart the courses of outward-bound and returning submarines that was intended to be so dense that no submarine could safely penetrate it. The British claimed that it couldn't be done, but at Franklin's insistence, the sowing of mines began in June 1918. The war ended before the effectiveness of the North Sea Barrage could be fully tested, but at least six U-boats were believed to have been sunk in it. Fear of the deadly minefield was also said to have been a significant factor in the decline in morale in the German Navy that ultimately led to mutiny and defeat.

In September 1918 Franklin returned from an inspection of naval facilities in the war zone suffering from pneumonia. He was so sick that he was carried off the ship on a stretcher. Eleanor took over the handling of her husband's personal business—and made the shocking discovery that he was having an affair with Lucy Mercer. "The bottom dropped out of my own particular world," she told Joseph Lash, a quarter century later. "I faced myself, my surroundings, my world, honestly for the first time." For some time, she had been uneasy about the relationship between Franklin and her former social secretary, but had avoided facing the problem for as long as she could. Franklin and Lucy had often been seen together while Eleanor and the children spent the summer at Campobello, but she had determinedly brushed off all the rumors, including what may have been an attempt by Alice Longworth to tell her about the affair. One day, Eleanor had met Alice at the Capitol and, as she told Franklin, left her without "having allowed her to tell me any secrets. She inquired if you had told me and I said no and that I did not believe in knowing things which your husband did not wish you to know so I think that I will be spared any further mysterious secrets!"

As tall as Eleanor, pretty and vivacious, Lucy was a member of an impoverished branch of the Carroll family of Maryland and as much a patrician as the Roosevelts. One of the few ways in which a young lady of her class could earn a living was as a social secretary, and from all accounts she was able and efficient, quickly putting Eleanor's affairs in order. "When I was 10 or 11 I remember feeling happy and admiring when I was greeted one morning at home by Miss Lucy Mercer," Anna recalled in an unpublished magazine article. "I knew that she sat at a desk and wrote on cards; and I knew that I liked her warm and friendly manner and smile." Eleanor sometimes invited her to dinners and parties when an extra single woman was needed. The contrast between the two women was obvious. Although Eleanor was less awkward than when she had first come to Washington, she was serious to the point of humorlessness, sometimes puritanical and unable to let down her guard. Lucy, on the other hand, was feminine, charming, and skilled at putting men at their ease. In all probability, Franklin loved his wife, but weighed down with the heavy responsibility of mobilizing the Navy for war, he may have sought gayer and more yielding companionship.

Various versions exist of what happened after Eleanor confronted Franklin with Lucy's letters, but Anna's account, based largely on what her mother told her, seems the most logical. Bitter at being discarded after thirteen years of marriage and five children for a younger and more beautiful woman, she offered him a divorce but advised him "to think things over carefully before giving her a definite answer." Whether Franklin hesitated is unknown, but according to Anna, he voluntarily promised to end any "romantic relationship" with Lucy. There were many reasons for this decision. The effect of a divorce on the children, the realization that Lucy, a devout Catholic, would be reluctant to marry a divorced man, a threat from his mother to cut him off if he left Eleanor, and the fatal impact of a divorce on his political career all made it inevitable. Eventually, Eleanor and Franklin reconciled, but the relationship between them was never the same again. She became more independent, less a reflection of her husband, and with her own life to live. Eleanor never wrote about this harrowing episode, but a passage in *This Is My Story* ostensibly concerning her war work in a hospital may have been an indirect reference to it:

> I think I learned then that practically no one in the world is entirely bad or entirely good, and that motives are often more important than actions. I had spent most of my life in an atmosphere where everyone was sure of what was right and what was wrong, and as life has progressed I have gradually come to believe that human

beings who try to judge other human beings are undertaking a
somewhat difficult job. When your duty does not thrust ultimate
judgments upon you, perhaps it is as well to keep an open and charitable mind, and to try to understand why people do things instead
of condemning the acts themselves.

Tragedy also stalked the Oyster Bay Roosevelts. Despite his
visual problem, Quentin had gotten through flight training and
went to the front as a fighter pilot. He was engaged to a young
lady named Flora Payne Whitney and they had wanted to get
married in France but were denied permission by the War Department. Theodore tried hard to have this "idiotic ruling" suspended, telling Ted, "It is well to have had happiness, to have
achieved the great ends of life, when one must walk boldly and
warily close to death." The Colonel was pleased and proud when
he learned early in July 1918 that Quentin had scored his first
victory, but on Bastille Day he was shot down in a duel with two
German planes. Edith and Theodore were self-controlled in public, but his friend Hermann Hagedorn said that with Quentin's
death, Roosevelt's old exuberance was gone and the "boy in him
had died." Paying tribute to his son, Theodore wrote: "Only
those are fit to live who do not fear to die; and none are fit to die
who have shrunk from the joy of life and the duty of life. Both
life and death are parts of the same Great Adventure. . . ."

With the war grinding to a end, some political observers were
already looking to the future and touting the Colonel for the Republican presidential nomination in 1920. "By George, if they
take me, they'll have to take me without a single modification of
the things that I have always stood for!" he declared with a flash
of the old fire. Worn out at sixty by a lifetime of strenuous living,
he brushed off warnings that he might be confined to a wheelchair for as long as he lived if he did not slow down. "All right! I
can work that way, too!" he replied, and plunged into an attack
on Woodrow Wilson's proposal for a League of Nations on
grounds that it was inimical to America's interests. But Theodore's own "Great Adventure" was rapidly drawing to a close,
and early in the morning of January 6, 1919, he passed away at
his beloved Sagamore Hill. "Death had to take him sleeping," observed Vice-President Thomas Marshall, "for if Roosevelt had
been awake, there would have been a fight."

Chapter XVIII
TRIAL AND TRIUMPH

"Take wine, women and song, add plenty of A-No. 1 victuals, the belch and bellow of oratory, a balmy but stimulating climate and the whiff of patriotism, and it must be obvious that you have a dose with a very powerful kick in it." So wrote Henry L. Mencken in fond recollection of the Democratic national convention of 1920 which met in San Francisco and nominated James M. Cox for President and Franklin Roosevelt as his running mate. Roosevelt professed surprise at being chosen for Vice-President, saying he had gone to the convention toying with the idea of announcing his candidacy for senator or governor of New York upon his return home. And some political observers were taken aback, for on the day the convention opened, the New York *Herald* had printed a list of thirty-nine possible candidates and Roosevelt's name was not among them.

Yet Franklin's nomination was logical. Despite his claim to surprise, Louis Howe had been working hard behind the scenes to win it for him. And he was a desirable addition to the ticket. Although Theodore Roosevelt was dead, the family name still had political magic; he had a good record as Assistant Secretary of the Navy; as a New Yorker he provided geographic balance to a ticket headed by a former governor of Ohio; he straddled the Prohibition issue while Cox was a "wet," and he supported Woodrow Wilson's dream of a League of Nations while Cox was cool to the idea.

Wilson himself was a hopeless invalid and a virtual prisoner in the White House, his beloved League in tatters about him. He had returned from the Paris Peace Conference in 1919 as a demigod, but Cabot Lodge and other "irreconcilables" blocked approval of the Versailles Treaty to which was attached the covenant establishing the League. Wilson's shrewd political judgment completely failed him. Although he had agreed to a raft of compromises in Paris to obtain British and French acquiescence to the League, he stubbornly refused to give a single inch to obtain ratification of the treaty by two thirds of the Senate. By refusing to accept even the simplest reservation—such as one reaffirming that the Constitution should be paramount in cases where it and the Covenant of the League were in conflict—Wilson inadvertently did more than Lodge to ensure that the United States did not join the League of Nations.

Throughout the fifteen months of the battle, Alice Longworth cajoled, advised, and succored the so-called "Battalion of Death" which opposed the League and helped devise its strategy and tactics. Nicholas Longworth had been returned to Congress in 1914, and she made her home on Massachusetts Avenue their headquarters. No task was too insignificant for Alice if it promoted the anti-Wilson cause. When she learned that Eleanor and Franklin had persuaded Bamie's son, a young naval officer named Sheffield Cowles, Jr., of the logic of the League, she moved swiftly to enlist him in her cause. Eleanor found her "very partisan," and Franklin was "rather annoyed" at her. Day after day, Alice haunted the Senate gallery like a latter-day Madame La-Farge, grimly entering the names of those who supported the League or wavered in their opposition on her blacklist. She revealed an infinite capacity for hatred and viperish comment. Not even Lodge was safe from her sharp tongue when she discovered that he was "peddling a compromise" on one of the articles around the Senate. "Good morning, Mr. Wobbly," was her greeting for him until he returned to full opposition. In the end, she had her way—and the League of Nations was dead.

The struggle over the League had left the Democrats in complete disarray. Wilson was discredited, his treaty rejected, and the American people disillusioned with great moral crusades. Weary of Wilson's appeals to idealism and his visionary preachments, they wanted to shape their own lives without interference from the government. The prospects for the party in 1920 were grim, and Franklin Roosevelt was convinced that only one man could turn the tide for the Democrats—Herbert Hoover, the able director of European relief and wartime Food Administrator. "Hoover is certainly a wonder and I wish we could make him President of the United States," Franklin told a friend. "There could not be a better one." But Hoover opted for the Republican party and Roosevelt went to the convention supporting the favorite-son candidacy of New York's Governor Alfred E. Smith.

By the time the delegates began assembling in San Francisco, however, the prospects for the Democrats seemed less bleak, thanks to the Republicans. Meeting in Chicago, they had bypassed General Leonard Wood, whose nomination had been seconded by Corinne R. Robinson, to nominate Senator Warren G. Harding, a silver-haired mediocrity from Ohio, and Calvin Coolidge, the equally conservative governor of Massachusetts. William Allen White, the Kansas editor, said he had never seen a convention "so completely dominated by sinister predatory economic forces"—particularly the oil industry—and Harding was handpicked by a small group of party leaders in "a smoke-filled hotel room."

Even before the convention was gaveled to order, Howe and other Roosevelt supporters were buttonholing delegates and drumming up support for the vice-presidential nomination, while Franklin stood ready to seize any opportunity to gain prominence. Such an opportunity was not long in appearing. The convention opened with the unveiling of a huge portrait of Wilson which touched off a demonstration that sent most of the delegates swirling into the aisles bearing their state standards before them. But the New York delegation, under orders from Boss Charles F. Murphy, who disliked the President, remained conspicuously in their seats. Unable to bear the taunts of the demonstrators, Franklin scuffled with the Tammany stalwart clutching the state's standard and bore it away in triumph into the parading mob, much to the delight of pro-Wilson southern delegates. Roosevelt also attracted favorable attention with a graceful seconding speech for Smith when the governor's name was put in nomination for the presidency.

Throughout the early balloting, New York held firm for Smith, but Murphy, realizing that the delegation's favorite son could not be nominated, because he was a Catholic, a "wet," and a representative of the big cities, ordered a switch to Cox. Most of the delegates followed instructions, but a handful, including Roosevelt, shifted to William G. McAdoo, the Secretary of Treasury and Wilson's son-in-law. Frances Perkins remembers Franklin "vaulting over a row of chairs to get to the platform in a hurry" at one point. Ballot after ballot followed in which McAdoo's strength steadily waned, and on the forty-fourth ballot Cox won the nomination. That night he selected Roosevelt as his running mate, but knowing Murphy's antipathy toward him, told an aide to clear it with the Tammany leader. "I don't like Roosevelt," the Boss declared. "He is not well known in the country, but . . . this is the first time a Democratic nominee for the Presidency has shown me courtesy. That's why I would vote for the devil himself if Cox wanted me to. Tell him we will nominate Roosevelt on the first ballot as soon as we assemble."

The Democratic ticket was doomed to defeat, but Cox and Roosevelt made a fight of it. Treating the election as a referendum on American participation in the League of Nations, they barnstormed across the country, with Franklin, alone, making no fewer than eight hundred speeches, talks, and appearances. Harding stayed close to his home in Marion, Ohio, mouthing canned platitudes. His campaign slogan was "back to normalcy"— and it struck a responsive chord among the voters.* "There might be no such word in the dictionary," Frederick Lewis Allen has written, "but normalcy is what [Americans] wanted" in an age of kaleidoscopic change.

Women were voting for the first time in 1920, so Eleanor accompanied her husband on the campaign trail. Unprepared for the organized chaos of campaigning and often the only woman present, she had difficulty in adjusting. There was little for her to do but appear to be listening with rapt attention to speeches which she had heard over and over again and to effusively greet complete strangers no matter how tired she was. And Franklin had little time for her. He was either preparing speeches, plotting strategy, or relaxing around the poker table. The one person who took an interest in her was Louis Howe. Realizing

* In one of his speeches, Harding had meant to say "normality" but stumbled over the word.

that she wanted to have an active part in the campaign, he began coming to her at night to discuss speeches, points of political strategy, and the ways of the press. "I was flattered and before long I found myself discussing a wide range of subjects," she later recalled. For the first time, Eleanor sensed the keen intelligence behind Howe's gargoylelike figure, to understand the relationship between her husband and Howe, and no longer resented the intimacy between them. She and Howe became warm friends.

On the other hand, however, the 1920 campaign created a rupture between the Hyde Park and Oyster Bay branches of the Roosevelt family, which had but a single name to give the country. The Oyster Bay Roosevelts, Alice in particular, resented Franklin as an upstart exploiting her father's reputation and believed that if any Roosevelt should be running for national office, it ought to be her brother Ted. As Franklin stumped the country, people shouted, "I voted for your father!" and "You're just like the Old Man!"—which was too much for the Republican Roosevelts. Theodore Roosevelt, Jr., was dispatched by the Republican National Committee as a one-man "truth squad" to dog Franklin's trail. "He is a maverick," Ted said of his distant cousin. "He does not have the brand of our family." Eleanor was deeply hurt by the attack, and it is said she refused to speak to Ted for several years afterward. Franklin struck back by bitingly recalling that "in 1912 Senator Harding called Theodore Roosevelt, first a Benedict Arnold and then an Aaron Burr. This is one thing, at least some members of the Roosevelt family will not forget."

When the votes had been counted, Harding and Coolidge won by the largest popular margin since well before the Civil War. "It wasn't a landslide," said Joe Tumulty, Wilson's secretary. "It was an earthquake." If Franklin was depressed by this disappointing showing, he hid it well. Within a few days he was good-humoredly calling himself "Franklin D. Roosevelt, Ex. V.P., Canned. (Erroneously reported dead.)" Examining his situation, he found that in fact he had lost little. He had received national political exposure for the first time, had developed a national following, and had built a team of dedicated assistants who added their skills to those of Louis Howe. He could look forward to the future with expectation, for as Frank Freidel has said, the campaign of 1920 "was not so much a lost crusade as a dress rehearsal."

Long before Warren Harding became President, his father had an inkling of the disasters that lay in the future. "Warren, it's a good thing you wasn't born a girl because you'd be in a family way all the time," allowed the old man. "You can't say no." Friendly and gregarious, Harding brought with him to the White House as jolly a gang of small-town sports and backroom fixers as were to be found in any Ohio county courthouse. Big-bellied and good-natured, they descended upon Washington as if it were a big rock candy mountain, and it wasn't long before they were trying to pry the dome off the Capitol.

The scandals associated with Harding's name represent the lowest ebb of American political life since the post–Civil War era. His administration was a carnival of unrestrained corruption. Although there is no evidence that Harding stole so much as a nickel, members of his Cabinet, his friends and associates were in league with crooked businessmen to plunder the nation. His Secretary of the Interior was the first cabinet officer to go to jail, his Attorney General and political mentor only narrowly escaped a similar fate, and his Secretary of the Navy was forced to resign because of a mixture of stupidity and criminal negligence. Besides Teapot Dome, Harding's legacy included fraud in the Veterans Bureau, graft in the Office of Alien Property Custodian, and conspiracy in the Justice Department. Yet, as Alice Longworth remarked, the President who presided over these revels "was not a bad man. He was just a slob."

Harding paid off his campaign debt to the Oyster Bay Roosevelts by naming Theodore Roosevelt, Jr., as Assistant Secretary of the Navy, a post the family seemed to regard as its own. "I have had to stand two Roosevelts," groaned an admiral. "I cannot stand another." Fate had destined Ted to follow in the footsteps of his father, and he worked hard to live up to the family's expectations. But he was not entirely happy with this burden. "I will always be honest and upright, and I hope some day to be a great soldier," he told a boyhood friend, "but I will always be spoken of as Theodore Roosevelt's son."

He had served ably and well in France, and following the war helped organize the American Legion, to see the veterans got a square deal. "You know, Father, Ted has always worried for fear he would not be worthy of you," the younger Roosevelt's wife told Theodore one day near the end of the war. "Worthy of me?" replied the Colonel. "Darling, I'm so very proud of him. He has won high honor not only for his children but like the Chinese, he has ennobled his ancestors."

Upon his return to New York, Ted had taken the first step on the political path designed to lead to the White House. He ran for the State Assembly from Nassau County on Long Island against an opponent who sarcastically recalled the elder Roosevelt's famous statement: "My hat's in the ring—and it isn't my father's." Ted won without trouble, the only election he was to win in a lifetime in politics. As a freshman legislator during the Great Red Scare of 1919–20, he showed the same courage that had distinguished him on the battlefield. Opposing the popular hysteria, he bitterly denounced the expulsion of five Socialist assemblymen on grounds that they were "traitors," declaring that it would completely destroy the principle of representative government. The Speaker rebuked him by reading passages from his father's writings, so that the "Americanism" of the father might be "painfully" contrasted with the "un-Americanism" of the son.

The other surviving Roosevelt sons, Kermit and Archie, took no part in politics. Kermit, who had in 1914 married Belle Willard, whose family owned Washington's famous Willard Hotel, organized his own shipping company and eventually became a vice-president of United States Lines. With an ear for languages and a spirit as restless as his father's, he carried on the family tradition established by Robert B. Roosevelt of the writer-sportsman. Refusing to follow a routine career, he hunted tigers in India and Korea and organized expeditions to the most remote corners of China and Central Asia, and wrote copiously about them. Archie, among the most fun-loving of the Roosevelts, was invalided home from France with a complete disability and launched his business career as a vice-president of one of the companies owned by Harry F. Sinclair, the oil baron. Theodore, who had been a Sinclair director before entering politics, had been instrumental in getting him the job.

While Theodore and Franklin Roosevelt both had the joy of overseeing the expansion of the U. S. Navy, Theodore, Jr., had the unenviable task of presiding over its decline. He played a leading role in formulating the American position at the Washington Conference for the Limitation of Naval Armaments in 1921, the Strategic Arms Limitation Talks of the day. The American proposals, unveiled by Secretary of State Charles Evans Hughes, exploded with the force of a sixteen-inch shell among the delegates. They called for the wholesale scrapping of dozens of battleships and limitations on the future construction of such vessels. "In less than fifteen minutes," declared a British observer, Hughes had sent more tonnage to the bottom "than all the admirals of the world have sunk in a cycle of centuries."

Many American naval officers were as stunned by the audacity of the proposals that Roosevelt had helped work out in secret. Most of these recommendations were accepted after considerable haggling. The general public hailed the outcome of the conference as a victory for American diplomacy, but some naval officers complained that the United States had scrapped modern vessels, while other nations had merely junked worn-out ships and torn-up blueprints. More recent studies have shown, however, that the United States fared better at the conference table than thought at the time. The battleships it retained were newer than those that remained in the British and Japanese fleets and they incorporated considerable improvements resulting from wartime experience.

This was the high point of Ted's service as Assistant Secretary of the Navy, for he was soon inadvertently besmirched by the Teapot Dome scandal. Teapot Dome, located in Wyoming, was one of several naval petroleum reserves that had been established to stockpile fuel for the Navy in case of emergency, and private oil companies had been trying to gain access to them almost from their inception. Josephus Daniels recalled that during the close of a congressional session in the Wilson years, "Mr. [Franklin] Roosevelt and I remained at the Capitol all night long watching the legislation . . . fearing some act might be passed that would turn over these invaluable oil reserves to parties who laid claim to them without even decent show of title." Control of the reserves was now vested in Edwin Denby, the new Secretary of the Navy, who seemed to have had little interest in his department except to administer it with the least possible annoyance to himself.

But Albert B. Fall, the Secretary of the Interior, had long been eyeing the rich petroleum reserves at Elk Hills, California, as well as Teapot Dome. With his drooping moustache, string tie, and wide-brimmed hat, Fall looked like the sheriff in a Western movie. Friendly with Harding since he had served with him as senator from New Mexico, he had been rewarded with a seat in the Cabinet. Almost as soon as he was firmly in the saddle, Fall launched a campaign to wrest control of the reserves from the Navy Department. He convinced Harding that it would be more efficient to have the reserves administered by his department rather than by the Navy, and prepared an executive order for the President's signature. Naval officers aware of what was going on were anxious to preserve the reserves from Fall's grasp. They briefed Ted on the details, and convinced the transfer would be a mistake, he asked Denby to hold it up. When the Secretary declined to do so, Ted went to Fall to seek a modification of the order.

Following a meeting between Fall and Roosevelt, the order was amended to provide that no drilling would be permitted unless the Secretary of the Navy or Acting Secretary had been consulted—which meant Fall had obtained full authority to do anything he wanted after merely informing Denby, or in his absence, Roosevelt, of what he planned to do. Harding signed the order without seeking any explanation. Moving quickly, Fall awarded a lease to the Elks Hills reserve to the Pan-American Petroleum and Transport Company, headed by Edward Doheny. Not long afterward, Doheny's son presented Fall with a little black bag containing $100,000 in cash. Teapot Dome went to Harry Sinclair for little more than $300,000 in cash and negotiable bonds. So, in exchange for about $400,000, Albert Fall had given away naval petroleum reserves then conservatively valued at $200 million.†

Fall's neighbors in New Mexico were soon surprised to see a rapid change in his fortunes. Back taxes were paid on his run-down ranch, new fences were erected, the house was repaired, and blooded stock appeared on his range. Questions began to be asked about his sudden prosperity, but the scandal did not gush over until after Harding died on August 2, 1923, while on a speaking tour. A Senate committee began looking into the oil leases, but with the Republicans loath to investigate, the leader-

† In 1975 the oil in the Elk Hills reserve alone was valued at from $30 to $50 billion.

ship passed to Senator Thomas Walsh, a Montana Democrat. With patient thoroughness and grim determination, he pursued Fall through a jungle of confusing documents and a long train of lying witnesses. Archie Roosevelt helped supply a link between Fall and Sinclair. With rumors afloat that Sinclair was involved in the Teapot Dome lease, the tycoon fled to Europe causing Roosevelt to start asking questions about his employer. Alarmed by what he had learned, he immediately resigned his position with Sinclair. "I may be wrong," he told Ted, "but I'm afraid there's been dirty work at the crossroads on this oil business."

Urged by Ted and Alice to appear before Walsh's committee, Archie testified that he had discussed Sinclair's hasty departure with Gustav D. Wahlberg, the oilman's secretary. He asked Wahlberg point-blank if he thought Sinclair had bribed Fall in order to get the lease. Bribery was a nasty word, the secretary was purported to have replied. "I think somebody may have lent Mr. Fall money," he added as an afterthought. According to Roosevelt, Wahlberg acknowledged being worried about "a payment which was made to a foreman of Mr. Fall's ranch; the amount was $68,000; and that he had the cancelled checks." But Wahlberg claimed that Archie had misunderstood what he had been told. He had been talking about cattle shipped to Fall's ranch—"six or eight cows," not "sixty-eight thous."

Ted came under attack because of his role in the handling of the executive order shifting control of the petroleum reserves to Fall, and his past association with Sinclair. Representative William F. Stevenson of South Carolina demanded that he resign as Assistant Secretary because his wife, Eleanor, was said to own Sinclair stock. She had, in fact, disposed of it long before the scandal had broken. Returning home late at night from a trip out of town, Ted angrily resolved to beat up the congressman for dragging his wife's name into the affair. A worried Eleanor immediately telephoned Alice, getting her out of bed.

"Sister? Ted is back," she said. "He's just leaving to go and beat up Stevenson."

"Let me talk to him," replied Alice. "Ted? I hear you're going to beat up Stevenson. . . . Yes, of course he deserves it. . . . I know he's a rat. . . . By the way, he's a little elderly man and wears glasses. Remember to have him take them off before you hit him."

"Are you sure of that?" asked Ted, who had never met Stevenson.

"Positive."

"Oh, *damn*. Then I suppose I can't do it."

Ultimately, Fall went to jail for taking bribes—although Doheny and Sinclair who had given them to him escaped punishment—but Ted was bespattered from the fallout of Teapot Dome. Although no one questioned his honesty, the New York *World* said "he was too dull or too lazy to accept [the] responsibility of high office. He went about the routine of his work asking no questions that were impolite. . . ." This was too harsh a judgment by far and did not prevent Ted from trying to continue in his father's giant footsteps. He resigned as Assistant Secretary of the Navy in 1924 to seek the governorship of New York, and was succeeded by Theodore Douglas Robinson, Aunt Corinne's son, which kept the job in the family.

Throughout his campaign against Al Smith, Ted was bedeviled by the Hyde Park Roosevelts, still smarting from his attack on Franklin four years before. "Of course he [Smith] can win," declared Eleanor in a seconding speech at the Democratic State Convention. "How can he help it when the Republican convention . . . did everything to help him." This thrust against her first cousin was loudly applauded. Maliciously, Louis Howe persuaded Eleanor to tail Ted about the state with a giant-size teapot that spouted real steam mounted on the roof of her car to remind the voters of Teapot Dome. "It was a pretty base thing for her to do," declared an angry Alice. Years later, Eleanor tended to agree, saying: "In the thick of political fights one always feels that all methods of campaigning are honest and fair, but I do think now that this was a rough stunt. . . ." Ted lost the governorship by 108,000 votes, running nearly a million votes behind Calvin Coolidge, the victorious Republican presidential candidate. "We naturally said it was because they did something to the ballot boxes in New York," Alice observed. Nevertheless, Ted's career in elective politics had run into a dead end—just as Franklin Roosevelt was emerging from the great crisis of his life.

Out of office for the first time in a decade, Franklin helped establish a new law firm, but his heart was not in the rather staid practice that it offered. The twenties were the heyday of the speculator, the plunger, and the smart operator, and Roosevelt followed the gravitation of power to Wall Street. Having emulated Theodore Roosevelt for ten years, he now tried to become a successful businessman like his father. His main interest during the period was a vice-presidency of the Fidelity & Deposit Company of Maryland, a leading surety bonding firm that paid him $25,000 a year to head its New York office. Although he had gotten the job through friendship with Van-Lear Black, major stockholder in the company and owner of the Baltimore *Sunpapers*, Franklin plunged into business with the same zest he had shown for politics. Wide-ranging political contacts in Albany and Washington helped him drum up much profitable business for the firm.

Eleanor had also outgrown the genteel life of teas and sewing circles she had known in New York before the war. She took courses in typing and shorthand, learned to cook, became active in the League of Women Voters, sat on the boards of several charities, and became friendly with social workers and activists. Franklin's mother was distressed that she was no longer available to pour tea for her friends or to keep her company, but Eleanor had, following the Lucy Mercer affair, proclaimed her own declaration of independence. She was no longer the timid girl of fifteen years before. "I was thinking things out for myself and becoming an individual," she said.

Having had little rest in recent years, Franklin was looking forward to spending the summer of 1921 with his family at Campobello—and to plotting strategy with Howe for the gubernatorial race the following year—but the press of business kept him in New York until early August. Marguerite LeHand, his secretary, wrote Eleanor that he "looked tired when he left." Even so, Franklin plunged into a typically active Roosevelt vacation as soon as he arrived on the island. While preparing bait for a codfishing expedition, he slipped and fell into the frigid Bay of Fundy, and even though he was pulled out almost immediately, he still remembered the shock a dozen years later. "I've never felt anything so cold as that water. . . . [It] was so cold it seemed paralyzing."

On the following day, August 10, he went sailing with his children. Sighting a cloud of blue smoke rising from a nearby shore, the Roosevelts landed and fought the forest fire, flailing away at the flames with evergreen branches. It was hard, hot, and dirty work. "Our eyes were bleary with smoke; we were begrimed and smarting with spark burns, exhausted," Franklin said. The best cure was a swim, so he led a two-mile jog across the island to a freshwater lake where the party took a dip which was topped by a plunge into the icy waters of the bay, a tonic that had always left him invigorated. Roosevelt was surprised to find that "I didn't feel the usual glow I'd expected."

Back at the house, he found the mail had arrived bringing some newspapers he hadn't seen and he sat down on the porch in his wet bathing suit to read them. After a while, he felt a chill but was too tired to dress. "I'd never felt quite that way before," he said later. Complaining of chills and aches, Franklin went to bed early, believing he was suffering from an attack of lumbago. Awakening the next morning, he swung out of bed to find his left leg was so weak it almost collapsed under him. "I tried to persuade myself that this trouble with my leg was muscular, that it would disappear as I used it. But presently it refused to work, and then the other."

"I don't know what's wrong with me, Louis," Franklin muttered to Howe over and over again a few days later. "I just don't know." Pain and desperation were etched on his face. A country doctor summoned by Eleanor had diagnosed his illness as a simple cold, and was puzzled when the patient's condition quickly worsened. Severe pains spread through Roosevelt's back and legs and he lost the power to move them. His temperature shot up to 102°, and he no longer had control of his bodily functions. Howe scoured the nearby resorts with the hope of finding a vacationing specialist and persuaded "a famous Philadelphia diagnostician" to come and examine Franklin. He concluded that Roosevelt was suffering from a blood clot on the spinal cord, and then, changing his mind, said it was a lesion. He prescribed massage and sent Eleanor a bill for $600. Each day, Franklin's condition grew worse, and even the weight of the bedclothes on his limbs was painful.

For two nightmarish weeks, Eleanor slept on a cot in his room, nursing her husband night and day. She bathed him, fed him, tried to keep up his spirits, while she alternated between hope and despair, her own anxiety made worse by the frightening inability of the doctors to even determine the nature of Franklin's illness. The only person she could turn to for help was Louis Howe. Refusing a lucrative job offer in the oil business, he remained with his afflicted friend, and as Eleanor said, "From that time on he put his entire heart into working for my husband's future." Following the misguided advice of the specialist, Eleanor and Howe massaged the sick man's limbs for hours on end, only to later learn that besides being painful, it further damaged his weakened muscles. Franklin was undergoing mental as well as physical agony. Overnight, he had been turned from a lithe, active man of thirty-nine with a brilliant future, into a bedridden cripple completely dependent on others for the simplest service. It was almost too much for him. Many years later, he told Frances Perkins that he had been "in utter despair" during the first days of his illness, "fearing that God had abandoned him." Nevertheless, his spirits began to revive, and before long he sometimes bantered with Eleanor and Howe in his usual flippant manner, despite the ever-present pain.

Two weeks after Franklin was stricken, his Uncle Fred Delano, acting on information provided by Eleanor, sent Dr. Robert W. Lovett, a Boston specialist on poliomyelitis, to Campobello. From what he had been told, Lovett suspected that Franklin was a victim of infantile paralysis, and an examination of the patient confirmed his hypothesis. He thought the attack a mild one and said Franklin's chances of recovery were excellent. Everyone exuded optimism for Franklin's benefit, including his mother, who had just returned from her annual trip to Europe. "I realized that I had to be courageous for Franklin's sake," Sallie said of her first visit to his bedside, "and since he was probably pretending to be unworried for mine, the meeting was quite a cheerful one."

Franklin was deeply concerned about the effect of his incapacity on the children. They knew only that their father was gravely ill in an upstairs room where the shades were always drawn and their mother was tense and worried. "We children were allowed only a few glimpses of him, a hurried exchange of words from a doorway," says Jimmy. "Yet from the beginning, even before the paralysis had receded fully from the upper reaches of his body, Father was unbelievedly concerned about how *we* would take it. He grinned at us, and he did his best to call out, or gasp out, some cheery response to our tremulous, just-this-side-of-tears greetings."

In mid-September, Franklin was moved to the Presbyterian Hospital in New York, while Howe skillfully brushed off press inquiries about the state of Roosevelt's health until Franklin's physician issued an optimistic bulletin on the prospects for his recovery. But Dr. George Draper, who had taken over the case, soon determined that this optimism had been unwarranted. Realizing that the state of his patient's morale was vital to his physical condition, Draper kept his misgivings to himself. Even so, it must have been a grim time for Franklin, as he faced the full consequences of his sickness. Sweat streaming down his face, he would spend hours concentrating on trying to wiggle his big toe. His eyesight failed temporarily and his right knee tightened, causing the leg to bend so badly that both legs were put in plaster casts to keep them straight. But the man who had often been called "a feather duster" and "a mama's boy" had hidden reserves of courage and he fought back. Presently, there were a few small hopeful signs. Both his arm and back muscles became stronger, and by the time he was discharged from the hospital, late in October, could, with the aid of a strap suspended from the ceiling, swing himself from his bed onto a wheelchair. Still, there was a certain finality about the last entry on his hospital chart: "Not improving."

While Franklin struggled to walk again, a behind-the-scenes battle of wills raged between his wife and mother over his future. Raised voices and sharp words were rarely exchanged, but the conflict was acrimonious and the emotional scars deep. Eleanor later described this period as "the most trying winter of my life." She and Howe wished Franklin to remain active in business and politics and to lead, as far as possible, a normal life. They brought interesting people to the house on Sixty-fifth Street to stimulate his imagination with the hope that it would assist in his recovery. Sallie, on the other hand, was convinced that Franklin's career was finished and protested they were burdening him unnecessarily. Like James Henry Roosevelt, who had withdrawn from active life after being stricken with polio nearly a century before, she believed he should retire to Springwood. Under her adoring eye, he could lead the quiet life that his father had enjoyed, overseeing the estate, indulging in his hobbies, perhaps even writing the books he always talked about. Franklin may have momentarily found the prospect alluring, but he had no intention of retiring into a life of genteel invalidism. Even before leaving Campobello, he had accepted membership on the State Democratic Committee.

The episode took a heavy toll of Eleanor's emotions. Harried and anxious, she nursed her husband, managed a household so overcrowded that she had to share a room with one of the smaller boys, fended off her mother-in-law, and tried to maintain a relationship with her children. Fifteen-year-old Anna was a particular trial. Doing poorly in school, she was encouraged in her rebelliousness by her grandmother and became convinced that her mother did not love her. Years later, Eleanor blamed herself for the situation. "She was an adolescent girl and I still treated her like a child. . . . It never occurred to me to take her into my confidence and consult with her about our difficulties." One day while reading aloud to two of the boys, she suddenly broke down and began crying uncontrollably. "I could not think why I was sobbing, nor could I stop," she said. "I sat on the sofa in the sitting room and sobbed and sobbed." Finally, she pulled herself together by going into an empty room. "That is the one and only time I ever remember in my entire life having gone to pieces in this particular manner." Eleanor's momentary breakdown did have a beneficial effect on her relations with Anna. Perceiving her mother's emotional stress for the first time, the girl poured out her troubles to her and they reached out to each other.

Franklin's struggle to regain his health is now a part of the American legend. With his useless legs encased in heavy steel braces, he hobbled about on crutches and set various challenges for himself. A major one was to reach the Post Road at the end of the driveway leading to Springwood, a quarter of a mile away. Each day, he managed to struggle a few more feet toward his goal than he had the day before. Sometimes he fell and had to lie waiting on the ground until someone came along to help him up. Anna vividly recalled this battle, seeing "the sweat pouring down his face," and hearing him say, "'I must get down the driveway today—all the way down to the driveway.'" Perhaps Roosevelt's most harrowing fear was being trapped in a fire, and he learned to crawl down the long halls and up and down the stairways of the house, pulling himself along by the force of his hands and arms. Yet he refused to indulge in self-pity. "Now, I don't want any sob stuff," he told one reporter who interviewed about his illness, and he was remarkably patient and good-humored considering his plight. But there were shadows. Eleanor said he never mentioned golf to her after his illness and he avoided a return to Campobello, with its painful memories, for a dozen years.

Roosevelt never learned to walk without braces and the support of crutches or someone's arm, but he continued the search for a cure. When he found swimming to be good exercise because the water buoyed up his legs, he had a pool built at Hyde Park and would crawl to the edge and lower himself into the water. Soon, he developed the powerful shoulders and deep chest which when he was sitting down gave him an appearance of strength. "The water put me where I am," he once said, blaming the frigid Bay of Fundy for his paralysis, "and water has to bring me back!"

In 1924 Franklin began to visit a dilapidated resort at Warm Springs, in southwest Georgia, where the mineral-laden waters were particularly buoyant and allowed him to exercise without tiring. "How wonderful it feels!" he cried as he lowered himself into the pool for the first time. The place had a link with Eleanor's side of the family, for the nearby town was called Bullochville. He came back year after year, and a newspaper report that he was "swimming his way back to health and strength" attracted other polio victims to Warm Springs. Franklin, who was referred to as "Dr. Roosevelt" by his fellow "polios," developed special therapeutic exercises for them and devoted much time to their case. Convinced of the curative powers of the mineral springs, he bought the resort in 1926 for $195,000—a substantial part of his fortune.‡ Warm Springs became his winter home and under his direction, it developed into an international center for the study of polio and for the treatment of its victims.

Just what effect did Roosevelt's paralysis have on his political career and personality? Legend has it that polio transformed him from a frivolous young aristocrat into a humanitarian with compassion and understanding for the downtrodden. Frances Perkins, for one, believed it. "Franklin Roosevelt underwent a spiritual transformation during the years of his illness," she wrote. ". . . The man emerged completely warmhearted, with humility of spirit and with a deeper philosophy. Having been to the

‡ FDR's mother, who opposed the investment, refused to put money into Warm Springs. The death of his half brother "Rosy" in 1927 provided him with a financial windfall in the form of a $100,000 legacy.

"The Long Trail." Cartoon by J. N. "Ding" Darling on the death of
T.R. Courtesy, Theodore Roosevelt Collection, Harvard College
Library.

Anna Hall Roosevelt (1863–92), Eleanor Roosevelt's mother. Courtesy, Franklin D. Roosevelt Library.

Eleanor Roosevelt (aged about eight) with her father, Elliott (1860–93), and her brothers, Elliott, Jr., and Hall. Courtesy, Franklin D. Roosevelt Library.

Eleanor Roosevelt (1884–1962) on her honeymoon in Venice. Photograph taken by FDR. Courtesy, Franklin D. Roosevelt Library.

Eleanor Roosevelt and her mother-in-law at Campobello. Courtesy,
Franklin D. Roosevelt Library.

Eleanor and Franklin with James and Anna in 1908. Courtesy, Franklin D. Roosevelt Library.

FDR inspecting a ship as Assistant Secretary of the Navy. Courtesy, Franklin D. Roosevelt Library.

Lucy Mercer, circa World War I.
Courtesy, Lyman Cotten.

On her own. Eleanor arriving in Washington in 1960. Courtesy,
Franklin D. Roosevelt Library.

depths of trouble, he understood the problems of people in trouble." But this implies a mystical metamorphosis—akin to being born again—and Roosevelt was too much a pragmatist to be a mystic. Besides, he had already exhibited considerable strength of character in reaching the position he held before being stricken and it made it possible for him to psychologically survive the shattering ordeal itself. Jimmy Roosevelt may probably have had a clearer view of the effect of his illness on his father when he wrote that while polio broadened his understanding of human suffering, it did not make him President. "Indeed, I believe that it was not polio that forged Father's character but that it was Father's character that enabled him to rise above the affliction. I believe his path would have led him to the White House regardless of polio. . . ."

Early in June 1924, one of Franklin's neighbors came upon him sitting on a blanket in the grass near Springwood, dictating to Missy LeHand. "What do you think I'm doing?" Roosevelt called out in greeting. "I'm writing a nominating speech to nominate Al Smith for President." The speech to the Democratic National Convention to be held later that month in Madison Square Garden was Louis Howe's idea. After three years of recuperation, exercise, and treatment, the time had come for Roosevelt to show the world that he had emerged victorious from his ordeal. Franklin decided he would walk up the long aisle from his seat on the floor to the convention platform on the arm of his son, Jimmy, and then propel himself to the rostrum under his own power.

"As we walked—struggled, really—down the aisle to the rear of the platform, he leaned heavily on my arm, gripping me so hard it hurt," Jimmy recalled more than a half century later. "It was hot, but the heat in that building did not alone account for the perspiration which beaded on his brow. His hands were wet. His breathing was labored. Leaning on me with one arm, working a crutch with the other, his legs locked stiffly in his braces, he went on his awkard way." Thunderous cheers greeted Roosevelt's arrival on the platform. Releasing his grip on Jimmy's arm, he took up his other crutch and swung forward, step by step, as the crowd held its breath, fearing that the gallant figure might stumble or fall. He reached the rostrum and, braced against the lectern, cast aside his crutches. Drawing himself erect and with a toss of his classic head that was to become famous, he smiled triumphantly into the glaring spotlights. And then he placed the name of the "Happy Warrior of the political battlefield" in nomination.

After this display of courage, Franklin was probably more popular at the convention than Smith, and some observers believed the image of the "Happy Warrior" better suited him than the man to whom it was applied. The convention settled into a deadlock between Smith and McAdoo, and after 103 ballots, the weary delegates finally turned to John W. Davis, a conservative constitutional lawyer. Pleading poor health, Franklin did not campaign for Davis—and it was just as well. The Democrats had destroyed whatever chance they had of winning the White House at their rancid convention, and Calvin Coolidge was elected by a lopsided margin, despite the odor of corruption that hung over the Republican party. Franklin had emerged from the Democratic debacle as the only real winner, according to observers as diverse as Walter Lippmann, the liberal pundit, and Tom Pendergast, the tough boss of Kansas City.

Throughout the Coolidge years he divided his efforts between seeking a cure at Warm Springs and attempts to make a fortune in Wall Street. Van-Lear Black had generously kept his job open for him at the Fidelity & Deposit Company, and he returned to it as soon as he was able to get around New York, doubling its share of the bonding business. Bored with "estates, wills, etc." with which his old law firm was primarily concerned, he dissolved the partnership and with an aggressive young attorney named D. Basil O'Connor, formed the firm of Roosevelt & O'Connor. Franklin liked excitement in business as well as politics and became involved in a number of speculative ventures. They ranged from practical projects such as a syndicate that purchased devalued German marks and used them to buy shares in German industry, to those that were ahead of their time such as automatic vending machines and taxicab advertising, to such visionary projects as establishing dirigible service between New York and Chicago. Only the German venture produced profits.

All the while Louis Howe labored over schemes designed to keep his name before the public and the politicians. Following Davis' defeat, Roosevelt sent out letters to each of the delegates to the convention suggesting reforms designed to give the party a liberal cast in contrast to Republican conservatism. "There is one common ground—Progressive Democracy—on which we can all agree," he declared. Conservatives torpedoed his plan for a conference to hammer out a reform program, but Franklin had succeeded in putting himself forward as the leader of a rejuvenated party. Eleanor was pressed into service by Howe as her husband's surrogate. He forced her to overcome her shyness, to suppress a nervous giggle, and to give speeches. "Think out what you want to say, and when you have said it, sit down," he advised her. She developed a highly refined reportorial skill, and the information that she brought back was valuable to Howe's machinations.

While Franklin was seeking power, Nicholas Longworth had it. In 1925 he became Speaker of the House, an office that one writer has said "fitted Longworth as snugly as his pearl-gray gloves." He was also in for a surprise. After eighteen years of childless marriage, Alice announced that she was pregnant. A baby girl was born to the couple on February 14, 1925—St. Valentine's Day—forty-one years to the day after the death of Alice Lee Roosevelt.* Alice decided to name the child Paulina, a name of her own devising, rather than one of the traditional family names in hopes that she would be able to have a normal life of her own. "Poor T.R., Jr.," Alice had once said. "Every time he crosses the street, someone has something to say because he doesn't do it as his father would. And if he navigates nicely, they say it was just as T.R. would have done."

In 1928, for the third time in eight years, Franklin Roosevelt placed Al Smith's name in nomination for President before a Democratic convention. Unlike the "Happy Warrior" speech of four years before, this one did not electrify the convention. Low-keyed and simple in style, it was designed for the 15 million listeners tuned in on the radio rather than the 15,000 delegates at Houston, and revealed Franklin's ability to make effective use of the new medium. Despite southern and western disapproval of his Catholicism, urban background, and opposition to Prohibi-

---

* When rumormongers began spreading the word that fifty-six-year-old Nick could not possibly be the baby's father, Alice told one notorious gossip that the child "really looks very much like Uncle Joe Cannon."

tion, Smith was nominated on the first ballot. Although Nick Longworth angled for the party's nod, the Republicans chose Herbert Hoover, who had served as Secretary of Commerce for eight years. Believing that his recovery was so far advanced that he was on the verge of learning to walk without braces, Franklin intended to take little part in the campaign and to spend the rest of the year in Warm Springs. Besides, Smith's candidacy had failed to catch fire, and with rumors circulating that his election would mean that the Pope would be installed in the White House it looked like another bad year for the Democrats. Eleanor, Howe, and Franklin all agreed that he could afford to bide his time in making his bid for office.

Realizing that they needed to carry New York with its forty-five electoral votes or the election was lost, Democratic party leaders appealed to Roosevelt to run for governor. A torrent of letters, telegrams, and telephone calls poured in upon him in Warm Springs, emphasizing that without his presence on the ticket, Smith would be unable to carry the state. Franklin resisted the pressure until October 2, when Smith himself added his personal appeal. Over the opposition of Eleanor and Howe, he reluctantly agreed to enter the race. Once in it, however, he waged a dynamic campaign designed to prove to the electorate that he was vigorous enough to handle the governorship despite his handicap. "If I could campaign six months, I could throw away my canes!" he proclaimed, buoyant about his return to the great game he loved. The campaign was short but election night was long. It appeared as if Roosevelt had been defeated, but early the next morning, it became clear that he had won by 25,000 votes out of some 4 million cast. Al Smith lost both New York and the presidency.

Franklin's two terms as governor of New York—he was reelected in 1930 by a million votes—were anticlimactic and dwarfed by the Stock Market crash of 1929 and the creeping cancer of the Great Depression. The giddy search for El Dorado had ended in disaster. Prosperity had shriveled and crumbled in Hoover's hand. All across the country, factories shut down and banks closed their doors. Weeds began to grow in the crevices of unfinished buildings. Farmers poured unsalable milk onto the highways and plowed under crops for which there were no markets while people scoured the garbage dumps in search of food. Millions of men and women wandered from plant gate to plant gate in search of jobs that no longer existed. Terror and despair were reflected in the breadlines and in the eyes of the dispossessed. When John Maynard Keynes was asked if there had ever before in history been anything like this, he replied that there had: It had lasted four hundred years and was called the Dark Ages. As spiritually paralyzed as Franklin was physically, Hoover assured everyone that the economic heart of America was sound—and prosperity was just around the corner.

Nine Democrats vied for the party's nomination in 1932 in the cruel heat of a Chicago summer, certain that the convention's choice would be elected President. Roosevelt, who remained in Albany, led on the first three ballots but could not get the two-thirds majority required for the nomination, and it was feared that if the convention continued much longer, his supporters would turn elsewhere. The time had come for a deal; Howe and Franklin's other managers, Jim Farley and Ed Flynn, were ready to strike it. In exchange for the votes of California and Texas, the vice-presidential nomination was offered to Texas' John Nance Garner, who had succeeded Nick Longworth as Speaker of the House the year before, and had the support of William Randolph Hearst, who controlled the California delegation. Early in the fourth ballot, William McAdoo rose to declare that California had come to Chicago not to deadlock the convention but to nominate a President, and a tremendous roar almost drowned out his shout: "California, forty-four votes for Franklin D. Roosevelt!"

Breaking all precedents, Franklin boarded a waiting plane and flew to Chicago to accept the nomination in person without waiting for the usual formal notice that he had been chosen. A trivial thing itself, it was symbolic of things to come. As an organ ground out the lilting rhythm of "Happy Days Are Here Again!" he stood at the lectern, his brilliant smile and the cock of his chin symbols of confidence. "Let us now and here highly resolve to resume the country's uninterrupted march along the path of real progress, real justice, of real equality for all of our citizens great and small," Roosevelt told the cheering delegates. "I pledge you, I pledge myself to a new deal for the American people."

Chapter XIX
RENDEZVOUS WITH DESTINY

A battered fedora . . .
   A cigarette holder cocked at a jaunty angle . . .
   A little dog named Fala . . .
   A patrician voice drawling "My friends" . . .
Franklin Roosevelt now belongs to history, but these familiar symbols still evoke his gay spirit and the unparalleled excitement of his twelve years in the White House. Few Americans have aroused greater admiration and hatred; even today, the mention of his name can result in a wistful look in the eye or a hard set of the jaw. An entire generation measures its leaders against his long shadow, and although sometimes devious, calculating, and cynical, no President has more effectively combined the qualities of politician, statesman, preacher, and teacher required for greatness.

Certainly, none has come close to matching the impact of his First Inaugural Address. Huddled anxiously around their radio sets, millions of Americans were lifted out of the depths of despondency and despair by the confident and vibrant voice that proclaimed "the only thing we have to fear is fear itself."

Inauguration Day—March 4, 1933—dawned dour and cheerless, matching the mood of the nation. Herbert Hoover had been overwhelmingly repudiated by the voters, leaving the new President a bitter legacy. Upwards of 15 million people, or more than a quarter of the work force, were unemployed; thousands of farms and homes faced foreclosure and hundreds of banks teetered on the brink of failure. There was a large floating popula-

tion of young people who had run away from families that could
no longer care for them, and one out of every seven Americans
was dependent on public or private charity for their next meal.
"We are at the end of our rope," a weary Hoover had murmured
shortly before joining Roosevelt for a somber ride up Pennsylvania Avenue to the Capitol. "There is nothing more that we can
do."

Bareheaded and unsmiling in a chill wind, Roosevelt began his
first speech as President, with a denunciation of "the money
changers" who have "fled from their high seats in the temples of
our civilization" and then outlined his plans for overcoming the
sickness of spirit and sense of drift that gripped the nation. "This
nation asks for action and action now," he declared amid the first
heavy applause of the day. "Our greatest primary task is to put
people to work." Congress would be summoned into special session to approve the measures required to get the "stricken nation"
moving again, but if it balked, he warned that he would not hesi-
tate to seek authority "as great as the power that would be given
to me if we were in fact invaded by a foreign foe." The American
people "have asked for discipline and direction under leadership," he grimly continued. "They have made me the present instrument of their wishes. In the spirit of the gift I take it."

Rarely has a political leader come so close to expressing the
popular temper. Welling up from some inner spring, these words
were like a call to battle. From the miserable lines of the hungry
waiting before the soup kitchens, from the shivering paupers
selling apples in the streets, from the dispossessed gathered in the
shabby Hoovervilles on the fringes of the big cities, and from the
farmers in the Dust Bowl watching their topsoil blowing away,
there came a tremendous outpouring of support. Eleanor Roosevelt found it "a little terrifying. You felt that they would do anything—if only someone told them what to do."

Over the next hundred days—a period carefully chosen for
effect—Roosevelt produced more than a dozen messages demanding immediate action on the nation's problems, guided fifteen important laws to enactment, and gave ten major speeches. "Bold
persistent experimentation" was the new President's watchword,
and although critics complained that he didn't know where he
was going, the people found the ride with this Roosevelt as exhil-
arating as the charge up San Juan Hill with Eleanor's Uncle Ted.

"This is the happiest day in three years," observed Will Rogers after Roosevelt closed the banks. "We have no jobs, we have no money, we have no banks; and if he had burned down the Capitol, we would have said, 'Thank God, he started a fire under something.'"

And so began the New Deal which altered for all time the relationship between Americans and their government. One of the few successful gradualist revolutions in history, it transformed the United States from a nation of individualists into a social-minded community that accepted the principle of the welfare state and a planned economy. On the international scene, it carried the United States from isolationism to global leadership and victory in the greatest war in history.

Recovery, relief, and reform jostled each other throughout the New Deal. Some of the measures unveiled by Roosevelt were designed to alleviate the worst aspects of the Depression; others were aimed at bringing about the recovery of the national economy, while the rest, cast in the mold of the reforms of Theodore Roosevelt and Woodrow Wilson, were intended to prevent a similar crisis from occurring again. Like their predecessors, Franklin Roosevelt was no radical. Basically an old-fashioned progressive, he believed that despite all the evidence to the contrary, democracy and capitalism could be saved if given an opportunity to work. Innovator and conservator at the same time, he dealt the American people a new hand but used the old deck of cards. Pragmatic and abhorring idealogy of any stripe, he was willing to try anything that looked as if it might have a chance of success.

Reflecting Roosevelt's own mercurial temperament, the New Deal was a mixture of naïveté, humanitarianism, practical politics, and economic experimentation. He likened himself to a football quarterback who knows what the next play is going to be but can't plan beyond that because "future plays will depend on how the next one works." One day a young reporter asked, "Mr. President, are you a Communist?"

"No."

"Are you a capitalist?"

"No."

"Are you a Socialist?"

"No."

"Well, what is your philosophy then?"

"Philosophy?" replied Roosevelt. "Philosophy? I am a Christian and a Democrat—that's all."

For two years, until a conservative Supreme Court declared the most important New Deal legislation unconstitutional, Roosevelt ruled as a benevolent dictator—and most of the country loved it. With only perfunctory debate, Congress rubberstamped the emergency legislation, placed before it. The banks were reopened, Prohibition was repealed, funds were provided to save homes and farms from foreclosure, the stock market was regulated, bank deposits were insured, temporary relief was provided for the needy, child labor was banned, labor was given the right to organize, some 3 million youths were enrolled in the Civilian Conservation Corps and put to work on flood control and reforestation projects, and the nation's first old-age assistance program was launched. The aim of the New Deal was a better life for all Americans, an end to blighted lives, a lessening of the fear of poverty, dignity for labor, decency for farmers, and an expanded public patrimony protected for future generations.

Roosevelt's policies failed, however, to ensure sustained economic growth. In fact, this did not occur until the onrush of World War II sent American factories into overtime. And there were also blunders such as the Supreme Court packing plan and the attempt to purge conservative Democratic congressmen. Undaunted, the President, who had a talent for obliterating past failures with bold new plans, brushed off these setbacks and embarked on new programs.

In common with Cousin Theodore, he regarded the presidency as "a bully pulpit," and used it to educate the public. Through his fireside chats on the radio, he kept the American people informed of what he was trying to accomplish. Roosevelt's success was the result not only of his magnetic personal style—the voice, the mannerisms, the delivery, the sheer physical presence that made him such an effective leader—he also had the gift of convincing people that they were being taken into his confidence. They trusted him as the champion of "the forgotten man," and he seemed to be able to project himself into the homes of his audience and to speak to them as individuals. The freshness of such a direct appeal, his seeming candor, and the development of the topic under discussion in terms that everyone could understand were all parts of his magic.

"I want to talk for a few minutes with the people about banking," was the way Roosevelt launched into his first fireside chat a week after taking office. "I want to tell you what has been done in the last few days, why it was done, and what the next steps are going to be." Each of these talks was specific and limited to a single subject, and promised no miracles or panaceas. The audience was provided with information on what the government was doing and the reason that he was following a certain course of action. The vast majority of Americans were convinced that they understood what Roosevelt's goals were, and as partners in a great endeavor, they gave him their unqualified support. After his death, Eleanor said the people would stop her on the street to tell her "how much they missed" the President and his talks to them. They'd say, "He used to talk to me about my government."

Roosevelt also showed remarkable skill in bringing together men and women of diverse outlook, winning their loyalty, and shaping their often conflicting ideas into a national program. "He is the best picker of brains I ever saw," said one aide. The Brain Trust, the team of professors, administrators, and idea men gathered for the presidential campaign, included his best known advisers, but after the "hundred days" the bulk of the work was done by bright young lawyers and academics who swarmed to Washington when the Depression cut them off from the normal outlets for their talent such as the prominent law firms and the topflight universities. They drafted the legislation that put the Roosevelt Revolution into motion and manned the alphabet soup of government agencies spawned to administer it. Contemptuous of the businessmen who had been discredited by their inability to deal with the economic collapse, the New Dealers reversed the usual relationship between government and business. Power passed from the paneled boardrooms of Wall Street to the warren of offices crammed with battered furniture that abruptly blossomed all over Washington.

But these lawyers, economists, and social workers marched to a different drummer from the progressives of the previous generation. Hard-boiled, arrogant, and often cynical like their master in the White House, they made a great show of avoiding the gushing sentimentality attributed to earlier reformers. To them reform meant economic change—nothing less than a redistribution of wealth—not McGuffy Reader morality in politics. Most New Dealers adopted the easy amorality that the end justifies the means. As Harry L. Hopkins, the Iowa-born social worker who directed Roosevelt's relief program, once told a group of aides: "I want to assure you that we are not afraid of exploring anything within the law, and we have a lawyer who will declare anything you want to do legal."

Unlike the progressives who had labored to dismantle the urban political machines, the New Dealers worked in tandem with the bosses—as long as the politicians cooperated in attaining larger national goals. Thus, Jersey City's Frank Hague, Ed Crump of Memphis, Chicago's Kelly-Nash machine, and Big Tom Pendergast of Kansas City were members in good standing of the Roosevelt coalition along with the urban masses, small farmers, organized labor, Jews, blacks, liberal intellectuals, and poor southerners. "He may be an S.O.B.," the President said of one obnoxious demagogue, "but at least he's our S.O.B."

Until the coming of the Democratic Roosevelts, the White House had not seen so much bustle since Cousin Theodore and his boisterous brood had made the place their home. The change from the sedate and formal atmosphere that surrounded the Hoovers was sudden and complete. E. W. Starling, chief of the White House Secret Service detail, returned from seeing the departing President off to find that the mansion "had been transformed during my absence into a gay place, full of people who oozed confidence. . . . The President was the most happy and confident of them all." As Roosevelt swore in his Cabinet that afternoon, a reporter noted that grandchildren romped in the halls and on the stairs, and coveys of visitors came and went. Eleanor invited about seventy-five relatives—including Archie Roosevelt and Alice Longworth, whose husband had died in 1931—to a buffet supper that evening and breaking with tradition, greeted her guests at the door.

Life in the Roosevelt White House had a cheerful informality. The permanent residents included Louis Howe, who died in 1936, and was followed by Harry Hopkins, in both the President's affections and place in the old mansion; Missy LeHand; and Anna and her two small children, Anna Eleanor and Curtis Dall,

known to everyone as Sisty and Buzzy. In May 1926 Anna, then a
tall and attractive girl of twenty, had married Curtis B. Dall, a
New York stockbroker ten years older than herself. Later, she
told her son by a second marriage that she had wed him to "get
away from the constraints of her family." Anna found Dall conventional and conservative, and after six years they separated.*

The older Roosevelt boys had also married and started families
of their own and soon the old mansion was crowded with grandchildren who begged candy bars from the policemen and got into
various scrapes. The younger sons also drifted in and out, bringing friends home from college for lively parties in the East Room.
Anna, who spent more time in the White House than her
brothers, enjoyed living there. "Despite the tremendous history
behind it, I found it a warm rather than oppressive place," she
said. John Roosevelt, her youngest brother, thought otherwise.
Out celebrating on Inauguration Night, he drove up to the gates
in a battered roadster, but the guards wouldn't let him in. "Go
on," they said. "No son of the President would be driving such a
junk heap." And so young Roosevelt passed the night in a hotel
lobby.

Anna also found romance in the White House. During the 1932
campaign she was attracted to John Boettiger, a reporter for the
Chicago *Tribune*. Although the paper soon became one of Roosevelt's severest critics, Anna and Boettiger fell in love. The affair
was encouraged by Anna's mother, who liked Boettiger and
called him "one of the people for whom I have a very special and
personal feeling." Anna and John's son has recently written that
their love "may have offered Eleanor an image of the kind of intimacy she had fantasied and deeply wished but never realized."
Both obtained divorces and they were married in 1935 after
Boettiger had left the *Tribune* for public relations.

During the years in which the Roosevelts lived in the White
House, the overcrowded living quarters on the second floor took
on the same comfortably cluttered look as Springwood. Family
pictures and snapshots of children and grandchildren and naval
prints filled its walls and assorted bric-a-brac and ship models
took up the rest of the space; books and magazines, often several
months old, were strewn about haphazardly. The furniture, some

* Dall later became a spokesman for the ultraright Liberty Lobby.

of which belonged to the family, was more comfortable than elegant. A few pieces, including Franklin's bed, were made to order in the Val-Kill shop which Eleanor had helped establish at Hyde Park to provide employment to the villagers through the manufacture of reproductions of early American furniture. Eleanor hung a portrait of her grandfather, Theodore Roosevelt, Sr., in the Monroe Room. She had planned to leave the picture in the house on Sixty-fifth Street which was to be rented out, but her husband had insisted: "You can't rent your grandfather, take him with us."

The President's day usually began at about 8:30 A.M. Until he had his morning coffee and the first of the two packs of Camels he smoked every day, he was usually in a bearish mood. While he breakfasted in bed, he scanned the morning newspapers. His grandchildren were the only ones allowed to interrupt this morning ritual, and sometimes Eleanor had to rescue him. Upon one occasion, she heard shouting and calls for help coming from Franklin's room and discovered two little girls bouncing up and down on the bed shouting: "He's my grandfather!" "No, he isn't, he's mine!" The harried President was trying to protect his breakfast tray with one hand and holding the telephone in the other. "Wait a minute, Hacky," he was desperately telling the operator. "I can't talk to Paris just yet."

Aides would filter in as Roosevelt completed his perusal of the newspapers, and the day's appointments and business would be discussed while he shaved himself. If it were a Tuesday or a Friday, Stephen Early, the press secretary, would go over points likely to come up at his news conference. The President worked over papers until about eleven o'clock, and having dressed with the help of his valet, would be taken down by elevator to his office in the West Wing. He used a small wheelchair without arms so that he could swing himself into the swivel chair behind his desk. Once there, he was imprisoned for the day because of his disability.

Visitors were ushered in at fifteen-minute intervals, but almost invariably, Roosevelt would get behind because of his delight in talking and seeing new faces. Conversation was also used as defense when he didn't want to commit himself, and callers sometimes left him convinced that he supported their proposals when he hadn't the slightest intention of doing so. Assistants were always coming and going with important business, and Henry L. Stimson, who had been Hoover's Secretary of State and was to serve Roosevelt as Secretary of War during World War II, told a friend he was amazed at Roosevelt's ability "to reach the kernel of a problem," despite the interruptions. "He could grasp the essentials, reach a decision and complete action with speed and clarity." The President disliked long memoranda, and when presented with one that could be shortened, he would say, "Boil it down to a single page." Despite his talkativeness and the fact that he spent about half his time on the telephone, he kept up with an enormous volume of mail, sometimes scribbling a personal note at the bottom of letters. John Gunther reported that on Christmas he dictated letters of thanks for presents while they were still being unwrapped.

At one o'clock, the President had lunch at his desk, usually with a visitor. The flow of talk did not cease, but Rexford G. Tugwell, one of the Brain Trust, developed a strategy for dealing with it. He would eat lunch before coming to the White House, and while the President's mouth was full, he made his points. Afternoons were given over to more visitors and fixed appointments such as press conferences. Although most newspaper editorial pages had turned against him before his first term was completed, Roosevelt was on good terms with the bulk of the correspondents who regularly covered the White House. In those days they gathered informally around his desk and the President nimbly fielded their questions, while calling the regulars by their first names. During his twelve years in office, he met the press 998 times and regarded these conferences as part of the nation's educational process. Usually jocular and preferring to use the rapier against critics, Roosevelt could be sharp at times, particularly when the reporters tried to pry information out of him that he refused to divulge. "That's an iffy question," he might say, or "No cross-examination please!" There was something of a conspiracy between the press and the White House regarding the President's paralysis. As if by agreement, no pictures were taken of him while he was being lifted from his car like a sack of potatoes and stood on his feet. And if any photographer didn't heed this unwritten rule, the Secret Service was on guard to prevent him from taking a picture.

The President relaxed between 5:30 P.M. and dinner at 9. He went for a swim in the pool installed shortly after he took office and sometimes conducted business there. When his distant cousin Nicholas returned from Hungary, where he had served as minister under Hoover, the President received his final report while they were splashing about in the water together. After a massage and a brief nap, the President was ready for cocktails in his second-floor study. Roosevelt mixed the drinks himself, favoring martinis and old-fashioneds. He usually limited himself to two drinks. During the period he fed tidbits to his pet Scottie, Fala, and put him through his bag of tricks.

Dinner might be either with the family in the private dining room or a more elaborate affair downstairs in the State Dining Room. Eleanor often invited to dinner people whom she thought the President should meet, and some fairly odd characters turned up at the White House table. One official placed beside an obviously nervous young woman asked her what she did and was told: "I'm the dietician at the Brooklyn YWCA."

Neither Eleanor nor Franklin had much interest in food—Franklin once said he had "a digestion like ten oxen"—and the White House cuisine reflected it. "Undistinguished" and "uninspired" were the most charitable words used to describe the menus prepared under the direction of Mrs. Henrietta Nesbitt, the Dutchess County matron whom Eleanor hired as housekeeper. People who stayed at the White House for any length of time claimed they could tell the day of the week by what was set before them; if it was boiled beef then this must be Tuesday. The President finally rebelled, and when he had important guests to entertain, he called in a chef from outside. After his mother's death in 1941, he brought the cook down from Hyde Park and installed her in the family kitchen on the third floor of the White House.

Until World War II altered his schedule, Roosevelt liked to attend the movies shown in the wide, book-lined second-floor hall almost any evening. He especially liked newsreels and Mickey Mouse cartoons and greatly enjoyed Charlie Chaplin's *The Great Dictator*. When his mother was present, he would playfully try to shock her by making ribald remarks about the physical charms of the women in the picture. If he disliked a film, however, his valet would assist him into his study, where he would work on his extensive stamp collection or deal with papers and reports. The President usually went to bed about midnight, but he would often chat with Eleanor or read a report or book or magazine for another hour or so before turning off the light. He seemed to have no trouble sleeping and told one aide, "During my waking, working hours, I give the best in me. . . . When time comes for rest, I can reflect that I could not have done it better if I had to do it all over again. . . . There is nothing left for me but to close my eyes and I am asleep."

As the pressures of office increased, Roosevelt looked forward to vacations away from the White House, at Warm Springs or sailing on Vincent Astor's yacht *Nourmahal*, or going on a long sea voyage on a navy cruiser. But it was to Springwood that he always returned. It was his home and he cherished it with a nostalgic affection. Even after his children were grown and dispersed, it was the place where they came for summer vacations and holidays with their own offspring—particularly at Christmas. The President's hearthside reading of Dickens' *A Christmas Carol* was a classic performance complete with stage voices and dramatic business that kept the smaller children on the edge of their seats. He loved to show the family acres to visiting friends, piloting them about in his specially built Ford coupé which was operated by hand controls. Franklin described his occupation as "tree-farmer" when he voted at Hyde Park. In four presidential elections, however, he never succeeded in carrying solidly Republican Dutchess County, but romped over the opposition in Meriwether County, in Georgia, where Warm Springs is located.

Sara Roosevelt lived to be eighty-seven and delighted in her role as "mother of the President." She was a one-woman cheering squad for her son among her staunchly Republican friends and would not stand for a word of criticism of him in her presence. As imperious as ever, she had strong views on almost everything. Questioned about the Oyster Bay Roosevelts' persistent antagonism to the Hyde Park branch, Sallie declared: "I can't imagine why unless it's because we're better looking than they are." She never became entirely used to the politicians who visited Springwood, however. "Who is that terrible man sitting next to my son?" she hissed while the President was entertaining Huey

Long. And some of the visitors that Eleanor brought home also aroused her ire. "Where does she get those people?" the dowager muttered.

Eleanor Roosevelt entered upon her duties as First Lady with considerable reluctance. Neither her husband nor Louis Howe had consulted her about the decision to run for President in 1932, and she had taken little part in the campaign. Fearing that she would be the captive of protocol and tradition, she told a friend, "I never wanted to be a President's wife." Having achieved a position of prominence on her own as leader in the fight for social reform and as a writer and magazine editor, she was convinced that Franklin's election "meant the end of any personal life of my own." Nevertheless, Eleanor exhibited a tireless energy and warm humanity in the White House that quickly captivated the public as much as her husband's own exuberant vitality. All her predecessors had led circumspect and self-effacing lives, but this was not Eleanor's style. Typically, she held her first news conference even before the President had met the press.

"I feel that my job is to help him as much as possible and to do whatever falls within my scope," she declared. And she lived up to this broad mandate. Having overcome the prejudice of her class against blacks and Jews, she became the administration's conscience. Once again, it was Howe who propelled her into the limelight. In the spring of 1933 a fresh contingent of the Bonus Army descended upon Washington demanding immediate payment of the World War I bonus that had been promised for 1945. The previous year, Hoover had refused to speak to the veterans, and troops under the personal command of General Douglas MacArthur, the chief of staff, had burned their shacks and sent them fleeing from the Capital at bayonet point. One afternoon, Howe invited Eleanor for a ride in the country and then told her they were going to visit the veterans' encampment. Pushing her out of the car into ankle-deep mud, he said he was going to take a nap—confident that she would defuse a potentially dangerous situation. Surprised at being visited by the First Lady, the marchers welcomed her and she listened to their problems. They talked about the war and sang old songs and Eleanor got jobs and tickets home for the men. "Hoover sent the Army," said one observer. "Roosevelt sent his wife."

At Howe's urging, Eleanor went out to meet the people and to serve as the President's legs. Far from being a prisoner in the White House, she traveled forty thousand miles during the first year alone and reported back to Franklin on what she had seen and heard. Over the years, she logged even more mileage, and during World War II, when aptly enough her code name was "Rover," she visited all of the war zones to see how the troops were being treated. Nothing touched her more deeply than a visit to the West Virginia coal country.

In a company house I visited . . . the man showed me his weekly pay slips. A small amount had been deducted toward his bill at the company store and for his rent and for oil for his mine lamp. These deductions left him less than a dollar in cash each week. There were six children in the family. . . . I noticed a bowl on the table filled with scraps, the kind that you or I might give to a dog, and I saw children . . . take a handful out of that bowl and go out munching. That was all they had to eat. As I went out, two of the children had gathered enough courage to stand by the door, the little boy holding a white rabbit in his arms. It was evident it was a most cherished pet. The little girl was thin and scrawny, and had a gleam in her eyes as she looked at her brother. Turning to me she said: 'He thinks we are not going to eat it, but we are,' and at that the small boy fled down the road clutching the rabbit closer than ever.

Eleanor's travels soon became part of American folklore. Radio comedians joked about where she might turn up next and it was not long before life imitated art. *The New Yorker* ran a cartoon in which a startled coal miner tells another: "Good gosh, here comes Mrs. Roosevelt!"—and before people had even stopped chuckling, Eleanor did visit a coal mine. Frances Perkins relates that Roosevelt was "enormously proud" of his wife, although he sometimes teased her about her reputation as a do-gooder. "You know, Eleanor really does put it over," he said upon more than one occasion. "She's got great talent with people." He had complete confidence in her reports and relied upon her observations in making policy decisions, Miss Perkins added, and no presidential wife has had a greater effect on policy and public opinion.

Yet there were areas in which the President and his wife were in conflict. Eleanor was more to the left than Franklin on social

issues and considerably ahead of him—and her time—in supporting such causes as civil rights. She tried to persuade him to appoint blacks to high places in the administration and to support
antilynching and other laws banning racial discrimination. In
1939, when the Daughters of the American Revolution refused to
allow Marian Anderson, the black contralto, to give a concert in
Constitution Hall, she resigned from the DAR in protest, just as
she had when the Colony Club in New York had refused to admit
Mrs. Henry Morgenthau, wife of the Secretary of the Treasury,
because she was Jewish.*

Although by no means a racist, the President had easily accommodated himself to the segregationist ways of the South while at
Warm Springs and can best be described as a gradualist on the
race issue. Roosevelt believed that rising living standards and
broadened educational opportunities for all Americans would
also improve conditions for blacks, but worried about losing the
support of powerful southern committee chairmen for his legislative program, resisted Eleanor's efforts to force him to take an
overt stand against white supremacy. Even so, he allowed her to
state her views publicly on the race issue, adding: "I can always say, 'Well, that is my wife; I can't do anything about her.'"
And, as Frank Freidel has pointed out, the New Deal helped
create the climate of social and economic progress in the South
that eventually made change possible.

Once the bankers and big business had picked themselves up
off the floor with the assistance of the New Deal they leaped to
the attack with charges that Roosevelt and the radicals around
him were wrecking the country. Alarmed at what was perceived
as a drift toward socialism and regimentation, some opponents
not only attacked Roosevelt's policies but unleashed a barrage of
vituperation against him and his family that exceeded the bounds
of political criticism. Perhaps it was because they regarded
Roosevelt as "a traitor to his class"—although as Joseph Alsop,
Theodore Roosevelt's grandnephew, has pointed out, the Hudson
River squirearchy that had produced him had long since
vanished before he entered the White House. No matter what the
cause, no President since Lincoln was subjected to attacks as bit-

* Miss Anderson sang instead from the steps of the Lincoln Memorial before a
crowd estimated at 75,000 people. Eleanor thought it wise not to attend.

ter or as intensive; no charge or joke seemed too wild or obscene
to be circulated. A doggerel that surfaced during the 1936 campaign had Franklin telling Eleanor:

> You kiss the niggers;
> I'll kiss the Jews,
> We'll stay in the White House
> As long as we choose.

Old campaigners that they were, Roosevelt and his wife
brushed off such personal attacks, but it was not so easy for their
brood.† Unaccustomed to the merciless glare of publicity, the
spotlight always seemed to catch them in an awkward moment.
They discovered that such ordinary missteps as traffic accidents,
speeding tickets, and arguments in public became front-page
news. The older children were also vulnerable to attack for supposedly using their father's position to secure favors for those
who gave them lucrative positions. Accustomed to the trappings
of wealth without being wealthy, they were susceptible to deals
designed to make big money quickly. Anna was criticized when
William Randolph Hearst named John Boettiger as publisher of
one of his newspapers, the Seattle *Post-Intelligencer;* Jimmy was
accused of using political influence to make huge profits for his
insurance agency; and Elliott came under fire for his links to the
airline industry which was seeking special favors from the White
House and for his ties to a chain of Texas radio stations owned by
Hearst.

The President expressed concern that his family might profit
from their position, but his warnings seemed to have had little
effect. Jimmy, for one, later realized that despite their protestations about not using their influence, the Roosevelt children
had sailed close to the wind in some of their business arrangements. "Possibly I should have been sufficiently mature and considerate enough of Father's position to have withdrawn from the
insurance business entirely," he later wrote. "But I was young,
ambitious, spoiled—in the sense of having been conditioned to
require a good deal of spending money—so I went ahead in pursuit of what seemed to me the easiest solution."

† FDR could sometimes be vengeful, however. Upon several occasions, he ordered
special audits of the tax returns of his bitterest critics with the hope of turning up
irregularities.

Usually careful about inciting charges of nepotism, Franklin couldn't resist naming a member of the family as Assistant Secretary of the Navy, a post that had become almost its personal fiefdom. The fifth of the dynasty to fill the job was Henry Latrobe Roosevelt, a great-grandson of Nicholas the steamboat inventor, and a graduate of the Naval Academy. Jimmy also served briefly on the White House staff, arousing charges of favoritism and mixed reviews on his performance.

The chaotic domestic lives of the Roosevelt children—in all, they have accounted for seventeen marriages—provided considerable ammunition for the President's critics. Elliott was a special trial. The most rebellious of the boys, he refused to attend college after Groton, and like Anna rushed into an early marriage which he quickly regretted. At about the time of his father's inauguration, he left his wife and child in New York and went to Texas, where he announced that he was not only getting a divorce but immediately remarrying. Although divorce had become common among upper-class Americans, this was a first for a presidential family, and Roosevelt's opponents seized upon it. Although he and Eleanor were hurt by the marital problems of their children, they gave up trying to interfere. Perhaps they adopted this detached attitude because Franklin's mother had meddled so much in their marriage and they didn't want to do the same. And having made a deal to live together after the Lucy Mercer affair, they may also have sympathized with the children who wanted their freedom. "I probably carried this thing too far," Eleanor later said of this hands-off policy. Asked upon one occasion if his offsprings' problems caused him any political damage, the President replied: "I believe that a politician should be judged on his politics."

Probably reflecting some of her own anger, Eleanor partially blamed the early marriages of her children on Franklin's failure to make a break with his mother. As a result, she said, the family had always lived in homes that belonged to her and they never had a place of their own. "They were not rooted in any particular home and were seeking to establish homes of their own," she explained. "This added to their need to make money quickly." The children may not have had the parental attention they wanted, she added, because in their formative years, Franklin had been preoccupied with his fight against polio; in later years his time had been taken up by politics. Eleanor was also convinced that a quirk in her husband's personality made it difficult for him to talk to anyone about intimate matters. Ouwardly warm and friendly, he had apparently cultivated an inner reserve in order to combat his mother's attempts to control his life. Upon one occasion, Eleanor related, one of the children came to him for counsel about his personal problems. After listening, Franklin picked up a paper from his desk and remarked: "This is a most important document. I should like to have your opinion on it." Indignant, the boy angrily told his mother, "Never again will I try to talk to Father about anything personal."

"It may strike you as strange, but I spent relatively little time with Father," Franklin, Jr., told an interviewer. "The longest period I spent with him was an unforgettable five weeks in July 1934. It was on a cruise." One family event that Roosevelt particularly enjoyed was the wedding in June 1937 of Franklin, Jr., to Ethel DuPont. The marriage of the son of "that man in the White House" into a family he had lambasted as "economic royalists" appealed to Roosevelt's lively sense of humor. To add to the overtones of Montague and Capulet which surrounded the wedding, the DuPonts had given about $375,000 to the Liberty League which had vainly tried to bring about the President's defeat in the 1936 election. Mischievously, he brought such arch New Dealers as Harry Hopkins, Henry Morgenthau, and Frances Perkins to the DuPont's ancestral enclave in Delaware, and enjoying himself immensely, would not leave until he had kissed all the bridesmaids.

The Oyster Bay branch of the family—which became known as "the out-of-season Roosevelts"—faded from the news after Franklin entered the White House. Only the apolitical Kermit was on friendly terms with his cousin sometimes accompanying him on yachting trips. In 1940, Kermit and his wife Belle, supported Franklin for a third term, and four years later, their daughter headed the Servicemen's Wives to Re-elect Roosevelt. But the opinion of most of the family was succinctly expressed by Theodore Roosevelt's widow, Edith, who emerged from retirement in 1932 to introduce Herbert Hoover at a rally in Madison Square

Garden.‡ It was she who observed that Franklin was "nine-tenths mush and one-tenth Eleanor"—a remark usually attributed to Alice. In Manila, Ted, who had been appointed governor-general of the Philippines by Hoover, was asked his relationship to the new President and cracked: "Fifth cousin—about to be removed."

Looking back forty years later, Alice laughed about the "Greek tragedy of the Oyster Bay Roosevelts" and said that "it's high time someone realized how idiotically we all carried on" about Franklin, but she didn't regard it as a joke then. The clan's sense of frustration was compounded by Ted's fate, for it appeared that any hope for him to follow his father into the White House had gone glimmering. He returned home from Manila to become vice-president of Doubleday, Doran & Company, and to write along with his wife a travel column for *House & Garden*. He was also active in several organizations, serving at one time as a member of the board of the National Association for the Advancement of Colored People. Periodically, Ted and Kermit went on big-game hunting expeditions, bringing back from Asia the first giant panda seen in America and bagging a rare mountain sheep known as the *Ovis poli*. "You don't know what an *Ovis poli* is?" asked Will Rogers. "It's a political sheep. You hunt it between elections." But for Ted there were to be no more elections. A bitter critic of the New Deal, he warned that Franklin was a potential dictator but could stir little popular support for another try at the governorship of New York.

While the enmity of most of the Oyster Bay family toward Franklin was based on politics, some had financial reasons to feud with him. Following passage of the Federal Banking Act which provided for the separation of commercial and investment banking, the firm of Roosevelt & Son spun off its investment banking and brokerage business to remain only in investment management. A story made the rounds of Wall Street in 1934 that Philip J. Roosevelt, a partner in the firm, had telegraphed the President asking what should be done about some of his wife's utility investments. "I have nothing to suggest," Franklin is

‡ Aunt Corinne, however, refused to campaign against Franklin and observed that Eleanor was more like her brother Theodore "than any of his children." Eleanor's other aunt, Bamie, had died in 1931. Corinne died shortly before the inauguration. Edith Roosevelt lived on until 1948.

supposed to have replied. "Investments are your business, not mine." Philip bided his time and then wrote Franklin to the effect: "We have liquidated the utility investments in question and have invested the proceeds in government bonds. Now it is your business."*

Unable to reconcile herself to the presence of Eleanor and Franklin in the White House, Alice embarked on a guerrilla campaign designed to annoy them. Her fame rested on her slashing wit, and her trademark was a pillow embroidered with the words "If you haven't got anything nice to say about anyone, come and sit here by me." Almost every political one-liner was credited to her and she was said to have described Calvin Coolidge as looking "as if he had been weaned on a pickle";† Wendell Willkie as springing "from the grassroots of the country clubs of America"; and Thomas E. Dewey as "a man who looks like the bridegroom on a wedding cake." Invited to the White House, she insisted on addressing her cousin as "Franklin" rather than "Mr. President," much to his annoyance. Her imitation of Eleanor, complete with fluttery voice, girlish gestures and protruding teeth, was much in demand among Washington's "cave dwellers" until Eleanor asked to see it and professed to be amused.

Jimmy Roosevelt, then serving as one of his father's aides, suggested Alice might be appeased by naming her to some harmless commission or other, but Franklin replied, "I don't want anything to do with that damn woman!" Over the years, invitations to the White House slowed to a trickle and finally stopped. "Perhaps it gave them pleasure not to have me, but they should have been better winners," Alice was later quoted as saying. "They could have said, 'Look here, you miserable worm, of course you feel upset because . . . you hoped your brother Ted would finally achieve this, and now he hasn't. But after all, here we are. Just come if it amuses you.' But they took it all seriously. They took the meanness in the spirit in which it was meant."

One of the great curiosities of history is the intertwining of the fates of Franklin Roosevelt and Adolf Hitler. Both came to power within a few weeks of each other, both saw their task as lifting their peoples out of the malaise of defeat and to restore their

---

* Roosevelt & Son finally closed its doors in 1973 after having joined the parts together again in 1971.
† Alice credited this one to her dentist.

confidence, both made eloquent appeals to the emotions, and both died within a few weeks of each other. The great difference between them lay in the methods adopted to bring about change. Roosevelt appealed to the best instincts of man; Hitler appealed to the worst. Thus, it was inevitable that they should be in conflict.

Just when Roosevelt sensed the danger inherent in the aggressive policies of Hitler and his Japanese allies is an unresolved question. He had supported the League of Nations during the 1920 election, but the early New Deal had overtones of isolationism. Economic recovery was attainable only through independent domestic action rather than by international arrangements, according to the President. In fact, Eleanor invited Anne O'Hare McCormick of the New York *Times* to dinner in 1933 with the suggestion, "I wonder if you would try to get the President more interested in foreign affairs." Although aides have said he wanted "to do something" about Hitler and Japanese penetration of China as early as 1935, Roosevelt made no effort to challenge the pacifist and isolationist mood of the nation. It was not until October 1937 that he showed signs of a swing toward collective security with a proposal to "quarantine" the aggressor nations. This speech marked the beginning of the end of the policy of strict isolation that had prevailed since the profound disillusionment following World War I.

When war came in 1939, the American people were not neutral as they had been in 1914. Along with the President, they sympathized with the democracies in their struggle against fascism but were wary of being drawn into another European conflict. The collapse of France under the swift sword of the German blitzkrieg in the summer of 1940 created a crisis for the United States—and for Roosevelt. Britain now stood alone against the full fury of the Nazi onslaught, and sooner than most Americans, he sensed the danger to the United States should Britain fall. But never getting too far ahead of public opinion, he emphasized during his campaign for a tradition-breaking third term that his policy was aimed at keeping "war away from our country and our people" while describing the United States as "the great arsenal of democracy." Following this triumphant reelection, Roosevelt sponsored numerous measures aimed at helping bombed, beleagured Britain to resist, including the Lend-Lease Act which ended the fiction of American neutrality and signaled the beginning of an undeclared war with Germany.

Resistance to these moves was vigorous, however, with the Oyster Bay Roosevelts arrayed on the side of the isolationists. "Anything to annoy Franklin," said Alice. But after initially opposing any American entanglement in European affairs, Ted supported Lend-Lease. By April 1941 he was on active duty with his old regiment, the Twenty-sixth Infantry. And once again, Kermit did not wait for the United States to enter the conflict. As soon as Britain declared war on Germany, he joined the British Army. "He thinks it vitally important for the Allies to win and he should do everything possible to further the cause," said Belle. Kermit formed a contingent of volunteers to help Finland, under attack by the Soviet Union, but the war ended before they saw action. Returning to the British Army, he fought in Norway and the Middle East until invalided home. With the approach of war, the President's sons also volunteered for the armed forces, but the commissioning of Elliott as a captain in the Army Air Corps stirred criticism because he had no previous military experience. Buttons emblazoned "I want to be a captain, too" appeared all over the nation. "Sometimes I really hope that one of us gets killed so that maybe they'll stop picking on the rest of the family," Elliott angrily told his father.

The United States girded for war in Europe, but when it finally came it was in the Pacific, where the imperial ambitions of Japan had been thwarted. The Japanese attack on Pearl Harbor on December 7, 1941—"a date which will live in infamy"—made Roosevelt's task easier by unifying the American people not only against Japan but also against Germany, which declared war on the United States. Critics charged that Roosevelt had conspired to provoke the Japanese into attacking the American fleet to achieve this result. While it is true that the attack rescued him from an impossible dilemma, the conspiratorial views of Pearl Harbor ignore the fact that the United States had shown a willingness to negotiate its differences with Japan, but it was Tokyo that did not want a settlement. And one aide recalled that within moments of the Japanese attack on Pearl Harbor, he was on the telephone with the military commander in Hawaii and his reaction—"Damnit, you told me that!" repeated over and over—was hardly that of a triumphant schemer.

Roosevelt was unsurpassed as a war leader. He picked a first-class team of civilian and military advisers: Henry L. Stimson and Frank Knox‡ as civilian heads of the Army and Navy; General George C. Marshall and Admiral Ernest J. King to devise the strategy of the war; and such able theater commanders as Chester W. Nimitz, Dwight D. Eisenhower, and Douglas MacArthur, although he was deeply suspicious of the political ambitions of the latter. Roosevelt was instrumental in devising the "Germany first" strategy under which the war was fought, but unlike Winston Churchill, he had the good sense not to interfere with day-to-day military operations. Rather, as a master political tactician, he skillfully conciliated and coordinated the efforts of Allies with diverse and often conflicting interests. Roosevelt also realized that the war would be won by the preponderance of American industrial power and had the foresight to insist on production goals that appeared impossible of attainment. And few leaders matched him as a builder of morale. Even in the early months of the war when the Allied cause was nearly engulfed by a flood tide of disasters, he exuded an overwhelming confidence that buoyed the national spirit and faith in eventual victory. Roosevelt had his shortcomings as a war leader, however. The internment of the Japanese in concentration camps and his failure to do anything to halt the Nazi destruction of the European Jews are stains on his reputation.

By mid-1944, with the defeat of the Axis assured, Roosevelt was more concerned with the peace that was to follow the war than the fighting itself. His major concern was to preserve the Grand Alliance, and at Yalta made territorial concessions to the Russians in Eastern Europe and the Far East that were intended to preserve this unity. Using his own experience in American politics, he tried to conduct foreign policy on the basis of personal arrangements with Churchill and Joseph Stalin and believed that conflicting national interests could be resolved by bargaining in the back room. Stalin had different aims—and the Cold War was the result. Tragically, Roosevelt died on the threshold of victory, and the world will never know if he could have prevented the breakup of the Alliance which he had so feared. While he may

‡ Knox, Republican candidate for Vice-President in 1936, had been one of Theodore Roosevelt's Rough Riders. Stimson had been Secretary of State under Hoover and earlier, a protégé of T.R.

not have been able to prevent a rift from appearing among the Allies, he probably would have worked harder than his successor to close it.

Worn out by the pressures of his campaign for a fourth term and the meeting at Yalta, the President looked wan and much older than his sixty-three years when he arrived at the Little White House in Warm Springs at the end of March 1945. Observers noted that during Easter services in the little chapel that his hands shook and he dropped both his prayer book and glasses. But a few days of rest in the warm Georgia sun revived him, and Franklin was soon in good spirits. The war in Europe was drawing to a victorious close, and despite rumblings from the Russians, the future looked bright. Four women were with him in the bright, chintzy living room of his cottage shortly before lunch on April 12. Three of them were his spinster cousins Laura Delano and Daisy Suckley—his "handmaidens" as Eleanor called them—and Madame Elizabeth Shoumatoff, an artist making sketches for a portrait of the President. The fourth was Lucy Mercer.

Unknown to most people, Franklin had again begun seeing Lucy, now the widow of Winthrop Rutherfurd, during the latter years of the war. Usually accompanied by her daughter and one or two of her stepchildren, she came to tea or dinner at the White House while Eleanor was away. "Never was there anything clandestine about the occasions," wrote Anna, who served as her father's hostess, in her unpublished magazine article. "On the contrary they were occasions which I welcomed for my father because they were light-hearted and gay, affording a few hours of much-needed relaxation for a loved father and world leader in time of crises. . . . Never was I aware of anything self-conscious in Father's attitude, with me, about Mrs. Rutherfurd. . . . Never did Father and I discuss or mention any 'relationship' other than one of friendship with which I was familiar. As for me, I still found Mrs. Rutherfurd to be a most attractive, stately but warm and friendly person. She certainly had an innate dignity and poise which commanded respect."*

* Anna originally wrote, "She certainly had an innate dignity and poise which would have precluded any thought of a 'secret romance.'" She crossed out the last nine words.

Franklin was seated at a card table in his navy cape working on some papers while the artist painted. Laura bustled about and Daisy crocheted while Lucy sat quietly in front of him. Suddenly, he put his hand to his forehead, and murmuring, "I have a terrific headache," slumped unconscious into his chair. Servants carried him into a tiny adjoining bedroom where two hours later, Franklin Roosevelt died without having regained consciousness. On his table lay the text of a speech upon which he had been working. Its final paragraph read: "The only limit to our realization of tomorrow will be our doubts of today. Let us move forward with strong and active faith."

Chapter XX
"AN INDEPENDENT FAMILY"

"The story is over."

Less than a week after Franklin Roosevelt had been laid to rest in the hedge-trimmed rose garden at Springwood, Eleanor had packed possessions accumulated over a dozen years and moved out of the White House. The new President, Harry S. Truman, urged her to take as much time as needed but the task was completed in only a few days. Final farewells were exchanged with aides and servants, and the widow took the train to New York—and a new life. Night had fallen by the time she arrived at her apartment on Washington Square, an area redolent of the vanished society she had known as a girl. From out of the shadows stepped a waiting reporter, but Eleanor had nothing more to add. "The story is over," she said.

In reality, her story was barely beginning. The remaining seventeen years of Eleanor's life were to be her most active, and her fame was to transcend national barriers. But she faced starting a new life with uncertainty. Where would she live? What would she do? Anxiety was sharpened by the bitter discovery that Lucy Rutherfurd had been present at Warm Springs when Franklin was stricken. Old wounds reopened, her feelings of anger and rejection were revived, accounting perhaps for the "almost impersonal feeling" she later claimed to have experienced following Franklin's death. With a curious detachment, Eleanor acknowledged that his passing was "a terrible blow," but she did not regard it as "a personal sorrow." Rather, her sorrow was the universal sadness "of all those to whom this man who now lay dead, and who happened to be my husband, had been a symbol of strength and fortitude." Nevertheless, an alert newsman noted that at the funeral she wore at her throat a small pearl fleur-de-lis that had been Franklin's wedding gift forty years before.

Before the funeral there had been an angry confrontation with Anna about Lucy's presence at the Little White House. "Why was I not told about Mrs. Rutherfurd?" Eleanor demanded, according to an account published more than thirty years later by Elliott. "You certainly must have known about her. Why did you say nothing to me?"

"I didn't know she would be at Warm Springs."

"Has she ever been in the White House?"

Anna reluctantly acknowledged that Lucy had indeed been invited to the mansion by the President in his wife's absence and she had been present as hostess upon these occasions.

"Boy, am I in the doghouse!" Anna told Elliott, the only one of the Roosevelt sons able to return from the war in time for their father's funeral.

Eleanor's outward anger quickly passed, but it was a long time before she completely forgave her daughter for what she regarded as a betrayal. From Mrs. Rutherfurd, Anna received a message of a different kind. "This blow must be crushing to you—to all of you—but I know that you meant more to your Father than anyone and that makes it closer and harder to bear," she wrote. "He told me so often and with such feeling of all that you had meant of joy and comfort on the trip to Yalta. He said you were so extraordinary and what a difference it made to have you. . . . The world has lost one of the greatest men that ever lived—to me the greatest. He towers above them all. . . ."

Lying awake and listening to the clacking of the train wheels during the long trip from Warm Springs to Washington, Eleanor had made several basic decisions regarding her future. "I did not want to run an elaborate household again. I did not want to cease trying to be useful in some way. I did not want to feel old." There were books to be written, lectures to be given, people to see, mail to be answered, charities to be supported, causes to be championed. So much to be done, so little time to do it.

She decided to give up Springwood. Franklin had left the estate to his family if they chose to live there, and the house and immediately surrounding land was to go to the government at their deaths. Having always regarded the place as the domain of her mother-in-law and her husband, Eleanor had never been at home there, considering herself merely as a sojourner. Her bedroom is clear evidence of her feelings. Small and sparsely furnished, it seems to remind almost every visitor of a nun's cell.

Franklin had also left a private letter to Eleanor in which he urged the family to give Springwood to the government at once. The cost of maintaining the place would probably be prohibitive and they would have little privacy because of the influx of curious visitors. "Characteristically, he remarked that he would hate to think of us taking refuge in the attic or the cellar in search of privacy," Eleanor said. The children agreed with her decision, and on April 12, 1946, the first anniversary of Franklin's death, the formal transfer took place with President Truman in attendance. "It is with pleasure that our children and I see this house dedicated to the people and opened to them," Eleanor said. "It was the people, all of the people of this country and the world, whom my husband loved and kept constantly in his heart and mind. He would want them to enjoy themselves in these surroundings, and to draw from them rest and peace and strength, as he did all the days of his life."

Eleanor took up residence at Val-Kill Cottage, about a mile from Springwood, where she had once operated a furniture factory. At the insistence of Elliott, who had returned from the war as a brigadier general and was now married to his third wife, a movie actress named Faye Emerson, she purchased 1,200 acres of land from the estate on the west side of Route 9 which he planned to farm. Still to be resolved, however, was the problem of what to do with herself. Vigorous at sixty-one, she had no intention of retreating into a genteel retirement. She continued her daily newspaper column, *My Day*, as well as writing for magazines, and was gratified to find undiminished interest in her work which had a new frankness about it. "Because I was the wife of the President certain restrictions were imposed upon me," she said. "Now I am on my own and I hope to write as a newspaperwoman."

As the champion of Franklin's ideals, Eleanor played an important role in Democratic party politics—particularly its reform wing—in both New York State and on the national level but ruled out running for office herself. Although friends tried to persuade her to seek the nomination for U.S. senator, she turned her back on the idea. Running for office "is not the way in which I can be most useful," she said. "My children have labored for many years under the baffling necessity of considering their business of living as it affected their Father's position and I want them to feel in the future that any running for public office will be done by them."

In 1946 President Truman, who greatly admired Eleanor, pushed her back onto the center of the stage by appointing her to the American delegation to the United Nations, where her wide-ranging humanitarianism could be most effective. Some observers questioned her ability to stand up to Russian aggressiveness in the newly organized world body, but she displayed a toughness of mind and spirit that surprised enemies as well as admirers. While she urged the United States to make every effort to negotiate the end of the Cold War, Eleanor was critical of Soviet tactics. "She was in fact, a tough old bird who saw earth as well as stars," said Arthur M. Schlesinger, Jr. "People mixed with her at their peril. . . ."

Some of the positions adopted by Eleanor were considerably in advance of prevailing American diplomatic policy. She was an early advocate of a ban on nuclear testing in the atmosphere, supported the recognition of Red China, and opposing the State Department position, came out for the establishment of a Jewish state in Palestine. But her most important work was as chairman of the Commission on Human Rights of the U.N.'s Educational, Scientific and Cultural Organization. In this position she played a guiding role in drafting and securing approval of the Declaration of Human Rights and became, as Truman called her, "The First Lady of the World."*

Under no illusions about the effectiveness of this document in a world in which dictatorships and absolutist states flourished, she regarded it as a standard of measurement by which all nations could be judged. After two years of foot-dragging, semantic arguments, and legal pettifogging, the declaration was approved without a dissenting vote by the General Assembly on December 10, 1948. The Russians abstained. In a rare tribute to her work,

---

* Here, she followed in the footsteps of her uncle, Theodore Roosevelt. As early as 1903, he vigorously protested against the Russian pogroms against the Jews.

the Assembly gave her a standing ovation. The declaration "has entered the consciousness of the people of the world, has shaped the aspirations and has influenced the conscience of nations," Adlai E. Stevenson said later. And in an age in which the struggle for human rights is an issue that will not die, its provisions are a beacon to Soviet dissenters and civil rights protestors around the globe. As Eleanor wrote in 1953:

> Where, after all, do universal human rights begin? In small places, close to home—so close and so small that they cannot be seen on the maps of the world. Yet they *are* the world of the individual . . . the places where every man, woman and child seeks equal justice, equal opportunity, equal dignity without discrimination. Unless these rights have meaning there, they have little meaning anywhere.

Advancing age brought a stoop to Eleanor's tall, black-clad figure, and she became increasingly deaf, but her smile was triumphant over time. She had even gained a certain beauty when following an automobile accident her protruding front teeth were replaced with porcelain caps. About forty newspapers still subscribed to her column, which now appeared three times weekly rather than daily, and she continued to write books and was in demand as a lecturer. In some years, her income was in excess of $100,000, much of which she gave to her family, friends, and charity.

James, Franklin, Jr., and Elliott actively sought office, but Eleanor was the family's most prominent politician. "I know nothing of politics," she often told interviewers. "I have no influence." No one was fooled by her ingenuousness, and as America's most widely admired woman, her support buoyed the political fortunes of Adlai E. Stevenson. From the first time she met him at one of the early postwar meetings of the United Nations, Eleanor admired Stevenson and was among those who convinced him to make his first try at elective office, a successful bid for governor of Illinois in 1948. "Madly for Adlai," as she put it, she was a pivotal figure in his campaign for election as President in 1952 and 1956. On the other hand, John Roosevelt, who had gone into Wall Street and became a Republican, campaigned for Eisenhower in 1952. After the election, John was named to a presidential commission established to prevent discrimination in businesses with government contracts.

Suspicious of John F. Kennedy because of his father's isolationism before World War II and the senator's own failure to oppose Senator Joseph R. McCarthy's anticommunist witch-hunt, she urged the Hamlet-like Stevenson to again seek the Democratic presidential nomination in 1960. Franklin, Jr., and James both supported Kennedy, however. "If Stevenson's good enough for your mother, he ought to be good enough for you!" a demonstrator shouted to Jimmy at the party's national convention. "We are an independent family," he called back with a laugh. Later, Eleanor made her peace with Kennedy—who according to a friend "was absolutely smitten by her"—and campaigned actively for him, especially among black voters.

She believed that no matter what is wrong with society it can be put right by human action. A simple faith no doubt, but it gave her strength. Friends who visited Val-Kill were amazed at Eleanor's vitality. Whenever they were faced with sickness or family crisis, Eleanor's children turned to her for assistance and sympathy, and were not disappointed. She even remained on good terms with the many former daughters-in-law produced by the clan's marital ups and downs. Still, she could be angered by her children's antics. Gore Vidal, the novelist and a neighbor, was with her one day when the news broke that one of her sons had remarried. While they were talking the phone rang. "Yes, dear . . . yes, I'm very happy," Eleanor murmured over and over again. Then she hung up. "You would think that he might have told his mother *first,* before the press," she declared. Visiting grandchildren, grandnephews, and grandnieces splashed all day in the swimming pool and clamored at night for her to tell them stories. The telephone was constantly ringing with calls from reporters seeking her views on public affairs, chairmen of groups requesting support, or ordinary citizens wishing to speak with her. Eleanor did not suffer fools gladly, however. If bored with a conversation, she would turn off her hearing aid and periodically nod benignly. Political arguments were almost always in progress among her sons. Sometimes, outsiders were alarmed by their intensity, but Eleanor presided over the turmoil with serenity.

"When you cease to make a contribution, you begin to die,"

Eleanor once said. "I think it is a necessity to be doing something which you feel is helpful in order to grow old gracefully and contentedly." She followed this advice to the end, which came on November 7, 1962. "She thought of herself as an ugly ducking," said Adlai Stevenson in paying tribute to his old friend, "but she walked in beauty in the ghettos of the world. . . . And wherever she walked, beauty was forever there."

Two of Theodore Roosevelt's sons—Ted and Kermit—died while on active service during World War II and Archie was again severely wounded—making him probably the only man to be discharged from the Army in both world wars as totally disabled. As soon as the United States entered the war, Kermit, who had served with the British in both the Norwegian and Middle East campaigns, joined the U. S. Army with the rank of major and an assignment to Intelligence. Sent to Alaska, he took part in bombing raids on Japanese installations in the Aleutians despite deteriorating health. He was hospitalized for internal hemorrhages, but somehow persuaded an examining physician to allow him to remain on active duty. Plans were again being made to invalid him home when on June 4, 1943, he was found dead in his bed at the age of fifty-three. A year after his death, more than five hundred friends crowded into a New York church for a memorial service.

Although Ted was a brigadier general, he was no chair-borne commander. During training, he insisted on undergoing all the rigors of soldiers half his age and in North Africa, Italy, and Normandy, was in the vanguard of assaults on enemy positions and an inspiration to his men. He was assistant commander of the First Division, in which he had served in World War I, and in November 1942, personally led the combat team that attacked Oran in North Africa. Refusing to remain at headquarters, he was with the first infantry platoon to reach its objective. A few months later he was awarded an Oak Leaf Cluster to the Silver Star he had won in the previous war. Following service in the Italian campaign, he was transferred to England preparatory to the invasion of France.

Repeatedly, Ted sought permission to accompany the first wave of invading troops ashore on D-day, and finally his request was granted. "Although the enemy had the beach under constant direct fire, Brig. Gen. Roosevelt moved from one locality to another, rallying men around him, directed and personally led them against the enemy," said a War Department citation. "Under his seasoned, precise, calm and unfaltering leadership, assault troops reduced beach strong points and rapidly moved inland with minimum casualties. He thus contributed substantially to the successful establishment of the beachhead in France."

But at fifty-seven, his heart could not stand the strain of his strenuous life and there had been several warning attacks. Ted, however, kept his disability secret, fearing that he would be invalided home. On July 12, 1944, while his troops were waging a bitter battle among the hedgerows of Normandy, he died without knowing that an order had already been signed appointing him division commander. He was posthumously awarded the Medal of Honor for heroism on the Normandy beaches and the Bronze Star for bravery in action in North Africa—making him the recipient of every American combat medal. "He was a little man whose bravery had to be seen to be believed," said one correspondent. "He had an antique disregard for his personal safety and a great gift for holding men together. He never said 'Go!' He said 'Come!' "

Badly wounded and gassed during World War I, Archie somehow turned up in the Pacific as a lieutenant colonel, where in 1943 his men gave him credit for the capture of Salamaua, a Japanese stronghold on New Guinea. "Colonel Roosevelt, with two officers and three enlisted men, made a reconnaissance tour of Salamaua harbor," one soldier reported. "Under his orders we went close to the isthmus until Jap guns started firing at us, then turned west across the harbor. Colonel Roosevelt stood up with a map in his hand and every time a gun fired jotted down the position. They fired at us for half an hour, barely missing us several times. The Colonel noticed I was scared and said: 'You're safe with me. I was wounded three times in the last war and that's a lucky charm.' The next day our artillery landed squarely on those guns and the Japs never fired them again. That was when their resistance ended. . . ."

A year later, just about the time that Ted died, Archie was wounded by shrapnel during the fighting at Biak and invalided home. Commenting on the war record of Theodore Roosevelt's sons, the New York *Times* said, "Quentin, Kermit, Theodore

dead; Archibald wounded. . . . Here is a tradition of honor that
cannot die."

Under normal circumstances, any family group would be regarded as having done rather well if it included two congressmen, a cabinet undersecretary, a pair of gubernatorial candidates, a newspaper publisher, the mayor of a sizable city, a
general, a colonel, the winners of several military decorations, a
member of a leading Wall Street firm, and the authors of several
best-selling books. Yet the children of Eleanor and Franklin
Roosevelt are regarded as failures, and more attention is paid to
their seventeen marriages and their disappointments in business
and politics than to their accomplishments. Perhaps this is because they are measured against the long shadows cast by their
parents rather than the standards by which the rest of us are
judged. "One of the worst things in the world is being the child
of a president," Franklin had once said. "It's a terrible life they
lead."

Not even their severest critics could deny that all four brothers
had distinguished military careers. Despite recurrent stomach ul-
cers, James became second-in-command of Carlson's Raiders, one
of the Marine Corps's toughest outfits. "When he came to us," a
professional marine recalled, "he didn't know his ass from a hot
rock. But he was hot to trot." In August 1942 the unit attacked
Japanese-held Makin Island in the Gilberts as a diversion for a
major landing at Guadalcanal. It was a unique foray in American
military history, for the some two hundred marines were carried
into battle on a pair of submarines which surfaced off the
beaches. Although the invaders successfully made their way
ashore through reefs and surf in rubber boats, the Japanese
fought to the last. "A walkie-talkie was shot right out of my
hands," Jimmy later recalled. "I simply asked for another one. I
didn't have any sensation of fear until later. I was too busy with
the battle at the time to be frightened. The awful noise of the
gunfire blotted everything out."

Having destroyed the airfield, set a large gasoline dump afire,
and killed a number of the defenders, the marines evacuated the
island. Some of the rubber boats capsized in the heavy surf, however. Risking his own life, Jimmy saved three or four men from
drowning for which he was awarded the Navy Cross. The Presi-

dent's eldest son was the last man to scramble down the hatch-
way of one of the submarines as a Japanese plane flew over.
"Roosevelt . . . had just barely got his tail feathers down . . .
and the *Argonaut* had to go under," said an officer. "If the plane
had appeared fifteen or twenty seconds earlier, I'm afraid Major
Jimmy would have been swimming around in the Pacific." Fifteen months later, when Makin was captured, Jimmy, now a colonel, participated in the attack, and won the Silver Star. He also
took part in the bloody fighting at Guadalcanal and Tarawa.

Franklin, Jr., served in destroyers in almost every theater of
war. During the attack on Sicily, his ship, the *Mayrant*, was badly
damaged by German bombers and had to be towed into Palermo
harbor by a minesweeper. On August 1, 1943, the Germans
launched the heaviest aerial attack of the campaign against the
ships lying in the harbor. A line of railroad cars carrying nine
hundred tons of ammunition which were on a pier about fifty
yards from the *Mayrant* caught fire, and for four hours the vessel
was showered with shell fragments. One minute, Coxswain
Nunzio Cammarata said, he was standing on the bridge and the
next minute his leg "took off" and "laid beside me." Quickly,
Franklin, Jr., the ship's executive officer, applied a tourniquet to
prevent the wounded man from bleeding to death, and disregard-
ing the exploding ammunition, carried him over to the minesweeper, where he received medical assistance that saved his life.
Awarded the Silver Star and Purple Heart, Franklin, Jr., later
commanded his own destroyer-escort, which was credited with
sinking an enemy submarine.

John, the youngest of the brothers, a lieutenant in the Navy's
Supply Corps, persuaded his father to have him transferred to sea
duty as a logistics officer and won the Bronze Star and promotion
to lieutenant commander for gallantry while his aircraft carrier
was under attack by enemy planes.

As was to be expected, Elliott had the stormiest military career. Angered over the controversy surrounding his appointment
as a fledgling captain in the Army Air Corps, he sought the most
dangerous duty he could find—flying photographic reconnaissance planes often so small that he could not wear a para-
chute. In North Africa he was a specialist in "dicing," or flying as
low as one hundred feet over enemy targets for closeup pictures.
Piling up more combat flying time than anyone in his unit, he

photographed targets in Tunisia, Sicily, Sardinia, and Italy. Elliott was one of the first pilots to land on an airfield that the U. S. Army had constructed in Russia and was at his father's side at the conferences of Allied leaders at Casablanca and Teheran. The citation accompanying his Distinguished Flying Cross noted his "heroism and extraordinary achievement while participating in aerial flights."

But Elliott's military accomplishments were overshadowed in 1945 by stories that three homeward-bound enlisted men had been "bumped" off a military plane to make room for Elliott's dog, which was being shipped to his new wife in Hollywood. Denying that he had sought a priority for the animal, Elliott said the "bumping" was the work of an overzealous and unthinking officer.† The incident could not have come at a worse time, however. He had just been nominated for brigadier general, and the President's critics used the affair to try to block his promotion and to embarrass his father. Republicans noted that Robert E. Lee had thirty-six years of military service before he became a brigadier general; George C. Marshall had thirty-five years and Douglas MacArthur twenty-one. Elliott's supporters also mustered historical precedents, pointing out that Nathan Bedford Forrest rose from lieutenant to lieutenant general in only two years and Philip H. Sheridan had taken a year longer to cover the same ground. Despite the clamor, Elliott's promotion was finally confirmed by the Senate by a 53–11 vote. Observers noted, however, that thirty-one senators had abstained.

Controversy followed Elliott into civilian life. Shortly after his return to Hyde Park he published a book about his father, *As He Saw It*, that again propelled him into the headlines. Regarded as anti-British and pro-Russian, the book purported to present Franklin's table talk about his fellow Allied leaders and was full of re-created conversations. When the British were angered by

† When the Republicans launched a similar attack on FDR during the 1944 presidential campaign, he produced a classic response:

These Republican leaders have not been content with attacks on me, or my wife, or my sons. No, not content with that, they now include my little dog, Fala. Well, of course, I don't resent attacks, and my wife doesn't resent attacks, but Fala does resent attacks. You know, Fala is Scotch, and being a Scottie, as soon as he learned that the Republican fiction writers in Congress had concocted a story that I had left him behind on the Aleutian Islands and had sent a destroyer back to find him—at a cost to the taxpayers of two or three or eight or twenty million dollars—his Scotch soul was furious. He has not been the same dog since.

Elliott's characterization of Winston Churchill, Eleanor defended him in her column, saying he only meant to contrast the personalities of Franklin and Churchill. *Pravda* called Elliott a "sincere friend of the Soviet Union" while a London paper said the book merely demonstrated "that great men often have silly sons."

Shortly before John Boettiger's return from the war, Anna had written him: "I'd like to have some small place somewhere, the kind of place we can turn the key and leave without a qualm, but some place we would think of as 'home.' . . . I honestly have nothing definite in mind—it's just a huge vague hope that our years together in the future may be fraught with fewer worries. . . ." Unhappily, Anna was not to get her wish. Looking around for a newspaper of their own, after being eased out of Seattle by Hearst, they purchased a shopping news in Phoenix, Arizona. They poured every cent they had or could borrow into the paper, which they called the *Arizona Times*. Despite competition from a long-established conservative paper, the lack of well-known columnists, good comics, or wire services, they were optimistic about their chances of success. Beginning as a weekly, the liberally oriented *Times* became a daily in May 1947, nine months after its first issue appeared.

It turned out to be a disastrous venture, with losses eventually amounting to $30,000 a month. Both Eleanor and Anna's older brother, Jimmy, loaned them money in a last-ditch effort to keep the *Times* afloat. The paper's success became the gauge of the Boettigers' marriage, and under the pressure of its failure their marriage fell apart. Boettiger left Phoenix at the end of 1947, while Anna struggled to keep the paper alive. "I love a fight against a reactionary monopoly, and I hate to see the latter winning out in so many fields of endeavor in this country today," she wrote her mother. In the summer of 1948 she was finally forced to give up. The agony was compounded when she learned that her husband had been involved with another woman.

A year later, the Boettigers were divorced. John soon remarried, but engulfed by despair and depression, he leaped to his death from the seventh floor of a New York hotel on October 29, 1950. Among the letters he left behind was one addressed to Anna: "This is to say goodbye and to say thank you for all our wonderful years together. I'm sorry to have failed in many ways,

348 THE ROOSEVELT CHRONICLES

but my memories are filled with happiness. . . ." In 1952 Anna married James A. Halsted, a physician with a special interest in psychosomatic medicine, and at last enjoyed the quiet life out of the spotlight that she had desired. They lived in California, in Iran, where Dr. Halsted was a Fulbright professor, and in Washington, where he was with the Veterans Administration before retiring to upstate New York. Anna succumbed to throat cancer in 1975 and was buried in St. James' churchyard in Hyde Park.‡

Franklin, Jr., was the first of Eleanor and Franklin's sons to seek elective office. Having joined a New York City law firm and taken an active role in veterans' affairs, he ran in 1949 for Congress from the Twentieth District on the predominantly Jewish Upper West Side. Gifted with a startling resemblance to his father, young Roosevelt handily won election despite the opposition of Tammany, which tried to make an issue out of the fact that he didn't live in the district, and the decision of his wife, the former Ethel DuPont, to file for a divorce midway in the campaign. "Next stop Albany!" cried some of his jubilant supporters on election night; others shouted, "White House, there's a knock on your door!"

James, who had returned to California following the war, dabbled in liberal Democratic politics before deciding to run for governor in 1950. Although he had a sufficiency of the Roosevelt charm, he lacked his father's sensitive political antennae. As Democratic national committeeman two years before, he had backed Dwight Eisenhower for the party's presidential nomination—much to the anger of Harry Truman—and chose to make his political debut in a race against Earl Warren, California's biggest vote getter. Eleanor campaigned for Jimmy, but she could not transfer her popularity to him. She was so angered by Truman's failure to endorse Jimmy that she was persuaded only with difficulty from resigning from the United Nations. Roosevelt was

‡ Anna's son by her first marriage, Curtis Dall—the "Buzzy" of White House days—later changed his name to Roosevelt and is the only member of the current generation of the family to show a strong interest in public affairs. He is a member of the United Nations Secretariat, and like his mother has been married three times. His sister, Anna Eleanor—"Sisty"—has been married more than twenty years to Van H. Seagraves, and lives in Washington. John R. Boettiger, the only child of her second marriage, is a college professor and has written a sensitive account of his parents' lives, A Love in Shadow (New York: W. W. Norton & Co., 1978).

beaten by over a million votes—and was forced to borrow from his mother to pay off his campaign debts.

Undeterred, Jimmy bounced back again, and in 1954 won a congressional seat representing a Los Angeles district that encompassed the poverty of Watts and the affluence of Beverly Hills. He resided in Pasadena, but as in the case of Franklin, Jr., not living in his district was not a handicap. And like his brother, Jimmy even managed to overcome the scandal of a messy divorce action filed by his second wife. Shortly afterward, he married his secretary. Conscientiously serving his sprawling constituency, he was reelected five times, and became an important member of the House Committee on Education and Labor. He was identified with such liberal programs as increased minimum wages, civil rights, and fair employment legislation. Upon one occasion, L. Mendel Rivers, an alcoholic South Carolina congressman best known for his ability to snare defense installations for his district while denouncing welfare recipients, remarked that he was not surprised at Roosevelt's views since he was "the son of the greatest nigger-loving woman who ever lived in the White House." Fighting mad, Jimmy bounded from his chair with the intention of giving Rivers a well-deserved punch on the nose, but was restrained by his colleagues. The offending words were expunged from the record.

Political observers who had been looking forward to a Congress with two Roosevelt brothers vying against each other for national attention were disappointed, for in 1954, Franklin, Jr., announced that he was running for governor of New York. His candidacy was not helped by his record in Congress. Although he had an almost perfect liberal-labor voting record, he showed little interest in his job and as a boon companion of young Jack Kennedy, had a reputation as a playboy. "Gracious, let him start being a good congressman first," said Eleanor upon learning of his gubernatorial ambitions. Even so, Joseph Alsop, Roosevelt's distant relative, wrote that he was "an odds-on bet for the nomination." But Franklin, Jr., had failed to do his homework, and under the prodding of Tammany, the state convention chose Averell Harriman, who had been ambassador to Moscow during the war. Roosevelt was nominated as state attorney general instead. It was an empty honor, for he was snowed under by Jacob K. Javits, New York's most popular Republican. Tammany got its revenge for the earlier snub by ordering its supporters to "cut" him.*

Kennedy's advent into the White House revived Franklin, Jr.'s stalled political career. Roosevelt played an important role in helping his friend win the pivotal West Virginia primary—a victory he needed to continue his momentum toward the nomination. Kennedy's Catholicism was a serious handicap in West Virginia, and the endorsement by a son of Franklin Roosevelt, whose name was still influential in the state, may have provided the margin of victory over Senator Hubert H. Humphrey. "When John Kennedy took the oath as an ensign in the Navy in 1941, nobody asked him whether he was a Catholic, a Protestant or a Jew," Franklin, Jr., proclaimed throughout the hills and hollows of West Virginia. "All they asked him was whether he could run that PT boat." Roosevelt's campaign tactics were severely criticized, however, when he contrasted Kennedy's status as a war hero with Humphrey's failure to serve in World War II. The Washington *Star* called it "a new low in dirty politics," and even Eleanor was critical of her son.

In reward for his efforts, Kennedy, aware of the historic connection between the Roosevelt family and the Navy Department, wanted to name Franklin, Jr., as Secretary of the Navy, but Robert S. McNamara, the Defense secretary, turned thumbs down on the appointment. Following considerable delay, Roosevelt was finally named Undersecretary of Commerce, an appointment that opened him up to a grueling senatorial cross-examination about work done by his law firm for the Dominican Republic's Trujillo dictatorship. Herblock, the Washington *Post's* acerbic cartoonist, portrayed him sitting on a pile of Trujillo money and saying: "I'm broadminded—I'm just as willing to work for democracy." Franklin, Jr., was a frequent guest at the Kennedy White House and one of the President's sailing companions.

Following Kennedy's assassination, President Lyndon B. Johnson appointed Franklin, Jr., to head the newly organized Equal Employment Opportunities Commission, a post he left in 1966 to run for governor of New York on the Liberal ticket. It was his

---

* Some political observers believe that had FDR, Jr., made his peace with Tammany in 1954, he would have been elected governor of New York and would have been in line for the Democratic presidential nomination in 1960. John Kennedy was said to have been among them.

last political hurrah. Without a Louis Howe to make the shrewd calculations and to smooth the path before him, he had failed to capitalize on his political assets and his political career is a story of missed opportunities.

Unlucky in politics, Franklin, Jr., is the luckiest of the Roosevelt sons in business. He had obtained a Fiat dealership at the time foreign cars were first becoming popular in America and did so well with it that he became the company's national distributor. The arrangement proved to be so profitable that Fiat repurchased the rights from him at a considerable profit. Always an ardent horseman—in fact, Tammany had asked West Side voters back in 1954, "Do you want a congressman or a Master of Foxhounds?"—he retired to raise blooded cattle on his 2,300-acre estate north of New York City. In 1977 Roosevelt, then sixty-three, married for the fourth time to Patricia Oakes, twenty-seven-year-old adopted daughter of Nancy Oakes, Baroness Hueningen-Huene. They wed on horseback, the bride riding sidesaddle and the groom wearing hunting pinks.

Eleanor had once warned Elliott about going into politics— "You are better off out of politics. You will only get into a jam"— but he couldn't resist throwing his hat in the ring. Having moved to Florida, he ran for mayor of Miami Beach in 1965 after several business misadventures. When the opposition objected to the fact that his campaign literature was sent out with stamps bearing his mother's picture, a newspaper columnist declared: "If I had a mother with a postage stamp issued in her honor I'd use it on all my mail, too." Most of the voters were retired people to whom his father and mother were almost holy figures, and Elliott won handily. He worked hard at his job but was not reelected. His brother, James, attributed the defeat to "injudicious remarks about Jews" made by Elliott's fifth wife, which reached the ears of his mainly Jewish constituents.

Not long afterward, Elliott produced the first volume of a trilogy, *The Roosevelts of Hyde Park: An Untold Story,* that so angered his sister and brothers that they issued a formal statement disassociating themselves from it. Among other items, Elliott claimed that his father had had an affair with Missy LeHand, and even though he had been Eleanor's favorite, no mercy was granted his mother. She was depicted as a "detached, harried, fault-finding wife and parent." The two following books were in the same vein, but did not get a rise out of his brothers.

The Oyster Bay branch of the family is no longer centered on the cluster of homes on Long Island's north shore. After a successful career in finance, Archie Roosevelt, Theodore's last surviving son, has retired to Hobe Sound, Florida, where he keeps his hand in as chairman of the Hobe Sound National Bank. His sister, Ethel Roosevelt Derby, the most publicity-shy of the Roosevelts, was active in charitable work, particularly for the Red Cross and the American Museum of Natural History, until her death at the age of eighty-six in December 1977. She was one of the museum's first two woman trustees and helped found the Theodore Roosevelt Memorial Fund, an important source of grants in the fields of conservation, ecology, and natural history. Almost single-handedly, she preserved Sagamore Hill for future generations, and has been described by Leonard Hall, her godson and onetime Republican national chairman, as "the lady who led the charge of Sagamore Hill. 'No' was not in her vocabulary."

The Colonel's seventeen grandchildren have dispersed to all parts of the country, and like most American families their lives have followed no discernible pattern. Many served in World War II—Kermit, Jr., was in the cloak-and-dagger Office of Strategic Services; his brother Willard commanded a destroyer; and his other brother, Dirck, was with the British Eighth Army in Africa and the Middle East; and Ted's son Quentin II fought alongside his father in Africa and Normandy, and was decorated several times; his brother Cornelius was in the Navy. Quentin later joined the OSS and served in China, remaining there after the war. He became vice-president of the Chinese Nationalist Airline Corporation and during the civil war made airdrops to beleaguered Nationalist troops at considerable risk to himself. He was killed in a crash near Hong Kong in 1948, and some people believe his plane was sabotaged.

Like most well-educated, upper-class Americans, the new generation has become businessmen, lawyers, engineers, diplomats, and government officials, while their sisters have married men in similar positions. For the most part, they had shown little interest in politics, although Theodore Roosevelt III was at one time Pennsylvania's secretary of commerce. The interest of both branches of the family in conservation remains unabated, with Theodore III having given a wildlife preserve, the Theodore Roosevelt Natural Area State Park, to North Carolina, and Christopher Du Pont Roosevelt, the son of Franklin, Jr., is active in the Oceanic Society and other environmental organizations. Other young Roosevelts have gone into teaching, the law, and public interest work, forecasting what may be a new explosion of talent in the future.†

The Roosevelts still show a flair for the arts and writing. Willard composes avant-garde music; Cornelius, a prominent engineer, is an art collector of note, and one of Archie's daughters, Theodora, is a former dancer and a novelist whose work has been compared to Colette. Another daughter, Edith Kermit, once married to Alexander Barmine, a Soviet defector, writes a Washington column, and her sister-in-law, Selwa, was at one time a society columnist for the Washington *Star*. In an earlier generation, Nicholas has been both a diplomat and a newspaperman, and at one point wrote editorials for the New York *Times*. He has published a wide variety of books ranging from politics to cookbooks. George Emlen Roosevelt, onetime head of Roosevelt & Son, was a distinguished mathematician, and the mathematics center at Harvard is named for him.

Both Kermit, Jr., and Archibald, Jr., have had swashbuckling careers that would have been the envy of their rough-riding grandfather. Archibald joined the Foreign Service after the war and as a Middle Eastern expert, speaks Arabic, Kurdish, Uzbek, and Russian as well as several less esoteric languages, and lived with Arab, Kurdish, and Persian tribesmen. In recent years he was equally at home in diplomatic posts in Madrid and London as well as Washington. Mild-mannered and looking like the college professor that he once was, Kermit, or Kim, was the key Central Intelligence Agency operative in the Arab world. He is credited with personally arranging the 1953 Iranian coup that toppled Premier Mohammed Mossadegh, and restored the young Shah to power.

Born in Buenos Aires in 1916, while his father was working there for the National City Bank, he followed the familiar Rooseveltian path to Groton and Harvard and then taught his-

† The long-running feud between the Hyde Park and Oyster Bay Roosevelts seems to have abated and they have joined together in preparing a new family genealogy.

tory at Harvard and the California Institute of Technology. When World War II broke out, he joined the newly organized OSS and spent the war in intelligence work in the Middle East and Italy, where he soon had a reputation for courage. Shortly after the end of the war, he was injured in a jeep accident and while recuperating, was given the task of preparing the history of the OSS's clandestine wartime operations. The document remained in the secret files of the CIA, successor of the OSS, until declassified in 1976. Having become fascinated by the Middle East, Roosevelt traveled extensively in the area and following the upheaval resulting from the establishment of Israel, was active in groups sympathetic to the Arab cause in the United States.

Roosevelt joined the CIA in 1950 at the time of the Korean War, and as one observer has said, "for the next eight years he helped mold, and largely dominate, the CIA's Mideastern policies." Among his assignments was to try to persuade King Farouk of Egypt to get rid of corrupt advisers and to make reforms aimed at bringing the country into the twentieth century. When the weak-willed monarch failed to take these steps, Roosevelt, realizing his days on the throne were numbered, sought out among the young officers plotting to overthrow the monarchy the man most likely to succeed. He was Gamal Abdel Nasser. Soon on a "Gamal" and "Kim" basis, Nasser is said to have once jokingly suggested that Roosevelt become Egypt's ambassador to Washington, while his own man, who was constantly making excuses for the Eisenhower administration's erratic policies, should represent the United States in Cairo.

In 1953 the situation was deteriorating in Iran, where Premier Mossadegh, a crafty old man given to attacks of public weeping, had nationalized the British-owned, billion-dollar Anglo-Iranian Oil Company and sent the Shah into exile. Mossadegh was anti-Communist and the nationalization of the oil company was popular with Iranians, but John Foster Dulles, the Secretary of State, and Allen Dulles, his brother and chief of the CIA, feared the Russians would gain a stranglehold on Iran's huge oil reserves. Britain and the United States decided that Mossadegh had to go. The job of getting rid of him was given to Kim Roosevelt, then head of the CIA's Mideast division.

"It was a real James Bond operation," said an agent quoted by David Wise and Thomas B. Ross in their book *The Invisible Gov-*

ernment. Slipping over the border into Iran, Roosevelt orchestrated the overthrow of Mossadegh by the Iranian military and rioting street mobs at the cost of only $75,000. In return for the CIA's efforts to reseat him on the Peacock Throne, the Shah ended Anglo-Iranian's monopoly and granted several American oil companies a 40 percent share of Iran's production. "In so splendidly conceived and executed a mission," Winston Churchill told Roosevelt in his usual grandiloquent style, "it would, indeed, have been an honor to have served under your command." From his own government he received the National Security Medal.

Dazzled by this success, Foster Dulles tried to persuade Roosevelt to duplicate his feats in Guatemala, the Congo, Indonesia, and Egypt after the Eisenhower administration became disenchanted with Nasser. Pointing out the objective conditions for such intervention were lacking, Roosevelt says he resisted and resigned from the CIA in 1958. He joined Gulf Oil as vice-president in charge of government relations, a position in which he opened doors, gave advice, and made certain that the firm's interests were given careful consideration at the highest levels. In 1964 he branched out on his own, opening the Washington consulting firm of Kermit Roosevelt & Associates, which has specialized in serving well-heeled clients in the oil, armaments, and telecommunications industries, particularly those with interests in the Middle East. The disclosure in 1975 that one of his clients, the Northrop Corporation, had engaged in widespread bribery to sell its fighter planes abroad proved embarrassing. Roosevelt flatly denied having knowledge of the payoffs or having participated in them, and was quoted by a friend as saying: "I always stayed away from the payments side."

Jimmy Roosevelt was also embarrassed by a venture into international business. Badly beaten in a try for mayor of Los Angeles, he resigned his congressional seat in 1965 to accept an appointment from President Johnson as Ambassador to the U. N. Economic and Social Council. In this position, once held by his mother, he interested himself in the affairs of the underdeveloped nations. When the Russians proposed a resolution stating that each nation should be entitled to control and conserve its natural resources, he supported it without checking with his superiors. The resolution turned out to be in conflict with a State Department policy designed to protect American investments in natural resources in Third World countries and Jimmy's days in the U.N. were clearly numbered. Besides, Roosevelt was experiencing financial difficulties. The pressure of alimony payments and the expense of maintaining his official position without a sizable independent income was causing him to look elsewhere. Back in 1962, when he was still a congressman, the need for money had already inadvertently involved him in the Maryland savings and loan scandal when he had accepted a $6,000 annual fee for the use of his name by a questionable financial organization. He told newsmen that he ended the arrangement as soon as doubts were created in his mind about the operation.

While on U.N. business in Geneva, Roosevelt made the acquaintance of Bernard Cornfeld, a mercurial social worker turned financial wizard who had parlayed a few hundred dollars into the multibillion-dollar Investors Overseas Service. In trouble with various governments around the world because of IOS's freewheeling operations, Cornfeld needed someone to improve its international image and offered Roosevelt a $100,000-a-year salary, a generous expense account, and the use of a lavish home in Switzerland to become a vice-president of his operation. It was an offer that couldn't be refused by a man plagued with money troubles, and Jimmy resigned his ambassadorship at the end of 1966.

The Roosevelt name might have been controversial at home, but it was highly respected abroad, and Jimmy's presence lent a patina of respectability to IOS. He did more than supply window dressing, however. Roosevelt plunged enthusiastically into establishing mutual investment funds designed to channel money into developing countries. Among his other tasks, he solemnly presided over Pacem in Terris II, an international peace conference bankrolled by Cornfeld and attended by senators, intellectuals, archbishops, ambassadors, a gaggle of Nobel laureates and Cornfeld cronies "who may have thought Pacem in Terris was a stock traded over the counter."

Eventually, the bubble broke. By 1970 IOS was unable to generate enough profits to keep the operation going, revealing it to have been a chain-letter-like scheme designed primarily to enrich insiders at the expense of those persuaded to invest through hardsell, high-pressure salesmanship. And instead of channeling money into the Third World it was draining scarce resources from the poverty-stricken countries. The collapse of the Great Bull Market of the 1960s, which in turn was aggravated by the failure of Cornfeld's empire, did the rest. As the directors tried vainly to stem the tide, Jimmy Roosevelt made a somewhat tasteless comparison. "I feel like I did in 1933, when my father and I had meetings to sort out the problems of the United States," he was quoted as saying.

The financial wolves descended on the bloody carcass of IOS and Roosevelt bailed out in 1971. "I myself was burned by IOS and turned no profit in it," he claims. The years in Switzerland also produced a domestic crisis, with Roosevelt and his third wife engaging in bitter quarrels. One night she stabbed him in the back with a souvenir dagger. He was not severely injured, but the incident ended the marriage. Not long afterward, James married again, this time to an Englishwoman who had formerly taught at the Geneva school attended by the Roosevelts' adopted son, Delano, and was thirty years his junior. Returning to California, he started a new life and although over seventy, is active in a business consulting firm in Newport Beach and teaches a course in government at the University of California at Irvine. With a young wife and a daughter born when he was sixty-three, the eldest of the sons of Franklin and Eleanor Roosevelt seems to have found the peace that eluded him so long.

But not to be outdone by Elliott, he produced his own book on the tribulations of his parents. He denied his brother's allegation of an affair between Franklin and Missy LeHand, but in doing so raised the possibility that Eleanor may have had an affair with a state trooper who served as her chauffeur.

And there is Alice.

Astringent wit unimpaired by age, she views the vagaries of Washington with a mordant eye from the gently faded splendor of her home on Massachusetts Avenue. Both adored and detested but always talked about, she found herself in demand during the Kennedy years after the eclipse of the Truman and Eisenhower era. The new President—youngest man to hold the office since her father—was captivated by Mrs. L. and she again became a familiar figure at the White House, even though her vote had been cast for Richard M. Nixon in 1960. She admired the Kennedys for their wit, their sense of irony, and their solidarity. "They're one for all and all for one among themselves, which is quite different from our family, who were completely individualistic," she says. Lyndon Johnson was also a good friend, a fellow poker player, and the first Democratic presidential candidate for whom she ever voted. Always friendly with Nixon, her fondness for him cooled with Watergate, however.

Never one to dwell on her own troubles, Mrs. Longworth has had her share. In 1944 her only child, Paulina, married a young man named Alexander McCormick Sturm, who had published two children's books before graduating from college. But Sturm failed to live up to his early promise and after considerable indecision joined a partner in opening a small-arms plant in Connecticut. He died in 1951 at the age of twenty-eight after a long illness. Paulina was depressed by the death of her husband, and in 1957, her ten-year-old daughter, Joanna, found her unconscious on a sofa in the living room of their Georgetown home with an empty sleeping pill bottle nearby. Paulina's death was ruled accidental and Joanna went to live with her grandmother. Alice also survived two bouts with cancer but is as ready to mock herself as anyone else. Following her second mastectomy, she told a friend that she was the "only topless octogenarian in Georgetown Hospital."

The world beneath Mrs. L.'s window has changed rapidly, but for her, life goes on pretty much as before with a timeless ritual—arising about noon, tea and visitors at 5 P.M., and an all-night session of reading. Early one morning, shortly before her ninety-fifth birthday, a man with an official-sounding voice informed the Washington newspapers of her death. When a reporter called the Longworth home at 2 A.M. to confirm the story, a very much alive Princess Alice answered the telephone herself. "Oh, it's just too terribly funny," she said. "I've never felt better."

Appendix
A NOTE ON THE PRONUNCIATION
OF ROOSEVELT

Is Roosevelt pronounced *rews*-velt or *rose*-uh-velt?

The final word seems to have been written by Robert B. Roosevelt during an exchange of Letters to the Editor of the New York *Sun* in May 1903. It began with the following communication:

> To the Editor of The Sun—Sir: In the course of my daily work I recently had occasion to show that the name Roosevelt is subject to over 200 variations of pronunciation. The President pronounces his name Ro-zi-velt, the first vowel sound being like that in room, while the syllables are but two. . . . Perhaps our President does not think as deeply about the matter as academicians do. . . .
>
> Richard E. Mayne, Chairman,
> Department on Reading and Speech Culture
> New York State Teachers Association

A few days later, Uncle Rob fired back:

> To the editor of The Sun—Sir: My attention has been called to an amusing letter by Mr. Richard E. Mayne, chairman, department [on] reading and speech culture, New York State Teachers Association, calling the President to account for his pronunciation of his own name. . . . It is rather a dangerous proceeding to assume that a man does not know how to pronounce his own name, and the writer who attempts not only to criticise but to dictate may find himself in that unhappy position in which "angels fear to tread," even if he be a "chairman of reading and speech culture." A little culture and even less reading would teach most men and might teach a chairman that there is no analogy or usage of pronunciation according to spelling in the English language. . . . As there are readers of your paper who are justifiably anxious to know the proper pronunciation of the President's name, I will explain that it is Dutch. Now, I do not insist that the Dutch language is inherently superior to English . . . but that language possesses at least one advantage—

it has a positive pronunciation. In English when we try to distinguish the long from the short "o" we get into trouble. In Dutch they do not. The double "o" is simply a long "o." The word "Roos" means rose and is pronounced in identically the same way under all circumstances and all combinations. So the first syllable of the President's name is "Rose" pure and simple.

But the following "e" like the short German "e" or like the silent French "e" when read in poetry is slightly aspirated. An English analogy is the word "the," a word that our chairman must have come across in his "reading and speech culture." It is not pronounced at all as it is spelt, not like "thee," but with the sort of "the" and a breath stopped by the tongue on the teeth. So the name is "Rose-(uh)-velt." . . .

Robert B. Roosevelt

BIBLIOGRAPHY

I. MANUSCRIPT SOURCES

Roosevelt Family Papers; Delano Family Papers; Eleanor Roosevelt Papers; Anna Roosevelt Halstead Papers. Franklin D. Roosevelt Library, Hyde Park, New York.

Roosevelt Family Papers. Theodore Roosevelt Collection, Harvard College Library, Cambridge, Massachusetts.

Varick Papers; Livingston Papers; Roosevelt Papers. New-York Historical Society, New York, New York.

Roosevelt File. New York Public Library, New York, New York.

II. BOOKS AND ARTICLES

Alsop, Joseph, and Kintner, Robert. "The Roosevelt Family Album," *Life*, September 9, 1940.

Amory, Cleveland. *Who Killed Society?* New York: Harper & Bros., 1960.

Archdeacon, Thomas J. "Anglo-Dutch New York, 1676." In *New York: The Centennial Years 1676–1976*. Edited by Milton M. Klein. Port Washington, N.Y.: Kennikat Press, 1976.

———. *New York City, 1664–1710*. Ithaca, N.Y.: Cornell University Press, 1976.

Barrett, Walter (pseud. for J. A. Scoville). *The Old Merchants of New York City*. Fourth series. New York: Greenwood Press, 1968.

Beale, Howard K. "Theodore Roosevelt's Ancestry," *The New York Genealogical and Biographical Record*, October 1954.

———. *Theodore Roosevelt and the Rise of America to World Power*. Baltimore: The Johns Hopkins University Press, 1956.

Bliven, Bruce. *Under the Guns: New York 1775–1776*. New York: Harper & Row, 1972.

Blum, John M. *The Republican Roosevelt*. New York: Atheneum, 1965.

Boettiger, John R. *A Love in Shadow*. New York: W. W. Norton & Co., 1978.

Bradford, William. *Of Plymouth Plantation.* Edited by Samuel Eliot Morison. New York: Alfred A. Knopf, 1976.

Brough, James. *Princess Alice.* Boston: Little, Brown, 1975.

Burgess, George H., and Kennedy, Miles C. *Centennial History of the Pennsylvania Railroad 1846–1946.* Philadelphia: Pennsylvania Railroad Co., 1949.

Burke's Presidential Families of the United States of America. London: Burke's Peerage Ltd., 1975.

Burns, James MacGregor. *Roosevelt: The Lion and the Fox.* New York: Harcourt, Brace, 1956.

——. *Roosevelt: The Soldier of Freedom.* New York: Harcourt Brace Jovanovich, 1970.

Burt, Nathaniel. *First Families.* Boston: Little, Brown, 1970.

Byrdill, F. *History of the Locofoco, or Equal Rights Party* New York: Cleveland and Parker, 1842.

Churchill, Allen. *The Roosevelts.* London: Frederick Muller, Ltd., 1965.

"Claes Martenszen Van Rosenvelt," *The New Netherland Register,* January 1911.

Cobb, William T. *The Strenuous Life.* New York: William E. Rudge's Sons, 1946.

Copeland, Miles. *The Game of Nations.* New York: Simon & Schuster, 1969.

Daggett, Stuart. *Railroad Reorganization.* New York: A. M. Kelley, 1967.

Daniels, Jonathan. *Washington Quadrille.* Garden City, N.Y.: Doubleday & Co., 1968.

Davis, Kenneth S. *FDR: The Beckoning of Destiny 1882–1928.* New York: G. P. Putnam's Sons, 1972.

Davis, Richard Harding. *The Cuban and Puerto Rican Campaigns.* New York: Charles Scribner's Sons, 1898.

Day, Donald, ed. *Franklin Roosevelt's Own Story.* Boston: Little, Brown, 1951.

Delano, Daniel W., Jr. *Franklin Roosevelt and the Delano Influence.* Pittsburgh: James W. Nudi Publications, 1946.

Dictionary of American Biography

Divine, Robert A. *Roosevelt and World War II.* Baltimore: The Johns Hopkins University Press, 1969.

Dows, Olin. *Franklin Roosevelt at Hyde Park.* New York: American Artists Group, 1949.

Dunshee, Kenneth H. *As You Pass By.* New York: Hastings House, 1952.

Flexner, John T. *Steamboats Come True.* New York: Viking Press, 1944.

"Franklin and Eleanor Roosevelt's Fortune," *Fortune,* October 1932.

Freidel, Frank. *Franklin D. Roosevelt.* 4 vols. Boston: Little, Brown, 1952–73.

——. *F.D.R. and the South.* Baton Rouge, La.: Louisiana State University Press, 1965.

Gable, John A. *The Bull Moose Years: Theodore Roosevelt and the Progressive Party.* Port Washington, N.Y.: Kennikat Press, 1978.

Gipson, Lawrence H. *The Coming of the American Revolution.* New York: Harper & Row, 1954.

Gunther, John. *Roosevelt in Retrospect.* London: Hamish Hamilton, 1950.

Hagedorn, Hermann. *The Roosevelt Family of Sagamore Hill.* New York: The Macmillan Co., 1954.

———, and Roth, Gary G. *Sagamore Hill: An Historical Guide.* Oyster Bay, N.Y.: Theodore Roosevelt Association, 1977.

Hamm, Margherita. *Famous Families of New York.* Vol. 2. New York: G. P. Putnam's Sons, 1901.

Harbaugh, William H. *Power and Responsibility: The Life and Times of Theodore Roosevelt.* New York: Farrar, Straus & Cudahy, 1961.

Harrington, Virginia D. *The New York Merchants on the Eve of the Revolution.* New York: Columbia University Press, 1935.

Hassett, William D. *Off the Record With F.D.R.* New Brunswick, N.J.: Rutgers University Press, 1958.

Hellman, Geoffrey. "Roosevelt: From Breakfast to Bed . . . ," *Life,* January 20, 1941.

Hess, Stephen. *America's Political Dynasties.* Garden City, N.Y.: Doubleday & Co., 1966.

Hofstader, Richard. *The American Political Tradition and the Men Who Made It.* New York: Alfred A. Knopf, 1949.

Hone, Philip. *The Diary of Philip Hone.* Edited by Allan Nevins. New York: Dodd, Mead & Co., 1936.

Horsemanden, Daniel. *New York Conspiracy, or A History of the Negro Plot.* Edited by Thomas J. Davis. Boston: Beacon Press, 1971.

Johnson, Alvin P. *Franklin D. Roosevelt's Colonial Ancestors.* Boston: Lathrop, Lee & Shephard Co., 1933.

Johnson, Gerald. *Roosevelt: Dictator or Democrat?* New York: Harper & Bros., 1941.

Kammen, Michael. *Colonial New York.* New York: Charles Scribner's Sons, 1975.

Kessler, Henry H., and Rachlis, Eugene. *Peter Stuyvesant and His New York.* New York: Random House, 1959.

Kimmel, Stanley. *The Mad Booths of Maryland.* Indianapolis: Bobbs-Merrill, 1940.

Kleeman, Rita H. *Gracious Lady: The Life of Sara Delano Roosevelt.* New York: D. Appleton-Century Co., 1935.

Kouwenhoven, John A. *The Columbia Historical Portrait of New York.* New York: Harper & Row, 1972.

Lash, Joseph P. *Eleanor and Franklin.* New York: W. W. Norton & Co., 1971.

———. *Eleanor: The Years Alone.* New York: W. W. Norton & Co., 1972.

Latrobe, J. H. B. *The First Steamboat Voyage on the Western Waters.*
Edited by Carl R. Bogardus. Austin, Ind.: The Muscatatuck Press, 1961.
———. *A Lost Chapter in the History of the Steamboat.* Baltimore: Mary-
land Historical Society, 1871.
Leuchtenburg, William. *Franklin D. Roosevelt and the New Deal.* New
York: Harper & Row, 1963.
Lindley, Ernest K. *Franklin D. Roosevelt.* Indianapolis: Bobbs-Merrill,
1931.
Lippman, Theo, Jr. *The Squire of Warm Springs.* Chicago: Playboy
Press, 1977.
Longworth, Alice Roosevelt. *Crowded Hours.* New York: Charles Scrib-
ner's Sons, 1933.
Lorant, Stefan. *The Life and Times of Theodore Roosevelt.* Garden City,
N.Y.: Doubleday & Co., 1959.
Martin, Clarece. *A Glimpse of the Past; The History of Bulloch Hall.* Ros-
well, Ga.: Historic Roswell, 1973.
Mencken, H. L. *The Days of H. L. Mencken.* New York: Alfred A.
Knopf, 1947.
Miller, John C. *Origins of the American Revolution.* Boston: Little,
Brown, 1943.
Miller, Nathan. *The Founding Finaglers.* New York: David McKay,
1976.
———. *The U. S. Navy: An Illustrated History.* Annapolis, Md.: U. S.
Naval Institute, 1977.
The Minutes of the Orphan Masters of New Amsterdam 1655–1663.
Edited by Berthold Fernow. New York: Francis P. Harper, 1962.
Monaghan, Frank, and Lowenthal, Marvin. *This Was New York.* Garden
City, N.Y.: Doubleday, Doran, 1943.
Morison, Samuel Eliot. *Sicily–Salerno–Anzio.* Boston: Little, Brown,
1954.
Morris, Edmund. *The Rise of Theodore Roosevelt.* New York: Coward,
McCann & Geoghegan, 1979.
Mowry, George E. *The Era of Theodore Roosevelt.* New York: Harper &
Row, 1958.
———. *Theodore Roosevelt and the Progressive Movement.* Madison,
Wis.: University of Wisconsin Press, 1947.
Myers, Gustavus. *The History of Tammany Hall.* New York: Burt
Francis, 1968.
Nevins, Allan. *History of the Bank of New York and Trust Company.*
New York: Arno Press, 1976.
Nutting, Anthony. *Nasser.* New York: E. P. Dutton & Co., 1972.
O'Connor, Harvey. *The Astors.* New York: Alfred A. Knopf, 1941.
Partridge, Bellamy. *The Roosevelt Family in America.* New York: Hill-
man-Curl, 1936.
Perkins, Frances. *The Roosevelt I Knew.* New York: Viking Press, 1946.
Perling, Joseph J. *Presidents' Sons.* Freeport, N.Y.: Books for Libraries
Press, 1971.

Pickard, M. F. *The Roosevelts in America*. London: H. Joseph, Ltd., 1941.

Prebble, John. *The Darien Disaster*. London: Secker & Warburg, 1968.

Pringle, Henry F. *Theodore Roosevelt*. New York: Harcourt, Brace, 1956.

Putnam, Carleton. *Theodore Roosevelt: The Formative Years*. New York: Charles Scribner's Sons, 1958.

Raesly, Ellis L. *Portrait of New Netherland*. New York: Columbia University Press, 1945.

Raw, Charles; Page, Bruce; and Hodgson, Godfrey. *Do You Sincerely Want to Be Rich?* New York: Viking Press, 1971.

Reynolds, Cuyler. *Genealogical and Family History of Southern New York*. Vol. 3. New York: Lewis Historical Publishing Co., 1914.

Reynolds, Helen W. "Dutchess County Gives the State a Governor," *Year Book, Dutchess County Historical Society*, 1931.

Rixey, Lillian. *Bamie*. New York: David McKay Co., 1963.

Robinson, Corinne R. *My Brother, Theodore Roosevelt*. New York: Charles Scribner's Sons, 1921.

Rollins, Alfred B., Jr. *Roosevelt and Howe*. New York: Alfred A. Knopf, 1962.

Roosevelt, Clinton. *The Science of Government*. New York: Dean & Trevett, 1841.

Roosevelt, Eleanor. *Franklin D. Roosevelt at Hyde Park*. Washington, D.C.: U. S. Government Printing Office, 1949.

——. *On My Own*. New York: Harper & Bros., 1958.

——. *This I Remember*. New York: Harper & Bros., 1949.

——. *This Is My Story*. New York: Harper & Bros., 1937.

Roosevelt, Eleanor B. (Mrs. Theodore, Jr.). *Day Before Yesterday*. Garden City, N.Y.: Doubleday & Co., 1959.

Roosevelt, Elliott, and Brough, James. *Mother R*. New York: G. P. Putnam's Sons, 1977.

——. *An Untold Story: The Roosevelts of Hyde Park*. New York: Dell Publishing Co., 1974.

Roosevelt, Franklin D. *F.D.R. His Personal Letters*. Edited by Elliott Roosevelt. 4 vols. New York: Duell, Sloan & Pearce, 1947–50.

——. *The Public Papers and Addresses of Franklin D. Roosevelt*. Edited by Samuel Rosenman. 13 vols. New York: The Macmillan Co., 1938–50.

Roosevelt, G. Hall. *Odyssey of an American Family*. New York: Harper & Bros., 1938.

Roosevelt, James and Shallet, Sidney. *Affectionately, F.D.R.* New York: Avon Books, 1959.

——, and Libby, Bill. *My Parents*. Chicago: Playboy Press, 1976.

Roosevelt, Mrs. James, as told to Isabelle Leighton and Gabrielle Forbush. *My Boy Franklin*. New York: Crown Publishers, 1933.

Roosevelt, Nicholas. *A Front Row Seat*. Norman, Okla.: University of Oklahoma Press, 1953.

Roosevelt, Theodore. *An Autobiography*. New York: Charles Scribner's Sons, 1913.

——. *Letters to Kermit*. Edited by Will Irwin. New York: Charles Scribner's Sons, 1946.

——. *The Letters of Theodore Roosevelt*. Edited by Elting E. Morison and John M. Blum. 8 vols. Cambridge, Mass.: Harvard University Press, 1951–54.

——. *The Rough Riders*. New York: Charles Scribner's Sons, 1899.

——. *Theodore Roosevelt's Letters to His Children*. New York: Charles Scribner's Sons, 1919.

Runcie, John D. "The Problem of Anglo-American Politics in Bellomont's New York," *William and Mary Quarterly*, April 1969.

Schlesinger, Arthur M., Sr. *The Colonial Merchants and the American Revolution*. New York: Facsimile Library, 1939.

Schlesinger, Arthur M., Jr. *The Crisis of the Old Order*. Boston: Houghton Mifflin, 1957.

——. *A Thousand Days*. Boston: Houghton Mifflin, 1965.

Schriftgiesser, Karl. *The Amazing Roosevelt Family*. New York: Wilfred Funk, 1942.

——. *This Was Normalcy*. Boston: Little, Brown, 1948.

Scott, Kenneth. "The Slave Insurrection in New York in 1712," *The New-York Historical Society Quarterly*, January 1961.

Smelser, Marshall. "Clinton Roosevelt's 'Invulnerable Steam Battery' 1835," *The American Neptune*, July 1960.

Smith, Helen B. "Nicholas Roosevelt—Goldsmith," *The New-York Historical Society Quarterly*, October 1950.

Steelholm, Clara and Hardy. *The House at Hyde Park*. New York: Viking Press, 1950.

Still, Bayard. *Mirror for Gotham*. New York: New York University Press, 1956.

Stokes, I. N. P. *The Iconography of Manhattan Island*. 6 vols. New York: Robert H. Dodd, 1915–28.

Tugwell, Rexford G. *The Democratic Roosevelt*. Garden City, N.Y.: Doubleday & Co., 1957.

Valentine, David. *History of the City of New York*. New York: G. P. Putnam, 1853.

Van Rensselaer, Mariana. *History of the City of New York in the Seventeenth Century*. New York: The Macmillan Co., 1909.

Vidal, Gore. *Homage to Daniel Shays*. New York: Random House, 1972.

Welles, Benjamin. "Serving Oil, Arabs and the CIA," *The New Republic*, July 26, 1975.

Wertenbaker, Thomas J. *Father Knickerbocker Rebels*. New York: Charles Scribner's Sons, 1948.

White, Theodore H. *The Making of the President 1960*. New York: Atheneum, 1961.

Whittelsey, Charles B. *The Roosevelt Genealogy 1649–1902*. Hartford, Conn.: J. R. Burr & Co., 1902.

Willison, George. *Saints and Strangers.* New York: Reynal & Hitchcock, 1945.

Wilson, James G., ed. *Memorial History of the City of New York.* 4 vols. New York: New York History Company, 1892–93.

Wise, David, and Ross, Thomas B. *The Invisible Government.* New York: Random House, 1964.

Yeager, M. Hildegarde. *The Life of James Roosevelt Bayley.* Washington: Catholic University Press, 1947.

III. NEWSPAPERS AND MAGAZINES

New York *Times*
New York *Herald*
New York *Tribune*
New York *Herald-Tribune*
New York *Independent Reflector*
New York *Gazette and Weekly Mercury*
New York *Sun*
New York *World*
Baltimore *Sun*
Washington *Post*
Washington *Star*
Los Angeles *Times*
Time
Newsweek
New Republic
Nederland Mail

INDEX

death, 336–42, 348–49, 350; and Lucy
Mercer (*see* Mercer, Lucy Page);
marriage, 248, 266–71ff.; and
mother-in-law, 267–71, 283, 304, 323,
327–28; and politics and political activity,
275, 276, 278–79, 282–84, 291, 293–94,
300, 301, 309, 310, 323, 339–42; *This Is
My Story* by, 288–89; and uncle, TR, 246,
248, 258, 269, 267, 278; as U.N. delegate,
339–40
Roosevelt, Elliott (Eleanor Roosevelt's
father), 154, 164, 168, 169, 170, 184, 188,
191–93, 196, 231–33, 234–35, 236, 242,
243, 254
Roosevelt, Mrs. Elliott (Anna Rebecca
Hall, Eleanor Roosevelt's mother), 193,
231–33
Roosevelt, Elliott (son of Eleanor and
FDR), 243n, 246, 268, 270, 273, 326, 327,
332, 337, 338, 340, 351–52; *As He Saw It*
by, 346–47; *The Roosevelts of Hyde Park*
by, 351–52, 357; World War II record of,
345–47
Roosevelt, Elliott, Jr. (Eleanor Roosevelt's
brother), 232, 233, 234, 236
Roosevelt, Ethel (Mrs. Richard Derby),
207, 258, 286, 352
Roosevelt, Frank H., 130
Roosevelt, Franklin Delano (FDR), 46, 59,
108, 109, 128, 131, 132, 137, 171, 178,
224ff., 237–47, 297, 344, 346, 348, 351;
address to DAR, 1–2; Assistant Secretary
of Navy, 280ff., 296; attacks on, 325–26;
birth, early years, education, 185, 192,
224ff., 237–47; death of, 333–35, 336–38;
enters politics, 241, 265, 266ff.; fireside
chats, 315–16; First Inaugural Address,
312; as governor of New York, 310–11; at
Groton, 237–39, 242, 243; "Happy
Warrior" speech, 308, 309; at Harvard,
239–40; Harvard thesis on his family by,
1–2, 3, 4, 7, 45, 55, 69, 107, 113, 133, 134,
174, 182; and Howe (*see* Howe, Louis
McHenry); law practice and business
ventures, 271ff., 300–1, 308; marriage,
248, 266–71ff. (*see also* Roosevelt,
Eleanor); polio condition, 301–6ff.; as
President, style and accomplishments,
311, 312ff.; and TR, 225, 228, 239, 240,
241, 248, 254, 259, 260, 261, 265, 266,
273–74, 278; as VP candidate (1920),
290–95; at Warm Springs (*see* Warm
Springs, Ga.); and Woodrow Wilson,
278–80, 281, 282, 286; and World War I,
284–87; and World War II and Hitler,
330–34
Roosevelt, Franklin Delano, Jr. (the first,
died at eight months), 268, 269–70
Roosevelt, Franklin Delano, Jr. (the
second), viii, 174n, 268, 269, 328, 340,
341, 348, 353; political career and
business ventures, 349–51; World War II
record of, 345
Roosevelt, George Emlen, 353
Roosevelt, George Washington, 157
Roosevelt, Grace (Mrs. Guy Carleton
Bayley), 135
Roosevelt, Hall, 232, 245, 246, 286
Roosevelt, Helen, 228, 231n
Roosevelt, Helena (Mrs. Andrew Barclay),
61, 63
Roosevelt, Helena (sister of Isaac "the
Patriot"), 133
Roosevelt, Henry, 92

Roosevelt, Henry Latrobe, 327
Roosevelt, Hilborne Lewis, 129–31
Roosevelt, Isaac ("the Patriot"), 58–71,
72–90, 93, 108, 109, 110, 118, 133
Roosevelt, Mrs. Isaac (Cornelia Hoffman),
60, 63–64, 90
Roosevelt, Dr. Isaac (grandson of Isaac
"the Patriot"), 109, 110–14, 163, 170,
173–74, 175
Roosevelt, Mrs. Isaac (Mary Rebecca
Aspinwall), 112, 173
Roosevelt, Jacobus, 61, 62
Roosevelt, Jacobus (James, born 1692), 43,
45–46, 47, 48–50, 53–55, 57, 59, 60, 79, 82
Roosevelt, Mrs. Jacobus (Catharina
Hardenbroeck), 54, 59
Roosevelt, James (father of FDR), 113,
114, 163, 170–85, 192, 224, 225–26, 227,
228, 230–31, 237, 238
Roosevelt, Mrs. James (the first, Rebecca
Howland), 176–78
Roosevelt, Mrs. James (the second, Sara
"Sallie" Delano, FDR's mother), 170–73,
178–85, 192; and daughter-in-law,
Eleanor, 267–71, 283, 304, 323, 327–28;
and son, FDR, 224–28, 229–30, 237, 239,
242–44, 267–71, 272, 281n, 283, 288, 301,
303, 304, 306, 321, 322–23, 327–28
Roosevelt, James (Jacobus, 1760–1847), 64,
82, 83, 84–85, 87, 90, 92, 108–10, 111–12,
113–14, 127, 134, 135–36
Roosevelt, Mrs. James ([Jacobus], the first,
Mary Eliza Walton), 85, 109, 110
Roosevelt, Mrs. James ([Jacobus], the
second, Catherine Eliza Barclay), 110
Roosevelt, Mrs. James ([Jacobus] the
third, Harriet Howland), 111
Roosevelt, James (Jimmy, FDR's son),
241n, 243–44n, 268, 269, 326, 327, 330,
340, 341, 347, 348–49, 351, 355–57; and
Cornfeld and IOS, 356–57; *My Parents*
by, 241n, 270, 303, 307; World War II
record of, 344–45
Roosevelt, James (son of Johannes), 80–81,
84–85, 92, 93
Roosevelt, James I (hardware merchant),
81, 93, 94, 108–9, 114, 115, 123
Roosevelt, Mrs. James I (Maria Van
Schaack), 114
Roosevelt, James Alfred, 115, 130, 139, 163,
202n
Roosevelt, James Henry, 131–33, 304
Roosevelt, Mrs. James Henry (Julia Maria
Boardman), 132
Roosevelt, James J., 123–27, 128
Roosevelt, Mrs. James J. (Cornelia Van
Ness), 125–27
Roosevelt, James Roosevelt ("Rosy"),
177–78, 185, 228, 230–31, 283n, 306n
Roosevelt, Mrs. James Roosevelt (Helen
Schermerhorn Astor), 178, 185, 231n
Roosevelt, Mrs. James Roosevelt (Elizabeth
Riley), 283n
Roosevelt, James Roosevelt, Jr. (Taddy),
228, 231n, 237–38, 241
Roosevelt, Dr. James West, 187–88
Roosevelt, Janet, 119–22
Roosevelt, Johannes, 59
Roosevelt, Mrs. Johannes (Annetje
Luquier), 59
Roosevelt, Johannes (John), 43, 45–54, 57,
63
Roosevelt, Mrs. Johannes ([John], Heyltje
Sjoerts), 54

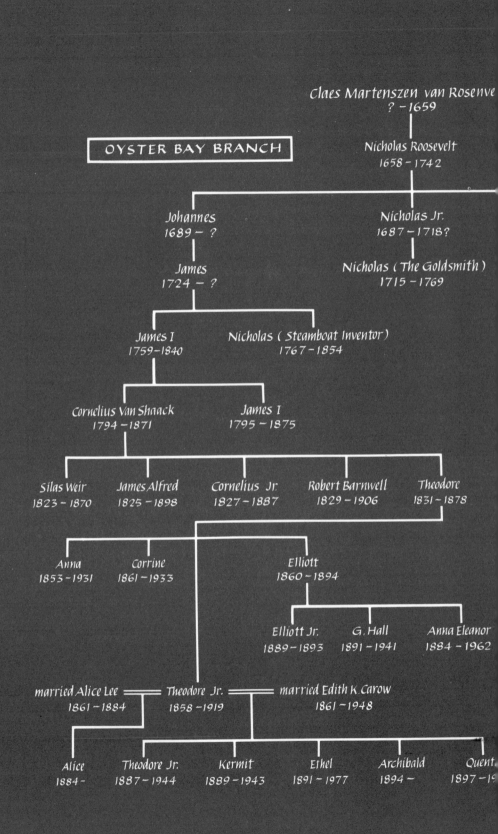

Claes Martenszen van Rosenve
? – 1659

Nicholas Roosevelt
1658 – 1742

OYSTER BAY BRANCH

Johannes
1689 – ?

Nicholas Jr.
1687 – 1718?

James
1724 – ?

Nicholas (The Goldsmith)
1715 – 1769

James I
1759 – 1840

Nicholas (Steamboat Inventor)
1767 – 1854

Cornelius Van Shaack
1794 – 1871

James I
1795 – 1875

Silas Weir
1823 – 1870

James Alfred
1825 – 1898

Cornelius Jr.
1827 – 1887

Robert Barnwell
1829 – 1906

Theodore
1831 – 1878

Anna
1853 – 1931

Corrine
1861 – 1933

Elliott
1860 – 1894

Elliott Jr.
1889 – 1893

G. Hall
1891 – 1941

Anna Eleanor
1884 – 1962

married Alice Lee
1861 – 1884

Theodore Jr.
1858 – 1919

married Edith K. Carow
1861 – 1948

Alice
1884 –

Theodore Jr.
1887 – 1944

Kermit
1889 – 1943

Ethel
1891 – 1977

Archibald
1894 –

Quent
1897 – 19